The Glasnost Papers

The Glasnost Papers
Voices on Reform from Moscow

edited by Andrei Melville
and Gail W. Lapidus

**compiled and with a commentary by
O. Aliakrinskii, S. Filatov, P. Gladkov, I. Isakova,
A. Melville, A. Nikitin, A. Pankin, V. Vlasikhin**

Westview Press
Boulder • San Francisco • Oxford

Published in 1990 in the United States of America by Westview Press, Inc., 5500 Central Avenue, Boulder, Colorado 80301, and in the United Kingdom by Westview Press, 36 Lonsdale Road, Summertown, Oxford OX2 7EW

Library of Congress Cataloging-in-Publication Data
The Glasnost papers: voices on reform from Moscow /
    edited by Andrei Melville and Gail W. Lapidus; compiled and with a
    commentary by O. Aliakrinskii . . . [et al.].
        p.   cm.
    ISBN 0-8133-0921-2.—ISBN 0-8311-0922-0 (pbk.)
    1. Soviet Union—Politics and government—1985-   . 2. Soviet Union—
Economic policy—1986-   . 3. Perestroika. 4. Glasnost.
I. Mel'vil', A. IU. (Andreĭ IUr'evich).   II. Lapidus, Gail.
Warshofsky.
DK286.5.G52 1990
320.947—dc20   90-34117
                                                                         CIP

Printed and bound in the United States of America

The paper used in this publication meets the requirements
of the American National Standard for Permanence of Paper
for Printed Library Materials Z39.48-1984.

10   9   8   7   6   5   4   3   2   1

Contents

Acknowledgments

We would like to express our appreciation to David Foglesong, Nellie Ohr, Bertrand Patenaude, Susan Zayer Rupp, David Schearer, Sylvia Townsend, and Tim Whipple for their translation services; to Andrew Kuchins, Jody Jensen, and Tony Reese for their editorial assistance; and to Susan McEachern and Bev LeSuer at Westview Press for shepherding this project through to completion and for showing extraordinary patience with the complications and delays involved in such an undertaking.

Gail W. Lapidus
Andrei Melville

ANDREI MELVILLE

A Personal Introduction

I want to begin with myself. For the first time in my life I feel optimistic and hopeful. Of course, I am not alone in this. There is a spirit of change in the air, of social upheaval. After many years of lethargy, Soviet society is finally on the move.

For me now my country is the most interesting place in the world. This feeling is shared by a great many people, and not just here in the USSR. I can barely remember 1956 and the 20th Party Congress (I was just six years old at that time), but the atmosphere of enthusiasm in the early 1960s and the ensuing bitterness at the end of that decade are preserved in my memory. People of an older generation will some-times say that enthusiasms and letdowns in society are nothing unusual. And yet, I am convinced that I am living through a unique time in the history of my country, a time of dramatic transformation.

Human beings are by nature conservative, and many people feel uneasy when their usual way of life changes, when the established order of things collapses. But when you know that you cannot continue in the old way, and when you see that the old way of doing things cannot be improved, no matter how hard you try; when you know that change is the only way out, and you are anticipating this change with eagerness and hope, then the time has come for a radical solution—to break with the old ways and create new ones. One might call this "revolution."

History knows various types of revolution, including ones not nec-essarily accompanied by bloodshed. For example, the New Deal of Franklin Delano Roosevelt was, in its own way, revolutionary in scale. I would like to believe that what is going on in my own country will become revolutionary in much the same way. Of course there are no barricades in the streets, but an intense struggle—both political and ideological—is taking place. And those in the Soviet Union who want radical, revolutionary changes in our society are no longer satisfied with attempts simply to "improve" the model of socialism that we inherited from the past. They want to dismantle it and create a new, different society.

Thus we are not talking about re-papering the walls of an old house and refurnishing it but about erecting a completely new structure on the same foundation. Yes, our foundation will remain socialist, but we want to build an entirely different model of socialism upon it.

It strikes me that this is precisely what distinguishes events today from those of other periods in our postwar history when the country was likewise moving forward. For in actual fact, in the 1950s and early 1960s, society's attention was focused on the figure of Stalin, and the problem we faced was diagnosed as the "cult of personality" and its consequences: that is, not a social pathology but rather a malignant growth on a healthy body.

Today everything is different. Today we perceive the fundamental problem neither in particular personalities nor in the wrongdoings and even crimes of one or another leader. And although our press today is actively involved in exposing highly placed officials of the not-too-distant past, it is not primarily this that has riveted people's attention. These are all symptoms of a disease, not the disease itself, which goes far deeper. Because this is a disease of the system, a disease of the society, and not simply of the individual, the medicine used to cure it will have to be potent. The question today is not about the window dressing of the system's functioning but about the very nature of its internal characteristics.

In the past, when we in the Soviet Union talked about socialism, all too often we substituted the ideal for the real as we tried to draw, down to the tiniest detail, the image of the ideal socialist society and, as it were, project it onto ourselves, for the most part ignoring the crying incompatibility between that ideal and reality. Today, with a much more sober and critical view of the reality with which we are dealing in our country, we are trying also to liberate our notions of the socialist ideal from the traditional utopianism, from the millenarian-chiliastic myths about an approaching "thousand-year kingdom" of Good and Justice.

So what remains unshakable in that foundation on which we are preparing to build a new social structure? I suppose it is the main features that distinguish the socialist ideal from other historical social structures, namely public (i.e., state and cooperative) ownership of the means of production and the absence of antagonistic classes and economic exploitation of human labor. Every possible new socialist model makes and will continue to make its "contribution," but in principle these characteristics will remain an integral part of socialism.

A great many people who were socialized and initiated into public life during the 1970s had the nagging feeling that all kinds of problems were piling up, were not being solved, and were looming ever larger. At first timid, we grew ever more determined in our conviction that the extreme crisis situation toward which our society and all its elements— the economy, social relations, political institutions, the intellectual sphere—were heading posed a grave threat. And all of this proceeded against a background of hypocritical self-glorification and panegyrics that no one even believed anymore, probably not even those who wrote them.

Thus, when Mikhail Gorbachev began to speak openly about the crisis situation in the country, most of us, despite the gravity of what he was saying, breathed a sigh of relief. Finally we stopped hiding what was painful and began speaking the truth out loud, saying what we were feeling and thinking.

Again let me stress that the majority of us had already sensed with our whole being this crisis situation developing, but we lacked knowledge and information. Go into any store, and you would feel it: In the economy, in management, there was discord, disorder. But as to what was really going on in the economy, you could not tell—in the newspapers and from the podiums you could hear only of achievements and accomplishments. You would encounter red tape and bureaucracy, a flagrant contempt for what should have been, by law, your rights and interests, and you would feel that all was not well, so to speak, in the social and political arena. But what exactly was wrong and how widespread was the problem, you could not know. And of events in the world, their whys and wherefores, you would not have an inkling from the newspapers or from the radio or television. Hence we had rumors and gossip, a virtual kingdom of hearsay, as if we were not even living in the twentieth century.

That is the way it was—and not just among the so-called ordinary people. Among professionals and intellectuals the situation was similar. True, in their own narrow fields they could still get some information, but under no circumstances were they allowed to look beyond that. At a library they could not usually take out a foreign book unless it was in their limited field of specialization.

It is tempting to use the familiar cliche "closed society" and to say, in effect, that nothing can be expected from such a society. However, even in those years of social lethargy everything was far from one-dimensional. In short, today, even as we subject ourselves to self-criticism, we should not simply dye the white black, or vice versa. We must see the variety of colors that always surrounded and now surround us.

In the West the Soviet Union has often been described as a one-dimensional society devoid of nuances or distinctions, a "totalitarian" society where everything is regulated from above, a society of universal conformity. In all honesty, I cannot lay all of the blame for the creation of this image on Western critics. Obviously one cannot dismiss the fact that there are influential figures and groups in the West who have vested interests in the image of the Soviet Union as "the enemy." Nevertheless, a certain degree of responsibility for this image must also be laid upon our own orthodox ideologues, who have propagandized about the un-fettered "monolithic unity" of Soviet society in which all people say only "yes."

But no matter what our demagogues or yours might say, in reality Soviet society has never been one-dimensional. A diversity of opinions, viewpoints, and intellectual currents has always existed. There have been disagreements as well as dissonance on all levels of Soviet society, as is the case in any normal society.

Of course, there have been periods (encompassing, unfortunately, a large portion of our history) when we have been forcibly compelled to think and act "like everyone else," when disagreements and dissonance were suppressed. But even then we always understood what was what and who was who and knew how to read between the lines even when we could barely read. And naturally there have also been periods (these occurred much less frequently) in Soviet history when, as it were, the floodgates have opened up and diversity, disagreements, and discussions have been welcomed. This was the situation during the de-Stalinization of the 1950s and the reforms of the early 1960s.

Speaking of this period, I feel compelled to mention the name of Nikita Khrushchev, one of the most ambiguous figures in Soviet history. Whatever one might think of his extravagances and, to put it mildly, his ill-considered actions (and although he himself was a product, in a sense, of the Stalinist system), his role—both political and psycho-logical—in undermining Stalinist totalitarianism and creating, even perhaps unconsciously, the basis for a future democratic movement, was considerable.

During the 1970s and the first half of the 1980s, while the official rhetoric was busy polishing its fictitious propagandistic images, we continued to argue—usually among close friends—about our country's social ills. That our economy was stagnating (or whatever scholars might choose to call it) and that technologically we were lagging behind other developed countries (and not just Western countries) were be-coming increasingly visible realities. We would lower our voices to talk about corruption, including corruption at the very top. We touched on various social pathologies as well: alcoholism, drug abuse, crime, vandalism, prostitution. We endured, intensely and bitterly, the almost ritualistic unresponsiveness on the part of our leadership, sensing in ourselves a deepening rift between expectations and reality, word and deed. We experienced a crisis of confidence in everything official—leaders, institutions of power, phraseology.

For some, conformity became an outlet. Others found a safety valve in their private lives, withdrawing into their particular interests, the enclosed world of their personal lives. But many others did not find an escape. There was growing alienation, apathy, and cynicism. People saw that an enormous and ineffective "welfare state" had been created that was excessive and inadequate. As a result, the work ethic itself was being eroded, with people becoming psychologically dependent on social guarantees, and very mediocre guarantees at that. At times the sense of arbitrariness and injustice spilled over into unconscious and poorly focused resentment. In short, these were not failures confined to a single sphere within the system; these were signs of a crisis of the system, which in turn led to the delegitimization of the official structures of the regime. The point is that the stagnation of the regime in the 1970s and early 1980s, and the decay—first and foremost of official structures—that accompanied stagnation still could not completely frustrate and obstruct the vitality of society.

During those years we were developing into a more modern, urban society. The population was growing ever more mobile. People were becoming better educated, and there was an increase in the number of professionals in the population. The standard of living was rising, and people were, I might mention, growing accustomed to this. Needs and expectations were growing quickly, and they were increasingly less likely to be satisfied or realized.

A variety of changes was also occurring in people's value systems. The poverty of meaning in the official rhetoric engendered a sort of spontaneous de-ideologization in the minds of many. People were drawn to moral and ethical questions about the human condition. Interests were becoming particularized, disconnected from one another, as if subject to some centrifugal force. It was only gradually and with difficulty that many people were overcoming some of the traditions of Russian-Soviet political culture and coming to the realization that diversity and pluralism in the life of a society are inevitable and natural.

Even while the word "pluralism" was still being used in quotation marks—as an indication of its "bourgeois" nature—we ourselves, though we did not use the word, were by degrees growing accustomed to the reality of diversity—diversity of life-styles and orientations, of interests and enthusiasms, of opinions and ideas. We were gradually becoming accustomed to somewhat broader definitions of individual rights as well as to the reality of diverse and often conflicting interests of different groups, in particular of "informal groups," as they were called by the media. The great majority of these groups were not at all political in nature, and their informality indicated that they had sprung up spontaneously—not by decree from above, but by their own initiative, as should be the case in any normal society (today, by official estimates, they number up to 30,000).

There was also growing autonomy in the sphere of information. On an unofficial level there arose alternative communications systems: People listened more and more often to foreign broadcasts on shortwave radio; they passed around unofficial printed matter, including foreign publications; video technology became more widespread; various types of contacts with foreigners, here and abroad, were increasing.

An independent public opinion was also taking shape, with an emphasis on social and ethical questions. And as this developing public opinion grew more and more active, it began to influence political decisions. For example, the campaign opposing a plan to divert the northern rivers, which at first seemed to be purely an economic and ecological cause, acquired a certain political significance.

Thus, even during the period of stagnation certain processes were developing at society's core; the preconditions were evolving for change, for overcoming the authoritarian-patriarchal order of things, for breaking through to modernity. And periodically one could glimpse, through the official varnishing of reality, those colors that were destined to determine the face of an emerging Soviet society. At the same time these pressures for changes at the deepest level of society often went against the grain of processes at the official, state level. In other words, there was a growing rift between the society and the state, between the people and the regime.

Seventy years after the October Revolution, the crisis situation had taken on a threatening aspect. We found ourselves at a crossroads in the fullest sense of the word. But many people didn't see any way out. A great many, of course, dreamed of changes, but when they tried to grasp the big picture, they almost lost heart: Changes were needed not just here and there, but everywhere.

The words with which Gorbachev addressed the country shook both the sleepers and the skeptics: We were on the brink of a dangerous precipice. The continuation of our old policies would lead us into a dead end; radical changes—both strategic and programmatic—were needed. But the solutions were not immediately forthcoming. At first, the focus was on attempting to force at least a few of the old social mechanisms to function differently under new conditions. Harsh measures were introduced against corruption and alcoholism and in favor of increased discipline. The measures were drastic and severe indeed. A definite effect, if only temporary and limited, was achieved fairly quickly; in any case, some disgraceful things that had been common in the past were diminished or ceased entirely. Further, these measures showed that the new leadership was serious in its intentions and would act decisively.

The new direction was identified with a term that was advanced for the first time: acceleration (*uskorenie*). In other words, it was thought that the pace of development had to be changed in order to pull society out of the mire of stagnation. Gradually, however, it became obvious that this was hardly the single, universal means of solving all the problems facing us. In a word, you cannot speed something up if it is not moving to begin with. First, it was necessary to clear aside the old obstacles and to create new mechanisms that would establish a new course and movement. Moreover, all this had to be done to a living social organism, one that could not be removed from circulation for repairs and could not be isolated from the external world.

So it was that in the process of radicalizing the reform impulse, the concept of perestroika was born: a program for the revolutionary restructuring of the entire society from the ground up. As Gorbachev said, perestroika is revolution. What we are trying to accomplish today is a radical break with the old society and the creation of a new one. This will not happen without intense conflicts between the old and the new. We have begun an immense experiment, whose very essence—the creation of a new society—strikes me as consonant with the spirit and psychology of America, that great land of innovators and first-comers. We do not want to build utopian schemes and rigid plans, because we know that "politics is the art of the possible." We do not have ready prescriptions for every situation, and there are no guarantees against mistakes. But seventy years after the October Revolution, this is the most interesting and dramatic period yet, both in its scale and in its social complexity; it is a potential watershed in the history of socialism, not only in the USSR but in other countries as well. Perestroika should reveal how and to what extent socialism today is capable of radical internal transformations and reform, whether it is possible to replace authoritarian, dogmatic socialism with a socialism that is free and democratic.

Not only do we believe that this is possible; we believe that for us it is the only solution. But we also recognize that it remains to be demonstrated in practice. In that sense, the fundamental question of our revolution today is in principle an open one: Is it possible to radically change the system that we inherited from the past? This is an open question not because we have doubts, but because we have never before attempted such sweeping changes. In the past, the system has functioned only in one mode of operation—an authoritarian, dogmatic system of administrative decrees. Now we want to transform society and switch it to another mode of operation. This aim presents a formidable challenge.

At times people say that we should return to Leninism, which was trampled on and distorted by Stalinism. And it is true that we must rehabilitate and restore our fundamentals before we can conceive of moving forward. But we also realize that we cannot look to the past for solutions to all the problems that we now face, many of which were unheard of in the past. Simply to copy the past, as Gorbachev has emphasized, would be the worst form of dogmatism; today we need bold quests for new solutions.

A completely justified question then arises: Where are these solutions to come from? Are they to come from the emancipated initiative of those below or from the enlightened impulse of those above? In fact, on this question we can now find adherents of both points of view. At times you even sense a kind of paradox: Democratization and decentralization of our society are difficult to accomplish without relying on a strong, authoritarian central power. For this reason "Gorbachev's revolution" is sometimes referred to as a "revolution from above."

There is a wealth of precedent for this type of revolution in our history. But revolution from above is not simply a coup d'état, a spontaneous impulse for fundamental social change initiated and directed by the country's leadership. There is an element of this, to be sure; the figure of a leader often proves to be a factor of enormous significance, as is the case with Gorbachev. But "Gorbachev's revolution" is not a one-man show. It is a movement of like-minded people at various levels of society. Its success depends on a "revolution from below," a broad-based and diverse coalition for reform.

It is difficult to believe that a revolution from above could be successful were it not met halfway from below and were it not supported by a mass movement. That movement itself can be internally heterogeneous, which lends it a special strength. In our case, perestroika is supported by various economic, political, ideological, and other forces and interests—not all of them necessarily in agreement about everything. But the main thing is that they are all moving emphatically in the same direction toward the radical reform of society.

What exactly are these forces and interests? First, there are those groups within the party that initiated the revolutionary changes. Then, of course, there are also many among the intelligentsia who yearn for the democratization of society. There are the professionals, especially the young ones, who aspire to modernize society and to create an environment in which they can better realize their own personal potential. There are those whose goal is the ideological purification of Marxism-Leninism, who want to rid it of the distortions and corruptions of the Stalinist era and the ensuing years. There are members of the military profession for whom industrial and scientific-technological development represents the only means of maintaining the country's security. Finally, there are also those heterogeneous national groups that are either dissatisfied with the state's decline or see in perestroika the only way to fulfill their national aspirations. It is impossible to name all the groups supporting perestroika. But the point is that a variety of people today are coming out in support of the restructuring and democratization of the entire society.

Sometimes observers in the West express the hope that the process of change in Soviet society will lead to its liberalization. It is a well-known fact that political categories such as liberalism and conservatism are employed differently in different political cultures. For this reason, those in the Soviet Union whom the West call "liberals" are not necessarily liberals in the traditional Western sense of the word. In our case, when one speaks of "liberalizing" the system, what one often has in mind is a mere "loosening of the bolts." But in reality we want much more—not just a slight weakening of the old system but its fundamental restructuring. It is for this reason that we seek not liberalization but fundamental democratization of the whole society, its political system and its social structures. And that, in turn, implies the institutionalization of political reforms as well as fundamental changes in the political culture that we inherited from the past.

We are often asked: And how do you define democracy, what meaning does that concept have for you today? My own view is that when we speak of the democratization of Soviet society, we have in mind two dimensions of democracy: the universal and the specific. Democracy in any society, under any conditions, implies some general, universal principles: democratic freedoms, civil and social rights, and so forth. But at the same time democracy is a relative concept determined by historical, cultural, and national traditions, which, naturally, are different in different countries and among different peoples. Therefore it is hardly worth fostering hopes that sooner or later everything will be reduced to a single common denominator. Even after the implementation of all the proposed changes in the USSR, and even in the case of their complete success (and the obstacles in their path are enormous), we will not become the same type of society as, for example, the United States. Our economy, our political system, our way of life—all will retain our stamp.

Today our slogan is, "Learning democracy!" This is precisely how Gorbachev has formulated one of our fundamental tasks. "What do you mean by that?" many people ask us. We spent seventy years trying to convince ourselves and others that the Soviet Union was the most democratic state in the world, that we should be proud of our democracy. Whether we always believed this is no longer important. Many believed, while others did not. What is important is that we want much more democracy. To us, more democracy means more socialism, but a different kind of socialism—not authoritarian-administrative, but free and democratic.

The democratic revolution that has begun in our country, like any revolution, conflicts with many private interests both of groups and of individuals. Revolution is impossible without opposition. So here too, while the majority of people have long been convinced that we could no longer continue in the old ways, not everyone has taken an enthusiastic view of Gorbachev's revolution.

The danger is posed not so much by organized opposition (which, to tell the truth, is hardly visible) as by passive resistance, boycotting, and social inertia. This opposition most resembles cotton wadding: There are almost no open collisions, but movement forward becomes incredibly difficult, impeded, deflected. The long-awaited laws are enacted but never carried out; radical declarations are pronounced but come to nothing. Let us be honest: There is political and ideological conflict in Soviet society, and it will not die down soon. More likely the opposite will happen. The opponents of reform did not at first believe that their interests were threatened. When they realized, when they understood, the opposition became tougher and, I would say, smarter. And their counterarguments began to appear: "We could go too far with this democracy," "We should not shake the foundations," "We would not want to lose the principles we hold dear," and so forth.

Of course we are all children of the age, products of our social conditions. Even those of us who ardently believe in radical reform find it hard (to use Lenin's phrase) "to squeeze the slave out of ourselves," to overcome the forces of conservatism and inertia in our thinking. But in speaking about opposition and resistance to democratic revolution we should not stop here. We must talk about the concrete interests that stand in the way of change. Who exactly is "against" it?

The bureaucracies within the party and the state defending their own privileged sphere are naturally against democratic reforms. And then there are the doctrinaire ideologues, and not necessarily just professional ones, who imbibed with their mothers' milk a rigid set of stereotypes and who jealously guard its "purity." All sorts of crooks are also against reform—those shady elements who warm their hands over the flames of the corruption, venality, and criminality of the stagnated regime. Sometimes these are crooks on a large scale, who are an integral part of the state apparatus and have become a powerful mafia. There are likewise many groups whose particular interests—and not just material interests—are threatened by perestroika and glasnost.

But perhaps the biggest problem is presented by ordinary people (including ourselves) who are faced with the prospect of having to change radically their opinions and habits, and above all, their attitudes toward work, toward their responsibilities and rights—in short, toward their customary interrelations with society and the state. This unavoidable problem arises so sharply because there is in the very logic of perestroika a kind of paradox: The long-term, radical transformation of our society may in the short term (or possibly in the medium term) demand measures that will have unfavorable economic and social consequences— a rise in prices, bankruptcy, the prospect of relative unemployment, a rise in inequality of wages, and so forth. We are not used to dealing with such problems, and we have much to learn.

We are waking up from long years of sleep, becoming active, responsible, enterprising, capable of shouldering the responsibility for ourselves as well as for society. We can no longer delegate that responsibility, as we have in the past, to some sort of abstraction that exists above and beyond the individual—to a group, a collective, an organization, a society. Today we make our own decisions. And this is an unusual situation for Russian-Soviet political culture. Five, ten, or fifteen years ago I knew exactly what was permissible and what was not; I knew exactly where the boundaries were drawn between the prohibited and the possible. Today I do not know this anymore, because society itself has been transformed. And today I must determine for myself what I think I can and should do. For example, in my books and articles I never intentionally deceived my readers, but, clearly, I was not able to say everything I wanted to because of external and internal censorship. Today I may not be concerned about censorship, but I do not know what the limits of glasnost are, and nobody will tell me. I have to decide for myself, which is sometimes very difficult politically and emotionally. I may very well be reprimanded for my decisions, but nonetheless nobody will make them for me. In making these choices, each person, by his or her very actions, either narrows the range of his or her freedom or broadens it and extends the possibilities in society from within the society itself.

The main instrument of democratization today is openness, glasnost. Real democratization is unthinkable without the creation of new democratic institutions and without structural changes in political, social, and public life; in short, organizationally secured changes are needed. Glasnost is the path to this type of change. More than anything, people want to know the truth, no matter how painful, that has been concealed from them in the past. Therefore, we believe that without glasnost, perestroika is impossible.

It is true that here we have distinctions and nuances in our opinions that are sometimes substantial. Glasnost here is sometimes regarded in the Soviet Union exclusively as a means of achieving perestroika. But many people, myself included, are convinced that glasnost is a very important goal in its own right. Glasnost cannot be regarded as something subordinate to other tasks, as something instrumental. Our people have already developed a taste for the truth, for openness. An acute moral sense has been awakened in them by which they judge politics, and society is growing bolder before our very eyes.

But not everyone understands yet that glasnost is not manna from heaven. Glasnost is an intense, difficult process, and it has a price. Is everyone prepared to pay it? The cost of glasnost is the open expression by others of views and ideas that might be alien and unacceptable to you personally and that you may even find repulsive. Glasnost's cost means the protests of the Crimean Tatars, the activities of the chauvinistic society Pamiat, the demonstrations of the refuseniks, the meetings in Nagornyi Karabakh, and the outrageous behavior of our own primitive "rockers" and "punks." Glasnost applies equally to the Stalinists and to those fighting Stalinism, for neither one nor the other is able to repress their opponents. How often one would like to take "practical steps" against those who, you are quite sure, are incorrect, and what's worse, who you are convinced are hindering progress. But it is the whole idea of a state governed by law, an idea at which we have finally arrived in the eighth decade of our development, that one's convictions, sympathies, and dislikes should never, even in the slightest degree, put into question the rights of others to have different convictions, sympathies, and dislikes. The only intermediary between oneself and society, or between society and the state, is law. This can hardly be regarded as an established tradition in our history. So we also realize that we are talking about a task that is fundamental in its complexity and scope: that of creating a new political culture in society and ridding it of a great many of its former components, including some that are a product of ancient traditions of Russian history.

Many of us today are growing discouraged: Where are the visible, palpable, material results of perestroika, democratization, and glasnost? To this question I would answer thus: Today in Soviet society a most important psychological groundwork is being laid, the preconditions for more radical changes to follow. Without such preconditions these changes would simply not be possible because they would be psychologically alien and would not become a necessity of life. And sooner or later we will have to choose: We can either allow the gradual dying out of reform or pursue its further radicalization. And we need to be prepared to face this dilemma both politically and emotionally.

Thus when we talk about glasnost, we are not talking simply about removing prohibitions and permitting what was not allowed yesterday. Glasnost and perestroika presuppose much deeper changes both in society and in the individual. Their goal is the formation of a new, autonomous—that is, nongovernmental—political culture. Their goal is a new social contract between the individual, the society, and the state.

We have a great deal to learn in order to reach these goals. We must learn democracy. We must learn tolerance. We must learn pluralism. And this process has already begun. We are better able to recognize the diversity of social groups. Even our conceptions of the state and the party itself are losing their exclusive character, as we begin to perceive them as situated among a whole group of other, independent social institutions. And even pluralism itself is beginning to be perceived as characteristic of any normal society; it no longer smacks of whatever foreign political and ideological overtones it once had. This pluralism should have definite limits—Gorbachev is quite open about this. It is a pluralism of opinions, interests, necessities, and orientations within the framework of a socialist society. But this very framework is being immeasurably broadened, so much so that "our" and "your" orthodoxies can even discern a movement beyond the boundaries of socialism. Some orthodox ideologues will fear this; others will welcome it. But both will be wrong, because they will be essentially operating from a one-dimensional and absolutely dogmatic conception of socialism that has its roots in the Stalinism of the past. We reject such a conception of socialism and are trying to change it.

Of course, a great many of us proved to be unprepared for all of this. Absolutely everyone must readjust. We must confront the real costs of democratization and glasnost, for unless we do, it will be impossible for us to create a new society based upon democracy and socialism.

We are often asked if there are limits to glasnost. We will be frank: Yes, there are. Until recently very little was written or said about Afghanistan. There are government institutions—for example, the KGB— that are largely shielded, for various reasons, from the bright light of glasnost. We are ignorant of many details, sometimes extremely vital ones, about the lives, opinions, and differences among those in the ranks of our leadership. Our foreign policy is only gradually becoming more open. We have not yet witnessed the death of many ideological "sacred cows."

Glasnost is undergoing some serious tests, and its every success is greeted with a sigh of relief. Chernobyl, the "Yeltsin affair," Nagornyi Karabakh, and many others all represent both sore trials for glasnost and its partial triumph. Glasnost is in danger of rhetorical impoverish-ment by those who only "talk glasnost." It is threatened by demagogic populism and leftist extremism. Nor have the conservatives made their peace with glasnost, and that is a major threat to it today. But no less dangerous is the potential for dissatisfaction and bitterness from below when glasnost is measured by only one criterion: What goods are available on the shelves of the local supermarket?

That question is far from simple: People's real standard of living is extremely low, and the first years of perestroika are not likely to improve that situation. Soviet economists who advocate reform warn that short-term sacrifices will be necessary for the sake of achieving long-term goals. But beyond that, there is the larger question of the correlation between glasnost and perestroika. Of course, a person cannot live by bread alone, but, although for me personally there is now nothing of higher value in our reforms than glasnost, it is clear that glasnost alone will not feed people either. For that reason the understandable temptation of many is to see in glasnost only the satisfaction of intelligentsia ambitions and not the necessary prerequisite for a complex (economic, political, ideological, and psychological) transformation of society.

Glasnost is not a decree that has been promulgated, nor a condition that has been attained, but a process—a complex, painful process, which often proceeds haltingly, but which, like the air we breathe, is essential to our society as it tries to reform itself.

Glasnost has its own stages of development. What was taboo three years ago was being openly discussed just last year. And what we still do not dare to discuss today will become the subject of stormy discussion tomorrow. I have written "will become," and it occurs to me: What grounds are there to believe in the inevitability and invincibility of this process? In the progress of history, nothing is "inevitable" or "irrever-sible." Glasnost is inevitable and irreversible only to the extent that we ourselves, through our own efforts, make it so. We should recall the period of chilled silence in the press and public discussions from 13 March through 5 April 1988, the period from the publication of the sensational article by Nina Andreeva—the "anti-perestroika," "anti-glas-nost" manifesto—to the well-known editorial in *Pravda* reiterating the correctness of perestroika and the democratization of society. For three full weeks there were very few indeed who dared openly challenge this conservative manifesto—which only proves that glasnost is still fragile and needs nurturing.

The 21st Party Conference (June 1988) established the guidelines for our movement toward democracy. And even if, as some maintain, it did not give us a sufficiently strong push forward, its significance lies elsewhere. It secured and legitimized the progress made thus far, and it did so under new and unusual conditions—conditions of much more marked opposition and counteraction by political and ideological forces in our country than we are used to. So all in all I am convinced that the 21st Party Conference was a major success for perestroika and glasnost.

Yet I must share one more feeling. Intellectually, we are thoroughly aware of the immense difficulties on the path of perestroika and glasnost, all the huge obstacles that will undoubtedly continue to arise on this path, and even the absence of the inevitability of our success. But with all my heart, I, and all of us who have started off on the road of radical reform, flatly refuse to allow the possibility of failure. As the Americans say, all our eggs are in one basket.

It is not just the heart speaking. The mind has its own arguments for the irreversibility of Gorbachev's revolution. What seems particularly important here is the psychological factor—the feeling that there is no alternative to perestroika and glasnost. At times the mood approaches the apocalyptic. This is our last chance; if we do not now accomplish what we have set out to do, we will enter the twenty-first century as an inferior power, as a stagnating society that appeals to nobody, as an underdeveloped giant bristling with its terrible weapons of mass destruction.

A sociological analysis should likewise strengthen our optimism. The genie has been let out of the bottle, and the social momentum for change grows ever stronger. The further it goes, the harder it will be to stop the democratic movement—that is why at this point literally every month is crucial. It appears to me that a widening of the social base for change is also taking place; right now, young people and the educated and professional strata are the main supporters of reform, but the average worker, who wants to determine for himself his own social conditions, is waking up little by little. Of course these workers' opinions are not unanimous, but the mere fact that they are becoming more active at the workplace and are more willing to determine their own fate is an important factor in our favor. And we have many other motivated, informal groups in society on our side.

We face an uphill battle. True, it is not the best solution, but all others are worse.

———————

The idea for this book was born a year and a half ago. I remember asking my American friends how much Americans knew, from their own newspapers, magazines, radio and television broadcasts, about the violent arguments and discussions, the diversity of opinions, ideas, and points of view that glasnost had made available to the Soviet people.

Yes, the words "perestroika" and "glasnost" are well known in the West, as was the word "sputnik" thirty years ago. But at times we ourselves in the USSR, especially early on, have tried to present these developments in a way that made it seem as if absolutely the whole of society was moving in orderly rows, monolithically and unanimously, toward perestroika, glasnost, and democratization. The impression was that we could move toward this new way of thinking with the same unanimity with which in former times we talked about maintaining other agendas.

Of course that is not so—it was not then, and it is not now. When the oppression that we had felt in the past was eased somewhat, nothing like unanimity of opinion ensued. At the risk of disappointing many Western observers and destroying many illusions, I have to say that the Soviet people never marched in orderly rows in the direction of the liberal democracy that seemed so "natural" to our opponents and to our friends across the sea. The result was the birth of a multitude of forces and tendencies, in many ways incompatible with each other, each arguing and insisting that it had a corner on the truth. In short, the result was the formation of a whole spectrum of positions on virtually every question.

Some of us were frightened and dismayed: What is this? Are we not undermining our own foundations? Are we not chipping away little by little at what is most important? It was not a simple thing for people to get used to a diversity of points of view, from which no single idea, strictly speaking, can lay claim to a monopoly on truth. But I am convinced that the real strength of a society—its vigor, its readiness for change—lies only in such diversity and in the conflict between various forces and tendencies. Thus, when in our discussions today we encounter conflict and at times passionate, polarized opinions, I see it as a sign of strength, not weakness. As in the world of nature diversity ensures development, so in society, reductionism, boiling everything down to one type of mode or position, carries the threat of stagnation and decay, while diversity moves things forward and stimulates development.

So when a year and a half ago I asked my American friends whether Americans know about the passions that are seething here around perestroika and glasnost, they immediately answered my question with another question: Would I undertake to prepare a collection of pieces from the Soviet press for American readers? These American friends of mine were Dulce and Michael Murphy of the Esalen Institute, who have spent many years pursuing citizen diplomacy, arranging various contacts and connections with the Soviet Union. At first I had my doubts. After all, my professional work lies in a completely different area, the study of American society. But it was also true that I was more excited by everything that was going on in my country than by anything in my professional work. And so I decided to give it a try. I talked to Soviet friends and colleagues from the Institute of the USA and Canada about our idea and suggested that we compile a selection of the most interesting materials that had been published in Soviet newspapers and magazines on the most important questions under discussion in our country today. Without dedication and participation in this effort of Oleg Aliakrinskii, Sergei Filatov, Peter Gladkov, Irina Isakova, Aleksandr Nikitin, Alexei Pankin, and Vasilii Vlasikhin, this book would not have been possible.

Why was this book necessary? Naturally we keep up with publications in the American press and know the serious work being done by such well-known specialists on the Soviet Union as Seweryn Bialer, Marshall Shulman, Gail Lapidus, Alexander Dallin, George Breslauer, Robert Legvold, Steven Cohen, Jerry Hough, Frederick Starr, Archie Brown, and others. But we wanted to offer the American reader the opportunity to judge the changes in Soviet society on a first-hand basis.

Of course we had to limit ourselves in many ways. It was not possible to find room in one book for everything of interest being discussed in the Soviet Union today. Obviously, not everything that is important for the Soviet people will be equally interesting and comprehensible to Americans. For this reason we decided to focus on a limited number of themes, selecting relevant excerpts from Soviet publications and abridging them in places where they were not directly related to our central focus. We also had to define our chronological boundaries. We chose the period from the end of 1986 to the end of 1988, because it was precisely during this time that the most dramatic events occurred in the Soviet Union and that decisions were made that in many respects would determine our future. We confined ourselves only to those materials that were published in Russian in our open national press, and primarily in the mainstream press—in such newspapers as *Pravda*, *Izvestiia*, *Moskovskie Novosti*, or its English-language edition, *Moscow News*, *Sovetskaia Kul'tura* (Soviet Culture), *Literaturnaia Gazeta* (Literary Gazette), *Nedelia* (The Week), *Literaturnaia Rossiia* (Literary Russia) and in the journals *Novyi Mir* (New World), *Znamia* (The Banner), *Voprosy Filosofii* (Problems of Philosophy), *SShA: Ekonomika, Politika, Ideologiia* (The USA: Economy, Politics, Ideology), *Argumenty i Fakty* (Arguments and Facts), and *Novoe Vremia* (New Times), among others.

In some sense this choice limits our presentation of the political and ideological spectrum that really exists in the Soviet Union today. For example, we did not draw on the many interesting publications and materials of many "informal groups," nor of the provincial and local press. We did not try to cover the unofficial extremes of the political spectrum emerging today in the Soviet Union. But at the same time, even our very limited focus demonstrates the immense expansion of glasnost's reach and the spheres of more open discussion in the mainstream press.

This book could not have been produced without the help and useful comments and suggestions from colleagues and friends in Soviet studies at Berkeley and Stanford, especially Gail Lapidus and Alexander Dallin. If Gail had not committed herself to this project, worked with me as coeditor, and undertaken a crusade to have the manuscript published, you would not be able to read it now.

We hope that the materials collected here might be of use to the American reader who is interested in the changes taking place today in the Soviet Union.

GAIL W. LAPIDUS

Overview—The Role of Glasnost in Gorbachev's Reform Strategy

"Glasnost" has become a household word in Western discussions of the Soviet Union, indeed an all-embracing symbol of the entire Gorbachev era. It has been indiscriminately applied to virtually every aspect of Gorbachev's policies and sometimes used as a synonym for perestroika (restructuring) itself. The expanding scope of glasnost in the past few years has been the single most dramatic manifestation of the far-reaching process of change in state-society relations now under way in the Soviet Union.

Perhaps best translated as "public disclosure," with its simultaneous connotation of candor and publicity, glasnost is not only an end in itself but also a central instrument in Gorbachev's larger campaign for reform. It reflects a recognition that building support at home and abroad for major changes in Soviet domestic and foreign policy requires a less secretive approach to Soviet reality: a more candid acknowledgment of Soviet shortcomings and errors and an expansion of the boundaries of public discussion, although by no means an abrogation of its limits. At bottom, it reflects a serious rethinking of how the Soviet leadership should relate to its own population as well as to the wider international community.

The years since Gorbachev became general secretary have been marked by a gradual widening of the role and scope of glasnost, a trend that is closely connected to the progressive radicalization of Gorbachev's conception of reform. Since the summer of 1986 Gorbachev has expressed a growing realization that the problems he inherited were more complex, and the obstacles to reform more daunting, than he initially thought.

His original focus on economic reform, with its emphasis on *uskorenie* (acceleration), was progressively supplanted by a recognition that more fundamental structural changes were essential to achieve a revitalization of the Soviet system. His campaign for perestroika is a call for far-reaching departures from prevailing practices and norms in virtually every area of Soviet life. Indeed, in July 1986 Gorbachev described "restructuring" as nothing short of revolution, encompassing "not only the economy but all other sides of society's life: social relations, the political system, the spiritual and ideological sphere, the style and work methods of the party and of all our cadres. . . . I would equate restructuring with revolution . . . genuine revolution in the minds and hearts of people."

Glasnost is a central instrument of this effort. "We need glasnost," Gorbachev put it, "as we need air." But the novelty and strategic significance of this instrument derive from his recognition that Soviet society has reached a level of maturity that requires a new approach to its governance. The Soviet people, and particularly the educated middle classes, can no longer be treated as the passive objects of official policy but must be brought into some form of partnership.

Khrushchev launched the process of inclusion—a shift, however erratic, from the centralized, coercive statism of the Stalinist system to a more conciliatory and flexible approach to social forces. Gorbachev seeks to extend it further. His advocacy of glasnost, as of cultural liberalization and democratization, is not merely a tactical device to secure the support of the scientific and cultural intelligentsia for his economic and political program or a public relations effort aimed at world opinion. It reflects a profound recognition that successful reform depends on fundamentally redefining the relationship of state and society.

The espousal of glasnost stands at the center of this effort. At one level it is, of course, a policy of preemption, intended to reduce the reliance of the Soviet population on foreign and unofficial sources of information. As the new Soviet leadership clearly recognized, dreary uniformity had robbed the Soviet media of credibility. On domestic as well as international issues, foreign sources of information, ranging from radio broadcasts to gossip, filled the void created by official silence.

The Chernobyl disaster gave enormous impetus to the advocates of change in information policy. The fact that the Soviet people first learned of a major domestic catastrophe with far-reaching implications for their own welfare from foreign broadcasts, and that the news was initially denied by their own government, was a major political embarrassment. It dramatized as never before the high costs of traditional Soviet secretiveness, both domestically and internationally. It demonstrated the extent to which new technologies had fostered a revolution in communications that was undermining the Soviet state's monopoly over information and breaching the Iron Curtain, which had long insulated the Soviet population from the outside world. After Chernobyl, Gorbachev became more determined to expand and enliven the flow of information in order to enhance his credibility at home and abroad.

In its early phases glasnost meant a more candid discussion of troublesome subjects, including subjects previously absent from the Soviet media. Accidents and disasters now found their way into the Soviet press, along with discussions of an increasing range of social pathologies, from drug addiction to prostitution, whose very existence had long been denied. Soviet television, giving unprecedented attention to political discontent, even showed the nationalist demonstrations in Alma-Ata in 1986.

Glasnost also served as an instrument for consolidating Gorbachev's political position. The enormity of the task he has undertaken, and the limited institutional support on which it is based, compelled the Soviet leader to seek new ways of mobilizing support for his programs. In the process he has turned to the media as a novel and influential political resource. The relatively recent spread of television to even the remotest corners of the Soviet Union has rendered obsolete the entire agitprop system that was long the linchpin of Soviet political socialization. Furthermore, industrialization and increasing educational attainments transformed the passive and inarticulate peasant society of the Stalin era into an urban society with an increasingly articulate and assertive middle class.

Gorbachev is the first Soviet leader to appreciate the way in which new technologies and new social forces impinge on Soviet political life and to recognize the potential power of the mass media in reaching this new "attentive public." By placing supporters of reform in key positions in ideological and cultural institutions or as editors of influential journals and newspapers and by making skillful use of Soviet television, he has sought to use the media to shape the terms of debate over reform to his political advantage and to compensate for his relative weakness in the more traditional organs of power.

Moreover, although Gorbachev's use of the media to attack and expose political opponents has a long tradition in Soviet political history, it is a double-edged sword with potentially broader implications. Glasnost encourages an expanded and more independent role for the media in exposing abuses of power and position by officials. For example, by promoting serious investigative reporting by journalists, it not only supports the principle of political accountability but provides an instrument for holding officials accountable for their actions.

Glasnost extends to the treatment of the Soviet past as well as the present and has been invoked on behalf of a more critical assessment of the Stalin as well as the Brezhnev eras. The process of de-Stalinization, initiated by Khrushchev but interrupted and partially reversed under Brezhnev, has regained momentum and provoked some of the sharpest public debates of the Gorbachev era. Gorbachev's endorsement of a fuller and more accurate account of early Soviet history has encouraged the publication of previously unpublished memoirs and documents that shed new light on highly sensitive historical events, such as the forcible collectivization of agriculture, the assassination of Sergei Kirov in 1934 and the Great Purges that followed, and even of Stalin's foreign policy and the events surrounding World War II. It has also invited a re-examination of the alternatives to Stalin. One consequence is the emergence of Lenin's associates and the later victims of Stalinism—Bukharin, Trotsky, Zinoviev, and others—from decades of oblivion and calumny. The Khrushchev and Brezhnev periods have also come in for serious reexamination.

If one motive in the "unrewriting" of history is the plain quest for truth, for Gorbachev and his followers historical revisionism also serves more instrumental goals. By removing the layers of varnish that had long prettified the Soviet past and present, and by highlighting previously ignored failures of earlier Soviet policies, glasnost delegitimizes certain features of Stalinism, demonstrates the urgency of reform, and serves to validate fresh approaches.

Historical revisionism has its parallel in the new approaches to Soviet culture. The most far-reaching and tangible of Gorbachev's reforms have been the publication of long-suppressed poems and novels and the public screening of controversial films. They represent a form of reconciliation with the intelligentsia and an expression of a more tolerant and ecumenical approach to Soviet culture. The publication of such novels as Anatolii Rybakov's *Children of the Arbat* and the screening of Tengiz Abuladze's powerful film *Repentance,* for example, brought unprecedentedly frank and powerful evocations of the crimes of the Stalin era into the open. At the same time, the literary and cultural journals that review these works have become a forum for major public debates with clear political ramifications. The reappraisal of the contributions of such writers and poets as Mikhail Bulgakov, Boris Pasternak, Marina Tsvetaeva, and Anna Akhmatova, once scorned for their deviation from "socialist realism," and the publication of works like *Dr. Zhivago,* and, more recently, of works by Solzhenitsyn, extend the boundaries of licit literature to figures and works of art previously excluded. Overtures to artists who emigrated seek to reunite the two streams of Russian culture at home and abroad.

During the cultural thaw of the Khrushchev era, the personal intervention of Khrushchev himself was required to authorize the publication of novels like Solzhenitsyn's *One Day in the Life of Ivan Denisovich*. By contrast, current approaches involve a partial devolution of cultural decision making from the center. Editors of journals and newspapers and directors of film studios and theaters now have responsibility for the contents of what they produce. This policy promotes a greater diversity in the cultural realm and narrows the degree of direct state intervention in the arts and letters.

Glasnost is also perceived by the present leadership as an instrument of feedback allowing it to monitor the pulse of Soviet society. The new regime has given support to the significantly wider use of surveys and opinion polls and has recognized the critical role of sociological research in understanding attitudes and behavior. As Gorbachev has put it: "We regard the development of glasnost as a way of accumulating the various diverse ideas and views which reflect the interests of all strata, of all trades and professions in Soviet society. We won't be able to advance if we don't check how our policy responds to criticism, especially criticism from below." Clearly seeking to defend himself against the charge that the West might use criticism to discredit socialism, he insisted: "I myself do not fear criticism. A critical review of our own experience is a sign of strength, not weakness. . . . Criticism is a bitter medicine, but the ills that plague society make it a necessity. You make a wry face, but you swallow it."

In broadening the boundaries of legitimate public discussion, glasnost opened the door to a transformation of Soviet ideology itself, most visible in the party's ideological journal, *Kommunist*. Lenin's conception of a single truth no longer holds sway, nor does the idea that there can be an infallible approach to any problem; instead, its articles present diverse and even conflicting approaches to current problems, and readers' letters often include sharp critiques of their key points. The very introduction of formal debate on Soviet television, with its presentation of two diametrically opposed positions on major issues of the day without any final resolution, is a dramatic departure from long-standing behavior.

Gorbachev clearly aligned himself with the advocates of ideological flexibility at the January 1987 Central Committee Plenum when he criticized what he called a "schematic and dogmatic approach" to party ideology. He attacked the persistence of theoretical concepts that remained at the level of the 1930s and the 1940s while the country's needs had fundamentally changed, the disappearance of vigorous debates and creative ideas, the absence of competition and conflict, and the absolutizing of particular points of view that should have been treated as contingent and context-dependent. And he explicitly criticized portrayals of Soviet society that denied the diversity of groups and interests, and the possibility of conflicts among them, as a denial of social dynamism itself.

This speech echoed a striking article that had appeared in late 1986 in *Izvestiia* calling for greater debate and controversy on major issues of the day. "We must get used to the idea that a multiplicity of voices is a natural part of openness," its author had argued.

> We must treat diversity normally, as the natural state of the world; not with clenched teeth, as in the past, but normally as an immutable feature of social life. . . . We need in the economy and other areas of Soviet life a situation where multiple variants and alternative solutions are in and of themselves development tools and preconditions for obtaining optimal results and where the coexistence of two opposing points of view on a single subject is most fruitful.

Reminding his audience of the high price paid in the past for intolerance toward other opinions, the author said: "We must learn to live under democratic conditions."

If glasnost serves these multiple purposes in Gorbachev's strategy of reform, it also has a deeper significance. At bottom, glasnost is also a symbol of trust. It reflects a recognition by the Soviet leadership of the maturity of the Soviet people and a partial repudiation of the patronizing notion that only a small elite could be entrusted with truth. It constitutes a potential challenge to the entire Bolshevik conception of a vanguard party, premised as it was on the need for tutelage over backward masses.

It is equally an expression of confidence in the basic legitimacy of the Soviet system and in its leadership, a recognition that the pretense of infallibility is no longer necessary to command popular allegiance and support. Indeed, greater publicity for shortcomings and problems— ranging from the shoddy construction of nuclear power plants to the spread of drug addiction—is an indispensable precondition for addressing them successfully.

The case for glasnost and its intimate connection to the prospects for reform was most eloquently put by Tat'iana Zaslavskaya, the reformist sociologist, who argued in a remarkable article in *Pravda:* "If we continue to keep from the people information about the conditions under which they live, say the degree of environmental pollution, the number of industrial accidents, or the extent of crime, we cannot expect them to assume a more active role in economic or in political life. People will trust and support you only if you trust them."

This realization of the interdependence of openness and trust is reflected in Soviet foreign policy as well, and particularly in relations with the United States. Traditional Soviet secretiveness and xenophobia are challenged by the advocates of a more forthcoming approach that is more sensitive to the concerns of potential partners abroad. A series of unprecedented Soviet initiatives manifest this new approach—from the testimony of a young embassy official before a congressional committee in the aftermath of the Chernobyl disaster, to the opening of the Krasnoyarsk radar installation to a group of visiting members of the U.S. Congress, to Soviet agreement to intrusive on-site inspection under the new INF treaty, to Gorbachev's disclosure of the size of the Soviet military budget. This new approach also involves opening Soviet television and the pages of the Soviet press to occasional presentations by Western political figures and scholars not known for their sympathy to the Soviet regime, from Margaret Thatcher to Richard Pipes.

As glasnost expands the scope of public discussion and gives voice to previously silenced views, the limits to the range of topics and points of view that can be expressed publicly are themselves changing over time. The basic features of the Soviet system—such as the role of public ownership and the monopoly of power by the Communist party—were initially immune to challenge but were later opened to discussion. Leadership politics, previously beyond public scrutiny, began to be exposed to public view. The speeches made by top party leaders who were compelled to resign their positions in April 1989 were published in full. And the first meetings of the newly elected Congress of People's Deputies and Supreme Soviet were televised live to millions of Soviet viewers.

Although foreign and security policy remain to a considerable degree "closed zones," a number of taboos have begun to be breached here as well. In journals of limited circulation and in interviews abroad, Soviet officials and scholars have begun to acknowledge that erroneous policies were pursued in a number of important areas. Questions have been raised regarding Stalin's approach to Nazism, the Molotov-Ribbentrop Pact of 1939, the Katyn massacre, the deployment of the SS-20s in Europe, and the scale of Soviet military expenditures; but most of the relevant archives remain sealed to this day. Even military and security affairs, long exempted from public discussion, have begun to receive closer scrutiny, and the actions of senior officials to be openly challenged. The use of military force against demonstrators in Tblisi, and the subsequent secrecy and disinformation concerning the circumstances of its use, evoked unprecedented public criticism in the media as well as among the newly elected deputies.

In the view of the Soviet leadership, glasnost does not enshrine the principle of freedom of expression. On the one hand, as Gorbachev himself has affirmed, freedom extends only to that which serves the cause of socialism. On the other hand, the boundaries of this novel "socialist pluralism" are fluid and hotly contested. Editors of different journals are willing to take different degrees of risk in publishing unorthodox pieces, while divisions within the political leadership provide some degree of protection to different views. On many issues, most notably nationality questions, the central media are less forthcoming than the local language press. A variety of individuals and groups seek to push these boundaries of tolerated expression and organization still further.

The emergence of a rich variety of unofficial groups and journals concerned with public affairs, and the ambiguity of their status, is testimony to the fluidity and novelty of the present Soviet scene. At one end of the political spectrum, a leading unofficial journal as well as a number of political clubs have appropriated the very title of "glasnost" to legitimize their activities, and their fate will serve as a barometer of the reforms in general. At the same time, current policies have elicited a reactionary backlash, most visible in the activities of Pamiat ("Memory"), which has sought to use glasnost on behalf of Great Russian nationalist, anti-Western, and xenophobic policies.

In the United States, glasnost must be seen as a welcome development, even if it does not meet the full range of Western concerns. It remains politically bounded and constrained by the nature of the Soviet system. It is dependent on the priorities of particular leaders, unbuttressed by firm legal guarantees, and vulnerable to reversal in a political culture still imbued with a strong commitment to control and an intense fear that spontaneity will lead to anarchy. The Soviet regime has had considerable experience at repressing deviance but relatively little in managing diversity.

To the extent that glasnost moves the Soviet Union in the direction of greater openness, responsiveness, and diversity, it can only be applauded and deserves to be encouraged. We should not delude ourselves into expecting that openness is synonymous with liberalism and that it will encourage the expression only of more humane, tolerant, and decent views. But the new information policy offers the Soviet population a more accurate picture of their own country and of the world abroad, as well as more informed input into Soviet policy-making. It also offers some degree of legitimation to the assimilation of Western standards, values, and ideas. Above all, glasnost is an essential prerequisite to the real liberalization and democratization of the Soviet system and to the transformation of subjects into citizens.

This volume is intended to convey something of the richness and diversity of the sociopolitical debate that has emerged in the USSR as a consequence of glasnost. Itself a collaborative effort by a Soviet-American "team," *The Glasnost Papers* is testimony of the new possibilities for Soviet-American cooperation that have been created by the process of reform.

ONE

The Anatomy of Glasnost

"And there poured out, like a sea, beneficent glasnost. . . . Oh, do not believe, do not believe, venerable foreigners, that we are afraid of beneficent glasnost, that we only now introduced it—and we are frightened by it and are hiding from it. No, we love glasnost and we caress it like a newborn child. We love this little imp who has just cut small, strong, and healthy teeth. . . . No, we are not afraid of glasnost, we do not shy away from it. It is all healthy, it is the young juices, a young inexperienced force that pulsates like a healthy spring and gushes to the surface."

—Fedor Dostoevskii

These words, which today sound so relevant, were pronounced by Fedor Dostoevskii more than 120 years ago in connection with the slight weakening of censorship that occurred after the abolition of serfdom in Russia in 1861. Since that time, glasnost has appeared more than once in our intellectual history. Glasnost, now elevated to the rank of state policy, has become an integral part of Gorbachev's revolution.

What Is Glasnost?

In the West, this typical Russian word was given wide currency after April 1985, having quickly become a kind of watchword for perestroika. At first, people attempting to discover its exact meaning tried to translate it very precisely, at times as "criticism," at other times as "openness," even as "advertisement." Then they stopped translating it and began to write simply "glasnost."

The basic principles of the policy of glasnost proclaimed by the new Soviet leadership were formulated by General Secretary Mikhail Gorbachev in his book *Perestroika: New Thinking for Our Country and the World* (pp. 75–78):

We want more openness about public affairs in every sphere of life. People should know what is good, and what is bad, too. . . . Truth is the main thing. . . . Today, glasnost is a vivid example of a normal and favorable spiritual and moral atmosphere in society, which makes it possible for people to understand better what happened to us in the past, what is taking place now, what we are striving for. . . . The people should know life with all its contradictions and complexities. Working people must have complete and truthful information on achievements and impediments, on what stands in the way of progress and thwarts it. . . . People are becoming increasingly convinced that glasnost is an effective form of public control over the activities of all government bodies, without exception, and a powerful lever in correcting shortcomings. . . . We regard the development of glasnost as a way of accumulating the various diverse views and ideas which reflect the interests of all strata, of all trades and professions in Soviet society. . . . We need glasnost as we need air.

The word "glasnost" comes from the adjective *glasnyi*. The authoritative dictionary of the Russian language of Vladimir Dal' (the Russian equivalent of Webster's) provides the following definition of glasnyi: "that which is known or evident to all, not concealed, everywhere made public." Glasnost is openness; it is the adoption of democratic forms for the expression of one's opinion, position, or interests. Glasnost also means the public disclosure of all that was formerly secret or hidden.

In the Russian language the word "glasnost" conjures up a whole succession of associations: It is "voice," but it is also "eye." Glasnost is sight, enlightenment, publication. Glasnost is the voice pronouncing the revealed truth. The proper field of the vital activity of glasnost is the public forum. In Russia the public forum has long since been the printed page. Today it also includes radio and television, but the newspaper and the journal still remain the principal estate of contemporary glasnost. Newspapers have become our necessary spiritual sustenance and the most important part of our daily life. Since the end of 1986, the number of subscribers to the major Soviet newspapers has sharply risen. People began to read *Pravda* and other Soviet publications with even more interest than they listened to the Voice of America or the BBC. The reason for this is the appearance of more open and honest information about what is happening in the country, the polemical spirit, the discussions, and the confrontation of various opposing points of view and opinions.

In order to fully understand the social and intellectual impact of glasnost, the Western reader should keep in mind that glasnost destroyed the monstrous empire of censorship where for many decades the Soviet media and ordinary Soviets had been doomed to dwell. It is easier to describe what was allowed to be discussed on the printed page than to enumerate what was banned. The latter embraced a vast area of information: the military budget, the crime rate in Moscow, grain imports, railroad crashes, Afghanistan, the monthly salaries of Olympic champions, slave labor on cotton fields in Uzbekistan, and prostitutes at "Intourist" hotels. The Soviet media was only allowed to comment on official statements reported in *Pravda*. Hence the unanimity and "single-voicedness" of Soviet pre-glasnost newspapers, whose correspondents just parroted the central party daily.

With glasnost this monolithic pyramid tumbled down. Newspapers and magazines gradually became voices of different minds. The spectrum of opinions reflected in the print media now ranges from the liberal and anti-Stalinist *Moskovskie Novosti* (published by the Novosti press agency), *Izvestiia* (the Supreme Soviet's daily), *Literaturnaia Gazeta* (published by the Soviet Writers' Union), *Sovetskaia Kul'tura* (published jointly by the Communist party and the Ministry of Culture) to the more traditionalist, if not orthodox, *Pravda* (the Communist party officials' daily), *Sovetskaia Rossiia* (published by the Russian Federation Supreme Soviet), and *Krasnaia Zvezda* (the Defense Ministry's daily). Somewhere in between is the influential *Komsomolskaia Pravda* (the Komsomol's League of Young Communists' daily). The diversity of liberal and conservative opinions is even more obvious in monthly magazines, many of them enjoying an audience of several million readers. *Ogonyok*, *Znamia*, *Novyi Mir*, *Druzhba Narodov*, *Yunost'* (all Moscow-based), and *Neva* (Leningrad), *Daugava* (Riga, Latvia), and *Raduga* (Tallinn, Estonia) are uncompromisingly anti-Stalinist and anti-Brezhnevist, advocating more freedom and democracy. *Nash Sovremennik* and *Molodaia Gvardia* tend to cling to old dogmas in ideology while promulgating an idea of "patriotism" which is but a euphemism for Russian nationalist and isolationist sentiments. Battles of words between the two camps are now waged on the pages of these newspapers and magazines, something unthinkable in the pre-glasnost era.

Before glasnost, the Soviet Union, according to the Soviet media, was a society without any grave problems or contradictions; no disputes were necessary. And what was published in the West or broadcast by Voice of America on current affairs in the Soviet Union was "anti-communist slander" that justified jamming Western radios and banning sales of *The New York Times* in Soviet cities. With glasnost all these restrictions have been lifted. A closed society, obsessed with secrecy, is being transformed into a normal one.

How have the Soviet media changed under the conditions of glasnost? What possibilities and unexpected obstacles has glasnost created for the journalist? Ivan Laptev, the editor in chief of *Izvestiia*, addressed these questions directly in an interview in the journal *Ogonyok* (1987, no. 32):

> I am absolutely convinced that glasnost is in no way simply the communication of information or even simply the expression of one or another position. Glasnost is a form of public self-government and self-control. And its task, in the words of Lenin, is to have an informed public that can make judgments about everything and can make conscious decisions. That is why you must think not only about the kind of information you circulate, but also what kind of impact it will have on people's consciousness and to what ends it will motivate them. . . .
>
> That is why the question of whether or not there exists in us an "internal editor" has to be connected with our past. Of course, the internal editor exists in each of us. But it manifests itself in different ways. In some people it is so strong that it does not allow them to take a single step. Leaf through some newpapers and you cannot tell when they came out—today or five years ago. In this is one of the aspects of perestroika: the problem of personal perestroika, the problem of internal transformation. . . .
>
> When I came to work at *Izvestiia* a little over three years ago, there were a lot of problems because of the reactions to the newspaper's articles. And the reactions were quite strange. For example, some of our leaders thought that if we came out in an article against a thief and a swindler who had set himself up in Yeliseevskii [the largest food store in Moscow] and established an entire crime network, this portrayed Moscow in an unfavorable light before the Soviet people and before the entire world.
>
> Criticism aimed at one or another ministry or department also evoked a similar response or peremptory cry. The telephone calls would begin. The ministers—now practically all are already former ministers—would start the process of halting publication of the article under the pretext that it would undermine the authority of the country. "We are trying to enter the world market," went their reasoning, "and here you are writing that we have shortcomings and you are under- mining our position." In general they portrayed it as a political blunder.
>
> Similar calls and pressure continued after the April (1985) Plenum of the Central Committee of the Communist Party of the Soviet Union (CPSU). But then our opponents understood that times had changed and that pressure was not the best way to fight for the truth, for the cause, and for perestroika.
>
> **Q:** Are there relapses of such a reaction in the criticism of newspapers occurring now?
>
> **A:** I must say that they occur. Even now when we print something about one or another controversial issue, once in a while it smells of the past. True, the tactics have changed.

Q: In what way?

A: For example, the suppression of a critical article. Such a maneuver was used before, but now the approach is different. They write or call the editor's office and say, "You want to raise this problem, but we ourselves have known about it for a long time and we are working on a solution. So there is no need to hurry."

More often they have begun to use the collective telegram and the collective letter. The correspondent has not yet returned from an assignment, is still writing the story, and we have not had the chance to work out the topic, and already telegrams and letters are arriving with long lists of signatures attached. You can find all kinds of things in these communications, starting with a refutation of the crux of the matter and ending with accusations against our correspondent: that he behaved improperly, that he did not talk to the right people, that he was overly aggressive, and so on and so forth. If he had a button undone on his shirt even this was reason for reproach.

When we begin to check, it turns out that the majority of the signatories have never read and in some cases have never even seen the text of the telegram or letter. Others never signed it at all. Several explain that they signed thinking that the newspaper would not bother with such a thing.

In my opinion, the behavior of such people is the main obstacle to glasnost. Such people do not take it seriously enough; that is, they still consider glasnost a source of information, not a process to work out their civic position, not as their own responsibility for what is going on.

Q: Are there groups whose interests have been dealt with directly by the critical publications?

A: Of course, perestroika has affected—and will continue to affect—the interests of many layers of our population and our professional groups. It has touched strings in the human soul that no one had ever heard before or knew what they sounded like. One could say that it touched the long-standing, immovable, petrified notion that one person is permitted to do something while another is prohibited. We are dealing with living people just like ourselves, and, I repeat, this is something that must be taken into account. . . .

When we speak about the influential groups, about their opposition to glasnost, we should firmly and clearly express ourselves. In my opinion, any confrontation over the problems of glasnost is a struggle between democratic and bureaucratic methods and approaches, a struggle manifesting itself at times in a multitude of different ways . . . through a mass of channels, branches, positions. In its time, one of our classics expressed this in its own peculiar acute and graphic way: In order to exist a bureaucracy needs secrecy; that is, secrecy guarantees the existence of bureaucratism. The bureaucrat is strong because he allegedly knows something that the person who has come to him does not know. The bureaucrat is, as it were, let in on something, and is therefore distinct from the common mortal. The bureaucrat keeps the "secret" and affects an air of secrecy about himself, his work, and his position. On this, the information he has that, ostensibly, no one else has, he flourishes.

To this there is only one counterbalance: glasnost.

In spite of the fact that the daily newspaper *Izvestiia* has an army of more than 10 million readers, the outspoken *Moskovskie Novosti* (Moscow News) enjoys no less popularity today. One hundred thousand copies of it are snapped up in an instant every Wednesday morning in Moscow, and approximately 50,000 copies are sold on Fridays or Saturdays in other major cities in the European part of the Soviet Union.

In the West this daily newspaper (in its English, French, German, Spanish, and other language editions) is often considered to be something of an export version of glasnost, that is, a kind of advertisement. But this ignores the fact that its most interested and captious reader is Soviet. The editor of *Moskovskie Novosti*, Yegor Yakovlev, defended it against a variety of accusations and explained his policies in a recent interview:

> **Q:** Yegor Vladimirovich [Yakovlev], do you share the opinion that our journalism more actively pursues domestic than international topics?
>
> **A:** Of course. One reason for this is that up to now we have not publicly analyzed errors in our international policy as we have our internal political life. In my opinion, it is less interesting to be an international observer these days. By the way, I do not consider myself an international observer and so personally I have ended up in a more favorable situation. Today there are no issues that our foreign correspondents deal with which we cannot freely respond to and reflect upon. Yes, before we had to, if you will, "mumble" when we could not find a convincing answer to a question posed at the intellectual level of a high school student.

The well-known television commentator Vladimir Posner, who has organized and conducted television "space bridges" with the United States, defended the extension of glasnost to Soviet TV in an interview in *Sovetskaia Kul'tura* (7 July 1987).

> It turns out that we are not very good at discussion. And that is not surprising, because for many years discussion has not been encouraged.

But if one speaks about glasnost the same way one speaks about politics, then glasnost presupposes the existence of various opinions and the ability to defend them. In this respect, not only were the Donahue broadcasts useful, but the interviews with the heads of state and with the major political figures—be it Thatcher, Shultz, or Chirac—were as well. They graphically confirmed how important it is to learn how to debate and argue one's point of view, while at the same time hearing out one's opponent. By the way, the art of polemics is not that difficult to master, but for that to happen it is necessary that discussion and debate become part of everyday life.

Posner criticized people who earlier complained about the lack of democracy in our society but who now, instead of actively fighting for the establishment of such necessary principles as glasnost and democracy, stand aside with a skeptical smile observing what is taking place and frightening those around them by saying, "Look, look! They are starting to tighten the screws again."

There cannot be two glasnosts—one for internal use and a totally different one for external use. Either there is glasnost or there is not. This is the same with journalism. In fact, it has turned out that journalism now occupies a leading position. But of course journalism does not exist in a vacuum, separated from society, where everything is closely interrelated. It is not possible that society would not as yet have rid itself of negative things, but that journalism has freed itself completely from them. Journalism, of course, is still fettered to a considerable degree. It is no secret that every journalist knows the limits of the permissible—what he can and cannot say. In each of us sits the internal editor; each of us remembers that we have an immediate boss and higher organizations looking down. . . .
I think that the liberation of the mass media has had salutary results not only for journalism itself, but also on society as a whole. The thing is that the talented and highly qualified journalist can be not only a conscientious propagandist of ideas expressed from above, but he is also capable of expressing ideas and proposals that are useful to society.

We see no less noticeable results of glasnost in our artistic literature. In Russia, writers have always been the spiritual leaders. These writers have not, however, always been guaranteed the right to their own points of view when they differed from the official viewpoint. Today the open or tacit ban has been lifted from the names of many authors. Silent, unheard, and forgotten voices ring out anew. Since the end of 1985, dozens of novels, poems, and plays have surfaced that for many years, even decades, were kept in doleful silence, patiently awaiting permission to return from exile.

Literary journals have become the best-sellers of our day. *Novyi Mir* (New World) and *Znamia* (The Banner), *Druzhba Narodov* (Friendship of Peoples) and *Neva*, *Yunost'* (Youth) and *Oktiabr'* (October)—the list goes on—are publishing the poetry of Nikolai Gumilev and Vladislav Khodasevich, the novels of Mikhail Bulgakov, Andrei Platonov, and many others. The works of Vladimir Nabokov and Joseph Brodsky, Vladimir Voinovich and Georgi Vladimov, once considered "anti-Soviet," are returning home. The taboo on Evgenii Zamiatin's satirical fantasy, *My* (We), and on Boris Pasternak's historical epic, *Doctor Zhivago*, has been removed. Of course, not all taboos are lifted. One still cannot read most of the works of Alexander Solzhenitsyn.

Just as glasnost means a normalization of the activities of the Soviet press, so does it signal in literature a return to normalcy. Igor Dedkov wrote about this in an article in *Moskovskie Novosti* (21 June 1987) under the characteristic title, "A Sense of the Norm."

A few years ago, reading the manuscript of a novel, I thought of how bad and shameful it was that it could not be published. Today that novel has been read by hundreds of thousands, maybe already millions, of people. The impossible has become possible.

And nothing was shaken: The walls did not crumble; the foundation did not shift; the birds sang; the lilacs blossomed. . . . And how much else is now in print that was only yesterday reputed to be "dangerous," "undesirable," and "harmful"? These books were not "designed" to destroy our lives, as it appeared to someone. They only resisted the thing within our lives that for a long time selfishly had the upper hand, that insulted the people with a lack of faith in their reason, consciousness, and initiative. They resisted, using the sharpest dramatical material, using the creation [*sozidanie*] of history, which had not as yet cooled down, was still burning. . . .

And here is what is noticeable: Although now and again we are reminded of the singularity of the literary situation (someone, strange as it may seem, from the writers' circles once in a while expresses his obvious dissatisfaction), it begins to be interpreted differently than the month before. It is as if the possibility of the impossible ceases to surprise.

But does everyone welcome these changes? Does everyone accept the removal of the nonsensical "forbidden" from the outstanding literary works as the norm? By no means. Even in writers' circles, there are ardent opponents of the normalization of our spiritual situation. From the pages of *Pravda* (26 April 1987) comes this warning from the writer Petr Proskurin:

> Our "thick" and "thin" literary journals in eager rivalry have thrown themselves into seeking out and publishing the works of the past decades that, for one reason or another, either never came to light or were published only in the West. Most often they transport the reader to a life that long ago died out. . . . In this connection is it not time to consider whether it is worth devoting so much space in the journals, which are intended above all for the publication of new literary works, to old works and to not always accomplished poetry and prose? Would it not be a better idea to take all of the material that deserves attention and to publish it in separate books, maybe even in an appropriate book series, such as *Literaturnye Pamiatniki* (Literary Heritage). For these old voices, muffled by whole epochs of burned-out passions, cataclysms, tragedies, accomplishments and defeats, nonetheless belong to the past. Attempts to write them into the continuous living literary process, into the context of the contemporary scene—whether we want that or not—not only slow down the flow of this process, but bring to it the smell of a kind of literary necrophilia.

The euphemism "our 'thick' and 'thin' literary journals" was easily deciphered by Soviet readers: *Novyi Mir, Znamia, Druzhba Narodov, Oktiabr', Yunost'*—because it was precisely in these journals that many formerly forbidden works were appearing. Not only did they publish classics of Soviet literature, but also the works of contemporary writers: for example, Anatolii Rybakov's *Children of the Arbat*, Anatolii Pristavkin's *The Little Golden Cloud Spent the Night*, Vladimir Dudintsev's *White Clothing*, the short stories of Andrei Bitov, Fazil' Iskander, Bulat Okudzhava, and many others.

Objecting to the charge of "literary necrophilia," Andrei Voznesenskii, in *Literaturnaia Gazeta* (6 May 1987) answered Petr Proskurin's challenge this way:

> Now is a time of glasnost, so let us open the parentheses. Who are these Soviet "necrophiles"? Maybe it's M[ikhail] Alekseev, who [as editor of the journal *Moskva*] published Nabokov's "The Defense of Luzhin"? Or V. Karpov, who wrote an article about Nikolai Gumilev? Or Grigorii Baklanov, who [as editor of *Znamia*] published the novel of A. Bek and A. Platonov's "The Juveline Sea?" Or A. Deent'ev, who placed in the journal *Yunost'* a wonderful article about I. Severianin? These are all healthy people, not necrophiles.
>
> A restoration of our culture is going on. So who are these "corpses"? Is it A[leksandr] Tvardovsky, whose poem "Memory" has today become the tuning fork of Soviet poetry? Is it A[nna] Akhmatova, whose

"Requiem" was for so long forbidden? I think that none of you can deny that she, Akhmatova, is now more alive than all of us, the living writers.

All of this is being done above all for the restoration of historical justice, for the restoration of the living literary process that is necessary for the new authors so that they write in earnest. And the people who stand in line at six in the morning waiting to buy those journals— they are not gourmands, they are not snobs, not necrophiles. These are the people, by the millions, standing there. This is necessary to them. Millions want to know the truth. They are voting for glasnost.

Voznesenskii was supported by other writers who shared an understanding that glasnost made it possible to return to Soviet readers everything that was secretly taken away from them, first in the Stalin, and then in the Brezhnev years. As Grigorii Baklanov put it (*Literaturnaia Gazeta,* 6 May 1987):

Glasnost is not the embellishment of life, and glasnost also does not exist so that we can make a good impression on someone abroad. It is not only that without glasnost there is no morality. Glasnost is necessary also because without the confrontation of various points of view, without the searches of several variants, the development of economics and of science is impossible. And without that you have the stagnation and death of a society.

The arguments and disagreements in writers' circles go beyond the borders of literary debates. In their essence they reflect the confrontation of diverse, often polar opposite approaches to the key problems of glasnost and perestroika. In them, as in a drop of water, are reflected concrete interests, various ideals, and various understandings of the role of glasnost in our society.

The Broadening Boundaries of Glasnost

So what are the limits of glasnost?

Without the confrontation—and, we would add, struggle—of diverse points of view, glasnost is unthinkable. But the formation of these diverse points of view, considering our tradition of silence, closedness, and secretiveness, is not a simple matter. It demands political courage and emotional readiness. And it will demand something else as well: the indivisibility of glasnost.

Here it seems to us extremely important to remember that glasnost is not a condition but a process. It is a continual movement forward, the conquest of new bridgeheads of the truth. It is a movement ahead—

for now a difficult and painful one—to an ever more truthful and deeper comprehension of problems, from the most general and principal to the most concrete and particular, which earlier were closed to discussion.

The development of glasnost is a process filled with contradictions, not a straight line steadily moving toward new heights. For several years we have been witnesses both of victories and defeats (fortunately temporary ones) for glasnost. For example, the removal of numerous taboos about names or subjects takes place unexpectedly and follows no apparent logic. The name of the former first secretary of the Moscow City Party Committee, Boris Yeltsin, was twice banished from our press: the first time when he was removed from his position in November 1987 (the stenographic report of the party plenum that discussed his removal was concealed for a year and a half), and the second time after the 19th Party Conference of July 1988 when an open clash took place between Yeltsin and Yegor Ligachev, then the Politburo's chief ideologist. But during the 1989 election campaign, Yeltsin won a triumphant victory in the elections in Moscow, garnering 90 percent of the votes in a struggle against an opponent supported by the Moscow party bureaucracy, and was ultimately elected to the Supreme Soviet as a leading figure of the "loyal opposition."

The paradoxical character of the process of expanding glasnost is reflected in the fact that today it is not completely clear what is "permitted" and what is "forbidden" in the press. In the past year many were outraged by criticisms of Stalin; today hardly anyone is surprised by criticism directed at Lenin.

In order to give the reader an idea of the issues that are the focus of glasnost today and how the boundaries of glasnost are broadening, we offer several selections dealing with themes that were traditionally outside the scope of possible public discussion.

The first involves a debate about the very meaning of socialism itself and the extent to which it has been realized in the Soviet Union. In the article "The Socialist Perspective and Utopian Consciousness," published in the party journal, *Kommunist* (1988, no. 3), Eduard Batalov stated the issue provocatively: Is it possible to call genuine socialism that which we imagined it to be in the past?

In recent years it has become increasingly obvious—and this has been pointed out in the party press—that many notions that circulate in Soviet society about real socialism and about the socialist ideal as a model, as a higher social goal, defining the activity of the individual do not reflect the genuine condition of that society nor the real tendencies of its development, which lie at the foundation of the ideal. . . . In other words, behind the existing notions about this social order are orientations and ideas peculiar to utopian consciousness—the very same consciousness that long ago was declared once and for all surpassed, but against whose resurrection, as it now can be seen, neither proclamations of faithfulness to Marxism-Leninism nor the construction of socialism is a guarantee.

Marx and Engels did not reject this ideal in itself but rejected attempts to construct it in speculative fashion, to present it as a timeless absolute. They insisted that the socialist ideal not stem from abstract notions about "justice," "truth," "good," and so on but from the objective tendencies of social development; that it be the embodiment not of dreams about heaven on earth but sober notions about real needs already ripening inside of society. . . .

Another principal difference between the Marxist treatment of the socialist ideal and the utopian is that Marx, Engels, and Lenin viewed it not as a hardened scheme but as a model subject to continual changes and transformations. . . .

This, of course, in no way means that today socialism will be understood one way, tomorrow another, and the day after another. Marx, Engels, and Lenin, when considering the features of the future society, invariably tried to derive them from some kind of general "root," to separate the stable nucleus of a socialist ideal, the essential features that distinguish socialism (communism) from the preceding formations and without which there could be no socialism. Marx, Engels, and Lenin saw the embodiment of the essence of socialism in the public ownership of the means of production; in the absence of antagonistic classes; in free labor (the absence of the exploitation of man by man). It is these features taken together that differentiate socialism from capitalism.

Of course, the above-enumerated features do not constitute socialism; they are not the whole content of the socialist ideal. The task itself of identifying socialism cannot be decided once and for all. However, in the past:

> Instead of studying real, living socialism, preference was given to the designing of speculative models. This tendency became especially noticeable in the 1970s. . . . We closed our eyes to the "unwanted" features of reality, acting according to the principle "there is none of this because under socialism there should not be any of it." This is not simply a tendentious approach, but indeed a utopian one oriented on the arbitrary construction of an "ideal," "best" way of life.
>
> We run up against this kind of thinking today in our consciousness, when just about everything that is positive, advanced, progressive in social, political, and spiritual life is made synonymous with socialism, while everything negative is associated with capitalism, denying both multidimensionality and turning them into stale symbols of "good"

and "evil." According to the logic of this thinking, just about all negative things in our life are the "leftovers" of capitalism, its "birth-marks." Meanwhile, the possibility of the effective functioning under the conditions of a socialist society of the mechanisms active under capitalism—even if in reformed condition—is denied because it is said that these develop or operate only within the confines of bourgeois civilization. . . .

The notion of socialism as a straightforward and simple society in many ways flows out of a utopian thesis about a society without internal contradictions, "monolithic," harmonious, and problem-free. In a purely formal sense, it is true, the existence of contradictions under socialism has always been recognized by us. However, the analysis of concrete situations in categories of contradictions became in recent years, to put it mildly, unpopular. Even where there was obvious conflict, we preferred to talk about "unsolved problems," "difficulties" (most often "temporary"), "discrepancies," "incongruities," and so forth—in a word, about anything, but not about contradictions and conflict. It came to the point where under socialism there could be no events that brought elements of drama and even tragedy to our daily life.
. . .

. . . The critical zeal that today informs many judgments of Soviet citizens about their socialist existence is directed not against socialism as a system of relations but against that which is considered a "de-viation" from socialism—its distortion, that is, as nonsocialism. The critics of the existing order want "more" socialism, not "less." Fur-thermore, there is a consensus with respect to the question of what constitutes the "nucleus" of the socialist ideal. In other words, public ownership of the means of production, the absence of antagonistic classes, and free labor are considered integral features of socialism.

The transition to the new thinking and the realization of perestroika under conditions of glasnost compel us to take a fresh look at many fundamental issues of world outlook that just yesterday were in their own way "sacred cows." Even to touch them was dangerous, because they were consecrated by the indisputable authority of unshakable philosophical "truths." But what kind of "truths" are these that exist on their own, without any kind of connection to real life, with its dramas, contradictions, errors, and quests? Was it that philosophy they taught us in school and in the university?

Two graduate students of the Institute of Philosophy of the Academy of Sciences of the USSR, Mikhail Mayatskii and Eduard Nadtochii, described the numbing impact of the "parrot-like incantations" that replaced the serious study of philosophy in the journal *Yunost'* (1987, no. 10):

When we studied in the university, it seemed to us that the thing was not our philosophy itself, but the heavy torpor hanging over all our life. It seemed as though we had to burst the soapy bubble of authoritarian self-satisfaction and then everything would change; that a new life would begin in which philosophy again would be at the epicenter of changes, as has happened more than once in Russian life; that everything would be filled with the sparkle of light, intellect, and imagination.

But the philosophers, as it turned out, had nothing to impart to the world. We had a dead style. . . .

. . . There are no fresh ideas, which would allow a radical change in the condition of our "nationwide" philosophy, an escape from the conventionalism and demagogy in philosophical work. The texts now appearing all too depressingly remind one of a jammed street organ playing the text of the regulations of sentry guard service. . . .

What kind of philosophy is this that leaped out of the control of people and trampled them under itself? In an inconceivable way everything in it that makes a philosophy a philosophy evaporated. In it the thinnest threads reaching into the unfathomable depths of the human spirit have been ruthlessly cut. Philosophy has always been understood as the knowledge of initial causes and beginnings. In it a person could find a basis for genuine judgment, moral demands, aesthetic appraisals, find support for any of his actions. But contemporary philosophy contains in itself also a few risks, doubts, and secrets. If philosophy becomes petrified in the satisfaction of captured truth, if it banishes all doubt, then it unavoidably pushes the limitless riches of the cosmos into the quadrature of daily life in the kitchen.
. . .

To the philosophy that already "exactly knows" everything and only thirsts for its earliest "practical application," it is impossible to turn with questions that from time immemorial have given impulse to the human spiritual quest—questions about the meaning of life, about purpose, fate, and death. To discuss this was considered the prerogative of bourgeois philosophy and a symptom of its decay. . . .

Probably, some of our teachers at this point will ask with wide eyes: Just what are you raising your voice against? Are you not calling for a rejection of the bases of our worldview? Our system of education is supported by this "terrible" question, unshakable up to now. The entire horror in it is that a very small group of people have assigned to themselves the right categorically to judge what is Marxism and what is not. . . .

As long as the imperative of the monopoly holds sway, all arguments will be conducted on behalf of Marxism-Leninism, and he who outdoes all others in sapping this sacred thing is victorious. Is it not time to gather up the courage to speak in our own names?

Supporting this line of judgment, Y. Furmanov wrote in *Sovetskaia Kul'tura* (12 March 1988):

> The wave of criticism and self-criticism in the social sciences, having reached the broad layers of the intelligentsia in the recent period, it seems, is capable once again, as occurred after the 20th Party Congress, of turning into a real tenth wave. On the pages of newspapers and journals and in our scientific and educational institutions there are hot discussions going on about the reasons for the stagnant and even crisis phenomena in social knowledge. Once again, as in the 1960s, the "Stalinist times" are coming under sharp criticism.
>
> Well, all of this is correct, because without criticism of our ideological past, the ideological perestroika of the present cannot rise up and go forward at full speed. . . . We will not understand the reasons for the stagnating phenomena in the social sciences until we make clear to ourselves that dogmatism is not simply a defined social institution. Dogmatism arose when the Marxist critical method was turned into an organized method of criticism of all "different-mindedness," when bureaucratic parasitizing of the writings of classics of Marxism-Leninism for protective ends was disseminated, when the methods of scientific, philosophical discussion among Marxist schools in our country that took place in the 1920s were reduced to forms of political struggle.

Y. Furmanov further argued that dogmatism was inculcated into the consciousness of the intelligentsia through various methods.

> The struggle with the real enemies of Marxism and socialism gradually started to take on ugly, doctrinaire forms of struggle with every different-mindedness. As the pretenses of Stalin and his accomplices to a command of the true interpretation of Marxism-Leninism were strengthened, the intolerance toward different-mindedness took on ever more authoritarian forms. "Mistaken" intellectuals were "corrected," and soon they either "fell into line" or they disappeared physically or ideologically and spiritually. . . . Marxist-Leninist philosophy does not deny and even presupposes a pluralism of actual positions.

The struggle over ideas in contemporary Soviet life is inextricably connected to a clash of interests, and open discussion of that relationship is important evidence that the borders of glasnost are opening up. A roundtable discussion entitled "Barricades of Perestroika," published in the journal *Vek XX i Mir* (1988, no. 2), addressed this confrontation of ideas and interests openly:

A. Arsen'ev: My relationship to perestroika is two-edged. On the one hand, I, of course, am fully "for" it, as a person, and as a philosopher whom the absence of glasnost doomed, in the course of dozens of years, to muteness and to the agonizing feeling of the impossibility of self-realization. On the other hand, I am extremely doubtful of the possibility of its realization in the foreseeable future. . . .

. . . The most powerful drag on perestroika, one holding practically unlimited power, will be the bureaucracy. At the expense of the state it commands a mass of caste privileges, not only material (apartments, automobiles, special services, food products from special farms, etc.), but also, for example, juridical impunity.

It is characteristic that the bureaucracy has used its caste privileges secretly, "like a cat in the night," and that until recently public discussion about them was punished as slander against Soviet power. And in general, preserving its power and privilege, the bureaucracy created a universal system of lies and hypocrisy. For that reason the immediate task on the road to perestroika is, in my view, the task of extricating ourselves from the colossal system, formed over many decades, of lies, deception, hypocrisy, and the distortion of all concepts, among them moral ones. Without that all arguments about perestroika will be meaningless. . . .

G. Pel'man: We have already spoken here about the clear enemies of perestroika—that is, the elitist, caste groups and prohibitive forces. But perestroika is threatened by its own future processes, inasmuch as perestroika in the sphere of social relations will lead to the rise of new social sovereigns, to the change of the political functions within social groups, and also between groups, and will lead to the perestroika of the mechanism of interaction between soviet, party, and social organizations and groups.

There will occur a "partition" of the zones of influence around the centers of decision making. And this process will not only be painful, but full of conflict. Already now it is necessary to have a special map to chart the dislocation of political forces in society, the regrouping of zones of political power, some of which are expanding their borders, changing their contours, while for others there is an unavoidable constricting, reduction. . . .

There can be various ways to contour such zones—for example, the categorical prohibition of the interference of the party organs in economic activity.

On the other hand, it should be recognized that the announced course toward democratization, glasnost, and "more socialism" unavoidably gives birth to a tendency of the personal complicity of citizens in the radical transformations. The variety of positions, of points of view on perestroika, naturally will give impulse to the creation of groups whose purpose will be to "defend" public opinion, democratically "rushing into" the sphere of democratic relations. This is a positive process, and already now it is necessary to prepare ourselves thoroughly, to get used to the "demilitarization" of political relations.

Marxism at the end of the twentieth century cannot exist in the same form it used to. . . .

Well known, for example, is the notion of three sources and three ingredients of Marxism—German classical philosophy, English political economy, and French utopian socialism. But what about new sources? You see, the above-named are associated with the eighteenth and nineteenth centuries. Are they to remain as before the basic sources of Marxism? But why not state the issue in this way: The sources of contemporary Marxism are all of the more talented and powerful intellectual directions of the contemporary world, of course, with the preservation and deepening by Marxism of its own inherent characteristics.

First of all, the dialectic. It should, on the one hand, reinterpret all new achievements of natural science. The theory of relativity, quantum physics, contemporary genetics, the theory of superconductivity—all these and many other branches of knowledge in a fundamental way have changed our notion of the macro- and micro-world, and it is absolutely impossible to boil down all the ideas contained in them, or even any one of them . . . to the Hegelian triad. . . .

Second, historical materialism. It needs to take account of new information, in part about traditional societies. One cannot forget that Marx and Engels, yes, and to a significant degree Lenin as well, worked in situations when little was known about China in ancient times and in the Middle Ages, about India, etc. But now a great amount of material has been collected, which offers the possibility to place in the foundation of the materialistic understanding of history not only the European model, which has been studied thoroughly and for a long time, but also contemporary Eastern models. Aside from that there is the notion of sociocultural models, which to a significant degree surpass the overly schematic, sharp juxtaposition of the economic base and the superstructure. That is, all that accumulated by the philosophical historical spheres of knowlege offers the possibility of constructing a much more complex picture of the correlation of the economy and the so-called noneconomic factors and of the entire picture of the movement of society as a whole.

Further, both Marx and Lenin started with the following premise: Capitalism has played out its role; it already developed its civil forces and created those relations and those political superstructures which it remains only to take and to begin using for socialist development.

History has turned out differently in the sense that that condition, which Marx observed (and even Lenin, having called it the imperialist stage of the development of capitalism), was one of the early conditions of capitalism. Today that is clear. But no one, not one genius, could foresee the first scientific revolution, the second, etc. They thought, speaking in contemporary terms, that once an industrial society was created, that meant the creation of the preconditions for socialism. . . .

Third, there should be a new teaching about socialism. In this it is still poorly developed, although some elements can be found among the Western Marxists, in particular the Italians [Antonio] Gramsci and [Palmiro] Togliatti. In this new teaching we have to rethink much— for example, the role of the political, state factor and the danger of the statization of society. We have to reanalyze the correlation between socialism and personal interest—from NEP to contemporary perestroika, including also the experience of China and of other socialist countries. We have to regard socialism not as some kind of short-term, intermediate measure where collective factors appear in pure form. Socialism should not simply use the possibilities of classical capitalism—these are absolutely inadequate—but should use, in competition with contemporary, developing capitalism, those new possibilities that reveal themselves within ·capitalism and not give way to it in that.

L. Saraskina: I was very young when Stalin died. At the age of seven I heard about the "anti-party group" and [Lavrentii] Beria, "the spy of British intelligence." As a student in school, I saw how year after year the ideas of the 20th Party Congress and the reforms of Nikita Khrushchev were discredited. Then Khrushchev was removed and called a voluntarist. At the institute they lowered my grade on an examination on the history of the CPSU for the expression "in the era of the cult of the personality." "There was no such epoch!" yelled the furious examiner. "You have to read the party documents better." In the "epoch of stagnating phenomena" I became a university student, and then an instructor of literature, and for fifteen years attempted internally to withstand the sticking cobwebs weaved from demagogy and lies. The impulse of October was handed down to me and to those of my generation, whose conscious, adult life fell on stagnation, to a significant degree distorted and tarnished. And in what condition did it reach today's sixteen-year-olds, born in the odious 1970s? . . .

The political and social self-knowledge of the zealots of orthodoxy operate on three old dogmas.

Dogma number one: We are a society of victors, of "hegemony," having received from history indulgence for all times. However, not history, but we ourselves in the name of history, issued ourselves the charter of immunity about our eternal and unalterable rightness. Our "solely true" theory serves as a justification for our practice, and our policy is obligated and summoned to serve as the confirmation of history.

Dogma number two: We have traversed a glorious path, and every day of that path is unique. To know about the monstrous crimes committed against the people and to insist upon the value of each day, and even of those days, months, and years when the country was ruled by a "huge, mischievous, enormous monster"—is at minimum immoral . . . especially if you know, if only approximately, about the number of victims of the Gulag. The sinister nonsense of the formula of the "glorious path" has haunted me my whole life. Is it possible today to repeat this incantation so unthinkingly?

And, finally, the third dogma, not, in general, of national origin, having swum to us from other shores. It says: The leader is always right. In Russian translation this comes out as: The leadership never makes a mistake.

Thóse using this slogan mastered the idea that in order to get ahead and prosper, you have to fall in obediently with the general line. But are these the cadres for perestroika—people without a moral core, without their own convictions?

As long as these three dogmas remain part of the foundation of perestroika, perestroika itself will be considered a test-tube baby emotionally unacceptable for the young. They have to learn that the leader may, perhaps, not be right. In my lifetime there has not been in our country a better leader than Mikhail Gorbachev, but if we do not learn the culture of polemics, the culture of dialogue with a leader of any rank, we will end up where we started. It cannot be that the very idea about the possibility of such a discussion is regarded as a provocation.

A. Nuikin: . . . We can assist perestroika now above all by criticizing it. Yes, it is time to criticize perestroika! To criticize not its wonderful intention, but the *besplotnost'* [incorporeality] of its form, the uselessness of several of the methods it uses, the concessions to the main opponent of perestroika—the multimillion apparatus of bureaucrats and administrators. We cannot waste time hoping for the irreversibility of the process. For now, alas, everything depends on the position of one or two people. And while this is so, perestroika can be cut short, never to develop properly. There are no guarantees. And for its successful development it is especially important, I think, that in the country there begin to develop open, distinct political structures reflecting the various programs for the construction of communism, with their own leaders, whose views and positions would be known to us and who would rally and organize those who agreed with their ideas. Yes, this will lead to a polarization of forces, but you cannot choose if there is no choice. And the possibility of a free political choice—that is what could become the basic guarantee of perestroika.

L. Karpinskii: What do we see today? A broad, multilayered bureaucratic community stores its eggs under the skin of perestroika and feeds its maggots at the expense of the latter's young, fresh flesh, tries to "work" in new categories in the old way. But meanwhile in the political ideology of perestroika, which we are not noting, the forces of stagnation and reversibility are already rising.

Y. Burtin: . . . It is asked: What hinders perestroika, what stands in its way? Well, everything hinders it, absolutely everything! The first difficulty is in the very objective of perestroika, in the fact that it is not a kind of sum of more or less accidental and partial disorders and breakages in an internally healthy social organism that have to be repaired without affecting the foundation. The objective of the transformation is the social system in its entirety. . . .

The third difficulty, and, on the other hand, hope, of course, is people and their interests. There is already a difficulty in that in the above-mentioned social institutions the leading positions at every level, just as before, with rare exceptions, are occupied by the same (or similar) people who five and ten years ago sat in the very same places. And others for now are nowhere to be found. . . . Everyone one way or another understands that it is impossible not to restructure— to push ahead with perestroika—otherwise we will face a catastrophe. However, for each person individually, in terms of his personal welfare, perestroika in the best case promises something in the future but today directly will give nothing, or practically nothing. . . . And the last question. In the total of the seventy years of our Soviet history in the contemporary developed world, there have existed two systems, the organic quality (and in that sense the viability) of which has been confirmed by time: capitalism and real socialism, in that form in which it has developed in our country. The question is this (I already touched upon it a bit earlier): Can there be at least as viable a third structure? . . . No one will remove from us the burdens of the question: Do we imagine a third path, and what concretely it should be?

L. Karpinskii: . . . Our social reality, as has been elucidated, contradicts socialism, and socialism in its pure sense, as it turned out, in essence is incompatible with the given reality. This very incompatibility became the point of departure for perestroika, the formula for its necessity and its powerful energetic charge. . . .

L. Batkin: . . . The bureaucrats brandish the bugbear of "pluralism." But we all understand that without real pluralism not one contemporary society ever existed, just as no economy ever existed and cannot exist without a market. The forbidden market becomes the "black market": Apparently, there also occurs a "black pluralism." But today without open cultural diversity you cannot even mention the construction of a European socialist society of a higher level, let alone European capitalism! Such a society should not remove pluralism, which arose on a capitalist foundation, but broaden it, deepen the sphere of democratic diversity in culture and in society. That is socialist pluralism.

We have an urgent need for independent newspapers and journals that are not departmental organs but are put out by groups of journalists, writers, of all those who want and are capable of doing it. What is so awful about that? If Soviet power in the 1920s did not collapse because of independent publications, then neither will it today in its seventy-first year. . . .

We turned on its head the classical Marxist correlation of politics and economics. Having handed over all the means of production to the state—and not society—and having created an apparatus possessed by the state, we made the apparatus the master of our own fates, which we are reaping today. That is why it is time to think far more consistently and radically about the return of power from the apparatus to society itself. The first steps are needed. These first steps suggest that glasnost will be transformed from a dangerous, rare animal into the normal public and printed expression of personal opinion. That opinion can be forbidden only in cases where it contains calls to violence or insults social morality.

But for now there is none of this; we have as yet no mechanism for the self-defense of perestroika and because of this there is a natural fear that everything could be shut down in one night. Yes, and there are those around us who have that temptation. . . .

I experience with regard to perestroika something like a gloomy optimism. Why gloomy it is not necessary to explain to anyone; and for optimism there is only one basis: the reality of the very deep crisis our country is living through and the absence at all levels, including the highest, of any alternatives to the course of Mikhail Gorbachev. But to proceed along this course means for an intellectual to struggle for the perestroika of perestroika, for the uninterrupted development of its conception, of its working structure and methods, for the expansion of its boundaries. To the extent that new, mass forces are drawn into it, perestroika will be imbued with new content. The new forces come into politics with new positions, with new ideas, which often do not elicit from us any kind of delight. It is enough to recall the Black Hundred slogans of the Pamiat society, where we confronted the introduction into perestroika of something unplanned, foreign, and even frightening.

. . . If this is a revolution, then it is impossible to plan it. People conceive of revolution and they begin it. There is no turning back.

Could it, however, unfold all differently? Let's be sober: It could! But in that case our country will cease to be a great world power. Just as in infant mortality we have fallen to fifty-second in the world, finding ourselves among the undeveloped countries, so in all other parameters, entering the new era, the era of the computer revolution, of superconductivity under normal temperatures, we will become a backward country! We are obligated to explain this to people: Without perestroika we for all times will lose the status of a world power even in military terms, and also in foreign political, in foreign economic, and in foreign cultural terms—even in areas where there is little left to lose. And given that all the same we to a growing degree will turn

into a secondary force in the contemporary world, which will not
wait for us, this threatens to bring horrifying shocks—to us and to
the whole world!

Today the struggle for glasnost is above all the struggle against the
artificial limitations placed upon freedom of information, against senseless censorship, and against the cult of secrecy that sustained it. Compared with our recent past a tremendous amount has already been done.
We feel the air of freedom; we live as if in another world. But these
are only our first steps; the obstacles along this path remain considerable.
We hear fundamentally new ideas and new voices, and they are all the
more important to us because in the recent past they spoke in a
completely different tone. For example, the author of an article entitled
"From the 'Cult of Secrecy' to an Information Culture" (*Kommunist*,
1988, no. 13), Vladimir Rubanov, is the head of the KGB's Scientific-
Research Institute:

> The time has come to attract the attention of society to that tradi-
> tionally delicate sphere of state activity, inasmuch as it is becoming
> at minimum irrational to avoid a public discussion and resolution of
> the worsening problems of the defense of secrets under the conditions
> now developing. Among these problems are the circumstances obvious
> even to the nonspecialist of the absence of full-fledged legislation on
> questions of secrecy; the alienation of the mechanism of the defining
> and preservation of state secrets from democratic institutions; the
> unjustified limitation on access of Soviet citizens to information con-
> nected with the protection of secrets and with the measures of the
> regime. In addition, a constructive, official reaction to the developing
> social demands for such information is absent. This leads to a worsening
> of the problem; it negatively affects not only the political state of mind
> of the broad layers of the population of the country but also the
> condition of the very system of the protection of secrets. . . .
> The regime of secrecy as an attribute of power is a kind of indicator
> of the political development of the society, the level of democratization
> of its social institutions. In the construction and functioning of the
> formed system of the protection of secrets is reflected the low level
> of legal culture, the dogmatism of the ruling traditions, the dis-
> orientation in the definition of political, economic, and social priorities.
> This manifests itself in the juridical and organizational imperfection
> of regime-secret activity. But the measures of secrecy are not passive
> results of a naturally developing sociopolitical process. They are closely
> tied to the situation and interests of certain social elements of the
> society. . . .
> And so the bureaucratization of social life and unjustified secrecy
> are two sides of the same process of the alienation of society from

the political, material, and spiritual means of solving the tasks of self-government. . . .

Aside from direct threats to the moral development of the political process, unfounded and uncontrolled secrecy essentially traumatizes the self-consciousness and dignity of the Soviet person, weakens his ties to his government. The trust and support of the people can only be received in response to the trust placed in it. However, what kind of trust can you speak about when data reported in negotiations of a military-political and military-economic character, widely publicized afterward by foreign mass media, seldom are the property of our own society, when Soviet scholars are forced to draw upon foreign sources of information about the situation of affairs in one or another sphere of life in our country? It turns out that certain "state interests" are being protected not from a foreign threat but from Soviet citizens.

The extension of glasnost to previously secret aspects of foreign and defense policy is equally unprecedented. Although many commentators have deplored the fact that too many "closed zones" remain in this sphere, discussions have been initiated about such heretofore sensitive topics as Stalin's foreign policy in the 1920s and 1930s, his responsibility for Soviet unpreparedness in World War II, the harmful role of secrecy in precipitating the Cuban missile crisis as well as the Soviet intervention in Afghanistan, and the need for open information about Soviet military budgets and deployments.

These issues are discussed more fully in Chapter 7 ("What Is New About New Political Thinking?"), but one illustration of these new trends seems appropriate here. In an article entitled "In the Critical Light of Glasnost" (*Izvestiia,* 28 February 1989), veteran political commentator Stanislav Kondrashov argued that lessons must be drawn from the experience of the Cuban missile crisis about the dangers of making foreign policy without the necessary public information and scrutiny. The fact that Soviet missiles were sent to Cuba secretly, and that Soviet officials denied their presence, at a time when the American president had photographic evidence of their deployment, meant "a loss of trust in our representatives on the part of the Americans, which in turn did considerable damage to our state." Kondrashov went on to argue:

> However, the specific torments of Soviet diplomats and correspondents were only an insignificant detail next to a gigantic fact that somehow did not attract the proper attention: Our whole population was brought to the edge of the nuclear abyss without knowing about it, without having an opportunity to understand why—for just what reason! this extraordinary situation had arisen. This was the true, somber apotheosis of secrecy.

From an objective standpoint, it is quite possible to call this deception of the people or, in any event, total disregard for their right to know things that pose the question of their life or death. At the time, however, there was no talk about a right. Glasnost on this level just did not exist. It was only after 28 October—when, in an urgent exchange of messages between N.S. Khrushchev and J. Kennedy, the terms of a compromise were finally worked out—that this key word—"missiles"—began filtering into our press, and by no means immediately. Only after we had moved away from the brink did our people begin to understand exactly what sort of brink they had been standing on. . . . In 1962, Khrushchev was simply never confronted with the question of whether he and the other leaders of that time had the right to put the fate of their people at risk in order to aid another people, the Cubans. This right, like other authoritarian rights in the field of foreign policy, was implicit. This puzzled and intimidated the bourgeois-democratic governments of the West, which had no such rights, since they were hobbled in their actions by parliaments.

By the way, this divergence in the methods (in the methods, I emphasize, not in the social nature) of state administration deepens distrust, even without taking other factors into account, and makes the practice of cooperation more difficult, even when there is agreement concerning the general principles of peaceful coexistence between the two systems. The creation in the Soviet Union of a state based on the rule of law will eliminate many of these obstacles. Democracy is a complicated concept that is different for different countries, and especially for different systems, but any operating democracy—not one that is just for show—means a policy, domestic and foreign, that is attuned to the will of the people. And that means it is in full view of the whole world. The actions of a state based on the rule of law are more predictable than those of an authoritarian state, and this in itself facilitates dialogue and cooperation in the international arena.

We are not used to writing about how decisions "at the very top" were made in those days and how the various options were studied. In terms of his unique, half-century experience of participation in world politics, A.A. Gromyko occupied a special place. However, when he writes in his memoirs about his conversation with Kennedy, he does not reveal what he reported to Khrushchev in his diplomatic dispatches from Washington and on his return to Moscow. And the symposium did not do very much to break this silence.

How does one explain this traditional terseness of our statesmen when history itself demands that they openly share their experience and thereby make whatever contribution they can to the elimination of one of our most crucial shortages—our shortage of political sophistication, which also shows up in the current deficiencies in the democratic process? By the same mania for secrecy? By a distinctive vow of silence that our leaders—from generation to generation—

impose on themselves? Or by the clandestineness, which became second nature, that was institutionalized by Stalin so that he could keep in his own hands all elements of a power that was not accountable to the people?

Were any lessons drawn from the Caribbean crisis? In a narrow sense, yes, since we have not shipped any nuclear missiles overseas since then. As far as lessons on a broader level are concerned, a great deal continues to be shrouded in mystery, as they say. In the key area where foreign policy questions come into contact with military questions, the public has access only to documents of a general, often declaratory nature, but not to the key strategic decisions that were made in those years and now belong to history, decisions that determined our future military policy. . . .

Ten years after the Caribbean crisis, the 1972 Soviet-American Interim Agreement on the Limitation of Strategic Arms (SALT I), codifying approximate parity, froze for five years the then-existing ceilings on land- and submarine-based strategic missiles. But these data, which were included in readily accessible reference works overseas, in our country remained in the category of secret information for a long time. It goes without saying that the scope and rates of military construction continued to be strictly classified.

Unofficial Publications

The unprecedented spread of glasnost has reached beyond official (i.e., officially registered) publications and can be seen also in the greatly enlarged freedom for unofficial publications. They used to be called *samizdat*, whereas now more often one hears about "independent" publications which appear from the "underground."

Samizdat (which literally means "self-published," privately published) was widely used in the 1970s to refer to a variety of typed manuscripts—information bulletins, brochures, magazines, books—that could not be printed at state publishing houses. Usually, samizdat magazines and books existed in several dozen copies and circulated secretly. Banned novels, poems, and memoirs by Soviet and émigré writers were "published" by samizdat, many of which have found their way to readers legally only in the glasnost era.

Now samizdat is something different. It is no longer a "state crime" or an illegal activity. In a situation where there are as yet no private publishers in the Soviet Union, "self-publishing" faces many technical difficulties. The personal computer is one way out. Lately, with the slow advent of cooperative publishing houses, Soviets have been given an opportunity to bring out "real" printed publications. And one more change is telling. The very notion of samizdat has somehow disappeared from today's vocabulary and has been replaced by the notion of "unofficial" publications. The difference tells us something about the new political climate in the society, the new legal status of many things "unofficial" that are now tolerated by the state.

In an article in the Latvian journal *Daugava* (1988, no. 9), L. Britz and S. Maksimov discussed a conference of editors of independent publications that took place in Moscow, 7–8 May 1988. Here are some excerpts.

S. Maksimov: . . . The word *andergraund*, as is easy to guess, is of English origin. It means "underground." All publications that not without humor are united under that term, figuratively speaking, came out of the "underground." That is, even yesterday their existence was unthinkable—all the more so in that scope and in that range in which the editors of the "independent publications" gathered in Moscow at the conference.

Today the existence of such independent journals is a sign of the widest and deepest democracy. Indeed, each printed word is far from being taken as the "voice of God"—once something is printed, we are used to thinking, that's the way it is in reality. No way. It is not possible to agree with much that appears on the pages of these journals: Something might provoke an active (but healthy, not antagonistic) protest. But much is simply interesting, suggests ideas, as we say.

L. Britz: I guess that this movement was not born in a void. Indeed, it could not be otherwise. But when you try to understand historians. . . . You do not want to lie, but to speak the truth—even the truth as we understand it today—all the same it is a bit scary. But there's no escaping it.

S. Maksimov: The exact number of works of samizdat is practically unknown—perhaps it is known to the appropriate departments, but I doubt that they will divulge such specific information. Samizdat represented a whole branch of literature, encompassing practically all genres and existing outside and around "official literature." In it they wrote about things that the official press was silent about. But it is not correct to think that the seal of samizdat automatically means a sign of quality. There were weak works, imitative, written, paradoxically, in the full spirit of "official" literature—only with other symbols. . . .

Samizdat was the opposition literature, created by dissidents. *Dissidentura* sounds like a residential dwelling. But we are rethinking not only history but also the terminology connected with it. And among the dissidents there were different types. There were extremists, in spirit not tolerating anything connected with the Soviets. There were those who were "pushed out" into dissent—as a rule, people with a refined sense of justice, with aching conscientiousness, who could not be silent. They were not silent; they wrote. Wrote for their desks. And at times they put brilliant pieces there. . . .

L. Britz: . . . One can name several journals from the "era of stagnation" that succeeded in leaving their mark. First among these is the *Chronicle of Current Events.* I never got to see it, but from word of mouth I know that it was a sharply oppositional publication having secret but very well-informed sources of information, from which came facts about trials, about the situation of political prisoners, about the social adversity in various regions of the country. There were also the journals, if I am not mistaken, *Rus'* and *Veche*—as is not difficult to guess, of a *pochvennicheskogo,* Slavophile leaning. . . .

I think that for those who answer for the development of our ideological production, the existence of independent journals does not arouse great joy—this is said mildly. . . . I will not be surprised if I hear from some bureaucrat the open admission that his secret desire is to scatter all of these publishers. . . . This desire is for him understandable. But you cannot get away with that today. You have to accept the existence of such an unusual and dangerous form of social activity.

Everyone ought to have the right to speak. Only the strong voice cuts through and remains. That is, the voice which society needs, which everyone needs. Therefore, let them sing. And it is good that the voices no longer come to us from the underground.

The Opposition to Glasnost

It is very difficult to find among us a person who would openly and loudly declare that he or she is against glasnost and perestroika. In a word, all are sort of "for," but as soon as it comes down to practice, some—and there are many of these—say: "not all at once," "do not undermine the basic principles," "know moderation"; in a word—"yes, but . . ."

During the first three years of glasnost we have heard many times: "There must not be glasnost without boundaries." But, ironically, the alarmists hardly knew what the limits of glasnost should be, because glasnost, as a process, gradually transcends its limits. What is "allowed" or "not allowed" is an illusory thing, since the snowballing effect of glasnost makes all boundaries temporary. The same can be said about "socialist pluralism," a term that is highly ambiguous because the meaning of socialism itself is now in dispute. What is more important is that the issue of the limits of glasnost concerns mostly those who dislike the process itself.

To recognize those who are afraid of glasnost and are trying to castrate perestroika is at times not easy. Everyone has learned to speak the right words. Oftentimes, glasnost is a bitter pill both for the bureaucrat, who is afraid of losing his positions and his privileges, and for the "man on the street." The flow of truthful, but also alarming, information gushing through the locks opened by glasnost is throwing into confusion many people whose psychology and life-style were formed in the decades of silent "non-glasnost."

We still have to study and evaluate the full measure of the consequences for the national conscience of the era of non-glasnost. But even now, judging by the first reactions to glasnost, it is becoming obvious that the years when, using the expression of Aleksandr Pushkin, "the people kept silent" gave birth to several generations of people who did not even suspect that they had the right to know everything that happened in their country and to express their personal opinions about it. In the period of stagnation it was common practice to inform the population only about "exceptional achievements"—sometimes fictitious, but, according to the logic of those years, real (like the notorious "Kazakhstan billion" puds of grain collected every year—or more precisely, as it turned out, not collected). Everything that could even remotely undermine the prestige of Soviet society was passed over in silence as if it did not exist. And if, say, *U.S. News and World Report* reported on something that supposedly did not exist—for example, on the shortcomings in the health care system—then such information was treated as an ill-intentioned subversion, labeled a "bourgeois falsification." The era of non-glasnost spawned an ugly aberration of consciousness: Any critical word about Soviet reality or Soviet history was interpreted as a hostile action of Western propaganda directed at undermining the socialist order.

The popular reaction to the new role of the Soviet media, which are now beginning to work in normal fashion, is captured in a current anecdote: Two retired men meet and one bitterly laments, "All the same it was calmer before in this country—no railroad catastrophes, no natural calamities. But now you have submarines sinking and nuclear power stations blowing up."

But aside from jokes, glasnost can also provoke anger and disquiet among ordinary Soviet citizens, as the following letter to the newspaper *Moskovskie Novosti* reported (8 February 1987):

> I write to you with a feeling of deep concern about the serious shortcomings, and maybe even political mistakes, in the ideological positions of the newspaper published by Novosti, *Moskovskie Novosti*, which is distributed in 140 countries of the world.
>
> The ideological position of the newspaper changed radically after the change in its management.

I offer the following examples.

In the issue of 11 January 1987 on the first page in big letters is printed: "Let Us Learn Democracy." We have lived through seventy years and only now have we begun to learn democracy?

On page 40 of that same issue there is an article called "The Return" devoted to Tarkovskii, where his failure to return to his Motherland is excused. Furthermore, the author maintains that our film art is a "Potemkin village.". . .

In issue 45 of 9 November 1986, there is an article by Raikin, where he writes that in our country instead of "grandiose successes" there is "total bad management"; instead of "great achievements," ruin; instead of "heroic labor," drunkenness.

You would think that even an outright enemy of the USSR would be ashamed to say such things about our Motherland.

On 14 December 1986, the newspaper published the speech of Shatrov (real name Marshak) at the congress of theatrical workers. In his speech he maintained that after October the spiritual life of Soviet society was devastated, that there was basically a slave psychology, sociopolitical apathy. Further he argued that we have been given one more chance, and we cannot waste that chance. What kind of chance is he talking about?

Who is served by such an ideational position of a newspaper distributed around the world?

Glasnost needs bravery.

> Member of the CPSU since 1939, A.M.L.,
> Moscow, 1/13/87

The editor of *Moskovskie Novosti*, Yegor Yakovlev, answered this upset reader (8 February 1987):

You have written—and we anticipated it. . . . The reader evidently thought that with his letter he was complaining about the newspaper *Moskovskie Novosti*. In fact, he is complaining about time. He sees the reasons for the change in leadership of the editorial board and does not notice those ideational principles which, since the April Plenum of the Central Committee of the CPSU and the 27th Party Congress, have triumphed in Soviet journalism, which is now aggressive, open, socially just, and for which there are no forbidden themes, including those in our past.

Having entered the party on the eve of the Great Patriotic War, our reader obviously lived a difficult life, deserving of sincere respect. And one can understand, even sympathize with, how difficult it is late in life to renounce living axioms that before needed no proof, and which suddenly have become mere theories. But it is not befitting of a person whose youth went by with the song "Our locomotive, fly ahead . . ." to take a seat now in the train, draw the curtains, pretend the train is moving, and accuse those who are trying to rescue it from that condition.

Other protest letters continued to be published in *Moskovskie Novosti.* For example (1988, no. 45):

> With indignation and bitterness I have observed over the past three years how your newspaper has been turning increasingly into an organ working not for socialism and our Motherland but for our foreign foes. From issue to issue your newspaper prints material abusing and spitting upon our country, its history and past. Brandishing the flag of repressions, you have been trying to use them to overshadow the entire heroic past of our country, portraying them as the main aspect of the prewar and postwar periods. Our people's heroism in building the economic and social foundations of socialism (I emphasize: socialism) in our country is being obscured. Of course, the repressions against innocent people that took place in the prewar and postwar years are a great tragedy and pain for our whole people and country. They were carried out on orders from the top echelons of the ruling body, not controlled by the people. But the shadow of the repressions fell upon all our people, upon our entire system and upon the whole country. The innocent victims of repressions have to be rehabilitated. But to raise such a hullabaloo around the repressions, to put our tragedy on display for our foes to see and enjoy, is both unseemly and criminal. Whatever little bits bourgeois agents procured before to denigrate our Motherland in the eyes of their people you treat them to wholesale through your paper. How would you, Yegor Yakovlev, feel if your family affairs and secrets were read out for your neighbors and other strangers to enjoy? Even though it might be the truth about your family, you would not rejoice at it. You, Yegor Yakovlev, are by far not a first-class journalist, but you are a brilliant mediocrity, and you are supposed to possess an intellect enabling you to understand that denigrating our country's past in a newspaper by parading before the enemies data detrimental to the country's prestige is unworthy both of a Soviet newspaper and of a Soviet journalist. It was with a feeling of disgust that I read in your paper of 9 October 1988 the article entitled "Kuropaty." With what delight you relish the details of our people's execution near Minsk: How people were shot through the back of their head, from under the skull, or through the side. Who needs these details? After all, you provide the foes with material for educating their people in the feeling of disgust for our country and hostility for socialism as a system. I feel ashamed and hurt by your newspaper and by you, Yegor Yakovlev, as editor of this newspaper.
>
> Respectfully,
> Butivchenko, Alexei Fyodorovich,
> Veteran of the Great Patriotic War,
> D.Sc. (Military Sciences), Professor

These letters to *Moskovskie Novosti* are not isolated cases: The "open, everywhere made public" discussion of the dramatic events of distant and recent Soviet history has elicited acute hostility. Here the opponents of glasnost are unanimous: We have to put an end to the revelations of political crimes of the Stalin era and to the sharp criticism of the Brezhnev era of stagnation. Here is another random example, a letter to the journal *Ogonyok* (1987, no. 37):

It must be said that the defamation of an entire sixty-year period of Soviet history (1925–1985) renders the very idea of perestroika a bad service, inasmuch as people sooner understand it really as a means of self-assertion, in the manner of former comrade Khrushchev. . . .

. . . Inasmuch as it is exclusively the advocates of the degeneration of our society who have access to the pages of our press today, there can be no objective, businesslike discussion. To the accompaniment of the glorification of "glasnost and democracy," they have denied to those who are brave enough to make their own judgment the possibility to express it. This hysteria of subversion has no relation to perestroika, glasnost, and to all those wonderful things discussed at the 27th Party Congress and the subsequent plenums. For that reason, I consider those conducting this hysteria to be enemies of Soviet power and provocateurs who are discrediting the idea of perestroika and compromising the Leninist party.

> A. Berlizov,
> Senior Lieutenant,
> Born 1953,
> Krasnodar

The dissatisfaction of those who think "glasnost has gone too far" is dictated, as becomes clear from these letters, by a concern for the "benefit of the state" and the "interests of society." Meanwhile, people forget that the lawlessness of the 1930s and the pompous propaganda about "achievements" in the 1970s were conducted under the same slogans.

Yet another concern of the opponents of glasnost is its impact on Soviet international prestige. The hidden fear of "What will they say about us in the West?" is still strong in our social conscience, and the opponents of glasnost are quick to play on this neurosis. In the article "What Will They Say Abroad?" (*Izvestiia*, 2 January 1988), N. Propushin wrote:

Once in a while you hear: Are we not injuring the authority of the country when we openly speak about our shortcomings? Do we not by this render a service to hostile propaganda? Several readers have sounded this alarm. "We must tell about the abuses that were committed in the years of stagnation," writes V. Markova of Kiev. "However it is also worth thinking about what they will think of us abroad." V. Sviridenko of Moscow is more categorical: "We should be thinking more about our face in the world and not give various foreign 'voices' grounds for the gossip."

In N. Propushin's opinion, many are convinced that, in speaking aloud about a sore spot, we give arguments to our adversaries, who are ready to make noise about the "failure of socialism," the "crisis" of perestroika. Whether it be the appearance of an unusual film or a polemical article, for them the subject of anxiety is the same: What will they say in the West? Sensing in this a certain danger, they are quick to caution others. N. Propushin wrote:

> It is possible to understand people who are concerned for the prestige of our country in the international arena. However, those who most often invoke the theme "what will they say about us abroad?" are those who are afraid to be seen. They are the ones who, in answer to just remarks addressed to them, repeat over and over again about the undermining of the foundation, the damage to the whole society, beneficial only to "them," not "us." They identify their own prestige and the reputation of their department with the prestige of the state, of socialism, and again and again they warn: Do not pour water on the "mill of the enemy."

The realization that the admission of past mistakes and present problems is a sign of the strength, and not the weakness, of a society does not come easily. This seemingly elementary truth is grasped with difficulty—or is unceremoniously rejected by those who are used to keeping silent. But the majority of our people (judging by the many letters to the editors of the biggest newspapers and journals) understand how vitally important the medicine of glasnost is for the rehabilitation of society.

Andrei Nuikin sought to characterize the opponents of perestroika and glasnost in the article "Ideals and Interests?" published in two issues of the journal *Novyi Mir*. Nuikin's basic thought was that the opponents of the revolutionary transformation of our society are not simply dogmatists who prefer not to look truth in the eye. No, these are people who have fully defined interests—most often material—in the preservation of the past; in short, they are conservatives in the broad sense of the word. They can be fought only when a new economic mechanism of socialism, democratic methods of economic leadership, and the political and organizational structures of power have been worked out.

> All of us are in the same boat—no argument about that—but we are not all rowing in the same direction. It is for that reason, I think, that our boat circles in place, although we have not done a bad job recently of figuring out where we should be heading. . . . Of course, the situation for the bureaucracy suddenly is not so favorable. A whole series of high key positions was taken out of their control, yes, because of glasnost people are nervous; and to return the people to their former state of indifference and apathetic obedience is risky. Conflicts are possible, but the outcome would be hard to predict. It is better to wait and see. For the second time in the twentieth century in Russia a curious situation has come about, a kind of "dual power" where neither side is prepared to take a decisive step and each awaits its hour. It would be very naive on our part to suppose that the bureaucracy (as a social force) is wasting time right now. It has—one has to give it its due—detected the most vulnerable place of perestroika and, not advertising it, has carefully camouflaged its plans behind a glorification of the announced reforms (including the economic methods of management instead of administrative). It is preparing a broad attack. Its direction has been chosen, it seems to me, faultlessly. (*Novyi Mir*, 1988, no. 1)

Nuikin then spoke about "singers of ascetic socialism with faces beaming with childlike spontaneity who energetically elbow their way to the rostrum in order to start gabbing away in the old style," who present with enthusiasm worn-out, moldy arguments and intimidate with words about a capitalist degeneration in our country, about how excessive abundance and "satiation" are completely destroying our ideology, how the "game of democracy and people's power" will lead to complete anarchy, an undermining of the "leading role of the party," and so forth.

> Is it possible that our patient, trusting people once again will allow themselves to be deceived by the empty chaff of demagogy? How much can one go around blindfolded threshing someone else's sheaves? The reins of the government of the country have been fully in the hands of the advocates of the administrative model of socialism for over a half-century. Why don't they demonstrate in more than words the great advantages of that model? Isn't it time for them to offer not glowing promises, but a "final product," practical results?
>
> The experience of social impotence is a very dangerous experience. I think that for perestroika there is now nothing more dangerous, because it threatens to turn glasnost itself into a miserable farce. . . .

Democracy, as long as it has not constructed a mechanism of self-preservation, is not so much a means as a goal. In this situation it must not be "granted," not announced, but confirmed in deed, organized, won in battle. Revolution, it is said, is far from the most democratic mechanism of social progress, but without it not one democracy has up to now been consolidated. For this reason, a revolution must not be allowed to be toothless. Is it awkward to resort to undemocratic, repressive measures? So, then, work within the limits of the law and for the sake of legality. That is the first thing. And second, if perestroika is destroyed and the forces of stagnation take power fully into their hands, then they will show us how the question of cadres should be decided. They will make once again such a selection that for 100 years on the field of social life it will be impossible to come up with one healthy ear! (*Novyi Mir*, 1988, no. 2)

At first it was as if the opponents of glasnost and perestroika were merely onlookers wondering how these events would develop. When will there be a little balance? Won't all of this be limited, as it was so many times in the past, to a simple propaganda campaign? But gradually, when the lineup of positions became clearer and more defined, they, as Nuikin predicted, tried to launch a counteroffensive.

On 13 March 1988, the newspaper *Sovetskaia Rossiia* published the article "I Cannot Renounce My Principles," signed by Leningrad teacher Nina Andreeva, but expressing—beyond any doubt—far more than her personal position alone. This now-famous letter, devoted to a broad range of problems connected with perestroika, used the issue of glasnost as a point of departure for a radical critique of the reform of the Soviet political system. Extreme glasnost, from the point of view of Nina Andreeva, like proposals for bold political reform, would lead to the destruction of traditional socialist principles:

Already too often much has appeared which I cannot accept, with which I cannot agree. A crush of words about "terrorism," the "political servility of the people," the "barren social vegetation," "our spiritual slavery," "universal fear," the "dominance of boors in power." . . . From these threads alone the history of the transition to socialism in our country is often woven. For that reason we should not be surprised that, for instance, nihilistic moods are growing stronger among some of the students, that there is a confusion of ideas, a displacement of political points of reference, or even ideological omnivorousness. Yet again we have to hear the statements that it is time to bring to justice Communists who supposedly "dehumanized" life in our country after 1917. . . .

I read and reread sensational articles. What, for example, can our youth receive, aside from disorientation, from revelations about the "counterrevolution in the USSR at the start of the 1930s," about the "guilt" of Stalin for the coming to power in Germany of fascism and Hitler? Or from the public "computation" of the number of "Stalinists" in various generations and social groups?

N. Andreeva then turned to the place of Stalin in Soviet history. Although the "entire obsession of critical attacks" focuses on Stalin, she argued, the problems themselves had more to do with the complicated era of transition than the historical person of Stalin himself. This era involved the "unparalleled feats of a whole generation of Soviet people who today are leading more active political and social lives." Into the formula "cult of the personality" are crammed, in N. Andreeva's view, industrialization, collectivization, and the cultural revolution, all of which pulled our country into the ranks of the great world powers. "All of this is now placed in doubt," she lamented.

> Together with all Soviet people I share the anger and indignation at the mass repressions that took place in the 1930s and 1940s through the fault of the then party-state leadership. But a healthy attitude decisively protests against painting contradictory events in one color, as has begun to happen today in several organs of the press. . . .
> . . . Alongside the professional anti-communist in the West, who long ago took up the supposed democratic slogan of "anti-Stalinism," there live and thrive the successors of the classes overthrown in the October Revolution, far from all of whom were able to forget the material and social losses of their ancestors. It is appropriate to include in this category the spiritual successors of [Fyodor] Dan and [Iulii] Martov, of others in the ranks of Russian social-democracy, of the spiritual followers of Trotsky or Yagoda, of the offspring of Nepmen bearing a grudge against socialism, of the *basmachis* [Central Asian "bandits" during the Civil War] and *kulaks*.

Andreeva went on to analyze the "counterrevolutionary" spirit of perestroika. The first and most fundamental ideological stream to make an appearance in the course of perestroika offers a model of a kind of left-liberal intellectual socialism, the supposed expression of the truest humanism, the most "purified" of class stratification. Its advocates oppose proletarian collectivism with "self-worth of the individual"—with modernistic searchings in the area of culture, God-seeking tendencies, and technocratic idols; they preach about the "democratic" charms of contemporary capitalism, fawning before its real and imaginary achievements. Its representatives state that we built the wrong socialism and that only today "for the first time in history a union of the political leadership and the progressive intelligentsia has been formed."

Andreeva described the advocates of "left-liberal socialism" as falsifiers of the history of socialism. Claiming absolute historical truth, they substitute for sociopolitical criteria of social development "the scholasticism of ethical categories." Further, she asked "whom it serves" to have "every major leader of the Central Committee of the party and of the Soviet government compromised after leaving their post, discredited in connection with their real and imaginary mistakes and miscalculations." She continued:

> Here is another thing that disturbs me: Connected with militant cosmopolitanism today is the practice of the "repudiationism" of socialism. Unfortunately, we come to our senses only when its neophytes with their outrages are an eyesore outside Smol'nyi or under the walls of the Kremlin. Moreover, they are trying somehow gradually to train us to see in the above-mentioned phenomenon a kind of almost harmless replacement of "residence," and not a class and national betrayal of figures, the majority of whom on our national means finished college and graduate school. In general some people are inclined to look upon "repudiationism" as a sort of display of "democracy" and the "rights of the individual," whose talents were hindered by the flowering of "stagnating socialism." Well, and if there, too, in the "free world," they do not value vigorous enterprise and "genius," and the trade in conscience does not hold the interest of the special services [*spetssluzhby*], you can always return. . . .

If "neoliberals," in N. Andreeva's view, are oriented toward the West, "conservatives and traditionalists" strive to "overcome socialism at the expense of backward movement," to return to the social forms of presocialist Russia:

> In the views of the ideologues of "peasant socialism" there is an incomprehension of the historical significance of October for the fate of the Fatherland, a one-sided appraisal of collectivization as "an act of horrible tyranny over the peasantry," uncritical views of religious-mystical Russian philosophy, old tsarist conceptions in native historical science, and an unwillingness to see the postrevolutionary stratification of the peasantry and the revolutionary role of the working class.

She summed up her article as follows:

> As it has been presented, today the question about the role and place of socialist ideology has taken on a very acute form. The authors

of the opportunistic forgeries under the aegis of the moral and spiritual "cleansing" erode the boundaries and criteria of a scientific ideology; manipulating glasnost, they propagate supra-socialist pluralism, which objectively hampers perestroika in the social conscience. This is reflected especially painfully on our youth, which, I repeat, is distinctly felt by us, teachers in institutions of higher education, schoolteachers, and all those who deal with the problems of youth. As M.S. Gorbachev said at the February Plenum of the Central Committee of the CPSU, "We should also act in the spiritual sphere—and maybe precisely there in the first instance—guided by our Marxist-Leninist principles. We should not forego the principles, comrades, under any pretexts."

On this we stand and will stand. Principles were not given to us as a gift but have been achieved by us through much suffering in the sudden turns in the history of our Fatherland.

This article was like an exploding bomb. Opponents of perestroika seized on the article and began to reprint it in local newspapers, using it to intimidate all those who stand for "glasnost without shores."

But this publication not only alarmed advocates of reform but stimulated them to respond to this direct challenge. On 5 April 1988, *Pravda* published an editorial entitled, "The Principles of Perestroika: Revolutionary Thoughts and Deeds," which presented a comprehensive rebuttal of the Nina Andreeva article and a restatement of the need for further reform:

Many difficult, painful questions are being raised. Glasnost has shown that in arguments at times there is not enough of political culture, of the ability to listen to one another, to scientifically analyze social processes, and, too, there is simply not enough knowledge, arguments.

Yes, and glasnost itself is often variously understood. For some it is another cosmetic repair job. Others see in glasnost the possibility for a kind of "dismantling" of the entire socialist system, and as soon as it comes to this, then the whole path traversed after October is declared to be false and the values and principles of socialism bankrupt. A third group gets carried away by radical phraseology, entertaining themselves and others with the illusion of leaping over necessary stages. . . .

Such a variety of reactions to the practical business of perestroika is understandable, especially if you consider also the weight of the former conservative habits and the complexity and unusual nature of the new problems that have been concentrated into this short, three-year stage.

. . . The struggle for perestroika is conducted in production as well as in the intellectual sphere. And although this struggle does not take the form of class antagonism, it is acute. The appearance of something new always strains the relations to it and the judgments made about it.

Already in themselves the discussions, their character and direction, testify to the democratization of our society. The diversity of judgments, appraisals, and positions takes up one of the most important signs of the time, evidence of a socialist pluralism of ideas really existing today.

But one cannot but notice in that discussion a very specific tendency. It now and then manifests itself not as an aspiration to make sense of what is going on, to figure it out, not as the desire to move things forward, but, on the contrary, to put a brake on them, shouting out the usual incantations: "They are betraying the ideals!" "They are renouncing principles!" "They are undermining the foundations!"

One of the ABCs of Marxism is that ideas and interests are mutually related categories. Any interest is expressed in certain ideas. Behind any ideas there unfailingly stands one or another interest. The conservative resistance to perestroika is due to the weight of habit and to practices of thinking and acting carried over from the past; it is militant egotistical interests used to existing at someone else's expense and not wishing to renounce this practice. It is precisely these interests against which perestroika is objectively directed. Because perestroika, like any revolution, is not only "for" but is also against something. Against everything that keeps us from living better, fuller lives, from moving ahead more quickly, from paying the smallest price for the mistakes and miscalculations that are unavoidable on a new path.

And in this complicated situation we must clearly differentiate between real discussion, genuine concern for actual problems, and searches for the best answers and solutions, and the aspiration to turn democratization and glasnost against these very same ends.

Some people's heads are filled with turmoil, confusion. The unfolding of democracy, the rejection of administrative-command methods of leadership and management, the broadening of glasnost, and the removal of all kinds of prohibitions and limitations have created a danger: Are we not shattering the very foundations of socialism? Are we not subjecting the principles of Marxism-Leninism to revision?

Some state: "We are moving in the direction of petty-bourgeois socialism, based on trade and money relations. . . ."

"Don't rock the boat!" others threaten. "You will overturn, destroy socialism!"

There are also those who directly suggest a halt be called, or even that we turn around and go back.

An echo of these moods was found in the long article "I Cannot Renounce Principles," which appeared on March 13 of this year in the newspaper *Sovestkaia Rossiia. . . .*

. . . Any author has the right to defend his or her point of view. It is this very approach that, thanks to glasnost and perestroika, is consolidating itself in our society. The rubric under which the article was published led one to assume that a polemic concerning the questions it raised would follow—if not immediately, then at least after a certain amount of time. This is all the more necessary because the questions are serious and are raised in a key [*kliuch*] that cannot be called anything but an ideological platform, a manifesto of the anti-perestroika forces.

Perhaps in this "letter to the editor" it was the first time readers saw in such a concentrated form not a search, not a reflection, and not even the expression of confusion, of turmoil in the face of complex and acute questions that life has presented, but the rejection of the very idea of renewal, a crude exposition of a very refined position, a position in essence conservative and dogmatic.

We are rehabilitating Truth, cleansing it of phony and cunning truths that lead us into the dead end of social apathy; we are learning the lesson of truth offered by the 27th Congress of the CPSU. But Truth has turned out to be in many ways bitter. And so already an attempt is undertaken using references only to the extreme situation to white-wash the past, to justify political deformations and crimes before socialism. . . .

Now and again voices are heard to say that Stalin did not know about acts of lawlessness. He not only knew—he organized them, directed them. Today this is already a proven fact. And Stalin's guilt, like the guilt of his close entourage, before the party and the people for the permitted mass repressions and lawlessness is enormous and unforgivable. . . .

But why is it just the same now, when the party has given a clear and direct answer to this question; why must we return to it again and again? We think there are two reasons. Above all because, in defending Stalin, they stand for the protection of our life and practice today, of methods they created for "solving" discussion questions, of the social and state structures they built, of the norms of party and social life. But the main thing is that they defend the right to tyranny. Tyranny, which at the top invariably turns out to be only a question of egotism—although one person may be motivated by the desire to take more and give less, another's outer wrapping is the respectable clothing of pretensions on a monopoly in science, personal infallibility in affairs, or something else. . . .

But some people in no way can escape from the nostalgia about the past, when some laid down the law and others had to listen and submissively carry it out. . . .

. . . Some people are ready to see all misfortunes, all troubles of current life, in the fact that the newspapers are "blabbering away, making judgments about everything, exciting public opinion," etc. It must be recognized: A newspaper is a secondary thing. The primary thing is life itself! In order not to have to read about shortcomings in our newspapers, we must remove them from our lives.

And again we see what value, what responsibility is the printed word. As at times unverified facts and pretensions can be used in a monopoly-mastery of truth, at times simply an adjustment of the facts to fit into a preconceived notion of the author can naturally turn against the very best motives. Conservatives take such mistakes to the absolute: that only they receive the fruits of democratism and glasnost. What is the result? Forces that at first glance are polar opposites in their convictions in fact form a bloc in the braking of perestroika.

The publication of this response in *Pravda* was of major significance; it clearly pointed to the surviving strength of the conservative forces and to the fact that the decisive battle with them still lies ahead. The well-known Soviet playwright Aleksandr Gel'man wrote about this several days later in *Sovetskaia Kul'tura* (9 April 1988):

Three years have gone by since the moment perestroika began. What is the major positive result? In my opinion it is that, despite the fact that three years have gone by, perestroika continues. What is the major negative result? In my opinion it is that, despite the fact that three years have gone by, perestroika has not as yet become irreversible.

The fact that there have as yet not been created sufficiently democratic structures that could make the democratic way of life reliable, self-reproducing, is for all those who associate perestroika with the fate of our future a source of great anxiety, or great nervousness, which does not let go of us for one day, for one hour. And that, I believe, will be the main question of the 19th Party Conference—to work out and pass decisions whose realization will guarantee the total irreversibility of the democratic process in society.

Open and hidden opponents of perestroika more and more clearly are aware that the ideals of perestroika with every day win over more and more hearts and minds. They understand that the segment of time during which perestroika can be suppressed or even appreciably knocked off the decisive revolutionary path is short. Sensing this deficit of allotted time, they are bristling. They understand that they have to hurry while those mechanisms of decision making, with whose help they can evade public opinion and strike a blow at perestroika, are still working. These mechanisms in many cases are in their hands. I allow that the preparation for the party conference or even the party conference itself may turn out to be the bridgehead on which they will try to make the decisive battle against perestroika.

It is possible that my fears are exaggerated. God willing that it were so. But we are talking about such serious things, about such possible tragic consequences, that I think I have the right not to hold back in the expression of my fears.

In this sense I consider the publication in *Sovetskaia Rossiia* of an article by Nina Andreeva expressing several programmatic positions of the conservative forces in the party not accidental. The main pathos of that article was to place in doubt the correctness of the moral criterion used to evaluate past and present Soviet society. In the capacity of a Marxist idea, she preaches the incompatibility of politics and morality, juxtaposes class and ethical approaches. . . . In general she is disturbed by the fact that little is being spoken or written today about the working enthusiasm of those times, only about tragedies and tragedies. She somehow cannot get it into her head that according to the laws of normal human sympathy, people are more disquieted by the fate of those who innocently and prematurely died in Stalinist camps than by the fate of those who without doubt are deserving of respect for their evident working heroism but who all the same lived and worked normally and who are still living or who died their own death. . . .

Whom does the position of Andreeva suit? The people? The party? Not by any chance. This position willingly or not serves the vital interests of the bureaucracy, including the party bureaucracy. It serves them to separate politics and morality; they need to avoid the condemnations of past sins so that nothing will prevent them from committing new ones.

The smarter, more farsighted opponents of perestroika use a different strategy—they strive to substitute liberalization for democratization. What is the difference? Democratization provides for the redistribution of power, rights, and freedoms, the creation of a series of independent structures of management and information. Liberalization is the preservation of all the bases of the administrative system, but in a softened variation. Liberalization is a released fist, but the hand is the same and at any moment it can again close into a fist. Only outwardly does liberalization at times resemble democratization, but in fact this is a fundamental and inadmissible substitution.

The opponents of perestroika do not have the conclusive logic, the convincing program, but in its stead they still have power. They have strength. For that reason, I think, we, rank-and-file Communists, should not sit with arms folded and wait for the decisions of the party conference according to the principle "whatever God will send." Our concern for the fate of perestroika must be transformed into real action. Not only into books, scripts, plays, and films, but into real, direct political action. . . .

Glasnost must be protected like the apple of one's eye. . . . We must inhale some air for a second wind, and now is the very time to do it. The struggle is not about to end; its decisive, most difficult stage is only beginning.

Nina Andreeva's article, the ideological platform of those conservatives who grew dissatisfied with the progress of glasnost, was the first attempt to halt the process. A second crusade against glasnost was carried out in the summer and fall of 1988, when the Ministry of Communication announced a limit on the subscriptions to many newspapers and magazines (as a rule, the most liberal of them), an action that was widely interpreted as the bureaucracy's effort to "yoke" glasnost. After severe public protests the restrictions were lifted. The journalist Andrei Romanov commented on the lessons of this experience in *Moscow News* (1988, no. 44):

> Restrictions on subscriptions to newspapers and magazines—which the public roundly protested—have been lifted. Hurray, comrades?
> Yes, we—readers and subscribers—can all congratulate one another. Last Thursday the press broke the news that no one thought possible: at a meeting of the USSR Council of Ministers the day before, the subscription limits had been abolished on virtually all national publications.
> In response to the subscribers' outcry, the government had found an extra 90,000 tons of newsprint for 1989 periodicals. Where to print the additional newspapers and magazines and how? This problem was also solved. Meanwhile the subscription period for 1989 was extended to November 15. . . .
> The current subscription campaign has revealed, most importantly, that the undemocratic mechanism enabling bureaucrats to disregard public opinion is still in place. A mechanism which continues to generate crisis-like situations.
> A mechanism which can only be countered when public opinion screams "Emergency!" It took an explosion of popular passion and protest at the top governmental level to stop this mechanism and secure something elementary—consideration of people's requirements. Perfectly reasonable requirements.
> Is this normal for a democratic society? Once again this has confirmed the vital need for a political reform and democratization of the entire society. Then glasnost, too, will be delivered from the threat of limits.

Though this new assault and the subsequent defeat of anti-glasnost forces undoubtedly showed that opponents of glasnost occupy high positions in government, they remained anonymous.

A final important event in the recent history of glasnost involved a public debate on the life and works of Alexander Solzhenitsyn. The debate opened with the publication in *Knizhnoye Obozrenie* of a short article by Yelena Chukovskaya proposing to restore Solzhenitsyn's Soviet citizenship and publish his books in the Soviet Union. This article evoked hundreds of responses from readers. Some, like these, wrote in support of Chukovskaya's proposal (*Knizhnoye Obozrenie,* 1988, no. 33):

> We need now both the works of Solzhenitsyn and he himself. The strength and artistic quality of his books about our past are unparalleled. We in Russia do not have now a writer of talent as strong as his. Alexander Issaevich must be with us.
>
> Vyacheslav Kondratiev

> The time has come to repudiate the injustice done to Solzhenitsyn. In the whole civilized world he is rightly considered one of the most outstanding Russian writers of the twentieth century. One may agree or disagree with his ideas and philosophy, but he belongs to Russia. . . .
>
> Ya. Etinger, Ph.D.

> Of course, Solzhenitsyn has nothing to do with socialist realism. But we want to read his books, to brood over them, to argue with him. . . . The writer, the artist, any man has a right to think freely. . . .
>
> Vladimir Lazarev

There were dissenting voices, too (*Knizhnoye Obozrenie,* 1988, no. 36):

> I am a war veteran. My opinion is shared by other readers of *Knizhnoye Obozrenie* who are veterans as well. . . . Let him stay over there, where he is generously paid by his CIA superiors.
>
> I. Kryukov

The "Solzhenitsyn affair" stirred considerable interest. Many voices for the rehabilitation of Solzhenitsyn could be found on the pages of newspapers and heard on TV. And *Novyi Mir*—where at the beginning of the 1960s Solzhenitsyn's works were published, *One Day in the Life of Ivan Denisovich* among them—announced *The Gulag Archipelago* for publication in 1989. But suddenly the whole project was cut short. At a regular press conference in Moscow, Vadim Medvedev, Politburo member responsible for ideology, informed journalists that he did not approve of the decision to publish Solzhenitsyn.

After this the name of Solzhenitsyn disappeared from the Soviet media. But not completely. A well-known literary critic, Igor Zolotussky, disagreed indirectly with the Politburo opinion while discussing the problem with his colleague Alexander Lanshikov:

> **Zolotussky:** You keep insisting that before we consolidate we need division. Here you are in league with Mikhail Shatrov who in his interview to *Ogonyok* suggested to divide ourselves from the author of *The Gulag Archipelago.* I understand that not everybody thinks it possible that such literature be published in this country. . . . But I am against a "struggle of ideas" promulgated by Shatrov. Because this struggle presupposes the division into "ours" and "not ours" and we have had enough of it.
> **Lanshikov:** What we need now is a dialogue with those for whom literature became fate and not mere gambling.
> **Zolotussky:** Yes, that's it, a dialogue, not a struggle. (*Literaturnaia Gazeta,* 1988, no. 3)

Among the important matters difficult to avoid when speaking of the development of glasnost is not only what we argue about but also how we do it. To learn tolerance, respect for the opinion that differs from one's own—this is not as simple a matter as it appears. As Eduard Batalov put it in the mouths of imaginary participants of a dialogue in the journal *Vek XX i Mir* (1988, no. 1):

> Tolerance requires in deed the recognition of the legality of the activities and views differing—possibly in the most radical way—from our own. You reject, but you do not destroy, forbid, liquidate, extirpate, close, remove, etc., that which you, possibly, would like to destroy, forbid, etc. But also toward your behavior and views, which might also appear to someone else a sharp knife, others will relate with just as much tolerance. . . .
> Tolerance, as with everything on this earth, has its limits. In principle, these are defined by the norms of law and by the simple norms of morality—do not kill, do not steal, etc.
> . . . I am speaking about serious things. And indeed about tolerance toward alternative opinions at the level of the adoption of a decision— in a word, about that which is sometimes called "socialist pluralism." Of course, all of this can become a real factor in social life only with the presence of corresponding legal guarantees and under the condition that your higher authority will not consider itself infallible and elected for life. No less important, of course, is support from below. Not simply agreement with that pronounced from above, not the latest "thank you, party and government," but initiative, vigor, criticism.
> . . . Several things and conversations make a strong impression. But I have come to the opinion that intolerance is seething in many souls. People want not simply to be liberated from the ballast, to seek out

the truth, but also to avenge themselves. Some with the old, others with the new. Several letters, published in your newspapers, letters from simple people, shake me with their cruelty and intolerance. Their authors do not simply express disagreement—that is just normal—but demand just about the execution of those who think differently than they themselves think. And some of these people, as follows from their letters, send a copy to the KGB.

Yes, we are clearly as yet lacking in tolerance toward political unlikemindedness [*inakomysliu*], although if you remember in what environment these people were raised, it is not difficult to understand the logic of their actions. Here we need years.

Professor Leonid Gol'din also wrote in *Sovetskaia Kul'tura* (16 February 1988) about the style of our discussions.

> Calls for dialogue, discussion, are audible everywhere. There grow stronger, however, the voices of those who think that we have already talked too much. For such people the concepts of discipline and order are like alternatives to the polyphony of opinions and positions (although we are talking about mutually connected things). You cannot embarrass them with a question about socialist pluralism. All that, they say, is for the newspapers and the thick journals, for Soviet-American "spacebridges"; but in their own department, if indeed there is any discussion, then it is only about how better to carry out the orders of the leadership. . . .
>
> But today those who consider broad social dialogue a necessary condition of democratization and progress are also confronted with a serious problem fundamentally weakening their position: the thirst for quick, uniform truths and solutions, good for all occasions. . . . Having discovered that the world is not decorated in one color, that it is multi-measured [*mnogomeren*], that there exist various positions, various appraisals, we, in any case many of us, were not so pleased by the multi-coloredness and by the problems that had opened themselves up to view along a huge front. . . .
>
> Naturally, in conditions when some led and others followed, when it was clearly known to whom belonged the monopoly on truth, life was simpler. The notion that someone possessed the key to the solution of all the world's complications, knew how to make everyone happy without asking what people wanted—this notion is comfortable; it creates a feeling of social stability. . . .
>
> Passions burn, there is a sharpness of tone, the clashes are furious. . . . On the one hand, there is gladness that various points of view can be heard, at times even controversial—gladness even if on the strength of the novelty of such a situation. But what is to be done if for one writer rock music is the embodiment of progress, while for another it is the moral equivalent of AIDS? How do you define whom

to admire, whom to applaud, and to whom to give reproach? And voices are heard to ask if it is not time to "set limits" to this polemic.

As to the style of the discussion, to the courteous conversation to which we historically are not accustomed. . . . You cannot consider people retrograde only on the basis that they do not like *Repentance* or *The Executioner's Block.* And even *Children of the Arbat* should not divide us along different sides of the barricade. It must be taken as a rule: The more meaningful an event in spiritual life, the sharper will be the controversies. . . .

That is why a statement of the type, "We have spoken and that's enough, now to work, comrades," is simply dangerous. The uninhibited word is the indispensable condition of creative work.

Mikhail Gorbachev said that "Every person has his social experience, his level of knowledge, of education, the peculiarities of his perception of what is happening. That is where the wide range of opinions, convictions, and appraisals comes from, which, naturally, demand attentive consideration, comparison." This multi-flowering of ideas and positions is our strength and not our weakness, and we should learn how to use it reasonably. . . .

Because the history of thought, of creativity, is the history of the struggle of ideas, of viewpoints. In order to know how to defend our positions, convictions, we need strong reason, developed intellectual muscles, which weaken without real competition. . . .

Active social dialogue accompanies stages of the ascent of renewal, of the broadening of scope of spiritual freedom. And, on the contrary, monologue thinking, truths in the final instance pronounced by leaders, is always an indicator of the strengthening of a totalitarian, feudal atmosphere in society. Certainly, social conditions define the possibility of genuine dialogue. . . . But dialogue in its own turn is a stimulator of citizenship, social activeness, is a necessary condition of the struggle against apathy and stagnation.

The struggle for glasnost, the battle with the opponents of glasnost, continues to unfold. Yes, and that is the way it should be if perestroika and glasnost mean not cosmetic changes but radical shifts in our way of thinking and acting, in the very social structure.

TWO

Debates over History: We Want to Know the Truth About Our Past

Let There Be No "Gaps" in Our History

During these years of enormous social breakthroughs when the prohibitions previously imposed by censorship are crumbling, people are not just looking toward the future. They are turning their gaze as well to the past, a past that until recently resounded with empty slogans, gleamed with official varnishing, and concealed, like an iceberg, nine-tenths of the truth. In order for people to be honestly and sincerely proud of all that is good in their past, in order for them to be able to look squarely ahead, they must know and understand their history.

The heated disputes concerning the "blank pages" of our history that have flared up recently in our press are evidence that this necessary but painful process is under way. The intensity of these discussions is unprecedented. Both in the breadth of their historical scope, encompassing virtually our entire past, and in the radical nature of their approach, involving the rejection of "truths" that were previously considered indisputable, they go far beyond the discussions of the Khrushchev era.

Professor Yuri Afanasyev, rector of the State Institute of Historical Archives, is one of the pioneers in these debates. Indeed, he has played the crucial role of catalyst, supplying the "jolt" that set discussion in motion. In an article published in *Moskovskie Novosti* (11 January 1987) about the problems facing Soviet scholars in the social sciences, he challenged the assumption of the superiority of Soviet scholarship:

It has been established [in the Soviet Union] as an unchallengeable principle that our social sciences cannot in any way be inferior to non-Marxist, bourgeois approaches. And inasmuch as it can be assumed that every historian is already—by virtue of his birth in the Soviet land, from the cradle of advanced education on—recognized as a "Marxist" and nothing else, it is therefore accepted that any book published here is superior—not only in its methodology, but also in terms of its primary content—to books published by "them." With machine tools and shoes this is not necessarily so. But research in the humanities—somehow even at the stage of conceptualization—takes on a qualitatively superior Marxist-Leninist stamp. Alas! In reality things are significantly more complicated. For after all, memorizing, as you would, a line of verse about the "natural succession of socio-economic stages of development," or even about how "Marxism is not a dogma, but a guide to action," still does not make you a Marxist. It takes, as is well known, a tremendous amount of work. It takes courage and subtlety of thinking, scientific talent, and fresh ideas and approaches, as yet unapproved by anyone (except by logic and the facts); in a word, it takes enormous effort to qualify for the high calling of a Marxist historian in the late twentieth century.

Afanasyev stated that there are still many questions to be answered about the historical experience of the Russian proletariat's conquest of power, the defense of the Revolution, and the building of socialism. In his view "the impetus provided by the party decisions of the 1956–1961 period began to run dry and were restrained in the subsequent fifteen to twenty years, and a decline ensued in the study of the history of the October Revolution." Of course not everything in the publications of that time was above reproach. Mistakes were made, and some assertions made by participants in the discussions were declared erroneous owing to misunderstanding (or, more precisely, owing to a lack of understanding). Under these conditions, working out the methodological problems of history should have been pursued with even greater intensity; instead it was brutally interrupted.

One important reason for the decline of Soviet historiography, according to Afanasyev, is that the old, "hardened stratifications that have oppressed research efforts since the 1930s made themselves felt."

This was exacerbated by the fact that we felt reassured by more sweeping conceptions not only of the state of our science, but also by the notion that this was a passing phase in the development of our society, during which, according to "theoretical" generalizations, there could be no room for contradiction of principles, ideological antagonisms, or serious contrasts. And so it was on the surface, but beneath the surface processes were occurring that would later give grounds for a bitter, alarming conclusion: We know little about the society in which we live.

Perhaps our gravest theoretical (and practical) mistake was that at times we forgot that the nature of the path on which we had decided to embark was revolutionary (and, consequently, it would inevitably be enormously difficult, full of dangers, and, if you will, agonizing, and at times tragic). A secret conviction was born, that once we were on the track, once we had received the initial world-historical impetus, from then on our system would glide smoothly along from achievement to achievement, from one triumphant stage to the next, from the good to the better. As if supreme efforts, resourcefulness, and self-denial were not called for. As if the "demonic force of ignorance," the inertia, and the cupidity of certain people and groups in the population had just disappeared.

According to Afanasyev, Soviet textbooks:

present a one-sided picture of many events in the actual history of the Communist Party of the Soviet Union, and about much they say nothing at all. Stalin's historical sketch of the triumph of the October Revolution and the building of socialism in the USSR, though far from the truth, remains unquestioned to this day in most textbooks, and is sometimes even reproduced directly in them. . . .

Let us just take the question of how Lenin's last letters and articles are presented in some of our textbooks. A sufficient number of pages are devoted to an exposition of his last letters and articles. But only one or two pages are devoted to Lenin's plan itself. The remainder are crammed full of platitudes that set the teeth on edge about the epoch of mankind's transition from capitalism to socialism, about the beginning of a "world-wide revolution," about the prospects for a transition to socialism that bypasses capitalism, about the fundamental conflict of the epoch, and so on and so forth—that is, about things of which Lenin made no mention at all (with a few exceptions) in his "testament." The integrity and the structure of Lenin's plan are not demonstrated. An even worse fate befell the descriptions that Lenin gave in his last letters of the leading members of the Central Committee. They are lifted from the exposition of his plan and transferred to the parts of the book that describe the 12th Congress of the RKP(b). They are quoted one-sidedly, with all positive descriptions of these future members of the opposition omitted, and only the negative ones retained. The result is that a fierce and complex battle of ideas and of specific individuals, the living dramatic tension of those days, is replaced either by detective stories or by lifeless oversimplification. All that remains is a bombastic pomposity which conceals the weakness of argumentation and the avoidance of pointed questions. . . .

The unfortunate student, on whom a wave of Stalinist definitions comes crashing down—"a brand of Menshevism," "a Menshevist deviation," "an antirevolutionary group," "agents of the kulaks," and so forth—must basically waste his intellectual abilities memorizing labels. At the same time he is deprived of the opportunity to delve into the essence of theoretical arguments and ideas about the formation of socialism, to compare the path of socialism in the USSR with the path that the building of socialism has taken in other countries. This is truly not the full-branched tree of life, but the planed-down telegraph pole! And in fact, given a high-quality, honest, thorough presentation of the material, our history can and should evoke profound interest, for there is nothing more dramatic or more interesting than the building of socialism in the USSR, a process which was accomplished by the country in the shortest possible historical time, with the greatest selflessness and sacrifices by the people, with enormous mistakes and political crimes, to a large degree connected with the personal qualities of Stalin.

All of this stated openly in print hit many like a bolt from the blue. Of course, a great many of us had the same thoughts even before, but few people would have dared to express such thoughts aloud. Sometimes, however, one example is sufficient to elicit a significant reaction. As controversy flared up, a clear demarcation of positions became immediately apparent.

In the middle of this controversy stood the very same Yuri Afanasyev, who insisted that only the serious study of Soviet history would make it possible to successfully address current problems. In an interview published in *Sovetskaia Kul'tura* (21 March 1987), he affirmed:

> To surmount [social passivity] and other problems as well, we need to have the truth about the society in which we live. This is perhaps one of the most decisive points for understanding our socialist future. Without the past, there can be no possibility of consciousness; the entire arena of contemporary meanings and meaninglessness, fears, hopes, and plans, becomes incomprehensible. It is part of our make-up that our very ability to part with the past requires that we understand it and find support in it. That is the principle.
>
> But at this precise moment, in light of the problems that our society is trying to solve, knowledge of two central periods in our Soviet history is particularly essential: 1917 to 1929—"during and after Lenin"—and 1956 to 1965—"the post-Stalin period, the 20th Party Congress, and attempts at reform." The triumphs and defeats of these two periods, enormously dynamic and rife with contradictions, deserve detailed study.

Afanasyev urged his audience to reread and understand the diverse proposals, ideas, and social projects that were proposed in Lenin's time and after his death and called for the republication of the materials of party congresses as well as of Stalin's reports and articles.

It is not just that we do not know our history. In recent years, historical science, and above all the history of the Soviet period, has ceased to influence social consciousness. Can this situation be remedied?

In order for a historian to speak authoritatively about the society in which we live—its problems and their scope—he must also have the moral right to do so. And this right can only be won by opposing those who would condemn history, as a science, to social passivity and all its attendant flaws—inertia, servility. It is not fitting for us, as historians, to judge society as if from the sidelines, to appear before it dressed in a white dressing gown or tails. Indeed who, if not we ourselves, should be the first to cure our own ills and, perhaps, to do penance as well. And let us hope that, in our own circle, restructuring still lies ahead. Yes, there have been more than enough appeals for debate and for theorizing. But ultimately everyone knows that theories and new knowledge in the historical sciences are only encouraged when they are not at variance with "generally accepted" opinions. The historian who deviates from the "norm" risks many consequences, including expulsion from the scientific arena. . . .

Just consider this: For twenty years the flow of ideas was cut off. Not entirely, of course. It is impossible to completely stop an idea. But nevertheless, all those years of artificial constraint! It has become fashionable to sigh over the general situation that has developed in our country, over the universal irreparability of these past years. And it is probably something that deserves thought. But there were, in fact, specific parties involved. It is no coincidence that Mikhail Gorbachev invariably returns to them, naming, among others, the Central Committee of the CPSU, the country's leadership. And everyone must do this. Anonymous criticism does not serve perestroika well. There have been and still are specific people who directly "created" the stagnation. At the very least we should know who they are, the more so as their pattern of thinking and modes of action are still operating in the same direction today. The campaign to curtail scientific research in historical science in the early 1970s was headed up by Sergei Trapeznikov, who enjoyed free rein in directing science and who filled virtually all the positions under him with people who were dependent upon him and who were connected by "business" ties. Some of them continue to "direct" historical science today and never tire of issuing appeals for "bold quests and discussions.". . . I believe that the polarization of positions in this sphere must increase. A new age is dawning, but a new campaign is not being conducted.

Which period in Soviet history is most in need of serious, critical reevaluation? On this question there is considerable consensus: the Stalin era. It is not simply a question of the "cult of personality" about which so much has been heard since the 20th Party Congress. It is a question of a societal phenomenon that can no longer be equated with the personality of one "great leader" alone. Afanasyev remarked that while non-Marxist historiography has produced thousands of publications on this subject, "we continue to ignore it."

> For example, it is clearly difficult to accept the assertion that the massive repressions directed against honest Soviet people in the 1930s were either a "mistake" or a "deficiency" "in the preservation of Soviet legality" (mentioned in the same breath with deficiencies "in consumer service") or even the "inevitable costs of the class struggle and the revolutionary reconstruction of society." The well-known party decisions characterize them differently: "distortions," "tyranny," "unlawful actions," "abuse of power during the period of the cult of personality," the activities of [Lavrentii] Beria's "criminal band." These phrases have become a part of public consciousness. No scientific data to suggest a reappraisal of this evaluation has appeared since 1956. . . . The party decisions have not been revoked. A reconsideration of them is therefore politically and morally untenable.

Afanasyev's articles stirred up a stormy debate. *Moskovskie Novosti* (10 May 1987) reported receiving a telephone call from the head of the Central Archives of the USSR, Professor F. Vaganov, who argued that the publication of Afanasyev's article was a mistake. The editors proposed that Vaganov himself set forth his point of view on the pages of the weekly. Three months later the following letter was submitted to the editors by a Professor A. Nosov, who mentioned that its writing had been coordinated by Professor F. Vaganov. This critical article was also signed by P.I. Sobolev, L.V. Shirikov, and S.I. Murashov, all professors and heads of departments of the history of the CPSU at various Moscow institutions of higher learning:

> The appearance in *Moskovskie Novosti* (11 January 1987, no. 2) of the article by Y.N. Afanasyev, "The Energy of Historical Knowledge," cannot but meet with the disapproval of specialists in non-Marxist historiography, promote confusion and bewilderment among young people, and provoke indignation among an older generation of Soviet historians of the CPSU and the USSR. What is at issue here? Why has this unscientific, sensational, pretentious article attracted such attention? To understand, you must delve into its contents, its basic idea.

Y.N. Afanasyev essentially calls on historians to re-evaluate the 70-year historical path of the Soviet people, as it has been revealed in the historiography of the history of the CPSU and the USSR. It turns out, in the author's opinion, that historical science "is stagnating, and in many ways not up to the standards of the rest of the modern world. . . ."

Perestroika seeks not to destroy, but to create, to ascend to new heights of historical science. And as we make this ascent we are taking with us all the best in the historiography of the history of the CPSU and the USSR. And there is something to take. Y.N. Afanasyev thinks that over the last 15–20 years historians' initiative in studying the October Revolution has been drying up, been stifled. But how then can we explain the fact that some very serious scientific works have been produced during this period, honoring the 100th anniversary of V.I. Lenin's birth, and the 50th, 60th, and 70th anniversaries of the October Revolution. . . .

We consider it essential to call attention to the strange, fallacious position taken by Y.N. Afanasyev in his evaluation of the party's general Leninist course in the building of socialism.

Y.N. Afanasyev deplores the fact that "Stalin's plan for the triumph of the October Revolution and the building of socialism in the USSR, although far from the truth, remains unquestioned to this day and is sometimes even reproduced directly." . . .

The author has advanced a postulate, without citing evidence or arguments of any sort, because there are none. In the program of the CPSU, accepted at the 27th Party Congress, it is stated that after the working classes had won political power, after victory had been achieved in civil war, and after foreign attempts at military intervention had been utterly defeated, the party set about putting into practice the Leninist plan for building socialism. "Supported by the enthusiasm of the masses, repelling attacks from both Right and 'Left' opportunists, strengthening its own ideological-political and organizational unity, the party steadfastly held to the general Leninist line of socialist construction" (Program of the CPSU, Moscow, 1986, p. 7). It is in fact this Leninist plan for building socialism and its realization that Soviet historians have illuminated in their books, and not Stalin's non-existent "plan" for revolution.

The only person in the party who aspired to his own plan for revolution was, as we all know, Trotsky. But everyone knows that our party rejected, decisively and irrevocably, Trotsky's ambition to replace Leninism with Trotskyism.

The four authors concluded:

The energy of historical knowledge must be directed toward the revolutionary restructuring of all aspects of the life and history of

Soviet society, and toward educating our young people in historical responsibility and pride in their homeland, in both its heroic history and its present.

Unfortunately, Y.N. Afanasyev's article does not serve these aims, and can only confuse foreign readers, even more so those who know the history of the CPSU and the USSR.

Just a few years ago such accusations could have had harsh consequences for the "accused." Today, the situation is different: The debate continued. In an article characteristically entitled "We Talk about the Past, but the Future of Socialism Is Being Decided" (*Moskovskie Novosti,* 10 May 1987), Afanasyev wrote:

> Here is what I consider the centerpiece, the core of the letter written by those four: "Perestroika is not the destruction, but the creation, the ascent to new heights of historical science." . . . [But perestroika] signifies in the Russian language a simultaneous destruction and creation; and no matter how you bend it, you cannot separate one side of the coin from the other. Creation, yes! But not on a vacant lot. Rather, so to speak, on developed land, in the thick of long-standing economic, political, and ideological structures and organizations. That which is valuable, which has justified its existence, which has potential, should serve as a support and a foundation, while whatever has been mere ballast and a brake on the development of the possibilities of socialism is discarded. Perhaps my opponents can explain how it is possible to establish new methods of management without destroying the old ones? How to master new ways of thinking without first overcoming the old, dogmatic ways? And likewise: how to take a new historical view of Soviet society, without first doing away with primitive cliches, silences, and sometimes even falsification? . . .
>
> If there has been no stagnation in historical science over the last decades, if "hundreds of books and articles" were so good, then please show me where even one of these pre-1985 publications dealt not with the "successes of developed communism" but rather, for example, with the mechanisms that impede development. I would not begin to pose this rhetorical question if the four authors of the letter did not evaluate the current state of the "historiography of the CPSU and the USSR" with a self-satisfaction so rare in these times. . . .
>
> My opponents believe that there is not and never has been a Stalinist plan for the triumph of the October Revolution and the building of socialism. But what, if not this plan (the essence of which, it would seem, has yet to be fully disclosed in our literature), provides the basis for the *Short Course*? . . .
>
> . . . Let me just point out the distinctive characteristics of this plan: the history of the party was essentially reduced to an inner-party and inter-party conflict within the working-class and democratic movement,

and the conflict of opinions, the search for the true paths of revolution, the disagreements within the party leadership were perceived as part of someone's evil design. The groups that formed during this period were subsequently labeled "anti-party," that is, prompted by counterrevolutionary motives. Divergences in political convictions and positions became the target of fantastic criminal accusations. It is precisely this version of the party's history, laid out in the *Short Course*, which was subsequently reproduced in literature on the history of the party.

Lenin's position, however, was completely different. Lenin thought in broad categories. His first concern was always an objective analysis of the position of the masses in the revolution, of class relationships. He insisted on evaluating historical figures by their actual contributions at various stages of the struggle. Never "blaming them personally" for this or that political vacillation, he endeavored instead to expose the societal roots of the divergences which occurred. Lenin took into consideration the political evolution of party figures: his judgment of their past performance was not influenced by his opinion of their more recent actions; but neither was that previous judgment allowed to interfere in circumstances that were new, unique. . . .

We must also bear in mind that the past, especially the recent, difficult past, does not disappear like landscape seen through the window of a racing train. Not only do we continue to talk about it, but we carry it with us, we preserve it in ourselves. The impending reform of socialist society also includes a new, unbiased reading of our own history as well.

This clash of opinions, involving fundamental ideological-political positions, did not leave readers indifferent. A number of readers' responses were published in *Moskovskie Novosti* (24 May 1987). Let us cite two typical examples:

> Yuri Afanasyev's article represents the fruit of scientific ignorance and cheap demagoguery. Historians have various specializations: the ancient world, the Middle Ages, general history, the history of the CPSU, the history of the USSR. I have never encountered the name of Yuri Afanasyev among Soviet historians of the history of the USSR and the history of the CPSU, among those of prominent specialists on the questions raised by this author. He has undertaken to address problems in areas in which he simply has no competence. Wittingly or unwittingly, he is playing into the hands of bourgeois historiography.
> . . .
> This letter expresses not just my own, personal opinion, but also the opinion of my colleagues in the department at the institute where I work, a number of scholars at the M.V. Lomonosov Moscow State University and at other Moscow institutions of higher learning, prom-

inent specialists on the problems discussed in the article, party veterans, members of the scientific-methodological council of the historical section of the Moscow regional branch of the Znanie [Knowledge] Society. All the colleagues whom I have lately chanced to meet and speak with about these problems have been of the same opinion: The author and the editors of the newspaper permitted serious mistakes; they were out of their depth on this subject and not qualified to discuss it. I think that the newspaper's editors should be more circumspect in their selection and coverage of materials concerning the problems of the science of party history, and only after consulting the appropriate specialists. In this respect certain other materials published of late in this newspaper deserve criticism.

As regards Y. Afanasyev's rebuttal in the article "We Talk about the Past, but the Future of Socialism Is Being Decided," it is so petty and shrill that it merits no special scrutiny. Attempts to embroil us in debates about the past can only distract us from the tasks of perestroika as set by the party at the 27th Congress of the CPSU and impede decisions and actions today.

> Member of the CPSU since 1947,
> World War II Veteran,
> Lecturer, Ph.D. Candidate in
> the Historical Sciences,
> Anatolii Borisov

I entirely support the statements made by comrade Y.N. Afanasyev and would like to express my own opinion (I am a worker, party member for over 40 years) to my respected comrades, scholars of historical science—and to voice my disagreement with their opinion on the question of the development of historical science in our country.

Over not the last 15–20, but the last 20–30 years historians' initiative has not only begun to dry up, but in the last 20 years has run completely dry. Why? The Soviet people are waiting for an answer to this difficult question from our scientist-historians; the people want to know the truth about what happened not only during the postwar years, but throughout the entire 70 years of the Soviet regime as well. We need the truth, not phrase-mongering. The truth about the administrations of Stalin, Khrushchev, and particularly Brezhnev. What was it like and what happened? Why didn't we stop the negative miscalculations in time, why were we silent? Why is it only at the 27th Congress that we have spoken with complete directness and honesty about our shortcomings and these negative phenomena? Y.N. Afanasyev is right. We do not in fact have real textbooks on the history of the party and the history of the USSR. We need the truth about the Great Patriotic War [World War II], about the role of individuals (leaders) in that war. Respected colleagues: Has it not occurred to you that what you are pursuing is not restructuring, but posturing? Or is the time not ripe? There have been enough unnecessary discussions. It's time to get down to the serious work that we, as workers and communists, expect from you. We need the truth and only the truth; without the truth there can be no authentic history of the nation, the party, or the people.

I. Khudiakov,
Monchegorsk, Murmansk Region

The polemical baton was shortly after seized by the newspaper *Sovetskaia Kul'tura*, which published an article by Professor F.M. Vaganov and Doctor of Historical Sciences A.N. Ponomarev, which, although critical, maintained a more moderate tone.

Several recent articles have used the pretext of perestroika to advance the idea that the reevaluation and reinterpretation of virtually the entire history of the CPSU and the history of Soviet society is a task demanding immediate attention. . . .

How can one characterize the past fifteen to twenty years from the point of view of the development of historical science? In Y.N. Afanasyev's opinion, historical science was oriented "toward deliberate passivity"; it was characterized by "inaction" and "servility"; the interpretation of theoretical problems was the province only of "a group of people who took on a great number of duties"; the pages of scholarly journals were "tightly barricaded by a wall of bureaucratic ice against fresh opinions." And as a result, "for twenty years the flow of ideas was cut off." It was a time when the development of historical science was "artificially impeded."

These are the kinds of gloomy colors with which this period is characterized. Although, it is worth noting, no proof or arguments are advanced to support these opinions.

We do not intend, nor do we want, to idealize the development of historical science during this period. But there is no call to dramatize it either. The truth should be what it is. Since the interview gave a one-sided and in many respects incorrect appraisal of the state of historical science, we want to call attention to the following actual facts. During the period under discussion more than 10,000 scholarly works by historians were published in which profound advances were made in our understanding of many pressing questions about history— from the most ancient times to the present. And to close one's eyes and pretend that nothing of the sort happened is to depart from the truth.

To assert that historical thought was stagnating is also untrue. It does not seem possible in this forum to go into detail about the extent and the substance of the quite serious advances made in our

scientific knowledge of history. What is indisputable, however, is that
it was not stagnating, but moving. Of course, it could have moved
faster and further, and the opportunities that existed in that respect
were not effectively utilized—that is also a fact. And it is imperative
that we now draw the appropriate conclusions from that.

In the same 4 July 1987 issue, *Sovetskaia Kul'tura* published an
article written by a doctor of philosophical sciences, Professor Genrikh
Volkov, that takes issue with the views of the preceding authors:

> Yu. Afanasyev is right: The history of the party is still being set
> forth according to the outline of the *Short Course*, whose author alone
> emerges in a halo of infallibility while his opponents are smeared
> with black tar. It is no secret to anyone today that the *Short Course*
> is a distorting mirror of history in which some figures appear dispro-
> portionately magnified while others are ludicrously diminished. Dwarves
> and giants. Strictly speaking, there is only one giant. The rest are
> pygmies, deviationists, enemies of the people.
>
> "Is it really necessary to correct history?" the authors of the article
> inquire testily. But how can we further correct it? In many works the
> history of our nation has been so warped, is so full of yawning gaps
> and tarred colors, that nothing further can be done. We do not need
> to correct history but to straighten out its distorting mirror. . . .
>
> It's time that the principles of glasnost were extended to the whole
> history of the party. There should be no gaps in it, no forbidden
> subjects or forbidden names. In political debates we should be able
> to compare the positions and arguments of various sides in their
> entirety. . . .
>
> An enormous and irreparable harm is done to new generations, as
> they come of age, by the very fact that Marxist-Leninist teaching is
> presented as a collection of ready-made truths with solutions for every
> problem, and the "stupid, unenlightened world" need only "open its
> mouth to catch the precooked morsels of absolute science."
>
> Hence the appearance in our midst of those who have become
> disillusioned, consider Marxism obsolete, and think that the truth can
> be found only in the new-fangled "isms" that spring up in the West
> and percolate through to us. It never even occurs to them that the
> conception of Marxism that they were taught during their student days
> is in great disagreement with true Marxism.

"Declassifying" our own history, abolishing forbidden names and
subjects, and exposing the "gaps" are tasks of enormous dimensions.
These tasks demand intensive efforts at the highest political level and
on the part of the broad masses; they require the efforts of professional
historians, social scientists, and figures in the cultural and historical

spheres. A great deal will depend, of course, on the attitudes of historians themselves in accomplishing these tasks, because the type of position they take in the debate that has opened up will ultimately determine the kind, the amount, and the interpretation of information that is presented to all of us. Therefore, it is important that the position taken by Yu. Afanasyev (as well as by G. Volkov and other specialists) is to a greater or lesser degree in keeping with the point of view held by other representatives of historical science.

The debate continued in the 29 July 1987 issue of *Literaturnaia Gazeta* in an interview with Yuri Poliakov, member of the USSR Academy of Sciences:

Distortions of history took on enormous proportions under the influence of Stalin's cult of personality. As early as 1929, works appeared exaggerating his role in the October Revolution and in the Civil War. For no less than a quarter of a century the avalanche of these distortions increased. At that time it was considered impossible to write any work on the history of Soviet society without demonstratively exaggerating Stalin's role as "leader and teacher," without unqualified eulogy. The remaking of history to glorify Stalin was carried to the limits of absurdity, but it was as if no one noticed. They got used to not noticing.

At that time it became the norm to violate the principles of historicism. People who had come out against the "general party line" in the 1920s began to be accused of subversive activities connected with the history of the Revolution of 1905–1907, the time of the October Revolution, and the Civil War. Their names were either not mentioned at all or were mentioned with the label "enemy of the people." In books of the time it would be impossible to run across such an elementary statement as, "Chairman of the Moscow Soviet L.B. Kamenev did such and such. . . ." Such a name could only be heard in this kind of standard context: "Having forced his way to the post of chairman of the Moscow Soviet, the enemy of the people Kamenev hindered in every way possible. . . ."

In most surveys and textbooks on [Soviet] history the reader would not even be able to find the names of all the chairmen of the Council of the People's Commissars and the Council of Ministers of the USSR. And no more than ten people have occupied that post over the entire seventy-year history of the Soviet regime.

The 20th Party Congress changed many things for the better. A significant portion of party, state, and military figures . . . have been restored to history.

It was not long, however, before new distortions of historical truth began. In works devoted to the 1960s and 1970s, more and more ceremonial motifs began to appear, and the history of those years gradually evolved into a "Guidebook to an Exhibition of Economic Achievements." A simplified, one-sided understanding of the concept of socialism led to a suppression of the negative phenomena, the dark side, the difficulties, the contradictions. The distortions affected other periods of time as well. Everyone remembers that during the 1970s a relatively small number of events of the past war were portrayed as the main, key events. The decisive significance of Brezhnev's actions in the Malaya Zemlya region was chronicled in monographs and in academic and popular articles and elaborated on to an extreme degree in collections of works and in respectable, multivolume works.

Later on, plainly exaggerated appraisals of Chernenko's role in the Great Patriotic War began to appear. It is sufficient to glance, for example, at the article devoted to him in the first edition of the encyclopedia *The Great Patriotic War.*

Why did it turn out this way? Let us not idealize the authors. Many of them displayed their opportunistic zeal willingly and happily, showing considerable initiative. But their zeal was encouraged by a situation that, as the January Plenary Session of the Central Committee of the CPSU noted, had developed on the theoretical front as a whole, when "animated debate and creative thought ceased to be part of theory and social science, and authoritarian evaluations and judgments became unquestionable truths subject only to commentary."

In the historical editing offices of publishers and journals a cautious mood began to prevail. Editors demonstrated particular zeal in removing anything that elicited doubt, that seemed debatable, or even if it did not seem so, that might appear so. More than once I have encountered the situation where an editor compared the formulations in the manuscript with formulations of official or reliably approved publications. If he found a "variant reading," he would demand its elimination. With matters thus arranged it would be difficult to put forward an original, fresh idea or a conclusion based on new principles, to give one's own definitions, deeper and more precise than the previous ones. And neither publishing houses nor the guiding authorities that direct science encouraged "liberties." . . .

. . . The majority of scholars, it seems to me, share the understanding that history must be "populated" and are prepared to remove the veil of darkness from the facts of the past. Only the densest retrogrades resist this. The dogmatics, who as before see their primary task as the retelling and superficial commentary on party documents, are still fairly powerful. On the other hand, the critics are emerging ever more actively and casting doubt on nearly every achievement of the Soviet regime. I have no doubt that with the open expression of their views, which was practically nonexistent before, the polarization in views will intensify. The essential debates are still ahead.

The arguments increasingly extend to the early years of the Soviet state and the role of Lenin himself. The publication of the play *Onward*

. . . onward . . . onward! by the well-known playwright Mikhail Shatrov, provoked considerable controversy. In the play, the author attempted a radical reexamination of the post-October period of our history, focusing his attention on the conflict between Lenin and Stalin and critically reevaluating the actual historical roles of the closest entourage. A roundtable discussion at the editorial offices of *Moscow News* (1988, no. 10) captured the debate sparked by the play:

> Most of those who have written about the play are historians. Reading these articles closely (there seem to have been no reviews so far discussing the play's artistic merits), one concludes that the main thing for their authors was not the play itself. It merely provided a pretext for discussion of the main point of contention, "heritage."
>
> If we take the extreme viewpoints, they look like this: some historians claim that Mikhail Shatrov makes null and void all our ideals and values; others insist that the dramatist uses the style of journalistic reporting to separate our values from their inhuman substitutes, to bring back Lenin's conception of these values.
>
> Both these opposite points of view can, naturally, be voiced and defended by their advocates. That's what discussions are for. Provided neither side claims to be in possession of the absolute truth, neither lapses into the "prosecutor's tone" or presumes that the opponent has malicious intents. If that should happen free contest of minds is out of the question. But it is this free contest of minds that we need.
> . . .
>
> **Eduard Klopov:** In order to study certain developments, a historian probes into and correlates facts, whereas a creative writer imaginatively interprets these facts—both minor and extremely important ones. We as historians have no right to interpret facts imaginatively. History, and historians, cannot use the subjunctive mood, while writers can. Shatrov used it to show the attitude of participants in the October Revolution to what took place on October 24, knowing the further course of events. So Shatrov's play should be judged from this point of view. Shatrov has described a situation utterly inconceivable in real life but quite conceivable in playwrighting. . . .
>
> **Yuri Polyakov:** The facts of Stalin's madness and Brezhnev's stagnation continue to stagger our hearts and trouble our minds. Again and again we come to the important conclusion: society sustains dramatic losses if it fails to ensure reliable protection against autocracy.
>
> It is hardly surprising that today's literature increasingly turns to Lenin's struggle against red tape, against officials cringing before the leader and punishing as perpetrators of crimes against the state anyone who comes up with original views that differ from those of the leader. Unity is power, says Lenin in Shatrov's play. But he stresses that blind unity based not on ideals but on the leader's unquestionable will, on personal devotion to him, on the absence of debate and clashes of

opinion point to the party's terrible weakness. This hardly differs from Bonapartism, disguised by some sort of Communist sign, or from worshipping and idolization. . . .

Genrikh Ioffe: The press sounds a loud alarm: would not we corrupt our readers? But the masses already have their own experience. When I hear that methods of historical analysis should be explained to the reader, I think this amounts to self-exposure. What on earth have we been doing all those years, whence all our degrees and titles, if our people are completely illiterate in history? Have we been plainly sponging on the people?

Eduard Klopov: It has become a tradition over the past years for a historian, a social scientist to offer to his readers certain judgments pronounced on figures or events of history rather than the results of his own reasoning. This approach rules out any serious research. What is still more sad is that this approach encourages the reader to reject alternatives that may suggest themselves in the analysis of a complex episode in history, to reject the very possibility of doubt. Many readers write to insist on being given one simple categorical answer in terms of yes or no, good or bad, friend or foe. . . .

Vitaly Lelchuk: We are responsible for what people know about history. Many readers of historical books find it easier to think about the past in old stereotypes. This approach can be seen also among higher-school teachers and researchers accustomed to viewing things in one dimension only.

But there have been some positive changes in recent times. This can be seen in particular in the debates about Shatrov's new play. Only a few periodicals pronounced their editorial judgment on the play. In each individual case the article's tenor depended on its writer's competence: the less conversant the writer was with history, the more categoric he was in his judgments. And still I think it is very gratifying to know that the principle of "go ahead without fear and doubt" has been encouraged.

Forgotten Names

In Orwell's Ministry of Truth, historical events and names of active participants in history are "forgotten" or rewritten in the interests of the present political situation. In the Soviet past as well it has too often happened that "inconvenient" or unwelcome names simply disappeared, with the result that our history was not merely "smoothed over," but took on an empty, jingoistic character.

In conditions of glasnost we want to know the truth both about historical events and about their participants. And the key figure here is Stalin. The majority of today's historical debates ultimately revolve around the question of how to evaluate him. Doctor of Historical Sciences

Professor Iu. Borisov, head of sector of the Academy of Sciences' Institute of the History of the USSR, wrote in the article "Man and Symbol" in the journal *Nauka i Zhizn'* (1987, no. 9):

> History played a fateful joke on Stalin. A man who in his day removed from books on the history of Soviet society other active figures himself became an "unmentionable figure."
>
> It is not easy to give his political portrait today. Here we have a man who, over the course of fifty-five years, was an active participant in the Russian revolutionary movement, in three revolutions. Then, after Lenin, he headed the party for more than thirty years during exceptionally critical periods—when the foundations for socialism were created, when victory was gained in World War II, when the restoration of the country's economy was under way, and when Soviet society began to make inroads into the scientific-technical revolution. More than thirty years have passed since his death, but the mystique surrounding his name has not dissipated, and his status as an "unmentionable figure" only perpetuates the fuss over his past cult.
>
> What kinds of associations does Stalin's name evoke? For a number of reasons it has become a sociological concept, an image used to define social phenomena connected with the building of socialism in our country. It is not the kind of neutral symbol common to mathematics that elicits no emotions, but a phenomenon of the moral, political culture of man and society.
>
> Until 1956 Stalin's name was a symbol that personified socialism. . . . His name was a symbol of the achievements that the people had attained under the party's leadership, under the system of socialism. At that time his name was connected neither with the tragic error on the eve of the war, nor with the massive repressions, nor with the mistakes in policy, nor with the replacement of the Leninist principle of democratic centralism by bureaucratic centralism, which became the basis for the "braking mechanism" on the building of socialism.

And once again, as has so often been the case in our experience, the impulse for a new, fresh view has been provided by literature: by novels such as *Children of the Arbat* by Anatolii Rybakov, *The Disappearance* by Yuri Trifonov, *A New Destination* by Aleksandr Bek; by the plays of Mikhail Shatrov; and by many other works. Rybakov's *Children of the Arbat*, for example, which dealt with Stalin's role in the 1930s, provoked a great outburst of readers' emotions. The responses to this novel dramatically reflect the diverse ideological and political attitudes held by various groups in the population. Several examples are taken from *Literaturnaia Gazeta* (19 August 1987):

Just a year ago I could not have imagined that we could hope for such things. In order to find out just an inkling of the truth about the 1930s, you had to take dozens of books, published in various years, and read the truth between the lines. I did not expect it, I did not hope for it, but it is a fact. A tremendous thanks to the party that this has finally happened.

Now I am celebrating. Finally we are printing what was previously banned. And the BBC and such is now just garbage to me; their broadcasts about our past are not worth the words of your novel.

Glasnost is the triumph of Lenin's ideas. The year 1985 is the continuation of the lives of all those who fought for our happiness, who defended our future during World War II, who worked for restoration after 1945, who opened up the virgin lands, who flew into outer space, and who fought for peace on earth. And I believe that we will not retreat.

I am thirty-two years old, and I work at a factory as an electrical worker of the sixth class.

> P. Parkhomenko,
> Dzhambul

Comrade Rybakov!

I cannot refrain from sharing my thoughts with you about your recently published "masterpiece," *Children of the Arbat.* In my opinion this book is harmful, untruthful, and contains subjectivist views about our nation's history. It is particularly harmful to our young people, who do not possess a thorough knowledge of historical developments from 1917 to 1956. Apparently you do not have the courage to admit honestly that you are embittered at fate and at the people who decided it. The fact that you suffered at a certain moment has left a deep imprint in the book. I feel no compassion for you. . . .

I will share any further thoughts about *Children of the Arbat* with the organs of the press. I may possibly send a letter to the KGB.

> L. Strizhakova,
> Office worker,
> Leningrad

I have waited for this book for forty years, since I came of age at the front and began to try to find out the truth. I had figured out many things, but to tell it like this—you proved to be the man for the job. Your work is painful, agonizing, but let our gratitude, our hope, and our impatient expectation be a help to you. After all, what you have written is essentially only the prologue. And we hope to discover with what ties HE managed to bind the most prominent figures and force them to tread in the blood of their comrades; why [Klement] Voroshilov allowed the army to be torn to pieces; why healthy forces were not able to oppose HIM; why HE felt the need to decimate HIS officer corps on the eve of the war; and so many other of these "whys" that will not leave us in peace.

P. Nikitenko,
Lieutenant General

Why muddy the waters? It was impossible to create the first socialist state in the world without mistakes. And in an entirely capitalist environment. My comrades and I, who are the same age as you, find your attitude strange. The publication of your novel *Children of the Arbat* is the latest mistake someone made. Do not deceive our young people, do not cast a shadow on your contemporaries' memories of a wonderful youth.

Your former admirer,
K. Sidorova

The publication in the journal *Znamia* of Aleksandr Tvardovsky's long-banned poem "Memory" occasioned the same kind of lively debate. The journal also published some of its readers' responses, from which we quote here (1987, no. 8):

I have never been one to write letters to the editor, but when I read A. Tvardovsky's poem "Memory" in your journal I decided to take up my pen. I want to convey how enormously grateful I am to you for publishing this poem.

I admit, I wept as I read. How true everything in it is!

Truly, nothing that happened has been forgotten. You cannot forget!

The fact is that I am the daughter of one such "enemy of the people."

My father was neither a kulak nor a priest. He was a simple worker, just an activist who stood solidly behind the Soviet regime.

We lived in the Leningrad district in a tiny town on the river Svir.
. . .

On 3 March 1938 he was summoned to the RONKVD, and he never returned home.

My mother was left alone with five children on her hands. At ten, I was the oldest, and my one-year-old twin brothers were the youngest. My grandmother also lived with us, my father's 86-year-old mother.

Today it is difficult to imagine how we survived. We were left entirely without means of existence. . . .

In 1939, my grandmother died, and soon after one of the twins died, too. . . .

We suffered many humiliations and injustices. And that is harder to bear than hunger and want. All these experiences could not help but affect our characters and our health. We are by nature withdrawn, unsociable, and neurotic. All four of us have been conscientious workers, and we have all been awarded the Veteran of Labor medal. My sister and I are already retired, but my brothers still work. Fate has scattered us all over the country. We have never returned to our native village, because it no longer exists: The fascists burnt it to the ground.

Before the war my mother often wrote to inquire about my father's fate, but she never got a reply. Similarly, when she made inquiries after we were liberated, she got no answer.

In 1955 I was summoned to the KGB and in answer to my question I was informed verbally that my father had been sentenced to ten years at a Corrective Labor Camp [ITL] and had died of sepsis in June 1943 while serving out his sentence.

After this I wrote an application requesting that my father's case be reviewed. (I had always believed that he was not guilty of anything.) And then, finally, in 1957 they sent me a document saying that my father's case had been reviewed and closed with his complete rehabilitation.

Almost twenty years of our sufferings! And for what! And how many others like us were there! Especially where we lived, in the Leningrad district.

We survived all of this, but it is impossible to forget it. It is good that we have begun to write about this. It makes those of us who suffered from the cult of personality feel a little better. Let the people know the whole truth.

My mother is now eighty-one years old and I greatly admire her for her courage and steadfastness. Under such conditions she raised and educated all those children! More precisely, we educated ourselves as adults, but she raised us to be honest and hardworking. Now she is still raising her grandchildren.

Please, excuse me for writing such a detailed letter, but I felt the desire to express the pain in my heart to someone.

> Respectfully,
> Kytmanova, M.A.,
> Volgograd District

We—students, blue-collar and white-collar workers—are profoundly disturbed by the publication in the journal *Znamia* (1987, no. 2) of the poem by Tvardovsky, "Memory" (1966–1969).

The author, who has been dead a half-decade, endeavored to show that Stalin was to blame for all the errors and mistakes. All the violations of socialist legality and democracy are the work of his hands alone.

This is a false view of I.V. Stalin's personality and actions worthy of Khrushchev or Solzhenitsyn. Here, in this vile, tendentious poem, Tvardovsky clearly aspires to paint Stalin in dark colors; to see all his actions as mistakes; to make Stalin shoulder the blame for the dark deeds of Beria's band and of others; and to turn the repressive measures against innocent citizens into deliberate actions by Stalin alone. . . .

Pathetic liberals!!! It is precisely because of liberals like Tvardovsky and his ilk that all these vices exist in our society, because of them that we have the lack of discipline, permissiveness, impunity, irresponsibility, the crimes committed without fear of reprisals!

There you have the results of your liberalism!

No, people—ours especially—need a strict, energetic, and stern leadership that puts demands on them. For our people have the strange peculiarity of turning into good-for-nothing, drunken swine, dirty pigs ready to drink, steal, and cheat whenever they get the chance.

There's your liberalism for you! The fruits of democracy.

And you editors foolishly smack your lips over the tendentious scribblings of Bek and Trifonov, and now Tvardovsky as well. Shame on you and curse you for such deeds!

We know that the party was not sold out under Stalin. We know that the children of Stalin, Molotov, and Voroshilov were never self-seekers, scroungers, drunkards, and traitors like the children and sons-in-law of your regular "true Leninists."

From Readers in Kiev
(unsigned and with no return address)

Much has already been accomplished recently; many questions have been raised. As they say, perestroika is under way. Here are its most recent steps as of today: The complete rehabilitation of Boris Pasternak and the poem "Memory" published in the journal *Znamia*. It is this poem that has directly inspired me to write this letter to the magazine.

Here is what gives me no peace. There is the Piskarev cemetery, the Mamaev burial mound. There will be a Poklonnaya gora. The Pioneers and enthusiasts have done a great deal and will do still more for the unknown heroes of World War II. And that is as it should be.

But what are we to do with the other memory, the one that A.T. Tvardovsky wrote about?

There should, there ought to be a Memorial to those who perished guiltlessly! And it is not important where: in Moscow, in Magadan, or in Vorkuta. After all, there is also the decision of the 22nd Party Congress, which, as I recall, no one has yet dared to revoke. It was quietly shelved, and we pretended that it had to be so.

Personally, this is how I picture the Memorial: a grey, granite wall, very long—almost endless—and on the wall outlines of human faces emerging through the stone. . . . Women's, children's, men's faces. . . . Thousands, tens of thousands of faces! And no names, no dates. Just faces, whose stone eyes hold the question frozen for eternity: "For what?"

And we will come to that wall, gaze into the stone eyes, and search for an answer to the unspoken question. And our children, grand-children, and great-grandchildren will search for the answer too. . . . Let an Eternal Flame burn by the wall, eternally reminding us that it is not only the struggle against international imperialism that demands vigilance.

The Memorial should be created on the basis of voluntary donations. Let the Ministry of Finance determine the expense, and it will im-mediately become clear—there will be a Memorial or all other un-dertakings will come to nothing.

We just need to understand that if we allow the agonizing memories of the 1930s to dissolve in time, they will return in some other era, slowly enveloping us in paralyzing fear.

I am Vladimir Ivanovich Kolesnik. I am thirty-nine years old. A worker. Not a party member. Married with three sons. As far as I know, there is no one in my family who suffered during the years of the cult, so any personal bias on my part can be ruled out.

We greeted the publication of the poem "Memory" in the journal *Znamia* with great indignation. The poem contains malicious, slan-derous attacks, such as we have seen before, on our history, on the period when Stalin led the country.

After the war I became a cadet at the Kremlin and later served in the renowned division of F.E. Dzerzhinsky. It was here that I entered Red Square for the first time in parade formation and that I saw I.V. Stalin for the first time. To serve by protecting the government and by making possible the glorious festive occasions on Red Square was both a great joy to us and a weighty responsibility.

It was also our lot to endure many anxious days during the funerals of eminent party and government figures, especially during the funeral of I.V. Stalin.

During those difficult days of mourning it also fell to me to stand guard in the Hall of Columns in the Trade Union House and to see how deeply and painfully the Soviet people suffered at Stalin's demise, how they came in an endless stream to look at him for the last time.

Many of them cried and thanked him for leading the country, for the victory he gained over the fascist invaders.

I stood there then and thought, will there really come a time when these anxious days and graveside tears are forgotten? And I firmly believed that our people would give I.V. Stalin his due, erect a majestic monument in his honor. . . .

In the military we sang popular songs that contained words like "Stalin and Mao are listening to us," "Gunners, Stalin has given the order," "When Comrade Stalin sends us into battle and the First Marshal leads us into battle," "The well-fed steeds pound their hooves, we will meet the enemy as Stalin would." We were taught loyalty to our homeland and to the party of Lenin-Stalin, but now they want to refashion and revise everything.

We have matured enough over time so that we mistrust you and can figure out everything ourselves.

> Sincerely yours,
> Demin, Ilia Petrovich,
> Moscow

We have not as yet had any serious scholarly research that would present a rigorous, unbiased, and complex evaluation of Stalin and his role in Soviet history. True, we have learned of many plans for such studies. One that is being readied for publication is a political biography of Stalin prepared by Lieutenant General and Doctor of Philosophical Sciences Professor D.A. Volkogonov. On 9 December 1987, *Literaturnaia Gazeta* published an abridged version of the book's preface entitled "The Phenomenon of Stalin." In it Volkogonov wrote:

Stalin is one of history's most complex personalities. Such people, whether we want it or not, belong not only to the past but also to the present and to the future. Their fate provides endless philosophical "food" for thought about existence, time, and conscience. One of the conclusions that suggests itself right at the beginning of research about Stalin is that the history of this individual, as if by magic, throws light on the most complex dialectic of our age. The personality at the head of the people and the party turned out to be as complex as the conditions of that time. If we are honest before truth and before history, we cannot but acknowledge I.V. Stalin's indisputable contribution to the struggle for socialism and its defense as well as his unforgivable political mistakes and crimes, which were manifested in the groundless repressions against many thousands of innocent people. By standing up for and defending Leninism in the political and ideological struggle, Stalin, the party's guiding center, created favorable conditions for accelerated socialist construction. And then, when it appeared that the most difficult stage (in terms of the inner-party struggle) was past, with the achievement of enormous successes in many spheres of innovation, a thoroughly erroneous thesis, blessed by Stalin, was born—that the class struggle must be intensified as progress forward demanded. And that meant that the dictatorship of the proletariat increasingly demonstrated its punitive rather than its constructive side. Hence it is no accident that evaluations of the figure of Stalin underwent cardinal changes to the extent that they were illuminated by the light of historical truth. . . .

When Stalin's name is mentioned, the first thing that comes to many people's minds is the tragic year of 1937, the repressive measures, the flouting of human decency. The Valkyries flitted unseen through the atmosphere of society, dispensing, as is well known, life and death. Yes, all that happened. There can be no forgiveness for those guilty of these crimes. But we remember that in those same years the Dneper hydroelectric power station and Magnitostroi were constructed; and there was Papanin, Angelina, Stakhanov, Busygin. . . . We owe the creation of the foundations of everything on which we stand today to those years; we owe the exalted soaring of the human spirit of the Soviet people, who withstood and defeated fascism in World War II, to that time. Thus it is a mistake in political terms and dishonest in moral terms, when condemning Stalin for his crimes, to cast doubt on the actual achievements of socialism, its basic potential. It is incorrect, when evaluating Stalin or the individuals in his immediate circle, to transfer mechanically those evaluations to the party, to the millions of simple people whose faith in the truth of the revolutionary ideals was not shaken. . . .

It is given to very few to outlive their own time. One of these few was Stalin. But his peaceful immortality is assured. The arguments about his role in our history—accompanied by epithets and tinged with reverence, and hate, and bitterness, and eternal bewilderment— will not fall silent for a long time. One way or another, Stalin's fate confirms our conviction that ultimately the power of great ideas is stronger than the power of people. And the tragic odyssey of Stalinist abuses could not, of course, undermine the enormous attractiveness of the ideals advanced by the luminaries of Marxism.

People's judgments can be illusory. The judgment of history is eternal.

There are various attitudes one can take to what Volkogonov wrote. But one thing is clear—he has hardly had the last say in our evaluation of Stalin and the Stalinist era. Many people will not agree with the opinions quoted above; those opinions will be criticized from both sides. Of course, even those who long for the times when a "strong arm" ruled the country and there were no differences of opinion find it difficult to openly defend either Stalin or his repressive regime. They will most likely recall the Russian proverb "You cannot make an omelette without breaking a few eggs," reasoning along the lines of "yes, there were repressive measures, but . . ." In other words, Stalin is a "great man," albeit with some shortcomings.

People from the other camp express their opinions and evaluations without any "buts" or "althoughs." For them, the logic of the "great man, but . . ." type of reasoning is unacceptable in principle. This point of view did not spring up yesterday. There were those who thought this way even more than twenty years ago, but for understandable reasons they were not able openly to defend this opinion.

The magazine *Druzhba Narodov* (1988, no. 3) recently published a letter written in the mid-1960s by one of our oldest international journalists, S.N. Rostovsky. Writing under the pseudonym of Ernst Henri, Rostovsky originally sent this letter to the well-known Soviet writer Ilya Ehrenburg criticizing Ehrenburg's portrait of Stalin in his memoirs *People, Years, Life*. Ehrenburg saw in Stalin the interlacing of "good and evil"; he emphasized Stalin's "reason and will" but also sharply condemned the repressions Stalin caused. Ernst Henri came down hard on this conception of "balance":

I will make so bold as to say that your evaluation of Stalin's mind and his role just as a state figure, and not as a moral individual, is completely at odds with historical reality, with the facts. . . .

I will touch on only one thing, that with which I am most familiar—the "reason and will" of Stalin in the area of international and related affairs, the role he played politically in the fate of our nation during that quarter-century of which you speak. . . .

You recall, Ilya Grigoryevich—none of us from the older generation can forget it—that a few years before the war against the most terrible enemy ever to oppose Russia, virtually the entire main body of the Red Army's high command was suddenly obliterated or dismissed. According to General [Aleksandr Ivanovich] Todorskii's data, repressive measures were taken against the following men:

of 5 marshals of the Soviet Union, 3
of 2 army commissars of the 1st rank, 2
of 4 army commanders of the 1st rank, 2
of 12 army commanders of the 2nd rank, 12
of 2 fleet flag officers of the 1st rank, 2
of 15 army commissars of the 2nd rank, 15
of 67 corps commanders, 60
of 28 corps commissars, 25
of 199 divisional commanders, 136
of 397 brigade commanders, 221
of 36 brigade commissars, 34

The data are incomplete. The total number of commanding officers subjected to repressions cannot be calculated. If we count only the highest commanding officers, from the marshals to the army commissars of the second rank inclusive, then it turns out that of 46 men, 42 were put out of action. If we count everyone and come up with an average figure, then two out of every three men of the Red Army's high command became victims. . . .

Here, in my view, are the results of Stalin's wisdom as a statesman toward the end of the 1930s (as I have said, I am speaking only about his international policy and matters directly related to it):

1. Devastating the Red Army's command personnel on the eve of the war.
2. Disrupting the anti-fascist unity of the working class in the West.
3. Affording Hitler the chance to finish off France, England, and to neutralize America before falling upon the Soviet Union.
4. Refusing to seriously fortify Soviet defenses along the lines of the Wehrmacht's impending attack.
5. Discrediting the Western Communist parties by the order to reject anti-fascism in 1939.
6. Affording Hitler the opportunity to launch a sudden, stunning attack on the USSR, despite the presence of a host of highly reliable warnings.

That is only over a span of four years—1937–1941.

Any one of the six points just enumerated would be sufficient to guarantee that the political figure who committed such a miscalculation, no matter who he was, no matter where he lived, would lose his reputation forever and be barred from the arena as unfit for his occupation.

Stalin and Stalinism today are the central focus of heated debates about our entire historical experience. The points of view are not simply "pro" and "con" but range over a diverse spectrum. One view of the problem, published in *Moscow News* (1988, no. 24), is that of our distinguished mathematician Igor Shafarevich, who sent his article to the editors with a note stating that he doubted that they would publish it:

The publication of Nina Andreyeva's notorious letter and the heated discussions that followed made me realize the importance of the issue I have been continually and even painfully preoccupied with of late. My question is *why such wide-scale inner resistance to all new reports about the cruelties and crimes of the Stalinist epoch?* . . .

One reason behind this is clear—fear of responsibility, reluctance to settle scores with one's conscience, fear of the fact that "the authorities" in general are condemned. But I think this is by no means all. The overwhelming majority of those whom I met are delighted to see how the language of the press is gradually becoming uninhibited; they wait and hope for changes in the economy and social life and are merciless in their appraisal of the closer past. Only stories about the bloody horrors of Stalin's 25-year rule are perceived with morbid bewilderment.

I will take the risk of expressing my own hypothesis. *The reason lies in the discrepancy between the scope of the tragedy which is gradually being revealed and that of the explanations usually given.* The explanations are either not available or are all incorporated into the notion of the perfidy and cruelty of one personality, and the concurrence of some unfortunate circumstances. . . .

If only the situation were so "simple" for everybody! For me it is still a mystery, though it has tormented me from my youth. I recall the loathing caused by these hypocrites who could shut their eyes and ears so well when they so desired. In fact, the axe of fear did not hang over their heads! Who will risk reproaching the miserable [Osip] Mandelshtam, who wrote a poem extolling Stalin in a hopeless attempt to save his own life? But how can we forgive Leon Feuchtwanger, who described in his book, *Moscow 1937*, the healthy appearance of the accused at the show trials, or how Stalin disliked the excessive number of his portraits and busts. Well, that's what these people are like! He finished the book with a quotation from Socrates: "All that I understood was fine, therefore, I think that what I did not understand is still better." When asked about the famine in the early 1930s (which took the lives of millions of peasants), Bernard Shaw jokingly retorted that he had eaten the best meals of his life in the USSR. When in 1934 A. Tolstaya and American publicist Don Levine addressed a request to Albert Einstein to support the protest against the bloodbath being organized by Stalin in Leningrad after the assassination of [Sergei Mironovich] Kirov, Einstein refused, saying: "I am disappointed that Russian politicians have been carried away. . . . Despite this I cannot join your venture. . . . I would like you to give it up. . . ." Late in the 1940s Jean-Paul Sartre wrote that the rumors about "forced labor" in the USSR must be ignored since they could result in the despair of the French proletariat! How can you explain the fact that at that time nothing was heard about the violation of human rights in the USSR, and that the "violations" were noticed when the crunching of bones was no longer to be heard and when the smell of blood no longer hung over our country? And Sartre, hurt by Khrushchev's report, found consolation in Mao's "cultural revolution"?

There is little doubt that Stalinism, rather than being the result of chance events, is connected with deep-rooted world-historic tendencies. Only realizing this can you understand and overcome its consequences. Hence, a broader view of it—the period of collectivization and war communism—is inevitable, especially in its international aspect and deeper roots. Only with this broader view can we remove the vexing shade of chance and absurdity which surrounds the disaster the country went though, shade which stops many people from trying to understand it.

The historian Roy Medvedev answered Shafarevich:

I think that Igor Shafarevich is not too far from the truth when he maintains that new reports about the cruelties of the Stalinist epoch arouse in many people not only morbid bewilderment but also inner resistance. Perhaps he is right that Stalinism is a "national disaster" of world importance (and this makes it difficult to understand). Perhaps, one can equally accept his theory that a profound logic led us to Stalinism, that it had fundamental causes. It is also difficult to disagree with my opponent's initial theory about the inadequate explanations of the tragedy experienced by our people, compared to its scope. We have still to overcome this last phenomenon, although, it has to be admitted, we have already arrived at quite a few conclusions.
. . .

Studying the events of the first 15 years of Soviet power, the conclusion must be drawn that somewhere at the turn of the 1930s Stalin usurped power in the party and the country, allegedly in the name of socialism. He claimed to be defending socialism from external and, still more, internal threats, which, according to his theory, increased along with people's successes in building a new life. Under these circumstances it became a sort of natural demand to promote "strong personalities," "heroes," to establish barrack discipline everywhere. . . .

As follows from his truly "fundamental" work—*Socialism as a Phenomenon of World History* (Paris, 1977)—Shafarevich, a Christian thinker, believes that socialism is an absolute evil and that Stalinism is one of the most logical manifestations of the essence of socialism. "Understanding socialism as one of the manifestations of mankind's striving for self-destruction," Shafarevich maintains, "makes clear its hostility to individuality, and its tendency to annihilate the forces which back and strengthen human personality: religion, culture, family and individual property. Consonant with this is the striving to reduce the human being to the level of a cog in the state machinery. . . ." Hence it is clear that our slogan "More socialism!" is perceived by him as a call for "More Stalinism!" But for the vast majority of Soviet people, for their friends, the appeal "More socialism!" sentences Stalinism, against which it is necessary to fight not with curses addressed to Stalin and not even with objective exposure of its root causes, but by perestroika, glasnost, democratization, and radical economic reform. This is what we are doing today.

The arguments today about Stalin and Stalinism often go beyond the limits of academic discussion; indeed, they have become an issue in legal proceedings. "I shall defend Stalin's honor and dignity as long as I live," declared Ivan Timofeyevich Shekhovtsov, a war veteran, a lawyer by education, and a retired investigator and procurator who brought charges against the writer Ales' Adamovich in a Moscow district court accusing him of insulting an individual and distorting historical truth. *Moscow News* (1988, no. 40) reported this surprising court session:

> For the claim: "A polarization of social views began after the April Plenary Meeting. Some people started to slander our history without grounds, to discredit the 1920s–1930s in terms which the BBC and Voice of America have long since abandoned. As an historian and a lawyer, I could not but analyze these statements, especially those denigrating a person who, as fate willed it, symbolized the nation for 30 years and headed the party and the state. . . . A person who cannot utter a single word in his own defense, who cannot be declared a criminal if he has never been convicted of a crime."
>
> In his article entitled "On the Eve" (*Sovetskaia Kul'tura*, 19 August 1988) Adamovich, quoting from one of Shekhovtsov's letters without naming the author, speaks about the "triumphant defenders of butchers who gloat over our liberalism." Said plaintiff Shekhovtsov, "in this article, I recognized myself." On recognizing himself, Shekhovtsov demanded that *Sovetskaia Kul'tura* apologize and suggested that it publish his own composition, "How Adamovich criticizes Stalin's resuscitators." Denying Stalin's complicity in mass repressions, denying the very fact of repressions, and referring to the presumption of innocence principle in so doing, Shekhovtsov formulated the claim in defense of his honor and dignity by analogy with the previous 16 suits in defence of Stalin's honor and dignity.
>
> From the claim: "I object to my being called a defender of investigators-butchers, because only a person who has been found guilty of using unlawful methods—torture—during the investigation can be called that. . . . Otherwise this amounts to fanning the flames of an anti-Stalin hysteria and other unhealthy phenomena in our society."

In the debate over Stalinism we are now encountering names that we either never knew, or forgot, or tried not to utter. One such name is Lavrentii Beria, the tough right-hand man of the "people's leader" who headed the secret police. After Beria's execution in 1953 his name was struck from our history. And today we are interested in Beria not for himself, but as a social type. A slew of materials has recently appeared on this subject, which have enabled our younger readers to discover—often for the first time—pages of our history that were previously closed. An article by Doctor of Historical Sciences S. Mikoyan entitled "Servant" offers a startling portrait of Beria (*Komsomolskaia Pravda*, 21 February 1988):

In her first book, which came out abroad, Svetlana Alliluyeva [Stalin's daughter] tried to create a "rose-colored legend," according to which Beria, that "evil genius," tricked and confused Stalin, exploiting his trust. Such a legend circulated even before Beria in connection with his predecessor, the sinister figure of Yezhov. . . .

And even today there are still a few ill-informed people who are not averse to thinking along these lines, who lack either the desire or the strength to accept historical truth the way it is.

But the truth is extremely simple: Before Beria, his role had been played first by [G.G.] Yagoda and then by Yezhov, but these puppets were invariably controlled by one person. After Beria, and parallel with him, were Merkulov, Abakumov, and many other underlings of lesser caliber. . . .

Beria was not squeamish about personally participating in interrogations. According to the testimony of contemporaries, he shot the first secretary of the Central Committee of the Communist Party of Armenia, Zandzhian, in cold blood in his study. He dealt ruthlessly not only with those who had worked with Stalin for a long time and knew his actual worth but also with those who had known him, Beria—even if only vaguely—before his own unprecedented rise. Therefore, the Communist Party of Georgia suffered perhaps more than the Communist parties of neighboring republics.

Beria was distinguished by his craft, his cunning, his ability to influence his "master" so that he did not and would not take a back seat and would remain useful for many years to come. And he did remain useful. . . .

Beria had, among other qualities, certain organizational abilities. During the war this helped him prove himself not only in the NKVD but also in matters related to defense. True, it also helped that he had free rein over the enormous work force concentrated in the camps. And just one reference along the lines of "Beria ordered . . ." worked absolutely unfailingly. . . .

And then in the summer of 1953, during one of the Politburo sessions (renamed the Presidium before Stalin's death), a group of marshals and generals of the Soviet Army were summoned to the Kremlin. They were instructed to arrest Beria and dispatch him to the headquarters of the Moscow garrison. . . .

Beria's trial was speedy. Possibly it was too speedy. Perhaps he should have been forced to tell many things that would have made the work of today's historians easier. . . . Perhaps the matter should have been more thoroughly investigated before he was written off as someone's "agent" in the heat of the moment (even if his work as an agent of the Musavatist intelligence service in 1919 in Baku was not in fact really the fulfillment of a party task, as Beria tried to assert).

But this is not really the point. The point is that a whole era was at an end.

For the sake of justice and for the sake of the future we are also beginning to talk about people whose names it was dangerous or "unnecessary" to utter in the past. These are names not only of those who were the victims of repressions in the Stalinist "purges," and who were rehabilitated after the 20th Party Congress, but also of those who until very recently were still numbered among the "enemies of the people." Lev Ovrutskii wrote in *Sovetskaia Kul'tura* (27 February 1988) in an article entitled "The Measure of the Law and the Excesses of Illegality":

As we begin to gain a clear view of things, we observe that life has become larger than life. Everyday events have disappeared somewhere. Today every event has a distinct meaning and import. But among all these unusual events, one of the most recent ones stands out in its magnitude. I have in mind the decision reached on February 4 of this year by the Supreme Court of the USSR to revoke the verdicts with regard to N.I. Bukharin, A.I. Rykov, A.P. Rozengolts, M.A. Chernov, P.P. Bulanov, L.G. Levin, I.N. Kazakov, V.A. Maksimov-Dikovskii, P.P. Kriuchkov, and Kh.G. Rakovskii. In March 1938 they were convicted in the case of the so-called anti-Soviet "Rightists and Trotskyites bloc."

The old dogmas are crumbling, withered as dried flowers. Social justice is turning into historical justice with increasing frequency. . . .

We have been waiting for this. . . .

We will remember.

I have in my hands the "Court Transcript of the Case of the anti-Soviet 'Rightists and Trotskyites bloc' " published at the time, in 1938. . . .

[Andrei] Vyshinskii: How would you sum up your aims?

Bukharin: Our prognosis was that there would be a big surge toward capitalism.

V: And as it turned out?

B: It turned out entirely differently.

V: It turned out that socialism was completely victorious.

B: It turned out that socialism was completely victorious.

V: And your prognosis was a complete failure.

B: And our prognosis was a complete failure.

V: In short, you slid into sheer, unbridled fascism.

B: Yes, that's true. . . . Allow me to proceed directly to an account of my criminal activities. . . .

And here is an episode from A.I. Rykov's "testimony":

Rykov: . . . The major national republics are gravitating away from the USSR.
Vyshinskii: Consequently, that is the dismemberment of the USSR, the seizure from it of a number of its republics?
R: Yes.
V: The preparation of a beachhead for the fascists' attack and victory?
R: Yes, that is indisputable.
V: Did you pursue your criminal goals at the cost of treason?
R: Of course.

How could the people believe this? That is the question to end all questions, and one that commentators on current affairs are pondering anxiously.

At that time class instincts were intensified to the utmost degree, writes one of them. It is difficult to agree with that. Class instinct is apparently manifested in an unfailing ability to distinguish one of your own from one of theirs. While here, as in theater of the absurd, a revolutionary is taken for a saboteur, a Bolshevik for a spy. Rather than talking about an intensification of the class instinct, we should talk about its atrophy.

Vyshinskii: To sum up briefly, to what do you plead guilty in this case?
[V.F.] Sharangovich: . . . I did all of this with the aim of overthrowing the Soviet regime, with the aim of ensuring the victory of fascism and the defeat of the Soviet Union in the event of a war with the fascist states.
Presiding Judge [V.V. Ulrikh]: Leading to the dismemberment of the USSR, the separation of Byelorussia, its transformation into . . .
Sh: Its transformation into a capitalist state under the yoke of Polish landowners and capitalists.

Sheer delirium, the reader will not hesitate to make the diagnosis.
But the signs are clear today, while yesterday they believed this delirium like a revelation, for fear lent a phantasmagoric quality to rational and sensible existence.

The article made another interesting point. The author particularly emphasized the fact that in regard to one person tried in the case of the anti-Soviet "Rightists and Trotskyites bloc" no protest was lodged by the Office of the Public Prosecutor of the USSR. That person was G.G. Yagoda. In the not-too-distant past it was unacceptable to utter his name as well.

Over the course of many years Yagoda directed the punitive organs, was responsible for one of the first waves of repression and ultimately fell victim to them himself, and finally stood trial in the same "Rightists and Trotskyites" case.

Yagoda "confessed" his guilt as one of the leaders of the "Rightists and Trotskyites underground bloc," whose goal was to topple the Soviet regime and to restore capitalism in the USSR. Yagoda "took" on himself the guilt for espionage and for transmitting government resources to Trotsky, for organizing the murders of Menzhinskii, Kuibyshev, and Gorky, and for making an attempt upon Yezhov's life by spraying poison on the blinds in his study. (How squalid the prosecutor's imagination!)

He gave, as the "Court Transcript" attests, criminal sentences to people whose innocence has today been attested to by the Supreme Court. Handing vials of poison to invisible beings, conspirators exchanging remarks with the empty air, Yagoda is frozen over eternity like a question mark, in a pose whose comic quality degrades justice. . . .

Today most people know that Yagoda was guilty—not of espionage on behalf of Trotsky and the like but of exactly the opposite, of organizing repressive measures against innocent people. Only a court can determine the measure of that guilt. But instead Yagoda has simply been "shut up."

To learn democracy means, among other things, not to exceed the bounds of legality in deed or in thought. In the ideal with which we associate our conception of the activities of the higher supervisory bodies, morality is completely contained and dissolved in the law; it does not reside in it heterogeneously in the form of a suspension or a sediment. The conflicts that arise here expose either the decline in ethical imperatives or the imperfection of legislative norms.

The inadequacy of the biblical principle—as you sow, so shall you reap—is revealed when it comes into contact even with everyday morality. Remember the "golden rule" of Stalin's prewar strategy: "We will answer the enemy's blow with a threefold blow!"

And if the blow is below the belt?

Answer baseness with baseness, vileness with vileness, meanness with meanness?

No. Only the measure of the law can withstand the excesses of illegality. By the very action of appealing to the law, we mark the boundary between revenge and retribution. There is one justice—for the saints and the self-righteous, for the murderers and their victims. Justice is indivisible as truth and fairness are indivisible.

The rehabilitation of party and government figures executed on Stalin's orders who had not been previously rehabilitated has been an important event in our lives today. Prominent among them is N.I. Bukharin, whom Lenin, in his day, called the "party favorite." Today, for the first time in half a century, we can read his works, many of which are being reissued, as well as the accounts of eyewitnesses, recollections that resurrect the historical truth and eliminate "gaps." The reminiscences of Bukharin's wife, A.M. Larina, published in *Ogonyok* (1987, no. 48) are among the most poignant. They begin with an excerpt from a letter that Larina sent to Mikhail Gorbachev requesting the posthumous rehabilitation of her husband:

Despite the tense international situation, I am submitting to you the question of the posthumous rehabilitation of my husband and the father of my son—Nikolai Ivanovich Bukharin. . . . This appeal comes to you not only from me, but at the request of Bukharin himself. Departing for the last time for the February-March Plenary Session in 1937 (the Plenary Session lasted for more than one day), Nikolai Ivanovich had a presentiment that he would not come back again and, bearing in mind my youth, asked me to fight for his posthumous vindication. That unbearably heavy moment will never die in my memory. Worn out by the investigation, by confrontations that were terrible and inexplicable to him, weakened by the hunger strike that was his sign of protest against these monstrous accusations, Bukharin fell on his knees before me and, with tears in his eyes, implored me not to forget a single word of the letter he had addressed to "A future generation of party leaders," implored me to fight for his vindication: "Swear that you will do it. Swear! Swear!" and I swore. To break that vow would be to go against my conscience.

Larina then recounted the tragic events surrounding Bukharin's arrest in 1937 and her husband's final "testament":

I remember 27 February 1937——that fateful day when Stalin's secretary called in the evening and informed us that Bukharin was to appear at the Plenary Session—as if it were yesterday.

The tragic moment of dreadful parting is indescribable, nor can I describe the heartfelt pain that lives on in my soul even today. Nikolai Ivanovich fell on his knees before me and with tears in his eyes begged my forgiveness for my ruined life. He asked me to raise our son as a Bolshevik. "Without fail as a Bolshevik," he repeated. He implored me to fight for his vindication and not to forget a single line of his letter-testament. . . .

He believed religiously in the ideals of the October Revolution and wanted me to regard this whole black period of history as temporary, to keep hoping for purification and justice. It is precisely for this reason that he charged me with raising our son as a Bolshevik. And for this same reason he addressed his letter "To a future generation of party leaders."

Bukharin wrote the letter several days before his arrest. He was already psychologically prepared to be arrested and to part with his wife. He had lost all hope of acquittal and decided to declare to future descendants that he was not involved in any criminal activity and to ask to be posthumously reinstated in the party. I was then twenty-three years old, and Nikolai Ivanovich was convinced that I would live to see the day when I could hand over the letter to the Central Committee. Since he was sure that his letter would be confiscated during a search and was afraid that in the event of its discovery I would be subjected to repressive measures, Nikolai Ivanovich asked me to learn the letter by heart. Many times he read his letter to me, and many times I repeated after him the lines he had written. Oh, how indignant he became when I made an error! Finally, when he was convinced that I had memorized the letter's contents thoroughly and completely, he destroyed the text of the manuscript.

Newspapers and magazines are publishing materials and recollections that have led to the rehabilitation of party and government figures, military leaders, and scholars who were repressed and about whom both the younger and the middle generations know very little: A.I. Rykov, A.A. Kuznetsov, A.V. Chaianov, A.I. Egorov, M.N. Tukhachevskii, V.Kh. Bliukher, and many, many others.

Recently a Plenary Session of the Supreme Court of the USSR was held that again took up the problem of people who were illegally repressed during the time of Stalin's cult of personality. Oleg Temushkin, doctor of jurisprudence and honored legal expert of the RSFSR, wrote in the weekly *Nedelia* (1988, no. 7):

> Thousands of cases of "rehabilitation" have been considered over the past thirty years by the Supreme Court of the USSR. And at the opening of the most recent Plenary Session a resolution was unanimously passed that revoked the sentence and abandoned the proceedings on the grounds that the elements of a crime were lacking with regard to Nikolai Ivanovich Bukharin, Aleksei Ivanovich Rykov, Arkadii Pavlovich Rozengolts, Mikhail Aleksandrovich Chernov, Pavel Petrovich Bulanov, Lev Grigorevich Levin, Ignatii Nikolaevich Kazakov, Veniamin Adamovich Maksimov-Dikovskii, Khristian Georgievich Rakovskii, Petr Petrovich Kriuchkov—the members of the so-called "Rightists and Trotskyites bloc."
>
> The organs of the NKVD carried out the investigation into the case of the "Rightists and Trotskyites bloc." It was personally directed by

the newly appointed people's commissar—N.I. Yezhov, who replaced in that post G.G. Yagoda, who had been arrested for "membership" in the very same "Rightists and Trotskyites bloc."

Incredible transformations indeed: Yagoda, who had directed the fabrication of numerous provocative cases that deprived thousands of honest people of their lives, now turned out to be numbered among those of the "enemy" bloc. It was essential to the producers of this farce that this criminal anti-Soviet organization be given the appearance of an enormous network.

But the inclusion of Yagoda in this "case" made sense in another way as well. He had already exhausted himself in organizing past trials. The time had come to replace him with another "creator" of provocations. Yezhov was chosen for this purpose. . . . But soon he too became "unsuitable."

. . . The Judicial Collegium presided over by Ulrikh adhered firmly to the principle that "a confession by the accused is the queen of proofs." This principle worked splendidly during medieval times and was the inquisitors' reliable tool in their battle with witches. Now it was revived by Vyshinskii (Vyshinskii's book, *The Theory of Legal Proof in Soviet Criminal Procedure,* which was awarded the Stalin Prize, contains the theoretical foundation of this principle). . . .

Returning, in thought, to the "case of the Rightists and Trotskyites bloc," I gave serious thought to the question, So then for whom was this last decision in the "case" made?

And I answered myself: for the wives and children who for fifty years bore the terrible, though gradually diminishing stigma of being "relatives of enemies of the people." For those who were deluded for so many years, having succumbed to the hypnosis of the cult of personality. But, mainly, it is not "for" but "for the sake of"—FOR THE SAKE OF TRUTH, FOR THE SAKE OF THE TRIUMPH OF JUSTICE.

Justice, which has now been restored forever.

Today we are restoring the historical truth concerning not just those who fell victim to Stalinist repressions but also those whose names have been hushed up for the past twenty to twenty-five years. Most prominent among them is N.S. Khrushchev. In an article published in *Literaturnaia Gazeta* on 24 February 1988, Fyodor Burlatsky sought to reopen a public discussion of the achievements as well as the failings of this key Soviet leader:

Khrushchev and his times. Unquestionably one of the most important and, perhaps, most complex periods in our history. Important, because it has a direct relation to the perestroika now under way in our country, to the current process of democratization. Complex, because we are dealing with a decade that was first called "glorious" and later condemned as a period of liberalism and subjectivism. During that time the 20th and 21st Party Congresses were held, which became reflections of the fierce political struggles that determined the country's new course. Under N.S. Khrushchev the first steps were made toward the revival of Leninist principles and the purification of the ideals of socialism. Then too the transition was begun from the cold war to peaceful coexistence, and a new window was opened up on the contemporary world. At this abrupt turn in history society inhaled a whole chestful of the air of renovation and choked . . . either from an excess or a lack of oxygen.

Burlatsky wrote that for a very long time Khrushchev's name was taboo. But in the address given by M.S. Gorbachev on the seventieth anniversary of the October Revolution, we heard a long-awaited speech about that era—about what was done and what was only partially done or not done properly, about what had survived into the 1980s and what had been eroded or lost in the period of stagnation.

Khrushchev came to power both by accident and not by accident. It was no accident, because he was the spokesman for a certain trend in the party, which in other circumstances and, probably, in a different way, turned out to have been represented by such very dissimilar figures as [Feliks] Dzerzhinsky, Bukharin, Rykov, [Yan] Rudzutak, [Sergei] Kirov. They were the advocates of NEP, democratization, and opponents of violent methods in industry and in agriculture, and especially in cultural life. In spite of Stalin's brutal repressions, that tendency did not die out. In that sense the advent of Khrushchev was natural. . . .

It was Khrushchev who, on his own initiative, advanced the task of creating lasting guarantees against recurrences of the cult of personality. He waged an uncompromising battle for this within the country and in the international arena without taking into consideration the costs that such a battle could entail with respect to some nations that were just entering the socialist camp.

Burlatsky noted that Khrushchev attached great significance to the ideological aspect of the matter, the necessity of telling the truth about the crimes of the 1930s and of other periods. But this truth was halfhearted, incomplete. Khrushchev stumbled over the problem of personal responsibility because of the role he himself had played in the persecution of personnel both in the Ukraine and in the Moscow party organization. Since he had not told the truth about himself, he was not able to tell the whole truth about others. For example, while opposing the role of V. Molotov and L. Kaganovich in the massacre of personnel in the 1930s, Khrushchev failed to mention the participation of A. Mikoyan, who subsequently became Khrushchev's trustworthy ally. In speaking about the 1930s, Khrushchev carefully skirted the period of collectivization because he had been personally mixed up in the excesses of that time.

> Today, almost a quarter of a century later, in comparing the period before and after October 1964, we see more clearly Khrushchev's strengths and weaknesses. His primary merit lies in the fact that he destroyed Stalin's cult of personality. This has proved irreversible, despite timorous attempts to establish the pedestal in its former place. Nothing came of them. That means that the plowing was sufficiently deep. It means that the plowman did not work in vain. The steadfast decision on the rehabilitation of many Communists and non–party members who were subjected to repressions and executions during the period of the cult of personality restored justice, truth, and honor in the life of the party and the state. This powerful blow, while not in all respects effective or skillful, was inflicted on centralism-from-above, bureaucracy and official arrogance.

According to Burlatsky, conservative forces were able to get the upper hand over reformers in the 1960s because both the administrative apparatus and the society as a whole were not yet ready for radical changes. That is why the very search for a conception of reforms and the means to realize them was based on traditional administrative and even bureaucratic methods. Today, supported by the experience of glasnost, we see particularly clearly how little was done even to inform people about the past, about the actual problems, the projected decisions, much less to include the broadest sections of society in the struggle for reforms.

> And one last lesson. It concerns Khrushchev himself. This man of keen natural political intelligence, bold and energetic, could not resist the temptation to glorify his own personality. "Our Nikita Sergeevich!" Is this not where the fall from grace of this acknowledged foe of the cult begins? Sycophants drowned him in a sea of flattery and eulogies, receiving in return high positions, the highest decorations, prizes, titles. And it is no accident that a whole chorus of sycophants and flatterers sang of the successes of "this great decade."

We have begun to speak about Brezhnev himself much more openly than even one or two years ago. Of course, this history is still too close to us, and it touches the interests of many people who are in the forefront of our political and social life. For that reason it is understandable that the historical reexamination of that period is going more slowly and that there are more reservations, nuances, and differences of opinion. Roy Medvedev published a particularly harsh assessment of Brezhnev in *Moscow News* (1988, no. 37):

> Brezhnev was neither a great nor even a distinguished personality. Frankly, I would describe him as weak in practically every respect. He lacked Lenin's intellectual power and political genius. He had none of Stalin's superhuman will and wicked craving for power. He was minus Khrushchev's exceptional independence, immense zeal for reform and capacity for work.
>
> In November 1982, Chernenko spoke about Brezhnev's outstanding abilities, acute wit and exceptional courage, about his resourcefulness, exactingness towards subordinates, intolerance of every sign of red tape, etc. With equal success he could have spoken about the deceased's outstanding literary gift (after all, he had received the Lenin Prize for literature), about his profound scientific erudition (after all, he had been awarded the Karl Marx Gold Medal) or his outstanding abilities as a military leader and a speaker. Many Western press reports described Brezhnev as a strong personality. All these assessments were far from the truth. Brezhnev was never a "strongman." He had a weak will and a weak character. . . .
>
> Brezhnev's surprising inclination for glittering honors and awards also provoked sneers. After the war, Major-General Brezhnev's breast was decorated with four Orders and two medals. After Brezhnev took over the country's leadership, awards came cascading down upon him as if from a horn of plenty. Towards the end of his life he had more medals than Stalin and Khrushchev together. On four occasions he was honored with the title of Hero of the Soviet Union. He was decorated with the Order of Victory which, under its statute, can be presented only to outstanding military leaders for major victories at fronts or groups of fronts. In 1976, Brezhnev was made a Marshal of the Soviet Union. Later, at a regular meeting with 18th Army veterans, Brezhnev arrived in an overcoat and commanded: "Attention! The Marshal is coming!" Removing his overcoat, he appeared before the veterans in a new marshal uniform. Pointing to the marshal stars on the shoulder straps, Brezhnev said proudly: "I have earned this."
>
> Not a talented orator, Brezhnev gave new speeches and reports almost weekly which were telecast nationally and included in special documentary film releases. He was a mere reader of the speeches and reports prepared for him. But even reading caused him much difficulty. He often mispronounced words, long words being the hardest for him. His speech writers were strictly instructed not to include long words in prepared texts.

Medvedev wrote that for nearly fifteen years all of our propaganda strove to portray Brezhnev as a "great fighter for peace," a "great

Leninist," a "great theoretician," etc. But this costly propaganda machine failed to produce a Brezhnev cult in the minds the Soviet people. Instead they treated him with indifference and, toward the end of Brezhnev's life, poorly disguised scorn.

But was everything so bad under Brezhnev? Didn't we call the 1970s the quietest decade in the USSR's history? Yes, but that was the tranquility of stagnation, when problems were not solved but put off, while the clouds continued to gather. The Soviet Union had recovered from the horrors of Stalin's terror. But on a lesser scale, unlawful repressions were carried out under Brezhnev. This preserved an atmosphere of "moderate" fear in society, which was reinforced by constant attempts to rehabilitate Stalin. There was no triumph of legality; there wasn't even elementary order in the country. Mismanagement, irresponsibility and the feeling that everything was possible took hold everywhere. The corruption eroding society became more unabashed and insolent, the abuses of power, the embezzling on large and small scales became the norm. Factionalism, mutual guarantee, nepotism and mafia practices were inculcated in every sphere of social and state activity from the national and regional party leadership to the editorial offices of literary magazines and the leadership of professional unions.

The reluctance and inability to work well, political passivity and apathy, indifference towards socialism's moral and political values, the moral degradation of millions of people, the reign of mediocrity from one end of the country to the other, the rift between words and deeds, and the promotion of a universal lie—this crippled the consciousness of an entire generation which we call (sometimes not without a reason) the "lost generation." From this point of view, "Brezhnevism's" overall consequences have proved as serious as those of Stalinism.

Brezhnev's regime scared everyone with its irrationality. Brezhnev spoke a lot about peace, but it was very difficult to trust a political group which ran a great nation on the principle "after us, the deluge." Brezhnev's physical death took a long and painful turn before the eyes of the whole world. His political death was much swifter. But to be done with Brezhnevism for all time, it is not enough to just take down the signs with his name from the city streets, squares and districts.

Glasnost and the new view of Soviet history are gradually extending to our own time. The rehabilitation of Andrei Sakharov and his return from exile in Gorky is just one piece of evidence that the attitude toward legal rights in the USSR is changing. Today we increasingly come across names that in the course of twenty years were erased from our history and hear the voices of those who, not in the far-off Stalinist times, but even very recently, were subject to repression. All of this is directly related to the reevaluation of individual rights and of those who have devoted themselves to its defense, which is still going on today.

The trial and sentencing of the writers Andrei Sinyavsky and Yuli Daniel in 1965 for disseminating propaganda with the purpose of undermining a weakening Soviet government was the first in a series of attacks on dissidence that took place from the end of the 1960s to the beginning of the 1980s. Today we are beginning to look differently on their ideas and their works. A sympathetic interview with Yuli Daniel was recently published in *Moscow News* (1988, no. 37):

> **MN:** What do you think today of that trial?
> **Yu.D.:** Strangely, I still remember that there were many well-wishing people in the courtroom, and that I literally sensed a wave of warm feelings. I remember [Yevgeny] Yevtushenko's despairing face and other faces, all expressing sympathy. I knew then that there were people who thought everything happening to us [was] a calamity. That helped me very much to stand [firm].
> **MN:** You both knew what sending your manuscripts abroad meant for you and still you did it. Why?
> **Yu.D.:** We, of course, had no political considerations. We were writers. We wished another sort of literature to have the right to exist too. A free literature, without forbidden subjects and problems. Why did we send our writings abroad? Simply because they could not be published here at that moment. . . . They tried hard, of course, to convince me that the enemies of our country had turned my stories into weapons in the ideological struggles. It was a serious charge, and 1937 was not a good year.

Perhaps even more significant than the reexamination of successive eras of Soviet history is the emergence of a wider discussion of the sources of the Bolshevik revolution in Russian and European history. In a series of articles published in *Nauka i Zhizn'* (November 1988– February 1989), Doctor of Philosophy A. Tsipko argued that the sources of Stalinism, as well as of the later distortions of Soviet policy, lie not in Stalin's aberrations from either Marxism or Leninism but rather in the purely philosophical doctrines—above all, a radical utopianism— that underlie all of them and that continue to shape Soviet life to this day.

> Why kid oneself, why mythologize Stalin and his works? Both he and his works were the progeny of a revolutionary movement that began long before Stalin assumed power. In the beginning there was the word. . . .

When cracks appear in the walls of a new building, the commission appointed to look into the problem generally begins with the blueprint for the building. . . . Once we are truly convinced that socialism is above all our choice, once we choose to improve our society, and once we dream of a democratic, humane socialism, then in analyzing the past, we must doubtless begin, nevertheless, at the beginning— with the word, the blueprint, with our theoretical principles. For socialism is precisely that historically unique society that is consciously built on the basis of a theoretical plan. And it is already clear that the defects in the structure are not just due to Stalin's departures from the original blueprint for socialism (it would be more correct to speak of his distortions of Marxism's values and understanding of the goals and sense of social transformations) but that they also represent departures of theoretical thinking from life, its inability to fully anticipate the future.

For example, it is common practice today to criticize the deformed, barracks-style, egalitarian socialism built in the 1930s. But that criticism diligently sidesteps the structural reasons for our barracks-style approach. And it avoids the central question: Can a nonbarracks-type, democratic socialism be built on a noncommodity, nonmarket foundation? That question is central, and not only for those seeking to understand the past. Why is it that in all cases without exception and in all countries, including Khomeini's present-day Iran, efforts to combat the market and commodity-money relations have always led to authoritarianism, to encroachments on the rights and dignity of the individual, and to an all-powerful administration and bureaucratic apparatus? . . .

This lack of conceptual thinking is also characteristic of Stalin's forced collectivization. The authors of articles published on this topic in *Oktiabr* (with the exception of G. Shmelev and V. Bashmachnikov) inadvertently create the illusion that the entire question boils down to a dilemma over whether to use "cavalry" methods in creating collective farms. But as our own experience and that of the other socialist countries indicates, the real question is whether there is a need to strive, in all cases, for cooperative production in the agrarian sector. Is the peasant family truly an anachronism? Just how sound, scientifically, was the plan to organize agriculture on a national scale? Is nationalization of the land truly necessary in all cases?

Apart from collectivization, there are dozens of other "difficult" questions in the closed zone that our scholars and even our journalists would not touch: Are sound guarantees of individual freedoms and democracy possible when all members of society work for the proletarian state for wages and have no independent sources of existence? Was violence against the peasant avoidable, given the firm conviction that socialized and collective labor on the land is an economic necessity? Doesn't the idea of a revolutionary vanguard lead to new forms of social inequality? Are "pure," unmediated forms of combining personal and public interest always more effective than "impure," mediated ones? Does the experience of human development in the twentieth century give grounds for maintaining the former belief in the possibility of fully overcoming worldview pluralism and religious belief and of overcoming the diversity of socioeconomic structures? Is it generally worthwhile to strive to overcome all the traditional structures of this kind, including the ones that we call patriarchal?

Tsipko argued that Stalin's thinking and his idea of socialism were in fact quite typical for Marxists of his time and did not differ fundamentally from those of a Kautsky, a Trotsky, a Bukharin, or a Lukacs. Its economic essence was the commitment to collectivist, nonmarket production; its political essence the view that only the vanguard policy knows what the proletariat "should" think:

> Naturally, making a distinction between what people should think and what they actually do think, and between the "advanced" views of the working-class vanguard and the "backward" views of the peasant masses, does not automatically lead to abuses of some sort or to repressions. It all depends on the legal culture of the society and on the moral and spiritual development of the people who are capable of influencing the course of events. But the conviction that one knows the truth better than others can be used to justify violence, particularly in extreme political circumstances. By exalting theoretical consciousness and subconsciousness of the revolutionary vanguard, the Marxists of those times unwittingly exalted the power of the leaders and of those who spoke on behalf of the laws of history. In the context of an uncritical attitude toward everything that acts in the name of Marxism and of the laws of social development, there was a sharply increased danger of subjectivism and arbitrariness where there was a perceived discrepancy with the theoretical forecasts of the future, and a sharply increased danger of political tyranny.

The Nina Andreeva article, he argued, is no more than a restatement of traditional views:

> As of this date, hundreds of cultural figures and scientists have taken a public stand against Nina Andreeva's so-called letter—against that anti-perestroika manifesto. But note that while all of them criticize her political views, no one has anything serious to say about their philosophical sources or about the conception of class struggle and the class approach to which she appeals. She said nothing new, after all. She simply reminded us of the philosophical and political truths that have been hammered into people's heads for decades, including

the dogmatist's traditional way of contrasting the political and social virtues of the industrial working class and its nucleus with the social and political flaws of all other nonproletarian classes, and of the peasantry and intelligentsia in particular.

Refusing to argue these principles with the apologists of Stalinism is tantamount to surrendering without a fight. It is a path that leads to the very half-truth that is worse than any lie. If, like O. Latsis, for example, you agree that the collective farm system—in other words, the organization of farm work by means of work orders of the type, "go here, go there, do this, do that"—is basically in keeping with the peasants' interests, and that "the trouble was not with collectivization per se but with the perverse methods by which it was carried out," then you disqualify yourself from substantiating the need for the present changes in the agrarian sector: the need for the family contract, leasing, and for returning farm autonomy to the peasant. If collective farms in the form in which their creators conceived of them are truly in keeping with the peasants' interests, then why do we need the new, present-day agrarian revolution that was planned at the July 1988 Plenary Session of the CPSU Central Committee? The answer is simple: The collective farm system that was created in accordance with Stalinist blueprints had nothing to do with the Leninist system of civilized cooperatives.

It is impossible to create a state ruled by law while maintaining the old conviction that there are classes and people who cannot understand their true interests by themselves, with their own minds, and who have to be taken by the ear and dragged to happiness. And in general, nothing sensible can be created while clinging to the old conviction that humanity achieves happiness only by destroying the old. The idea of a state ruled by law is also a legacy of bourgeois culture. Freedom of conscience was also born of that system.

If we continue to insist that class morality is of a higher order than universal human morality, that the peasantry is unable to find its place in history, that it does not know how to work or what is best for itself, and if we continue to insist that we do not need the market, that trade and enterprise inevitably lead to individual degeneration and dehumanization, then there is no need to beat around the bush. All we have to do is agree with Nina Andreeva and return to the none-too-distant past.

Tsipko asserted that it is the uncritical worship of an invented ideal flagrantly at odds with the realities of life that is responsible for the destruction of the Soviet system:

> In researching the past quarter-century, the historians of the future will doubtless be amazed by the massive resistance to the manifest truth of life and by our ability to disregard what is most important

and has direct relevance to our fate. They will be amazed by the fact that several generations that professed a devotion to materialism, that put scientific knowledge above all else and were highly active in combating idealism, never, in all their lives, so much as made mental contact with their surroundings, on the assumption that the important thing is not what exists and what they see, but what is hidden from the eye, what is assumed. I doubt that even the most fantastic mystics ever took such leave of the rudiments of concrete economic thinking as we have done—we, who consider ourselves to be materialists. . . .

We all know, for example, what a price our country and people paid for L.I. Brezhnev's and M.A. Suslov's "Communist orientation." It resulted in a shutting down of the 1965 economic reform and in the frustration of all attempts to put our economy on a rational basis; it put brakes on the Shchekino method and the brigade contract. It brought the country's economy to a state of crisis, put us far behind the developed countries in the area of scientific and technical progress, led to the exhaustion of the soil, and cost us many of our remaining hopes.

We also know the price to be paid for ignoring realities in order to worship an invented ideal. Isn't it abundantly clear, for example, that the notion of the mid-nineteenth century concerning a society of abundance where all limitations on consumption are removed is the purest of utopias given the approaching environmental, energy, and food crises?

Why are we afraid to tell the demagogues of the Communist ideal that they have done enough hoodwinking and kept enough people from thinking and working?! They cannot go on forever blackmailing the party and the people—after all, that is a crime too. Why are we afraid to tell these people that they are simply parasitizing on the society's political illiteracy and on what remains of the fear that has lodged in people's hearts since Stalin's times, and that the ideal that they are trying to impose on society is basically not an ideal?

The ideal of humanism, including the real humanism of Marx and Engels, was and is the dignity of the free human being, the autonomy— and above all the spiritual autonomy—of the individual, the right to one's own opinion, the right to err, to freely choose one's occupation and place of residence, to associate as one chooses, and to enjoy the culture of the past and the present; i.e., the right to everything that we are regaining in the context of perestroika.

We need to learn to distinguish between revolutionary doctrine as a necessary and justified form of resistance to violence, cruelty, and exploitation and ostentatious revolutionary doctrine that derives from human ambition, a passion for the new, or simply a desire to settle scores with a reality that has meant humiliation.

Excessive revolutionary fervor and leftist dogmatism that make revolution a goal in and of itself actually increase violence and injustice.

The policy of national self-destruction that resulted from Stalin's extreme leftist experiments, and the Pol Pot debacle that was born of students' radical leftist sentiments, led to nothing but destruction of the very bases of life. There was no constructive aspect to Stalin's domestic social policy.

In the debate that is raging today over possible alternative paths of development from the fateful year of 1929, many argue that there is no proving that any choice other than Stalin's was possible. But it is equally difficult to prove that Stalin's strategy of stripping the coun- tryside, of industrialization at the expense of the peasant's belly, had any scientific or socioeconomic basis. One has only to read his major speeches setting forth that strategy to convince oneself that Stalin's general policy was not backed by calculations of any sort or by a serious study of the possibilities offered by the existing forms of labor organization. All the arguments in favor of the new policy were strictly normative in nature. None was based on facts. Meanwhile, as we know, there were many serious warnings, such as those in the works of A.V. Chaianov. . . .

Even the father of the idea of industrializing the country at the peasants' expense, Ye.A. Preobrazhensky—reputed to have been a more learned Marxist and a more capable and honest researcher than Stalin—gives no indication of having felt a need to substantiate his leftist programs in any way. Had Preobrazhensky (not to mention Stalin) the slightest compassion for those peasants who were being condemned to lives of poverty, he and his ilk would have thought long and hard before enacting their laws. But human beings and human happiness are of no concern to leftist doctrinaires: Those "theoreticians" feel no responsibility to people.

I believe it is no accident that Nina Andreeva's anti-perestroika manifesto and her subsequent interview in the Yugoslav magazine *Vestnik* show no trace of materialism, not the merest suggestion of an effort to analyze our economic experience or shed light on the real economic and social situation in the society. She presents herself as a defender of the working people's interests, but she somehow manages to overlook the concerns of millions of Soviet people today, the things that cloud their daily lives and impede their happiness. She is absolutely unconcerned over the fact that "general lack of fitness," indifference toward work, and laziness have become a national tragedy, that our manufactured goods have gotten worse and worse, and that the USSR's prestige as a producer has fallen lower and lower.

One can show that such thinking is a relapse into the leveling type of utopian socialism that, by its very nature, is entirely obsessed with the problem of redistributing other people's wealth and has no idea of how to go about organizing production. This type of socialism, which is fighting perestroika, has absolutely no positive program to offer. And those pretending to defend the interests of the working class and society are misleading people and distracting attention from the main danger—the threat of the destruction of the very bases of production. It is a small step from this type of cynicism to an attempt to justify Stalin's crimes in terms of the laws of class struggle.

Profoundly egocentric and brutal people who are unfeeling toward others' fates have often garbed themselves as defenders of communism. But egocentricity has never been more terrible in defense of collectivist and socialist principles. Think of the social and philosophical meaning of Stalinism in action: Has history known another case in which humanist slogans have been invoked in sacrificing so many human lives to one criminal individual's ambition and thirst for power? Surely not.

These passages convey the scope of the process of historical rethinking that has begun in the Soviet Union. Yes, only "begun"—and for that reason the final word has not been spoken. However, we would like to think there will no longer even be a "final" word, because a pluralism of opinions, a diversity of points of view, is gradually beginning to be accepted in our country as "normal."

Of course, the excerpts from published materials that we have presented here represent only a small fraction of the enormous stream of information and opinions that we encounter today. It is difficult to speak of all the "gaps" in history that we are uncovering, all the forgotten names for which we are seeking justice, all the philosophical issues that are now being raised.

But perhaps the main point is that the heightened interest we have today in our own past is graphic evidence that our historical self-knowledge is developing, that we have taken upon ourselves the burden of our own past with all its pain and grandeur. Perestroika and glasnost are inconceivable without that.

THREE

The Church and Religion in Soviet Society

"Opiate of the People"
or Source of Morality and Culture?

The development of relations between the Soviet government and religious communities has been far from simple and at times tragic. In the first years after the revolution, the Russian Orthodox church, like other religious groups, was counted among the forces of counterrevolution, and repressive political measures were taken against the church and the clergy. Religion was treated, in Marx's words, as "the opiate of the people," and it was proclaimed that it had no place in a new socialist society. Believers themselves, millions of them, became the objects of massive brainwashing intended to inculcate atheism. Only in the mid-1920s did church-state relations begin slowly to change, and given the conditions of Stalinist politics, they could follow only a complex and painful course. Moreover, the Orthodox church itself was in the throes of factional struggle.

Somewhat new and different relations between church and state began to emerge during World War II, when the religious leadership played an active role in the struggle against fascism. The Council for Orthodox Church Affairs was created under the Council of Ministers to regulate church-state relations. Churches, monasteries. and seminaries were reopened. But the ensuing status quo was disturbed again in the early 1960s: In the atmosphere surrounding Khrushchev's hyperbolic promises of communism's speedy attainment and the withering away of religion, nearly half of the churches were closed.

The attitude toward church and religion from the late 1960s might be best characterized as "ostrich politics." No more old churches were closed, but no new ones opened. The church published copies of the

Gospels and the Bible in huge numbers, but they never enjoyed free distribution. The fact that religious organizations were contributing to the struggle for peace was acknowledged, as was their material support for restoration of Russian architectural monuments. But at the same time—and particularly in the provinces—administrative excesses directed against the church were far from rare, and the mass media carried periodic reminders of the need for atheistic education.

Literature was one area, though not the only one, in which the reconsideration of old assumptions—that religion is the "opiate of the people," that it is an irrational belief system that contradicts a "scientific world view," and that it is the product of spiritual impoverishment— took place. From time to time individual prose works treating the problem of religion and the church in an unusual and novel way survived the censor's maul; these gave the first stimulus to today's burgeoning discussions of religion and the church's role in society.

The year 1986 saw the publication of major new works by such diverse writers as Viktor Astaf'ev, Vasilii Bykov, and Chingiz Aitmatov that raised fundamental moral issues. What is important is that public opinion took them as reinterpreting some of the traditional features of oversimplified and negative attitudes toward religion. The musings of Victor Astaf'ev's lyric hero in *The Blind Fisherman* is an outcry against the destruction of moral values and religious belief:

> What has happened to us? Who has cast us into the abyss of evil and misfortune, and why? Who has put out the light of good in our souls? Who has blown out the icon-lamp of our consciousness, has knocked it down into a dark, impenetrable pit? There we grope our way, searching for a bottom and some guiding light from the future. What need do we have of that light that leads into the flames of hell?
>
> We lived with light in our souls; we did not stray in the darkness, did not run afoul of trees in the taiga or of one another in the world; neither did we scratch out one another's eyes, nor break the bones of anyone near to us. Why have they made off with all this and given nothing in return, spawning only unbelief—universal, ubiquitous unbelief? Who is there to pray to? Of whom do we ask forgiveness? For we surely once knew and have not yet forgotten how to forgive, to forgive even our enemies. (*Nash Sovremennik*, 1986, no. 5)

A new work by the widely read Kirghiz novelist Chingiz Aitmatov, entitled *Plakha* (The Executioner's Block), also stimulated enormous public controversy. One of the novel's main protagonists is Avdii Kallistratov, a young man of deep religious faith who has been expelled from a seminary for freethinking and socialist tendencies. Avdii falls in with a group of drug dealers and tries to mend these sinners' ways with a sermon, to which they respond by throwing Avdii off the train. Later he dies at the hands of a band of outcasts hired as deer poachers. Dying, Avdii calls on them to renounce their extermination of these rare creatures. The leader of the gang, clearly Stalinist in his convictions, addresses his victim with these harsh words(*Novyi Mir,* 1986, no. 8):

> So, you bastard, you reckoned God would give us a fright, you thought he'd put the wind up us, you wanted to shove God down our throats, you little vermin! You won't scare us with God—it's stronger types than that you're dealing with, you dog! Sure, I'll strangle you, you degenerate, as an enemy of the people, and people will thank me for it, seeing as how you're an agent of imperialism, you rat! You reckon that since there's no Stalin, justice will not be done to you? Get down on your knees, priest's spawn! I am your authority now—renounce your God or it's all over for you, you bastard!

Aitmatov's novel elicited harsh criticism from the defenders of political orthodoxy, and in particular from one of the nation's senior atheists, Dr. N. Kryvelev (*Komsomolskaia Pravda*, 30 July 1986):

> To reject principled, logical atheism is to reject the very foundations of a scientific and materialist worldview. And to farm out morality to religion—is this not some type of playing around with the good old Lord?
>
> It is more than strange to read such things in the Soviet press. Not only because this tendency to flirt with the good old Lord is so clearly expressed, but also because we have before us glaring examples of people forgetting all the well-known facts of history and the present, including such facts as have been clarified and given theoretical interpretation by Marxism and which, given their self-evidence, have long been beyond contention. . . . The best and loftiest minds in the history of humanity have selflessly fought against spiritual moonshine. A noble and heroic tradition of freethinking and atheism has ensued.
>
> We, Communists, have embraced this tradition and extended it. Our atheism is founded on a scientific worldview and is as unshakable as this worldview.

This article had broad repercussions. Such harsh expressions of opinion became unusual in the central press, not least of all because the author was specifically attacking the nation's foremost writers.

On 10 December 1987 *Komsomolskaia Pravda* published a letter to the editor from our famous poet Yevgeny Yevtushenko unusual for its outspoken defense of religion. Yevtushenko wrote:

The current fashion of wearing crosses outside of shirts or blouses has to do with a basic misunderstanding of what the crucifixion is and is in no way an indicator of religious fanaticism. What is more important: ignorance of religion or religious fanaticism? For it may be that these two phenomena are closely connected, and that we are simply not trying to understand them. . . .

Culture is the source of morality. But one cannot exclude religion from history's experience of morality, whether positive or negative; for the history of religion is inseparable from history as such. We must not deridingly interpret any treatment of religion that does not represent straightforward condemnation as "flirting with the good old Lord." Lenin's formulation is scathingly precise but was made at a particular time to a particular group; and to transfer it to the present, readdressing it to our leading writers, is out of place. It was precisely thus, unfortunately, that Dr. Kryvelev acted in his article "Flirting with the Good Old Lord." Kryvelev accused Aitmatov of "farming morality out to religion." At the same time, he accuses Bykov and Astaf'ev of the same thing. Kryvelev makes the elementary mistake of identifying Aitmatov's hero with the author.

Then Yevtushenko made an important argument, pointing out that the Soviet constitution speaks clearly and unambiguously about freedom of religion and separation of church from state. But nowhere is it written in Soviet law that atheism is inseparable from the state. Atheism should be a matter of choice, and not of forced adherence. Atheism ought to be one of society's rights, like religion.

Kryvelev accuses Christian teachings of being "consolidated, like something unshakable, essential for all times." It would appear that the author was against dogmatism. But a few paragraphs later he defends atheism with the most hackneyed of dogmatic rhetoric: "Our atheism is founded on a scientific worldview, and is as unshakable as this worldview." . . .

Kryvelev is correct when he finds a multitude of contradictions in the Bible, though in this respect he is hardly a Columbus. This book was written and rewritten by many people at different times. But the Bible itself is hardly guilty of Kryvelev's accusation that "in the contemporary Israeli soldier, Biblical teachings provide important material for the ideological reasoning behind the extermination of the Arabs." The Bible is a great cultural monument. I still cannot understand why the state press has published the Koran but not the Bible. Without some knowledge of the Bible our youth will miss much in Pushkin, Gogol', Dostoevskii, Tolstoi. All of early [Vladimir] Maiakovskii is drenched in biblical metaphors. Bibles command huge prices at second-hand book dealers and on the "black market." Kryvelev wants everyone to become atheists; but how can they if they do not know the Bible? Sweet, as they say, is the forbidden fruit. . . .

The religion that served social oppression was rightly labeled the opiate of the people. But can we forget how, during the war against fascism, our Church contributed massively to the collective victory? Can we forget how the Archbishop of Canterbury Hewlitt Johnson was one of the founders of the movement for peace? Can we forget how the priest Ernesto Cardinale became one of Latin America's leading poets in the struggle against imperialism?

Atheism in and of itself is not the source of morality. Culture is that source. The culture of human behavior. The culture of conscience that has no need of scientific diplomas.

A rebuttal by Suzen Kaltakhchian, a leading exponent of scientific atheism, was published alongside Yevtushenko's letter. Very much in the style of the earlier article by Kryvelev, it said:

Y. Yevtushenko's commentary forces us to seriously consider that lack of ideological clarity that, unfortunately, is not a rarity in our literature. . . . An attempt is sometimes made to justify dealing with religion by pointing out that religion is a part of culture and that culture is the source of morality. These claims are only true given one indispensable condition: that the concepts "culture" and "morality" and the place of religion in them be elucidated scientifically.

Kaltakhchian concluded:

Attempts to link religion with mythology are groundless, as are efforts to use this as a basis for seeing religion as a constituent part of true culture.

Religion developed by living as a parasite off of art—like a barren flower on the tree of living knowledge—and in a class society took the shape of a reactionary worldview. Religion did not enrich culture but took everything from it that could be turned to its own uses. From the very start religion made use of the artistic or figurative way of seeing the world from the viewpoint of primordial man. This selfsame myth could serve as the basis for art, for the aesthetic development of consciousness, and for the perversions of religious thinking. It is no secret that the church to this day exploits the imagery of art.

What has been said shows sufficiently clearly that the morality and arts that have been bound fast to religion over the centuries ("religious morality," "religious art") have, strictly speaking, nothing in common with the essence of religion. Their essence and content have been determined by the concrete, historical forms of socioeconomic life and the class struggle.

Kaltakhchian further said that one cannot credit the unsubstantiated claim that religion has enriched humanity with its moral principles. It has long been proven, he claimed, that it was not humanity that borrowed morality from religion, but rather the reverse, that religion borrowed and used for its own ends various parts of universal human morality. And he reminded us that the party points toward improving atheistic education (particularly among the young) and seeks new approaches, methods, and forms of atheistic propaganda. According to Kaltakhchian, efforts to restrain movements in this direction are shocking:

> The party has pointed more than once to instances of ideological shortcomings or unscrupulous worldviews in artistic and scientific works. It has been remarked in this respect that lack of discrimination in one's view of the world hinders ideological and educational work and can adversely affect even gifted people's work. Lastly, we cannot overlook the fact that our literature and art—which have made an invaluable contribution to the atheistic education of the workers— distracted from the problems of atheism. What is worse, we can trace in certain works of literature, film, and painting an admiration for church ceremoniousness, a taste for "charm," for saints' lives, for elders, church life, and religious morals.
>
> Our younger generation has a right to hope that the purveyors of culture will make a worthy contribution to the achievement of atheistic education, to the spread of new Soviet ceremonies and customs, and to the consolidation of Communist morality, which is alien to the hypocrisy and sanctimoniousness inseparable from religious morality.

A pause followed the publication of these articles in the central press, but by mid-1987 the controversy had flared up again. The first commentary on *Komsomolskaia Pravda*'s debate was Andrei Nuikin's article "The New God-Seeking and Old Dogmas" in *Novyi Mir* (1987, no. 4):

> It would not yet be correct to speak in our society of an even relative unanimity on questions concerning religion. There are certainly more than two opposing camps—and believers and atheists are not the only irreconcilable representatives of these far from monolithic frames of mind. As we learn to live under democratic conditions, we need to learn how to debate issues of religion. How to think. All of us. Without entrusting this gratifying and vitally important task to the specially initiated devotees of religion or atheism. Despite divergent understandings of it, the question of worldview is practically one of the most significant matters at hand, for upon its resolution depend not only individual action, not only our personal failures and successes, but the success of life as a whole. . . .

Do I share the opinions on religion that here and there creep into the books (or their heroes' words) and articles under review here? In essence, no. But still less do I share the position of Kryvelev, who rests assured of the invulnerability of his state atheist's formulation, broken in over the decades, but who is incapable of differentiating pseudo-intellectual shamans from those for whom God is a part of the people's consciousness or a despairing attempt somehow to argue for the necessity of good, conscience, love, compassion. . . .

As we discuss the interrelation of religion, mysticism, and art in our society, we ought to be aware of prospects. The forecast predicts that today's apparently comfortable situation will not last long. The spread of glasnost, honesty in the press, and democracy in general may prompt a wave of quite unexpected revelations of religiosity and mysticism in our culture, although in not as dominant a form as we have it in the works of V. Bykov, V. Astaf'ev, and Ch. Aitmatov.

There is no need to fear this wave, but one ought to be prepared for it. . . .

Why have I paid such special attention to a single episode in our social life, the publication of Kryvelev's and Kaltakhchian's articles? Because these articles are (one hopes) among the last bellows of the dogmatic atheism that enjoyed (while democracy and glasnost remained underdeveloped) a monopoly in ultimate truths and in the answer to questions of vital general interest that, if we are to be honest, were completely overlooked by the monopolists' answers.

Member of the Academy of Sciences Dmitrii Likhachev, today a leading proponent of cultural freedoms and the preservation of the cultural heritage of the nation, denounced even more rigorously survivals of this undifferentiated, hostile attitude toward church and religion in *Literaturnaia Gazeta* (9 September 1987):

Morality lies in human nature. Its sources are stable and eternal. Indeed what can we set in opposition to the commandment: "Thou shalt not kill"? "Kill?" And what about the commandments "Thou shalt not steal," or "Bear not false witness"?

This is one side of the coin, but there is a second side. I receive numerous letters telling of atheistic propaganda: that it often inculcates in our citizenry a hostile attitude toward believers and the church. Faith is considered a sign of ignorance, although one might note that it is more likely hostility toward believers that springs from ignorance, whether of church history or of history in general. In the mail I received in response to my article in *Literaturnaia Gazeta* was a letter disdainful in tone and free and easy in its treatment of believers and priests. This is not only the fruit of ignorance, but also of the absence of another culture—the culture of democracy. . . .

And apart from that, we know the church's role in Russia's history: In the time of feudalism's disintegration, for example, the church stood for unity and against civil strife, and it inspired the fight against foreign invaders. We speak of Dmitrii Donskoi's victory at the Battle of Kulikovo but stay silent on the subject of Sergei Radonezh, the inspiration for that victory, who (in the church's words) "proclaimed to the Grand Prince Dmitrii victory over the multitude of proud Hagarites, who had wanted to raze Russia with fire and the sword." And who spoke out against the cruelties of Ivan the Terrible's hard reign? Metropolitan Filipp, who fearlessly denounced the cruel tyrant.

Turning to the contemporary church, particularly today, on the eve of the thousandth anniversary of Russia's conversion, we need to underline that we are for full and effective separation of church and state. Our state should be outside religion and ought not to involve itself in church affairs. And the church, of course, ought not involve itself in the affairs of state. This is exactly what the Council for Religious Affairs' mission is. But, unfortunately, in the not-so-distant past the council was actively interfering in church affairs. And do we have to limit the church's right to publish in the necessary numbers those books needed by the faithful—the Bible, the church calendar, the writings of the holy fathers, and other works?

The clergy also contributed to the debate on the place of religion and the church. On 20 September 1987 *Moskovskie Novosti* published an unusual interview with the Metropolitan of Leningrad and Novgorod, Aleksei:

Q: What, in your opinion, defines today's relations between the Russian Orthodox church and the state?

A: I would say straight off that, in my opinion, there are no insoluble problems in our relations. There are no irreconcilable contradictions. But there are questions awaiting answers. And it seems to me that a clear and unambiguous answer could have great significance not only for the church, but for all of our society.

Let us first consider this. . . . The entire conscious lives of even the oldest members of the church have been spent under Soviet power. They have been educated under Soviet authority and are in every sense Soviet people, citizens of the USSR. An enormous number of believers are veterans of labor, of the Great Patriotic War, and the overwhelming majority are conscientious and honest toilers. So much the sadder, then, when at various times, in different places—and in obvious contradiction of the foundations of our common socialist government—believers are treated as "second-rate" people to be approached with suspicion and extreme care. Our present laws on cults are frequently broken by local organizations, and not to the benefit of believers. And the more this happens the easier it is for

Western propaganda to "latch on" to them and utilize them for its own ends. For this reason I consider it imperative to follow precisely the letter of our laws on cults.

But we ought to note that the Decree on Religious Associations that regulates church-state relations dates from 1929 and underwent only insignificant changes in 1975. It was adopted when the course of the revolution and ensuing events were still fresh in people's memories: a time, that is, when believers and church representatives were far from consistent in adopting the proper attitude. This was reflected in the laws promulgated. The real course of church-state relations has outgrown this framework, a point that is brought up in publications on this subject.

Q: What is your attitude toward perestroika?

A: I heartily support it. It gives me great satisfaction to see that a time of fundamental change has come in our society. It is the moral duty of every Soviet citizen to devote all his strength and creative energies to aiding perestroika.

Of course it is more complicated to restructure than it was to build the original structure. But I think the main goal has been achieved: We are rejecting the policies of selfishness and are sensitive to future generations and how we leave them the planet, and we have realized that economics is inseparable from morality.

The dialogue in our society between believers and atheists, now seventy years old, takes on particular significance in this light. This dialogue has not always gone smoothly. Today both sides are vitally interested in practical cooperation and in discussing those problems now facing our society in a quite new way. In a society that was the first to build socialism, this dialogue between atheists and believers is exceptionally important—not only for our country, but for the whole of humanity.

The dialogue prompts polemics and criticism. I would like to emphasize—without condemning in any way the atheist argument as such—that we call for conscientiousness in these polemics. When the atheists write books and articles hostile to believers and give insufficient documentation for their claims they do not contribute to a healthy atmosphere for dialogue.

For this reason I think that we ought to welcome any objective information on church and religion (I repeat, not apologetic, but objective information), which, we should acknowledge, is appearing in our press more than in years past. This information fulfills an important function: It eliminates nonbelievers' preconceived notions about the faithful and shows that believers and atheists alike stand as citizens at the same barricade. It thus consolidates our socialist society.

In the first years after the founding of our state many citizens saw the church as the exploiting class's spiritual support. But today both religious and nonreligious members of our society work hand in hand for the well-being of our Motherland, for the preservation of peace on earth, and to help solve the problems of perestroika and democratization addressed by our leaders. If one understands how the church exists in the reality of socialist conditions one can see that the Christian point of view does not lead man to abandon this world, but rather blesses his work for the good of all society. . . .

I believe that the church has something to say to contemporary man. The Christian tradition is centered on the human individual in all his uniqueness and moral responsibility. The church can counter the expansion of popular culture with the richness of its centuries-old spiritual inheritance as well as with its call to help one's beloved by giving of oneself. And it can oppose the cult of violence, cruelty, and war with the gospel of universal love and peace throughout the world.

Following the lead of *Moskovskie Novosti*, *Sotsiologicheskie Issledovaniia* opened its pages to the proponents of religion with the publication of extracts from W. Fletcher's book *Soviet Believers*, which first appeared in the United States in 1981. It also printed articles by a teacher in the Leningrad Seminary, Fr. Innokentii, and by a professor at the Institute of Scientific Atheism, V.I. Sherdakov. Fr. Innokentii's article contained a series of honest assessments of the church's situation in the USSR:

The fact that there is only one small church available in Sverdlovsk, or only two in Kaluga, deprives young believers of their anonymity. If the administration of local schools and institutions (given the momentum of past work on atheism) is harsh, then any student who believes or participates in services will try to hide his institutional religious activity from that administration. I know, for instance, of young people in Kaluga who will not attend the two local churches but instead travel to the country for services. In our country's educational system there is no discrimination against believers that is sanctioned by law. But still there is discrimination: The religious inclinations of a schoolchild or university student can at times be the source of unpleasantness in dealings with the administration. . . .

It happens that when church leaders prepare their reports, they anticipate the inclinations of the Soviet offices for which the reports are to be written: They intentionally understate the demand they satisfy in church. These "inverse entries" distort the statistics then used by Soviet religious researchers as well as Sovietologists. In any case, while crowning ceremonies are still not performed often in Moscow and Leningrad churches, they have nonetheless become more frequent than ten or fifteen years ago. This has to do with the growing number of young believers. . . . The church's situation grew significantly worse in the early 1960s: As a result of the voluntarism then characteristic of ideological work, the Orthodox church lost up to half its churches. The eastern Ukraine and Byelorussia suffered most in this respect.

V.I. Sherdakov's response was favorably disposed toward Fr. Innokentii's article and harshly criticized N. Kryvelev. He ended his article thus:

> Our goal cannot be to overcome religion by force, and still less to "liquidate" it, as the West often describes it. Communists have examined and reexamined the problem of religion in the context of the central task, social development. We cannot agree with the Enlightenment, rationalist point of view or, say, with that of the twentieth-century English philosopher Bertrand Russell, both of whom see religion as the main enemy of the social and moral process. Marxists look to more deeply embedded impediments to humanity's forward march. (*Sotsiologicheskie Issledovaniia,* 1987, no. 4)

Finally, a quite unusual occurrence—that stretched still further the limits of glasnost and the discussion of religion in the USSR—was the publication in a newspaper for Moscow youth of an article about a correspondent's meeting with some young nuns from the recently reopened Convent of the Intercession in Khot'kovo (outside Moscow).

> How often, when life's fuss and bustle has worn us out, we say with a touch of irony: "I have had it, I am joining a monastery." A popular idiom with pretensions to humor. But this is really the meaning of life for people who know that they will have to renounce much in life forever. They have made their decision, and now all their words and actions serve their chosen goal.
>
> I met with many young women and spent considerable time in discussion and argument with them, proving what seemed to be obvious. But it was as if my words ran up against a wall of incomprehension. To begin with, all their arguments seemed awkward, and it was tempting to negate them all at one fell swoop, resting my case on only a single premise: that the monastic life is unnatural. . . . How often, even as we proclaim the right of an individual to free choice, we are irritated to see someone contradict our expectations. We then try to explain it away as the product of shortcomings in upbringing or of an unfortunate life. The primitive habit of seeing one's own correctness as axiomatic, beyond any need for proof, can often unintentionally lead to arrogance and a desire to preach. I believe that our attitude toward democracy is defined by our attitude toward religious people. . . .
>
> Tania S. works in a maternity clinic in a youth collective. Suddenly she comments on her peers:

"Have you listened to their conversations! Everything revolves around clothes and parties. They cannot decide how to save up the money for a 400 ruble fur hat. Total spiritual impoverishment. They do not know how to work and do not want to. Utterly indifferent to our expectant mothers."

When I heard Tania's opinion that divorce and abortions are evil and the work of the devil, I was ready to go to the other extreme, but stopped short. To some extent she was right: The number of divorces and abortions can only give you pause.

Ira N. was recently christened and studied at the Moscow Institute of Architecture. She comes from a family of scientists. In school she was one of the first of her classmates to join the Komsomol.

"I deliberately underwent the rites of christening. Why? In Russia all the churches, every stone in them, were consecrated. The idea of serving God was precisely what gave rise to the Orthodox churches, and it preserved our culture. I am involved in restoration work: And if I remain unchristened, I do not have the moral right to work with Russia's spiritual inheritance. With every passing day we lose more of our Russian, Orthodox culture. Why are we so dissolute, why have so many forgotten their history, their roots? Why are drug addiction and alcoholism so widespread? Just try to say with some pride that you are Russian, and they will immediately castigate your nationalism."

Irina Z. used to play sports, studied the hard sciences and was interested in photography and painting. She graduated from a high school specializing in physics and mathematics. She dreamed about the heavens, and so she enrolled in the Moscow Institute for Astrophysics. She "hung out" with hippies, wore faded and patched American jeans. She played volleyball and was a good sportswoman. Then she transferred to the journalism department at Moscow State University. She became interested in painting and avant-garde art. She tried to follow the lead of Malevich's Suprematism.

Next she immersed herself in Russian philosophy. She defended a thesis on the works of F.M. Dostoevskii in the Russian literature department . . . and went to a convent. She did not go as a sightseer, but went specifically to live near the convent, to cleanse her spirit. Irina was soon christened and began her trips to various other convents.

"My soul was frustrated. For some reason I decided to show an elder my work 'A Tree in Its Cosmic State.' The old man spent a long time turning it this way and that, and then . . . advised me to burn it. It and all my other works. I went home tortured by this thought. Would it really be necessary to throw out everything? I collected everything into a pile and took it off to the rubbish heap. And I felt a great sense of freedom. . . ."

Irina is an uncommon person. She is driven by a thirst for knowledge. The only thing she regrets is that women are not admitted to seminaries. Her favorite pastime is delving into intricate questions of church dogma. Irina has a very strong will but her friends are a match for her. This is a fact worthy of attention, since it contradicts portrayals of believers as weak people. There are strong types among them, but they are people who have either lost or could not find ideals and values outside Christianity. The path that leads to the monastery or convent is far from the easiest to follow. Fortitude is needed to surmount the temptations confronted. From a faulty premise (that only weak people join the church) an opinion has formed: that with the strengthening of democracy, with the possibility of acting upon one's social convictions, the number of believers will sharply and steadily decrease. This is a delusion. A case in point are these "tyrants" of the future Convent of the Intercession in Khot'kovo, who could be led to the life of a nun by being consistent and acting upon their view of the world. (*Moskovskii Komsomolets*, 23 October 1987)

How did the representatives of orthodox, scientific atheism react to this? They are people whose life work is to maintain their original ideological virginity and who crudely criticize religion. The journalist E. Losoto, a well-known hardliner, expressed her opinion in her article "Heavenly Polemics":

As far as our personal lives are concerned, it is easy to see that the "new thinking" does not represent a rejection of materialism; that the restructuring [perestroika] of ideological work does not represent a rejection of our ideology; and that our thinking ought to develop further, but in the same direction—that is, based on Leninism. It is underhanded to take the term "new thinking" as meaning the possibility of basing an ideology on idealism—particularly when "new thinking" is cast as God-seeking. Regardless of whether it is labeled "new thinking" or consistent with new thinking, this seems to me a movement in reverse, like walking backwards. . . .

The religious (that is, the most conservative) consciousness has never found the real means to resolve urgent contradictions and has never been able to stand up against real evil. Whenever evil crops up, so does religiosity, as a protest against it in evil's own territory, as evil's other face. The attitudes of private ownership appear, and so does injustice, but powerless protest is the response, with some finding refuge in the bottle while others run away to religion. Rotgut religion acts like rotgut liquor: It obscures people's thoughts; it stifles them and weakens them.

Theft, corruption, and other crimes require a severe, party-minded response, nationwide evaluation and control by workers and peasants, and not the commandments given by God to Moses. . . .

Could there be a better symbol of submission and the inability to act than the crucifixion?

Yes, this is the opiate of the people. So it was, is, and for a while shall be. We need to be reminded of this as now the struggle for Marxism and its foundations is once again being fought. Attempts to divorce atheism from Marxism and to abandon it as a hindrance to "spirituality" are among the effects of this struggle. Another result is the attempt to substitute various types of religious morality, under the banner of "humanism," for atheism. . . .

It is murky waters that bear toward us saccharine religion in the name of "spirituality," or émigrés who hate socialism in the name of "our cultural inheritance," or drug addicts and homosexuals in the name of "truth" and "openness" [glasnost]. Murky waters that are becoming a flood, that may wash from our social consciousness—and particularly from that of our youth—what is truly valuable: our revolutionary traditions and Marxist theory. . . .

Some people tell me that soon not even the word for atheism will be left, that it will somehow be renamed. But it has not yet been renamed; it somehow manages to live on, no longer militant—God forbid!—but shy and diffident.

In fear I don my atheist's veil, no longer to walk with the "unspiritual" and the "leftovers." Well, well! Finally my appearance is more modern. Now my business is liberal discussion of "universal morality," timeless, classless, beyond the opposition of two systems, beyond rich and poor, worker and parasite.

And if I were to take off my atheist's veil? Well! Sure . . . the fit is not quite right, the cut's wrong, it's not today's look. But it really is important to take off this rubbish. (*Komsomolskaia Pravda*, 21 October 1987)

Losoto made it very clear that in her opinion atheism now needs not diffidence, but the strength to attack. It should not be on the defensive while religious morality is all the rage and declares itself "eternally valuable" and a panacea against evil. It forces her, in her own words, into a struggle for the authority of scientific truth.

But today all this is received differently, in a new way. Such an eruption of abuse, of complaints about the toleration of church and religion representing a threat to "democratic traditions"—and with homosexuality and drug addiction portrayed as the result of pernicious Western influence—all this is more likely to be taken in a comic vein by today's audience. The hysterical tone of this article reveals how little support the author finds in public opinion and how much moods have changed.

How Should the Principle of "Freedom of Conscience" Be Established?

The changes in attitudes toward religion, believers, and the church that are taking place in the context of perestroika and glasnost are now being widely discussed in our press. But there is an additional, but no less important, question that has also attracted society's attention: the civil rights of believers.

Previously, there was virtually never any discussion in the mass media of refusals to grant believers permission to form new communities (or, consequently, to open new churches) or of various other restraints and prohibitions. One of the sharpest publications on this subject, B. Soloukhin's short piece "Stepanida Ivanovna's Funeral," was first published in *Novyi Mir* in September 1987 (no. 9) but was actually written in 1967. In this work the author described all the difficulties and impediments that he came up against when he was arranging an Orthodox funeral service for his mother:

> If all this had happened in some war-ravaged land where the occupation forces kept the local population under such tight control and such a heavy yoke that they even forbade burials according to native customs without the express permission of those occupying forces, then it might be possible to understand this. But I do not know if such occupation forces exist on this earth, or if there exists a people that could submit to such control.

The rights of the believers were further discussed in S. Vlasov's article "If We Were to Pass Judgment as Humans . . ." (*Ogonyok*, 1987, no. 13). This article, devoted to the activities of the authorities in the Krasnodar area who systematically set about blocking the repair and construction of churches, elicited a wide response. Particular attention was paid to events in the village of Krasnoarmeiskaia.

> "I ask that my name not be printed in your article." Such was the request that the executive of the Krasnodar party regional committee made at the beginning of our conversation, and he repeated it twice after that. I thought that the man most likely hoped that later, when the conflict had died down, his name would not be associated with the regional committee's decisions. And it should be said that these decisions were rather harsh and provoked the overt displeasure of several groups of Soviet citizens. Collective letters were sent to various departments requesting "protection from the arbitrariness of our local authorities."
>
> One such letter came to our editorial desk. Three hundred people had signed it. This is how it opened:
>
> "We, the congregation of the Orthodox Church of the Nativity and Holy Mother, ask your assistance in protecting our legal rights as guaranteed by the Constitution of the USSR and legislation concerning cults. Confiscation of our place of worship, now being built to replace our old and now-decrepit church, is being justified by our failure to

receive the authorities' written permission before starting construction—although our application had been given oral approval by both the chair of the regional committee and his deputy, with witnesses present!

The old church had not been repaired since 1950 and had fallen into serious decay. In addition its main hall of worship was extremely small, with low ceilings, so that sometimes during services there were fatalities from lack of oxygen."

On 1 August 1986, construction was halted, precisely one and a half years after it had started. The most important point is that for a year and a half, in full view of the whole village, on its main street, 300 meters from the building housing the regional and party committees, the walls of a new building had been rising: a beautiful building, it must be said, one built with love, with soul, with concern for each stone and plank. Even the secretary of the party regional committee, A.D. Kudinov, used to say to his colleagues: "That's how we ought to build, as quickly and well as those old men and women."

Ogonyok's article gives examples of the tireless efforts of the believers to build their church. It often happened that bricks or other materials were delivered late at night or very early in the morning. Nevertheless, the elderly people would come out to unload the trucks. Sometimes someone would clutch at his or her heart then sit for a while to one side before getting back to work. No vacations or sick leave there. But suddenly construction was cut short when the regional committee adopted its resolution to confiscate the unfinished building and provide the believers with another building—a poor, old building that stood in need of full reconstruction and that was much smaller than the old church.

"Never will we leave this place!" The congregation announced this more than resolutely, in a single voice, as they surrounded me in a tight circle in the church courtyard. "We'll fight for our church. Kopeck by kopeck we collected funds for construction, contributing from our tiny pensions, giving our all to make our church beautiful. Each of us has suffered enough personal tragedies: Why create one more to afflict us all?"

For two days, a Saturday and Sunday, I listened to the stories of these people with the wrinkled faces, with the grey, wispy hair, and it was as if history passed before me. These people are no fanatics. Many of them are older than the Soviet state and helped to build it, defended it on the front lines, lost sons, husbands, fathers in the war.
. . .

It was not a comfortable life that led them to religion. Trouble, losses, and misfortune lined their paths.

Ogonyok marshaled facts about other communities in the Krasnodar region and showed that what happened in Krasnoarmeiskaia was not the exception. Similar things have happened in the towns and villages of Tbilisskaia, Temriuk, Krymsk, and others. In a long conversation, the archbishop of Krasnodar and Kuban', Vladimir, told the correspondent:

> Not long ago I was in the village of Otradnaia. . . . The church floors are so rotten that a woman's high heel simply sinks right through them. The building is in total disrepair: To worship there is to risk one's life. It is the same in Temriuk, where the ceiling is propped up with wooden supports. Who needs all this? Destroying a church building has nothing to do with destroying religion. On the contrary, it simply means rekindling the hostility between believers and non-believers, encouraging an anti-Soviet atmosphere. A myopic, unintelligent policy. The great Lenin said that the unity of the struggle "for the creation of paradise on earth is more important to us than the unity of proletarian opinion on the nature of paradise in heaven." The unity of believers and nonbelievers is the fundamental principle of our society. There are enough problems in the world that require our collective attention without our wasting effort on internecine conflict.

But are the believers justified in all their complaints? In *Ogonyok's* opinion, the situation is more complex than the letter from the church builders in Krasnoarmeiskaia would have us believe. For example, more than once believers themselves tried to use the ambiguities of existing laws on church and religion to outwit the law. And in the end, *Ogonyok* told the story's conclusion:

> When this article was ready for publication, we received two letters from the Krasnodar region. The first follows:
>
> In addition to the material that *Ogonyok's* special correspondent S. Vlasov gathered on the construction of a new house of worship in Krasnoarmeiskaia village, we inform you that the case in question was discussed by the CPSU district committee.
>
> The first secretary of the Krasnoarmeiskaia CPSU regional committee, comrade A.D. Kudinov, has been given a severe reprimand, duly recorded on his registration card, for his unchecked behavior leading to conflict with the believers. The CPSU regional and executive committees have taken measures to punish local party workers guilty of allowing the illegal construction.
>
> A resolution was adopted legalizing the church's construction, which in turn has allowed corrections to be made of errors in that project. In particular, specialists have concluded that the roof is not sufficiently

strong to support cupolas. Upon its completion the building will be given to the believers for their own uses.

With the authorization of the Council for Religious Affairs of the Krasnodar district executive committee, measures have been taken with regard to the church council leaders who endorsed serious breaches of the Soviet laws on religious cults.

With the adoption of these measures the conflict has been resolved and the situation in the village of Krasnoarmeiskaia normalized.

> B. Kivirev,
> Secretary of the CPSU district committee

Thus did we discover that the executive organ of the religious association responsible for breaking the law had been completely reselected.

We note, however, that this reply deals only with the fate of the church in Krasnoarmeiskaia. No further information has emerged concerning Temriuk, Otradnaia, Tbilisskaia, or Krymsk.

Several articles appeared in late 1987 (particularly in *Literaturnaia Gazeta* and *Moskovskie Novosti*) telling of unfounded persecution of the clergy and believers and of the resultant problems. The article containing the sharpest and most consistent defense of believers' constitutional rights was A. Nezhnyi's "Opinion Against the Law" in *Moskovskie Novosti* (16 August 1987). Some excerpts from it follow:

> Iurii Karacharov, secretary of the CPSU committee for Kirov *oblast'*, gave a stubborn reply to the assertion made both by us and the former inspector of the Council for Religious Affairs of the Council of Ministers that there can be no basis in law for refusing the Orthodox believers of Kirov the right to register a second religious society: "Out of the question!" And when we kept pestering Iurii Grigor'evich with our inflexible references to the constitution and law, he exploded: "I know all about it! You're inciting the believers!" We left the office and Podshibiakin said with a sad smile, "A hackneyed tactic!"

Moskovskie Novosti tells us that in Kirov there were two Orthodox religious societies and two functioning churches (Fedorovskaia and Serafimovskaia) until 1962. In keeping with the official rhetoric and approach they then adopted—that the communism soon to be achieved should come without believers, or at least with a minimal number of them—Fedorovskaia was closed, its community disbanded, and the church building destroyed in order to be replaced by a monument honoring the city's 600th anniversary. For twenty-five years since then, believers have visited the only church left in town, Serafimovskaia. For almost as long, they have been trying to get back what was taken from them.

But if their earlier petitions seemed to bear the stamp of doom, and could be silenced with a single, abrupt "no" from the city's CPSU executive committee, then now everything has changed. On 15 February 1987, the regional, district and city committees received completed applications and membership lists for a new religious society. On July 15, a telegraph of complaint was sent to the General Procurator of the USSR—the forty-second appeal to Moscow by Kirov's believers, still certain of their rights.

Do the city and *oblast'* authorities find such obstinacy pleasing? Do they like, for example, the letter that was sent to *Moskovskie Novosti* with two thousand signatures? Or the appeal to the General Secretary of the CPSU Central Committee, to the Presidium of the Supreme Soviet's President, and to the Chairman of the Council for Religious Affairs of the Council of Ministers? Why hide the truth: they hated it! "You are blocking up the Soviet postal system," A. Shalaginov (the Kirov *oblast'* representative of the Council for Religious Affairs) reproached the believers. . . .

. . . Time is the mainspring of Kirov's history. Thanks mostly to the new face of our times, the believers of this ancient Russian city, honest toilers, have begun to feel themselves full-fledged citizens. This is the feeling that the local authorities find so unattractive.

According to the story in *Moskovskie Novosti*, there are more than 400,000 inhabitants in Kirov, but only one church. (For comparison, Moscow has forty-four functioning Orthodox churches; Kostroma has six for a population of around 300,000 people). And the heated dispute between the believers and the local authorities has not died down. The believers unanimously assert that their church is full to overflowing, particularly in winter and on holidays and weekends. It is far from rare for some believer to faint from the stuffiness or to be rushed to the hospital because of bones broken in the crush. But what is the reaction of the authorities? Well, Valentina Charushina, the secretary of the city executive committee, insisted that the toilet be built right next to the main entrance to Serafimovskaia; she found it in herself to object to the church bells, labeling their ringing "a bourgeois survival."

The central concept of perestroika is, if you will, the idea that we will only be able to save our economy from its present near-critical state when respect for the law and complete observance of human rights (including the right to freedom of conscience) become the absolute norm of our lives. It seems that this notion is only beginning to take root in the Viatka area. The law, human rights, duty—all these can be sacrificed to the prevailing opinion, all these can be perverted in the local interest, all these can be driven to obsequious submission. . . .

I reminded Iu. Karacharov: "The state considered it possible to return Danilov Monastery to the Russian Orthodox Church." "Good for Moscow!" he shot back, and there was some sense in his harsh reply. You can do what you like up there in Moscow, but here in Kirov when we say "no" we stand by it unflinchingly.

The Kirov story ended more happily than the Krasnodar episode. On 25 October 1987 *Moskovskie Novosti* published the following short announcement:

> Just before this edition was sent to the presses the editor received a letter from the Council for Religious Affairs of the Council of Ministers: "The issue raised in your article 'Opinion Against the Law' has been removed from the agenda because, in accordance with the recommendations of the Kirov oblast' executive committee, registration has been approved for a second religious community of the Russian Orthodox church in Kirov, as well as the allotment to it of the religious building Troitskaia Church.
>
> The Russian Orthodox religious association in Viatskie Poliany (Kirov oblast') has also been registered and has been allotted a religious building."

This is yet another indication that the relations between church and local authorities (including protection of believers' civil rights) still require much attention, although things are changing little by little in this area as the result of the spread of glasnost. One more example of this can be found in another article by A. Nezhnyi in *Moskovskie Novosti* (24 April 1988). In this article he told of the difficulties that the believers encountered upon registering their new community.

> As long as members of the now registered second Orthodox community in Kirov did not complain to the *oblast'* procurator (pointing with good reason to infringement of the law by which, within two months, the community was to be allotted at least a temporary place of worship)—until that time the local authorities did what they could to delay acting on their resolution to give Troitskaia Church to the believers. It is not out of some desire to "finish off" those who broke the law, or abetted its breaking, that I call to mind Lenin's irreconcilability towards bureaucrats and officials. One must be wary of the hope that one beautiful morning we'll all wake up democrats. Over the decades the people have come to be treated like a child who

does not know what he wants, and this attitude cannot evaporate overnight. . . .

We received a letter from Naberezhnye Chelny, where an Orthodox community has spent many years petitioning for the return of their now decrepit Church of St. Dmitrii Solunskii. It contained the following bitter lines: "Oh, you people of authority, you leaders, what are you doing to us? To the people who from time immemorial have looked death straight in the eye; who have defended Mother Rus' from all her enemies and miscreants; who paid the price of life for peace; who went into battle, raised children, worked ceaselessly for forty years; who in minus forty degree weather took the gloves from our hands to send to the front; and who with our bare hands dug the trenches outside Moscow and Stalingrad that kept the satanic foe at bay?"

. . . Letters come from Michurinsk, where the believers have been left with only a small cemetery chapel. The Il'inskii Church—designed by [Bartolomeo] Rastrelli, a monument of architecture restored from ruins after the war by the labors and sacrifices of Orthodox locals— was taken from the community in 1964. It has since fallen into deplorable disrepair, as the local newspaper testifies.

We have letters from Gor'kii, Rovno, Sverdlovsk, Cheliabinsk, Tula, Novgorod, Kiev; and when one reads these letters, knowing that what they describe is true, then besides concern and pain one feels a certain burdensome bewilderment.

What is to be done? How? Glasnost', wide-ranging discussion of such issues, respect for the law and appropriate punishments for its breaking—absolutely. But each time we decide one case, we are immediately confronted with a second, a third, a tenth. . . . I believe that it would be in the common interest to create a special com- mission—perhaps affiliated with the Supreme Soviet's Presidium—in which public servants, deputies, and members of the Council for Religious Affairs, as well as church representatives and believers, would participate. Then this commission could finally answer the complaints of our country's believers, operating in a truly democratic way.

This open discussion of how the principle of freedom of conscience has been ignored is a first indication that the real state of affairs is changing. In this respect perhaps the most significant article was that by Chairman of the Council for Religious Affairs K. Kharchev, "Conscience is Free."

There is not yet reason to speak of a mass abandonment of religion. Believers number in the millions, even tens of millions. As we know, politics takes such millions as its starting point. And so the issue is absolutely clear and simple. If believers feel that perestroika is working, that it is finally eradicating perceptions of believers as "second-class" citizens, that it brooks no exceptions to the principle of freedom of conscience (or the laws based on it) at any level of society, then I am convinced that they will be the convinced partisans and participants of perestroika. . . .

. . . The church experienced what our whole society experienced, including administrative, harshly bureaucratic methods of control. Here I have in mind the 1929 law with its petty rules and regulations, with its efforts to legislate every step or act of the church, thus depriving it of all independence.

. . . We are now, I think, seeing an end to the difficult period when the registration of each new religious community was taken as a step backward, an ideological defeat, a concession to the believers. Such are the fruits of our recent past. These attitudes were an integral part of Stalinist rule, and we irrevocably renounce them. . . .

To deprive believers of the right to do good is to keep them from following the tenets of Christian teaching. It is fundamentally unjust. I assert that believers, as Soviet citizens, have the right to form their own cooperatives, to put out their own newspapers, and to publish church literature in larger quantities. (*Ogonyok*, 1988, no. 21)

The approach of the millennium of Rus's conversion to Christianity, 1988, provoked intensified debates and tested glasnost anew. The millennium offered an opportunity to reevaluate many of the sources affecting the development of society's consciousness, including research into the true role and significance of Christianity in the history of Russian culture and statehood.

Famous scholar and member of the International Academy of Astronautics B.V. Raushenbakh devoted an article to this anniversary in the party journal *Kommunist* ("Through the Depths of Time"). There he asked that we not take the thousandth anniversary of the conversion in a one-sided way focusing only on its religious component:

If we look only for the "darker aspects" of an event that occurred ten centuries ago, it will be impossible to fully evaluate its complex and contradictory nature, its objective sense and significance. . . . Today we have every reason to take pride in the acts of our great forefathers and to remember with gratitude their selfless labor. What happened 1,000 years ago (although this date, like others of its type, is a matter of convention) was an unambiguously progressive step forward on the long path of history. (*Kommunist,* 1987, no. 12)

Dmitrii Likhachev, in his interview on the millennium with the magazine *Ogonyok,* said:

The church ought not to meddle in affairs of state, just as the state ought not to meddle in the affairs of the church. . . . There is still much to be done; in particular, we need to calm the fears of bureaucrats. Here is a short example. Outside Gatchina, in front of the old Vyrskaia post station (now a museum), someone is afraid to put a cross on the reconstructed clock tower. Another type of superstition? And finally we need to publish the Bible, since the Bible contains the code of contemporary art. In other words, not only believers but also atheists suffer when it is not available. We encourage patriotism but ignore the richest Old Russian literature, knowing that it will remain inaccessible without our understanding Christianity's principles and framework. This is what encourages speculation, sects, involvement in all sorts of things. We can only hope that as long as we are not afraid of dialogue, the situation is reparable. (*Ogonyok,* 1988, no. 10)

On the threshold of the thousandth anniversary of the conversion, articles by believers began to appear more often than in the past. There was a true "breakthrough" following 29 April 1988, when M.S. Gorbachev himself met with Patriarch Pimen and the members of the Russian Orthodox Synod. At this meeting Gorbachev said:

The religious organizations were also affected by the tragic events that occurred during the cult of personality. This period has been conclusively evaluated as a deviation from socialist principles, which have now been returned to their rightful place. The mistakes made in dealings with the church and believers in the 1930s and later are being corrected. Our newspapers and magazines are now writing openly and objectively about this. On their pages we can hear the voice of the church and of those of you here today. (*Pravda,* 30 April 1988)

Between May and June 1988 most newspapers and magazines carried interviews with Orthodox bishops and priests and covered the anniversary celebrations in great detail. The majority of these articles were very circumspect and diplomatic. But the very fact of their publication changed the general atmosphere considerably and raised the level of tolerance shown toward the church. One of the most interesting and open interviews was with a Moscow priest, Vladimir Rozhkov.

People often complain that there are no churches in the capital's new suburbs, so that the faithful have to travel far for services, at great expense of time. Church writings are in short supply. I can see that there is live, active faith, that people are attracted to spiritual knowledge, but there is nowhere to learn about God's law, no book of commandments, no prayer books.

At the same time Fr. Vladimir sees some positive changes:

> People have grown more tolerant and respectful in their attitudes toward believers and the clergy. They have stopped noting down the addresses of people who christen their children. We have felt the influence of perestroika in our church too. In particular we have been allowed to enlarge our grounds when the opportunity presents itself. We were also allowed to build a new building for christenings on the church grounds. People in the church are happy at the changes: We have been waiting for this for a long time. Many people who come to pray have little notes with the name Mikhail—and I am certain that with great gratitude they are remembering Mikhail Sergeevich Gorbachev. (*Vecherniaia Moskva*, 13 June 1988)

This very peculiar combination of new and traditional approaches toward church and religion in the Soviet Union, the growth of tolerance, and the erosion of vulgar ideological stereotypes is characteristic of our life today. There can be no doubt that in respect to church and religion the debates have only begun and are going to continue. Broadening glasnost in this previously very sensitive area may also be judged as an important barometer of change in the Soviet Union.

Do We Need Perestroika in the Church?

In late 1988 and early 1989 the situation in church-state relations changed somewhat. During this short period more than 1,000 Orthodox churches alone were opened, including the Vladimirskii Cathedral in Leningrad and the central city cathedrals in Kostroma, Ivanov, and Krasnoyarsk. Monastery buildings were handed over to the church—for example, Nikolo-Golutvinskii and Iosifo-Volokolamskii near Moscow, Nikolo-Viazhishchenskii in Novgorod, Ionno-Bogoslovskii in Ryazan, Tolgskii in Yaroslavl', and others. Little by little the philanthropy and religious literature that had previously been prohibited began to be permitted. It was obvious that significant progress was being made, but we were still a long way from the norms of a rule-of-law state.

The enthusiastic reaction to the celebration of the thousandth anniversary of the baptism of Rus' was followed by a certain disappointment in the passive, extremely cautious—at times, even openly conservative—church circles.

The harshest appraisals again came from writers. In his novel *Greetings to You from Granny Lera*, B. Vasiliev, known for his progressive, democratic views, presented the following conversation between an old country peasant and a peasant woman who lived through the hell of the camps:

> "Why the hell should I go to see a priest? Where were they, those priests, when we, snot-nosed kids, were rummaging through people's ashes, robbing graves, blowing up churches in plain view and even laughing as we did so? They were shitting in their pants from fear. Those who were not were sent to Solovki. Have you heard of that place? That is why we do not have any church here. We have prostitutes wearing cassocks and holding crosses in their hands, and I do not trust them for two seconds. A man who has betrayed you once will betray you a hundred times. That is the truth, that is an iron-clad rule."
>
> "What will you say next, that there is no God either?" Onisia asked with unconcealed menace.
>
> She felt offended for the priests, because her memory of them was linked not to the churches but to the camps, where this appellation had been applied to believers of all sorts who had been deprived of their freedom for adhering to their conscience, for suffering in the name of what they believed in. They were members of the clergy and parishioners, Tolstoyans and Old Believers, sectarians and monks, dragged from their cells by the long arm of lawlessness. . . .
>
> "If God is conscience, then he exists," the peasant said softly. "If God is justice, then he should exist. But if he is holed up in the churches, then he should not." (*Neva*, 1988, no. 12, p. 57)

After this piece by the "liberal" B. Vasiliev was published, similar thoughts were expressed by V. Belov, whose reputation is that of a "conservative." Here are the thoughts of his priest, Nikolai, who regrets having joined the "living" ("Renovation") church, i.e., the faction that was distinguished in the 1920s by its extreme servility before the authorities:

> Yes, the adherents of the Living Church put themselves in the hands of the authorities, but what did the Renovationists obtain by this power? Very likely nothing at all, except new devastation. . . . They have done violence to the relics of Sergei Radonezhskii, as they did to the *solovetskii* saints. Graves have been defiled, altars destroyed. . . . They say they need the copper for tractor bearings. Good Lord, what bearings? That ringing metal glorified orthodox Rus', and frightened her devious enemies, driving them further away. Now they are melting it down to make spears of enmity. Was the body of Our Savior not pierced with such a spear? Father Nikolai could not bear the shame he felt for his own apostasy. ("The Year of the Great Turning Point," *Novyi Mir*, 1989, no. 3, p. 51)

Journalistic articles along similar lines also appeared:

> When the church held a local council in 1917–1918, that council
> was irreproachably representative. . . . The church demonstrated its
> ability, freed from state guardianship, to work out very democratic
> organizational forms. But then the same total bureaucratization that
> was occurring in the rest of society as a whole began to take place
> in the church. The state bureaucracy prefers to view the church, too,
> as a bureaucratic organization, whose director is, by virtue of con-
> servatism, called the "patriarch," whose heads of departments are
> "bishops," and so forth—but a submissive organization, one without
> full rights. (Speech by V. Makhnach at the roundtable, "A Dialogue
> for the Good of the Fatherland," *Vek XX i Mir*, 1988, no. 7, p. 47)

> How does the clergy, the internal life of the church, look from this
> standpoint? One is struck by the black "Volgas" of the bishops; is this
> the local *nomenklatura,* or foreign guests? The *Journal of the Moscow
> Patriarchate* (*ZhMP*) periodically reports on their trips abroad and
> their reception of foreign guests in their residences. Do they see
> anybody besides each other and foreigners? . . .
>   Let us leaf through last year's issues of *ZhMP*. . . . Reading the
> journal leaves one with a strange impression. Much is written about
> international, ecumenical contacts. There is a big official section.
> . . . There is a great deal about the Patriarch Pimen and the chairman
> of the publishing division (under whose jurisdiction *ZhMP* is located),
> Metropolitan [V.] Pitirim: where they have been and what they have
> been doing. Search as you may, you will not find anything in the
> journal about the internal problems of the church. Is there really
> absolutely no corruption, no incompetence in it? Are there no argu-
> ments over ideological and practical questions, no problems in the
> parishes? The journal is silent about social problems as well. . . .
>   Leafing through the official organ of the Orthodox church, you feel,
> surprisingly, that you are encountering something long familiar—the
> atmosphere of the recent past, what we now call "stagnation" . . .
> (S.B. Filatov, "Do We Need 'Internal Foreign Countries'?" *Sotsiologi-
> cheskie Issledovaniia*, 1988, no. 5, pp. 44–45)

During the second half of 1988, the public learned to its great
satisfaction of the transfer to the church of a number of monasteries.
B. Okudzhava wrote with bewilderment of the Optinaia Hermitage in
the spring of 1989:

Restoration works of sorts has begun in the monastery, but it is being conducted in a way that leaves much to be desired. . . . Instead of the parquet that was once there, the floor has been covered with flagstone, when in fact worshippers are accustomed to kneeling down . . . and so forth and so on. (*Nedelia*, 1989, no. 7, p. 17)

Journalists, in treating relations within the church—a subject that is new to them—are to their surprise uncovering scandalous facts. For example, V. Lebedev studied the complaints of parishioners of the Arkhangelskaia Church in a village in the Voronezh diocese. The parishioners told him that they disagreed with the dismissal of the respected priest Georgii Prilepin, an honest and talented pastor. Metropolitan Mefodii explained to the journalist that the Soviet authorities were entirely to blame. The metropolitan then evaded Lebedev until his departure on some metropolitan-related business to the United States. Lebedev evaluated Metropolitan Mefodii's behavior as follows:

The worshippers are suffering. Father Georgii, who has devoted thirty years of service to the worshippers and the church, is suffering. His wife and children live in poverty, in near destitution. In the name of what? And how does this accord with Christian morality? ("Father Georgii—Unemployed," *Nauki i Religiia* [Science and Religion], 1989, no. 2, pp. 34–35)

The bishops began to confront the necessity of answering the public's puzzled questions. Here is how Metropolitan Minskii Filiaret answered journalist P. Lukianchenko:

Q: It is no secret that the church, as a part of Soviet society, suffers from similar ailments. As the archbishops Khrizoston Irkutskii and Kirill Smolenskii declared at the local council, it is essential to raise the level of morality not just of the average worshippers and clerics but also of the higher clergy, "who do not always serve as a model of virtue." What is being done to treat these ailments?
A: The leitmotif of perestroika is the truth of life. That truth of life concerns the inner aspect of a person, his moral perfection. Where, if not in the church, is it necessary to pay vigilant attention to this very thing? In conditions of perestroika we should be more self-critical.
Q: In a number of letters received by the editorial department, worshippers complain about the anti-democratic nature of several decisions made by the church leadership. According to a letter signed by 700 parishioners of the Krasnodarskii Cathedral, Archbishop Vladimir—who actively fought corruption in the church milieu—was, by someone's secret order, removed from the eparchy and transferred to Pskov. Will the Synod address the wishes of the parishioners?

A: Conflict-ridden situations can occur where the only alternative is transfer to another eparchy. The church leadership tries to treat the requests of the worshippers attentively. . . . But perhaps here the interests of the church must also be taken into consideration. . . . (*Argumenty i Fakty*, 1989, no. 1)

The views of the conservative segment of the episcopate were perhaps most candidly expressed by Metropolitan Volokoamskii Pitirim in the dialogue "The Ecology of the Human Spirit," with Academician D.S. Likhachev. In response to Likhachev's statement that it is essential to guarantee the noninterference of the state in the affairs of the church and that "above all it must stop putting pressure on the church on questions concerning the appointment of priests, metropolitans, etc.," Pitirim answered:

In answering your question, I always recall the words spoken by our wise and venerable Patriarch Sergii in the late 1920s, that the church is separate from the state but not removed from it. (*Sovetskaia Kul'tura*, 23 March 1989)

Thus Pitirim openly identified himself with Patriarch Sergii, whose policies were directed at serving the Stalinist regime by faith and truth. Pitirim did not heed the writers' appeal. By mid-1989 it was becoming increasingly obvious that radical perestroika was necessary not only in relations between the state and the church, but within the church itself as well.

FOUR

The Debate over Justice and Individual Rights

Legal Nihilism: What Are Its Causes?

One of the most important tasks of perestroika and glasnost is the formation and development of an adequate legal system and the creation and safeguarding of the kind of social conditions that from time immemorial have been called the "rule of law." The painful shortcomings of the Soviet legal system are the subject of much discussion in today's media. Glasnost is coming into its own, unveiling many issues that in the past were cloaked in secrecy and silence. But unfortunately, the veil of secrecy has not yet been fully lifted. We are still unable to judge the state of crime in the nation; statistical data about the dynamics of crime are not yet made available to the public (as they are by the FBI in its yearly reports on the state of crime in the United States). Nor can the public fully judge the state of affairs in our prison facilities, as only scant information about them filters through to the press. The people do not really know the exact nature of the crimes and transgressions committed in the past by party and government officials who have since been removed from office.

Most important, perhaps, the problems that confront us today in the area of justice and individual rights cannot be reduced merely to the backwardness (or even the absence) of legal consciousness in our society. Let us be direct: We do not have independent legal institutions functioning effectively on the basis of law; we do not have a state bound by law.

The problem is one of principle. The lawlessness and arbitrariness, the paranoid secrecy, the lack of the necessary openness (glasnost)— all of this ultimately comes down to the relationship between law and politics. Which is more fundamental? In our country, politics—the politics of the party and the state—has traditionally taken precedence; politics has dictated the law. The sphere of justice has been perceived not as independent, but as serving, first and foremost, the interests of the party and the state.

Today we are well aware of the price that our society paid for this perception. On the pages of the Soviet press we have begun to see unprecedented discussions, conducted with far greater openness than in the past, about the accumulated problems in the sphere of justice, legality, and individual rights in the Soviet Union.

What then are the deep-seated sources of the problems that have arisen? Corresponding member of the Academy of Sciences of the USSR P. Volobuev located them in the long history of tsarist rule:

> Because of the lengthy domination of tsarist absolutism and the weakness of bourgeois liberalism, democratic institutions and traditions did not develop in Russia. . . . In the first place, we were beset by all the difficulties and trials, imaginable and unimaginable, that await those who are trailblazers on the unexplored road of social progress. In the second place, it is clear that even under socialism, historical development follows a zigzagging course. . . . The birth of a new type of democracy is a particularly difficult process. But this has been true, I would argue, throughout world history. (*Pravda,* 27 March 1987)

Another well-known Soviet legal expert, Academician Vladimir Kudriavtsev, placed some of the blame on the circumstances in which the new Soviet regime came to power:

> The first Soviet Constitution (1918) limited the political and civil rights of the overthrown exploiting classes. As the bitter class war raged on, the question being decided was: "Who is getting whom?" Under these conditions such democratic institutions as broad openness, freedom of expression, public monitoring of administrative decisions, and guarantees of the inviolability of the individual could not develop to their full extent. (*Pravda,* 3 April 1987)

The legal system that exists in our country today took shape gradually throughout the late 1920s and early 1930s. And it must be stated honestly that the legal institutions that developed did not entirely safeguard legality in the country. Thus, neither procuratorial supervision, nor the judiciary, nor for that matter the bar—that step-daughter of the Soviet legal system—prevented the widespread illegalities of the Stalin era.

In a letter published in *Moskovskie Novosti* (26 July 1987), Boris Lesniak wrote, "The tyranny of the thirties, forties, and the early fifties was made possible by the fact that the country lacked a firm legal foundation." In another article in this same newspaper (14 April 1988), Professor Aleksandr Iakovlev went into greater detail:

In our society there was a perception, which was artificially manufactured and inflamed, that a sinister threat loomed over the achievements of the revolution. This threat was personified by and embodied in its insidious bearers ("the enemies of the people"). Even selfless service to the revolution could be interpreted as a base masquerade perpetrated by villains. This threat was portrayed as all encompassing and ubiquitous ("a hornet's nest of enemies").

Battle was supposedly being done with blackest evil, and therefore concerns about evidence and the choice of methods took a back seat or were simply dismissed as the remnants of "corrupt bourgeois liberalism." Illegal practices crept into the methods of interrogation.

Those who did not throw themselves on the appointed victim at the first opportunity became "accomplices to the enemies of the people." And those who themselves were designated "enemies of the people" found themselves excluded from society, branded as misfits, doomed (and along with them their relatives, friends, and sometimes mere acquaintances). Those who would not confess guilt were considered dangerous because they would not "disarm themselves." Those who did confess were expected to "betray their accomplices." The ranks of the "doomed" widened. As a result, the punitive system itself manufactured its own "enemies," and their "existence" in turn justified the expansion of that system.

The lawlessness of the 1930s was compounded by the passage of cruel, inhuman criminal legislation. In 1932 a law was passed making the death penalty the punishment for stealing—the theft of property belonging to the state, a kolkhoz, or a cooperative. If there were "extenuating circumstances," ten years' imprisonment might replace execution. From 1935 on, individuals as young as 12 years old were subject to this law. Since 1937 such crimes have been punishable by terms of imprisonment of up to 25 years. Repressive methods against criminals, according to the accounts of contemporaries, were characterized by "a massive calling to account of the working people." There was "competition to produce quantitative indices of those against whom repressive measures were taken," a "massive calling to account and condemnation of the activities of the kholkhoz," and a "calling to account and taking of repressive measures for insignificant crimes, for paltry misdemeanors."

An editorial in the party journal *Kommunist* (1987, no. 5) commented on how these events diminished the authority of legal institutions and personnel:

Unfortunately, the most flagrant violations of socialist legality permitted in connection with the cult of personality, involving the curtailment of many democratic procedures, diminished the authority of law enforcement agencies and led to a decline in the public prestige of their representatives. Legal nihilism grew stronger: Lack of faith in the reality of such fundamental democratic principles as the inviolability of the individual, the equality of everyone before the law, fair trial procedures, and so forth, became widespread. For several decades, legal experts—both practicing lawyers and scholars—lost a certain degree of authority and respect in the eyes of the people.

The measures adopted after the 20th Congress of the CPSU in 1956—which were aimed both at overcoming the consequences of Stalin's cult of personality and preventing future acts of massive repression against Soviet citizens—at first had a positive effect on the strengthening of legality and on the operations of legal institutions. In the late 1950s a reform of Soviet law was undertaken. However, this reform was not radical enough.

Moreover, although the legal reforms carried out during the Khrushchev era took legality a significant step forward, they also introduced new problems. For example, the punishments for "economic crimes" were made more severe, and the definition of such crimes made it possible to include almost any individual economic initiative one wished. Harsh measures were introduced against so-called "spongers" ("parasites"), and the authorities resorted to these measures repeatedly for dealing with politically undesirable elements.

In the words of the Soviet philosopher Professor Anatolii Butenko (*Moscow News*, 7 May 1987): "The forces that prevented the full implementation of the decisions of the 20th Congress of the Communist Party of the Soviet Union (1956), which debunked and condemned the cult of personality, virtually brought to a halt the process of the renewal of our life."

During the subsequent decades, the nature of the country's legal system began to be determined by a rapidly growing "legal bureaucracy" that functioned according to its own rules, with anti-democratic roots, and in concert with the government bureaucracy and, not infrequently, with underground businessmen as well. Of course, this was not a return to the lawlessness of the Stalin era. The punitive apparatus lost its omnipotence, and people began to forget about the massive repressions. If under Stalin a person could easily wind up in a prison or a camp literally "for nothing," now one could no longer be imprisoned for no reason. But by the mid-1960s, the zone of relative and extremely limited democratization of our legal system, which had been opened up slightly by the 20th Party Congress, had already begun to narrow again. This is described in the magazine *Kommunist* (1987, no. 5):

> The forces of stagnation, which have been particularly prominent in the past two decades, could not but affect the political-legal sphere of public life. Democratic institutions "skidded off course"; openness was not guaranteed. Crime has been on the rise since the mid-1960s, while the battle with it has grown less effective. . . . Spheres that were above criticism (and consequently not subject to legal action) multiplied. At times law enforcement agencies, either on their own initiative or under pressure "from above" or "from the side," closed their eyes to many violations of the law.
>
> Red tape, bureaucratism, and corruption grew more and more evident in the work of legal institutions, which had lost a degree of the independence from local and departmental influences that is so essential to the successful protection of rights and law enforcement. The state of criminality and the activity of law enforcement agencies were often evaluated in terms of "gross output." Cases where, for the sake of these indices, legal procedures and the rights of the individual were violated in the course of an inquiry or a preliminary investigation were far from unique. . . . The situation reached the point where top officials of the USSR Ministry of Internal Affairs and of law enforcement agencies in a number of republics were found to be guilty of corruption and the inveterate abuse of their power.

Reading the materials that are currently being published in the press, one might justifiably conclude that almost every democratic principle of law and justice was either distorted or flagrantly violated in the course of actual investigative and judicial proceedings during the era of stagnation. As in the Stalinist period, the existing legal structures and law enforcement agencies could neither fully safeguard legal order nor act as firm guarantors of the rights of citizens. Perhaps the worst problem was that the punitive resources of law enforcement agencies were often placed at the service of corrupt politicians in the state and party apparatus. Here is a concrete example from a recent case in Uzbekistan. In 1983 a task force from the USSR Public Procurator General's Office was charged with conducting an investigation in Bukhara:

> At the very moment of receiving thousands of rubles worth in bribes, the head of the local Directorate of Internal Affairs' (IVD) unit fighting embezzlement and speculation [BKhSS], police Lieutenant Colonel A. Muzaffarov, was caught red-handed by KGB investigators. . . . When the police unit that investigates economic crimes arrived, the following officials were arrested: the regional head of the UVD, A. Dustov; the

director of the Urban Industrial Trade of Bukhara, Sh. Kudratov; and the head of the regional administration of the supply of technical equipment and material of the Gossnab [the state supply agency] of the Uzbekistan Republic, D. Sharipov.

"Modern day emirs" led the republic into a state of slow and agonizing decay where extortion and bribery became the norm, as did the collaboration of a large number of officials of law enforcement agencies, the party, and the agencies of the soviet with the criminal world. . . . During the course of five years a whole string of leading officials was placed under arrest, including former secretaries of the Central Committee of the Uzbekistan Communist Party; first secretaries of the regional committees, the city committees, and the district committees; the deputy chairman of the Presidium of the Uzbekistan Supreme Soviet; the manager of affairs of the Central Committee of the party; the first deputy minister of the Ministry of Internal Affairs of the USSR; the minister of internal affairs of Uzbekistan and three of his deputies; regional heads of the UVD; and officials of the state farms. (*Pravda*, 23 January 1988)

One of the "emirs"—the former general director of the Papsky agrarian-industrial complex, Akhmadzhan Adylov—created his own fiefdom in the territory under his control, which was fenced off and protected by his own personal security guards. The journalist Vladimir Sokolov described this situation on the pages of *Literaturnaia Gazeta* (29 January 1988):

Beneath a statue of Lenin, Adylov arranged public floggings of anyone whom he found displeasing or suspicious. In winter a stranger who had been captured would be brought to this place, and there, under the protection of Lenin's right hand and before the eyes of the common folk, ice water would be poured under his collar until he confessed who had sent him and why. . . .

Thus the master ruled his thousands in the name of the Soviet regime. . . . Of course, in a healthy climate this would have been impossible, but as it was Adylov walked all over the territorial and regional authorities. He assigned tasks to police officers, and if they did not perform them they were beaten or lost their jobs. . . . Not long before his arrest he even discussed with his inner circle the question of whom he should appoint as minister of the interior, who should be the republic's public prosecutor. . . . He was one of the most "powerful" men in the republic, with a huge amount of information at his disposal, his own apparatus of repression, and most important, the financial means to buy anyone and anything.

The concept of "organized crime" itself only very recently acquired a legitimate place in the Soviet lexicon. Just three years ago the question,

"Does organized crime exist in the USSR?" would most often have been
answered in the negative, owing to hypocrisy and inability to speak
the truth. Today, the situation is assessed differently.

Was the appearance of our "Soviet mafia" an inevitability or a paradox?
This is how the journalist Iurii Feofanov posed the question in his
article in *Moscow News* (1988, no. 33):

> Glasnost is upon us, and it is at its height. We read improbable
> reports, inconceivable disclosures. We are torn by controversies. We
> are proud about the bold exposures and are ashamed of the seamy
> side of our life.
>
> Much was known even before glasnost. There was that trial about
> the theft at the Okean fish shop. The Rostov thieves were shown on
> the television. The names of top officials of foreign trade were named
> in the press. The trials of Moscow trading officials were not hushed
> up either. But glasnost did not go all the way—it qualified these
> crimes as isolated and untypical. The words "organized crime" or
> especially "mafia" were attributed exclusively to the jungles of capi-
> talist business. That explains the public's shock upon hearing about
> the mafia here at home. Some people had a hunch that it existed.
> People freely discussed (without whispering) the rapaciousness of
> Brezhnev's clan and its circle. But all talk remains idle unless it is
> made public. Worse—it was officially known as "slandering our reality."
>
> *The Literary Gazette*, I think, came up with the most thorough
> research into the birth and blossoming of our mafia in its article "The
> Lion Has Jumped!" Frankly, I never imagined that organized crime
> could reach such proportions: the theft count was in the thousands
> of millions of rubles!
>
> Crime expert A. Gurov says: "Bearing in mind that the stakes in
> their card games could run as high as half a million, and that law
> enforcement officers were offered bribes of 300,000 or a million, you
> can well imagine what sort of income they have today."
>
> It turns out that our country has gangster clans on the order of
> those in Italy or the US. There are killings of rivals, street skirmishes,
> racketeering, sumptuous funerals for victims, and the newspaper lists
> these facts.
>
> But what we find most awful of all is that criminal gangs establish
> contacts with bribetakers in the higher echelons of power, and that
> leads to an alliance between criminal elements and corrupt officials.

The weakening of the legal system by those "invested with power,"
the exclusivity of the caste system, and the corruption all contributed
to the fact that by the mid-1980s the public trust in law enforcement
agencies had plummeted catastrophically: There was a widespread
impression of investigators, public prosecutors, and judges as bribe-

takers; the people had little faith that justice could be attained by means of legal institutions; legal nihilism was common. It is a great pity that the old Russian saying—"The law is like the shaft of a wagon; it goes wherever you turn it"—maintains a firm grasp on public consciousness, reflecting the failure of the legal system to protect the people vis-à-vis the law enforcement establishment.

Legal nihilism is also characteristic of the social and economic life of our society. The reason for this is essentially the absence of effective legal procedures that can mediate the relationship between the individual, the group, and the state. It is manifested in arbitrary administrative methods of management as well as in the huge number of administrative acts, which often contradict each other as well as other legal norms. These acts should be a concrete expression of the constitution and its statutes, but instead they too often undermine them by establishing exceptions and narrowing the sphere of their application. The actual breadth of a citizen's rights and responsibilities in a given sphere is established by administrative acts passed in secret, with no public participation and without regard for public opinion.

In quantitative terms Soviet law developed very energetically during the period of stagnation. The newspaper *Izvestiia* reported (22 September 1987):

> More than 10,000 so-called universally binding acts are in effect, promulgated by the ministries and agencies of the USSR; and these acts govern not just the officials of the ministries and agencies that passed them, but other agencies, organizations, and in many cases private citizens as well. . . . According to the calculations of specialists, there are more than 30,000 enforceable acts in effect, which were passed by the government of the USSR and its legislative agencies alone. . . . Moreover, the overall number of acts, far from decreasing, continues to grow. Approximately 600 legislative and governmental acts are passed every year, and since the constitution's ratification in 1977, 400 acts have been passed by the USSR legislature and more than 5,000 resolutions and regulations have been enacted by the USSR Council of Ministers.

Is the quantitative augmentation of the body of legal codes a good or a bad thing? Is quality perhaps not sacrificed to quantity? Here are the views of a number of legal experts on the quantitative increase in, for example, the provisions of criminal law.

Academy member Vladimir Kudriavtsev stated in an interview in *Izvestiia* (26 August 1987):

The criminal code . . . is currently overloaded with a mass of articles that appeared, one after the other, during the 1970s and 1980s. The reason is that instead of eliminating negative phenomena by means of economic and social change, we have relied on prohibitions and repressions. We are pursuing a foolish course, as scholars have warned for some time.

Professor Igor Karpets, a Soviet legal expert with a wealth of practical experience (he headed the Criminal Investigation Department for many years), described the negative impact that the quantitative accumulation of criminal law has had on legal order (*Pravda*, 9 October 1987):

A legislative "itch" possessed almost all the ministries and agencies. They all began to actively resort to the force of criminal law in attempting to patch up gaps and omissions in the system. Criminal sanctions were piled one on top of the other.

The number of new articles in the Criminal Codes of the union republics was growing rapidly. Punishments were made more severe for a number of crimes. . . . In the public's mind, wittingly or unwittingly, the idea became firmly established that all you have to do is introduce a criminal law, the tougher the better, and the harmful phenomenon that it punishes will disappear. Moreover, the struggle against crime is effective only when every kind of economic and educational leverage is applied. The strengthening of punitive trends in the law in general does not accord with a movement toward the democratization of social relations.

The criminologist Professor Aleksandr Sakharov is highly critical as well of the effectiveness of Soviet criminal law:

Our criminal law ranks among the harshest in the world. . . . Imprisonment has been employed more extensively as a punishment in recent years than it was (as analogous statistics show) in the first decade following the revolution. At the same time there is no indication that this has had a desirable effect on the crime rate: In the years of stagnation it rose. (*Sovetskaia Yustitsia* [Soviet Justice], 1988, no. 1)

The tendency toward punishments of greater severity, the criminalization of many types of behavior, and the faith in the effectiveness of coercion and force have all characterized the development of criminal law in the past decades. The implementation of the death penalty was broadened. The limits of freedom of expression shrank, dissent was suppressed, and dissidents were jailed. The magazine *Ogonyok* (1987, no. 33) gave some examples of these limitations:

In 1966, in the Criminal Code of the RSFSR, article 190.1 appeared, which made illegal the dissemination, either verbally or in any other form, of slander that defames the Soviet state and social system. This article covers actions that are not intended to undermine or weaken the Soviet state. Article 70 is one thing, providing as it does for actions aimed directly at undermining and weakening the system—truly a grave crime against the state. But article 190.1 can also include criticism that is "too" harsh, as well as conversations that are merely irresponsible or stupid. . . . Not so long ago *Pravda* reported that I. Kubrik, a worker who had uncovered petty thieves in the management of the enterprise, was convicted by a local court of "disseminating slanderous fabrications, which he knew to be false, defaming the administration." See how this formulation recalls, almost to a word, the text of article 190.1!

The prosecutorial bias in the administration of justice plays a pivotal role—penetrating and interconnecting inquiry, investigation, prosecution by the state, and court proceedings. An apt characterization of the situation appeared in *Pravda* (18 August 1987):

> Why do our courts so rarely return verdicts of "not guilty"? It seems that finding a person "not guilty" in court does more than just clear him of the charge and instill confidence in the fairness of the judicial system. A verdict of "not guilty" also cancels out all the work involved in the preliminary investigation. In addition, it represents a big "minus" in the work of the public prosecutor's office, whose responsibility it is to ensure that the law is discharged in the activities of the agencies of inquiry and preliminary investigation. The judges, not wishing to spoil relations with the investigative agencies and with the public prosecutor's office, often fall back on the "diplomatic" method: In the case of doubts as to the materials produced by the preliminary investigation, they do not interpret them in favor of the accused, as the presumption of innocence requires, but direct the case to supplemental investigation.

The unquestioning acceptance by judges of the prosecutorial version of a case is a shameful phenomenon and shows that the courts lack sufficient independence from outside influence. In the newspaper *Moskovskaia Pravda* (17 May 1987) Igor Petrukhin wrote:

> The Constitution of the USSR stipulates that the court be independent, and subordinate only to the law. In practice, however, the court is often bound by the conclusions of the investigative agencies, by the position of the state prosecutor, and by public opinion. Few judges can overcome this massive psychological pressure. Handing down a

"not guilty" verdict can be interpreted as a show of solidarity with the offender. . . . Research has shown that judges, as a rule, trust the conclusions of the preliminary investigation and are inclined to view nearly every defendant as a criminal. Of 736 judges questioned, 43 percent stated that they have always formed an impression of the defendant's guilt or innocence before the trial even begins. About half of the judges stated that they often form such a conviction. This means that many judges are not guided by the presumption of innocence, according to which the defendant is considered innocent.

If a judge holds firmly to the principles of the Constitution, he can expect an unpleasant time of it. Here, for example, is an excerpt from a letter to the editors of *Literaturnaia Gazeta* (5 August 1987) written by a member of the Krasnodar regional court, V. Kalachev, describing some of his personal experiences:

> During my eighteen years as a judge I have allowed myself to return more than a few verdicts of "not guilty." Here is what that led to. One day at 7:00 in the morning, officials from the office of the public prosecutor, the police, and witnesses to the investigative action appeared at my door and produced a search warrant signed by the public prosecutor of the city. The warrant stated that they were looking for . . . pornographic magazines and films, video and radio gear. . . . Two hours later the exact same search was conducted in my office on the premises of the regional court. . . . Of course, they found nothing reprehensible, but their real aim lay elsewhere: to show their power and strength to a disobedient, willful judge.

"In fact a judge today most often does not have sufficient guarantees that this most important constitutional principle of independence will truly be observed and adhered to," concluded Aleksandr Bovin in *Literaturnaia Gazeta* (3 February 1988).

Much is written these days about cases of honest, principled people who become victims of a corrupt law enforcement system functioning in concert with local authorities. Here is a story from *Pravda* (7 March 1988):

> It is not out of mere curiosity that we leaf through the pages of the case of Aleksandr Udalov. In 1960 he graduated from the police academy in Kaunas and was sent by the commissioner of the Criminal Investigation Department to the Krasnodar region. In two years he was elected by his comrades to membership in the Communist Party of the Soviet Union. Four years later he had earned his law degree, and four years after that he was appointed deputy chief of the Direc-

torate of Internal Affairs (UVD) of the Sochi Executive Committee and was given the rank of police colonel.

Glowing references, impressive connections—and suddenly, in one fell swoop—"he was dismissed."

"In Sochi we had to deal with a complex network of commercial mafia, and unfortunately it eluded our grasp," Aleksandr Fedorovich [Udalov] smiles bitterly. "The former chairman of the Sochi Executive Committee, Voronkov, about whom in his day a great deal was written in the national press, was far from the main figure in that large ring of operators," the colonel continues his story. "Much more powerful forces were at work."

Udalov himself was hardly what you might call a gift to these powerful forces. Nevertheless, operations of the department of criminal investigation were failing, one after the other, and it was no secret who was letting the criminals get away with it. Udalov, as deputy chairman of the UVD of the Executive Committee, gathered incriminating materials on the secretary of the city committee of the party, A. Merzlyi, following a thread that stretched all the way to the regional committee of the party, to the chairman of the party commission, G. Karnaukhov.

The reaction was lightning swift. A meeting of the bureau of the city committee of the party was held at which Udalov was expelled from the party. When he appealed to the regional committee, they created commissions—first one, then a second, and a third . . . twelve in all! He refuted the conclusions of all these commissions with the facts. But the pressure was mounting from all sides. Udalov's mother, Klavdiia Timofeevna, who had raised five children, was given a written warning not to leave her place of residence: She was alleged to have been receiving an extra 10 percent on her pension. . . . His brother, the manager of a boiler-house, was dismissed from his work. The operators of the ring collected 52,000 rubles to pay for the kidnapping of his daughter. (He managed to save her at the last minute.) They immediately began fabricating a "file" on him too. Eventually he was arrested. Incredible, but true!

Expelled from the party, defamed, he was suddenly transformed in the eyes of the public into the "source of all evil" in Sochi. (These rumors were inflamed by those very people who were responsible for it all—the corruption and the bribes . . .)

How did he get through it?

Well, justice cannot but prevail, and a fresh breeze cleared the air where not long before it had been so hard to breathe. Karnaukhov, Merzlyi, and others of their ilk were sentenced to long prison terms. Udalov was reinstated to the party and to the police agencies and regained his title of colonel.

Literaturnaia Gazeta reported on one of those monstrous miscarriages of justice that have, under glasnost, been made public for the first time (2 March 1988):

> For fourteen years in a row the same man was murdering young women in the region of Vitebsk and Polotsk. Every year the number of victims grew. During that time, fourteen innocent people were convicted in eleven separate court cases. By the time the real guilty party was caught, one of the convicted had already served ten years in prison; another, after eight years of confinement, had gone completely blind and was released as "not posing any danger"; a third, given the death sentence, had lost his life; and a fourth had tried to take his own life but was pulled alive from the noose.
>
> I saw the fourth man. I took a walk with him around the streets and parks of Riga, where the trial of the group of investigators who fabricated the case against him had been going on for six months. I saw this tall, thirty-year-old man tremble all over as he described the details of his "case," saw the tranquilizers spill out of his shaking hands. . . . It turned out that those who tried to defend themselves during the inquiry were beaten. They slammed the head of one against a safe; they struck another in the face with his own shoe. A third they beat with a copy of the Criminal Code of the Byelorussian SSR that happened to be handy, probably so he would not harbor any illusions that legality is respected in the process of criminal investigation. They turned one adolescent witness upside down and shook him. "To shake the nonsense out of him," the investigators explained later.

The magazine *Ogonyok* (1987, no. 7) told the story of an inquiry conducted by police officials in Petrozavodsk. Some citizens were arrested under suspicion of having stolen two tires from a car. The magazine reproduced their depositions:

> From the testimony of A.S. Velikainen, a moulder by profession: ". . . I did not see who hit me the first time. I shut up right away. Kapashinov started trying to persuade me that I should confess to the theft. He said that this was not a game, that they knew, even if I did not, that it would be better for me to confess. I did not say anything. Then Kapashinov stood up, walked around me, and hit me in the head. Then he grabbed my throat and began choking me so I could not breathe. My tongue was hanging out of my mouth, my eyes were popping out of my head, and someone told Kapashinov to lay off. He let me go, sat down opposite me again, and in that instant a man in a red shirt gave me a kick in the side that knocked me off my chair."

From the testimony of Konstantin Galashev, a metal worker–rigger:
"Then they started beating me up. There were three of them. One punched me several times in the stomach and hit me with his fists from behind in the kidneys. The second guy was thickset and older than the first, wearing shoes with tall heels. I remember those shoes well, since he struck me with one of them in the face. The third one hit me in the kidneys as well. They took a gas mask from the safe and put it on me. Then one of them said that nothing seemed to work. Another responded, 'I will go get the doctor. He will be able to do something.' The 'doctor' arrived. He advised them to 'torture' me for a period of two minutes, then to give me a respite of not more than a minute, and then to resume the torture. Then he left. They closed up the valve. I could not get any air. Sometimes I lost consciousness, and then they would open up the valve so I could get a couple of breaths of air."

The author of the piece in *Ogonyok* spoke with one of the police officials arrested for using illegal methods of interrogation, Evgenii Kalashnikov:

"How do such things happen? What could come over a man to turn him into a cruel sadist?"

"When you put on a uniform," Zhenia Kalashnikov said with sudden candor, "and walk around the city, you become another person. You know what I mean, you feel your own power. . . ."

What then, does that mean? That the power these agents of authority had over other people destroyed their weak souls? That, as it turns out, these guys simply grew stupider the higher they rose up in the power structure? That they did not understand, could not figure it out?

"The people," said Zhenia suddenly, "have the kind of police they deserve."

I was horrified to hear that.

Next we offer an account of a press conference conducted by the first deputy head of the Directorate of Internal Affairs (UVD), Iurii A. Tomashev:

In recent times the reputation which the Moscow police formerly enjoyed has been tarnished. There has been an increase in violations of socialist legality, and in cases of officials of law enforcement agencies abusing their authority.

Iu. A. Tomashev recounted a case which troubled him greatly. On May 4th police officials of the Lenin district of Moscow approached a group of young people—"hippies" as they are called—on Gogol

Boulevard. Although they were not breaking any laws, 58 of them were arrested and taken to the local police station. In the course of this two young people sustained bodily injuries. The actions of the officials of the District UVD were deemed errors in professionalism, and those involved were punished. Iu. A. Tomashev stressed that the Moscow police cannot always function perfectly in conditions of expanding democratization. . . . The greatest number of violations were found to have occurred among officials of the Department of Criminal Investigation and of the BKhSS. Thus in the first half of this year, 23 former officials of these offices were found guilty by the courts of corruption, assault, the theft of government property, and incidents connected with the highways and other means of transport. Ten of them committed their crimes while intoxicated, which only aggravates their guilt.

In talking about this, one occasionally feels misgivings: does not this information only promote the loss of faith in our police that the people feel? This was obviously the judgement of the Ministry of Internal Affairs itself not long ago when it decided not to make public a host of negative facts about the workings of the police. This decision, along with other factors, fostered the impression that the police enjoy unobstructed freedom and, as a result, are free to violate the law. It was they themselves, and not the stories about them, that undermined respect for the policeman's uniform. (*Moskovskie Novosti*, 23 August 1987)

In the Voroshilovgrad region, the following incident took place. A correspondent for the journal *Sovetskii Shokhtior* (Soviet Miner), V. Berkhin, conscientiously fulfilling his journalistic responsibilities, was gathering information about abuses by local authorities and party officials. He gave some of his information, which he felt was not likely to be printed in the local press, to a local *Pravda* bureau. The journalist's actions irritated the powers that be of the Voroshilovograd region, and they began to consider possible legal actions. Officials of the Directorate of Internal Affairs (UVD) arrested Berkhin on the street on his way to the local *Pravda* bureau; they searched his son's house looking for notes and critical materials. Berkhin was subjected to intensive interrogation and held in confinement. A search warrant and an order for his arrest were issued, but on grounds that were farfetched and insufficient. Besides that, the order was approved not by the Public Prosecutor's Office in the territorial jurisdiction in which Berkhin was alleged to have committed the violations, but in another district (the public prosecutor of the appropriate jurisdiction was a person of principles and was not under the thumb of the investigative authorities). Both party officials and local officials of the Public Prosecutor's Office, the UVD, and the Directorate of the KGB were involved in organizing Berkhin's persecution. The attempt to silence him was described in *Pravda* in a piece entitled "Crossing the Line" (4 January 1987).

The USSR Procurator General's Office intervened in the Berkhin affair, and all officials guilty of breaking the law were brought to justice. Glasnost yielded its results. What was unprecedented in this case was the fact that the unseemly role played by KGB officials was publicly acknowledged, perhaps for the first time. Up until this case, new items about the KGB had always concerned only its successes in exposing foreign spies and traitors to the homeland and stopping their activities. But now the public was being told how the KGB had exceeded its own authority in its treatment of a person who posed no threat of any kind to the state.

On the front page of *Pravda* (8 January 1987) in an article bearing his name, the chairman of the USSR State Security Committee (KGB), Viktor Chebrikov, reported the following:

> In connection with the publication in *Pravda* on 4 January 1987 of the article "Crossing the Line" we report on the measures that have been taken by the USSR State Security Committee in regard to the officers of the Ukrainian SSR State Security Committee in the Voroshilovgrad region involved in violations of Soviet law in the case of the chief of the news bureau of the magazine "Soviet Miner," V. Berkhin.
>
> An inspection conducted earlier established that A. Dichenko, then head of a Ukrainian SSR KGB Directorate, in violation of the rules of criminal procedure, was instrumental in instigating his arrest. By his directives Dichenko involved several of his subordinates in the UKGB in illegal actions against V. Berkhin and other persons.
>
> For committing the above-mentioned actions, which have discredited the high calling of Soviet officers, Dichenko has been relieved of his duties and dismissed from the agencies of the KGB.
>
> The chairman of the Ukrainian SSR KGB is charged with taking disciplinary action against the other officials of the Ukrainian SSR KGB Directorate in the Voroshilovgrad region who committed illegal actions.
>
> Supplementary measures to ensure that the actions of the state security agencies are in strict conformity with the law are being taken by the USSR State Security Committee.

Actual prison conditions have also recently come under the scrutiny of glasnost. The journalist Olga Chaikovskaya wrote about this subject in *Literaturnaia Gazeta* (15 July 1987):

> The time has finally come to describe in print what pretrial detention centers are like and how they got that way. The cheery "statistics" of

past years, which show the crime level falling year after year, have fostered, among other ill effects, the conviction that in our country the construction of prisons (ones that measure up to current standards in technology and living conditions and that conform to our sense of justice) was unnecessary and in fact damaging to the country's prestige. As a result, a situation arose that reflects strangely on that very prestige: In the USSR, the pretrial detention centers are located, as a rule, in old buildings, some dating back to prerevolutionary times, that are nightmarishly cramped and unsanitary. I had an opportunity to see these cells, to hear stories about what goes on there, and also to hear of the cruel domination of hard-core criminals. To start with, the conditions themselves are degrading, making the preliminary confinement itself a punishment (and a harsh punishment, when it has no right to be a punishment at all: The people in pretrial detainment centers are innocent in the eyes of the law). If arrest—and arrest itself represents an exceptional law enforcement measure—is necessary, if the investigative agencies are forced to deprive a person of his/her freedom, then that deprivation should not be compounded by others: not by dirt, nor cramped conditions, nor foul air, nor taunting by hard-core criminals. I suspect that some investigators have a vested interest in such conditions of preliminary incarceration and that therefore they are in a hurry to arrest—for the normal person who finds himself in these circumstances for the first time is ready out of sheer desperation to make many concessions.

The situation in our correctional institutions is described in an interview given by Professor Aleksandr Iakovlev to *Ogonyok* (1987, no. 33):

Q: You have spoken of the terrible conditions in the prisons and camps during those years. But have things really improved now?

A: The conditions now are different, somewhat better. But not everywhere. It is awful that many people think that the conditions in places of incarceration should be bad, as bad as the crime for which a prisoner is doing time. . . . The criminal is deprived of his freedom— his punishment consists in that. The law did not condemn him either to unsanitary conditions, or to the degradations of overcrowding, or to the cold, or to cruel, humiliating treatment. To suggest that by tormenting the prisoner we will somehow reform him is naive at best. . . . These days we read in the papers about an ill-intentioned investigator here, an unscrupulous judge there. The impression is created that those working in the labor camps are all sensitive human beings with hearts of gold! We never read anything about them. We all agree that there should not be zones that are closed off to criticism. Nevertheless certain zones are still off limits to criticism. What, exactly, is there to hide in a Correctional Labor Colony (ITK)? What secrets are there? In my opinion, the press today cannot be limited to courtroom news and case reporting. We must go beyond that.

In articles and materials currently being published about illegal actions committed by the "guarantors" of the law, the theme that sounds as a constant refrain is the necessity of the defense lawyer's participation in the preliminary investigation. One cannot talk about the consistent realization of the constitutional right to defense under conditions where the agencies of investigation and prosecution use every means to hinder the defense lawyer's participation in the preliminary investigation and where such participation itself is stipulated by the discretionary permission of the public prosecutor. Cases where the right to an attorney's help is violated at the stage of the investigation where such help is compulsory are not infrequent. Moscow lawyer Henry Reznik wrote:

> It is customary, . . . in discussing what a lawyer does to begin with his participation in his capacity as the defender in criminal cases— that is the front line in the fight for legality, for justice. But the types of legal help rendered by lawyers to citizens range significantly wider than that. The lawyer can represent someone who has suffered at the hands of the legal system, act as an attorney to plaintiffs, defendants, and third parties in civil cases, act as a consultant, give advice, and represent citizens in administrative agencies and in social agencies. In each case he has only one task—to teach citizens and to help them, as V.I. Lenin wrote, to fight for their rights following all the rules of the fight for rights under the law.
>
> One of the features of the period of stagnation has been the individual's feeling of powerlessness before injustice, his sense of helplessness in the struggle for his legal interests. (*Moskovskaia Pravda*, 9 October 1987)

In the meantime, it is inappropriate to talk about legal defense as if it were to any degree an influential component of the Soviet legal system and of the mechanisms that safeguard legality. Despite its constitutionally secured status, the Soviet bar is singularly frustrated within the legal system. In no other developed country in the world is there such a low per capita number of lawyers as there is in our country. There are only about 25,000 lawyers for the entire country. By comparison, in the United States there are approximately 650,000, and in Great Britain and Italy—50,000 lawyers each. The population is almost completely deprived of adequate legal services. A well-known specialist in the area of criminal justice, Professor Valerii Savitskii, wrote in *Pravda* (22 March 1987) about the low status of the defense attorney:

The legal profession, which renders legal aid to citizens and organizations, is one of the most important elements of the legal system. Stepping up its work should prevent many violations of the law and should more fully protect the rights and interests of the people.

Of course, how effective the defense will be depends most of all on the political maturity of the cadres of the bar, on their high degree of professionalism, on their civic courage, and on their keenly developed sense of justice. All these qualities are absolutely essential for every lawyer. Yet factors exist that lie outside of the individual characteristics of the lawyer himself but that nevertheless have a certain influence on his conduct, on his, if you will, attitude when he sets about carrying out his difficult responsibilities.

These factors can be summed up in four words: an environment of mistrust. . . . The constitutional principle that guarantees the accused the right to a defense presupposes a relationship of trust between the lawyer and his client, without which there is no possibility of legal assistance. Such a relationship has been guaranteed by the establishment of a legal ban on the questioning of the lawyer as a witness about circumstances that became known to him in connection with the fulfillment of his duties as a defense attorney.

Clear enough, it would seem. But recently, cases have come to light of certain investigators who were nevertheless attempting to turn defense attorneys into witnesses and by this means to lock them out of participation in the case. Such incidents have occurred in Moscow, Uzbekistan, Georgia. They should give us pause. After all, what we are dealing with here is essentially a sophisticated method of getting rid of defense attorneys who demonstrate too much "tenacity" in calling attention to gaps, contradictions, and other deficiencies in the preliminary investigation. Not only does this method grossly contradict the law, it leads to the undermining of the trust relationship between a lawyer and his client; that is, it virtually discredits the whole institution of legal defense. . . . There is a danger that when the defense takes a more active role in the preliminary investigation, some investigators will respond just as actively in opposition. After all, even now when the rights of the accused are limited, there are cases of attempts to discredit lawyers who take an active role, to make them more obedient, to discourage them and their colleagues from criticizing the defects of an investigation publicly in the press. This is the only way to explain the seizure in the Moscow City Bar of the registration cards of certain attorneys covering many years of their work. Such a mass seizure has a narrow aim—by any means to find material compromising to this or that lawyer—for instance, to prove that he received an honorarium in excess of the fixed rate. The application of such pressure can cause even the most uncompromising lawyer to lose heart. As a result it is not just the lawyer who suffers; the attainment of the truth and the fairness of the verdict are threatened as well.

So What Do We Need to Change?

Today, all our hopes for the perestroika, democratization, and humanization of the legal system are primarily connected with glasnost. Only widespread opportunities for open, honest, impartial public discussion of the problems of justice and legality can hold the doors open for the process of perestroika in this sphere. There can be no critical rethinking of tendencies in the development of the legal system, of its institutional defects, or of the direct violations of its declared principles and norms without public access to information and free expression of opinion on any given problem. This topic was discussed in an account of the Plenary Session of the Supreme Court of the USSR published in *Literaturnaia Gazeta* (17 December 1986):

> Glasnost! That is what they talked about at the top of their voices at the Plenary Session. Public control over the work of all law enforcement agencies! Of the courts above all: After all, the principle of glasnost is one of the most important principles of legal procedure.
>
> But is it to everyone's liking, this very glasnost? Probably not to those accustomed to giving "important instructions. . . ." Nor to those who receive the instructions and are protected by important figures. Nor, for that matter, to the "extractors" [those who beat the confessions out of the accused]. . . . Under glasnost you would not "extract" anything: Everything will always be under the public scrutiny. Recently, a student scientific research laboratory of the All-Union Correspondence Juridical Institute, under the direction of Assistant Professor M.A. Fedotov, conducted a survey of the capital's judges. Only 65 percent of those polled thought that glasnost in court proceedings furthers the administration of justice, and that was in Moscow! Here is an even more shocking result: To the question, "Does the publication of materials about the workings of the court help increase the public's sense of justice?" less than half of those polled answered yes. Do these figures represent mere opinion? They represent, alas, behavior. It is these people who are upset by glasnost, who are unnerved by the presence of representatives of the press in the courtroom ("unnerved," "upset"—some judges answered, unashamed, in precisely this way).

Glasnost, criticism, and the truth upset not only judges but also some officers of law enforcement departments and certain bureaucrats in the ministries. The results of a poll published by *Izvestiia* (12 December 1987) are symptomatic: Only 26 percent of the employees of law enforcement agencies polled believed that critical statements published in a newspaper raise the level of responsibility in their departments.

The majority of these people—67 percent—thought that pieces criticizing law enforcement agencies undermine the authority of the justice system. The negative phenomena in the workings of the law enforcement agencies that we read about in today's press can only be overcome through fundamental legal reform. This opinion is shared by the majority of specialists and ordinary citizens.

Today, for the first time, we have begun to discuss the necessity of creating a genuine rule-of-law state where the law is the sole principal arbiter and is not dependent on anyone—neither on an individual, nor on a ministry, nor on the party apparatus. Academician Vladimir Kudriavtsev, director of the Institute of State and Law of the Academy of Sciences of the USSR, and his coworker at the Institute, Elena Lukasheva, discussed the problem of the socialist rule-of-law state in their article in *Kommunist* (1988, no. 11):

> The attempt to establish the principles of the rule-of-law state is encountering and will inevitably continue to encounter resistance: After all, it requires the shattering of the ideological stereotypes that have taken shape; the total rejection of administrative-command style methods of management; the overcoming of legal nihilism, voluntarism, and subjectivism. On the theoretical plane, a serious inertial role is played by the fact that Soviet juridical doctrine long considered the very idea of the rule-of-law state unacceptable, since it was first advanced during the period of the bourgeois-democratic revolutions. In reality, this kind of dogmatic approach was only a reflection of the negative attitude toward those universal human values that were formed during the 1,000-year development of humanistic thought and that are the sum total of the incredibly broad historical experience of the emergence of social progress, freedom, and human equality. . . .
>
> In evaluating the lessons of the past, we justifiably devote a great deal of attention to the psychological characteristics of Stalin, to the criminal methods employed by him and by those around him in their activities, and to their enormous historical guilt before the people. But it is no less important to answer the question: How was all this possible? Can the social system be totally dependent on the psychological traits of its leader? Should not it have reliable means of defense against abuses, arbitrariness, willfulness, uncontrolled behavior on the part of any officials or organs? As is well known, in his last articles V.I. Lenin persistently sought the political guarantees and organizational measures necessary for the attainment of this goal. He was not able to realize them at that time. . . .
>
> Today, in conducting the consistent democratization of all spheres of life and developing a system of popular socialist self-government, we should concentrate our efforts first of all on restoring respect for the law and on establishing and maintaining the principles of legality.

But we need to accomplish much more: to create new, permanently functioning political and legal mechanisms that would eliminate the very possibility of the deformation of socialist principles in the future and would guarantee the normal, crisis-free development of society. This requires new political-legal thinking that is subsequently put into practice. That is how the 19th Party Conference set the task. . . .

The creation of a socialist rule-of-law state presupposes the reduction of state power in society, its liberation from petty regulation and from the interference of state organs in the resolution of questions that various public organizations are fully capable of handling. In order to ensure genuine democracy [rule of the people], the state must be subordinate to society, become the exponent of its interests, and be guided in its legislative activity by the democratically expressed popular will. The development of the principles of self-government in economic and political life, the perestroika of the economic mechanism, and the guaranteeing of the independence of enterprises and the rights of workers' collectives are of greatest significance. . . .

Today, the establishment of the principles of a socialist rule-of-law state has been put forward as a major condition without which society cannot be liberated from everything that is connected with the consequences of the cult of personality, with the administrative-command style methods of government, with the alienation of the workers from power, with bureaucratism, with the deviation of party and state life from Leninist norms. Such liberation demands a decisive reconsideration of the prevailing ideas about the relationship between the state and the law and a rejection of the stereotypes that have accumulated in this area over decades. . . .

Over the course of many years, Soviet jurisprudence established the position that the state had unconditional primacy over the law, which was considered merely an instrument of state power. The apparatus became the "creator" of laws. This role became the province of the "leader" as well, who was, for example, designated the creator of the 1936 Constitution of the USSR. Hence also such everyday formulations as: The state "grants citizens" a broad range of rights; and the conviction that these rights are a sort of "gift" from the state to the people. Such expressions, at first glance entirely innocent, in fact ideologically increase the dependence of the people on the will of the lawgiver, who can, if he so desires, "give rights," but who can also limit them at his own discretion. Thus a paternalistic psychology was established that has deformed the people's sense of justice, wounded their dignity, and cultivated far from the best of human qualities. . . .

Relapses into such an approach have not yet been overcome. That is why the idea of a socialist rule-of-law state is not only the basis for determining the practical measures and principles of perestroika in the legal sphere, but is also a major moral and ideological landmark in the reorientation of the people's consciousness and in the actual establishment of their sovereignty, of their determining role in the activity of the state. . . .

The formation of a rule-of-law state requires the consistent implementation of a number of basic principles. First among them is the supremacy of the law in all spheres of social life. This is an inalienable feature of socialist civilization, the manifestation of real democracy and rule of the people. . . .

That the state itself and its organs are bound by the law is the second critical legal and moral-political principle characterizing the rule-of-law state. It consists in the fact that a state that has promulgated a law does not have the right to violate that law itself. This principle counteracts all forms of arbitrariness, willfulness, and all-permissiveness. . . .

The third principle of the rule-of-law state is that the freedom of the individual is inviolable and that his rights and interests, honor and dignity, are protected and guaranteed. Indeed, the law embodies the norm of freedom. . . .

In this connection the articles of the Criminal Codes about anti-Soviet agitation and propaganda need to be reformulated. Reform is needed in the legislation dealing with freedom of conscience and with entering and leaving the country. It is essential that a law be passed establishing procedures for public meetings and demonstrations. In supporting and developing a socialist pluralism of opinions and interests, the state must provide firm guarantees of their realization. The problems of developing and ensuring the collective rights of nations and nationalities, public organizations, including informal ones, and also the rights of workers' collectives deserve serious attention. . . .

The reciprocal responsibility of the state and the individual is the fourth principle of the rule-of-law state. It expresses the moral principles of the relationship between the state as the repository of political power and the citizen as a participant in its implementation. In taking on itself, through the promulgation of laws, concrete obligations to its citizens, to public organizations, to other states, and to the entire international community, the state must also define the legal measures pertaining to the responsibility of its official representatives for actions committed in the name of the state and its organs.

In the rule-of-law state the executive organs must be responsible to the legislative branch. This is now far from widely observed. For example, according to item 3, article 131 of the Constitution of the USSR, the Council of Ministers implements measures to guarantee and protect the rights and freedoms of citizens. In the entire history of its existence, however, the government has never made a report to the Supreme Soviet of the USSR about this most important effect of its activity. . . .

The rule-of-law state must have effective forms of control and supervision over the implementation of laws and other normative juridical enactments. That is its fifth principle.

A more radical—if it can be so described—point of view on the problem of the rule-of-law state, the prospects for its creation in our country, and the difficulties in its path was expressed by Professor Yegor Yakovlev in an interview in *Ogonyok* (1988, no. 43):

> Alas, when, at an earlier stage in history, we proclaimed class criteria to be the highest and, essentially, the only important ones, we swept away the foundation of universal human values. And so, with no foundation, we started to erect a huge building. . . .
>
> The appeal to the idea of the rule-of-law state in fact reflects the understanding that socialism—if it is true democratic socialism—should not be a house built on sand, nor a building suspended in the air with no foundation, but a superstructure built on the progressive elements of humanity's development as a whole, including the progressive elements of the development of bourgeois democracy. . . .
>
> The idea of the rule-of-law state today represents a radical upheaval in our conceptions of social development, of revolution. Yes, revolution is a repudiation of what has gone before, but a repudiation with the aim of reconstructing the economic and political structure of society on a higher, more perfect, more moral level.
>
> **Q:** What, in your view, are the main obstacles to the transformation of the Soviet Union into a rule-of-law state?
>
> **A:** I see two such obstacles. First, the Soviet person does not possess a sense of his own economic worth. Second, the real power in the economy does not belong to those who should have it.
>
> You were expecting something else from a legal expert? This is not a conversation about economics? Well, I will even call physics to my aid: The law of communicating vessels is in strict operation in relations between economics and the law. . . .
>
> After all, the point is not that everybody should have a lot of everything, not that each person should rake in as much as possible for himself. The point is that there should be a lot of everything all around—accessible to every person. Because an abundance of available goods, the opportunity to get any commodity or service at any time, to get it without any additional conditions or superfluous exertions, by legal means, paying for it with one's labor, that is, to buy it—such an opportunity gives rise to an extremely important sociopsychological phenomenon: the feeling of economic worth. Which is the basis of human dignity in general!
>
> I would not, by any means, necessarily buy all of it, would not necessarily "rake it in." But the consciousness that with the money I have honestly earned I can buy everything I please, the consciousness

that under no circumstances will I be forced to demean myself and beg, the consciousness that I have full economic rights, engenders a feeling of confidence, serenity, dignity. On the other hand, I can rake in enormous riches, but I still would not have a feeling of worth, economic or otherwise, if it has all been seized, acquired through connections, bought from distributors, taken "out the back door," furtively and nervously. . . .

These days you hear all the time: You are on a lease/hire contract, so be daring, after all you are free! That is nonsense! A tenant/lessee does not have freedom. What, does he buy the equipment, the fertilizer? No, the state farm either gives them or does not give them. The product that the lease/hire contractor produces—what, does he sell it? No, that product is taken from him at a price that was previously fixed. Let us harbor no illusions here—he is no independent commodity producer. It is time we finally understood: Only when the elementary economic right to dispose of what you have produced— not to hand it over but to sell it, and not to receive but to buy—only when this is an inalienable right of the commodity producers, when it cannot be taken away, only then will they in fact attain real economic freedom and become subjects enjoying full rights before the law, or more simply, masters of their own lives, without any ironic or judgmental quotation marks. . . .

I consider it essential to speak about one more hurdle on the path to the supremacy of the law. That is the passport system.

Our Soviet passport is a completely illegal thing. It has only one legal function—its role as an identity card. A photograph, year of birth, my signature, and the state seal certifying that I am who I am. There should be no other "data" in the passport—for example, *propiska* [permanent residence registration and the police permit to have it], a concept that is not translatable into any other language. But it exists, and I can find no legal grounds of any sort for this institution. . . .

Q: Since we have gotten started on the passport, we cannot avoid the "nationality" reference. In Europe, for example, it no longer exists anywhere except here and in Czechoslovakia.

A: It is quite right that it does not! Just because it says in my passport that I am Russian does not make me feel any more Russian. I consider myself Russian because such are my language and my culture. I feel a responsibility weighing on me, beginning from the time of Ivan Kalita; I hate the *oprichniki* [a kind of security force established by Tsar Ivan the Terrible], because they are my oprichniki. Do you understand? Nationality is a real category and an extremely vital one. But its reality lies in striving to identify oneself with one's national culture and to reproduce that culture in one's activities.

Thus, nationality has cultural and historical significance. But nationality has no administrative significance whatsoever! It should not have. . . .

I am categorically opposed to the "nationality" reference in the passport; I am categorically opposed to the "fifth item" in forms, from the personal form you fill out when being hired for a new job to the library card. That is, I am against this cultural-ethnic category being in the hands of the state. The category of ethnicity belongs to society, not to the state. We know what sort of state elevated nationality to the status of a state symbol. The national socialist state. . . .

It has long been drummed into us (and quite successfully) that without a passport we are not citizens. We are not even customers, nor hotel guests, nor vacationers, nor patients—we are nobody at all.

But am I really a Soviet citizen because I have a passport? Quite the contrary. I have a passport because I am a Soviet citizen. The proof of that is not the passport but the fact that I was born here and live here.

You see, before 1932 a Soviet citizen was a Soviet citizen simply because he was born here, but since 1932 he has been a Soviet citizen only because the state permitted him this and issued him a passport.

The primal right to citizenship was replaced by the state-sanctioned right to be a citizen.

But this substitution took place not just on paper—in the perverted, distorted formulations of the Statute on the Passport System. The substitution took place in our lives, in our consciousness. We, the Soviet people, lost a very important sort of feeling. The feeling that even without this whole stack of papers and "authorizing" documents—without this red booklet, and without the labor book, and without the wage and payments book—without anything, but simply as we are, "naked," uncorroborated by anything, we are still free people, citizens with full rights.

Unless that feeling is revived, you will not succeed in building a rule-of-law state.

Q: Does not that explain why for so many years in our country Soviet people have so often and so easily been deprived of citizenship? Well, because it is not a primal right but somehow a blessing bestowed by the state, a transitory reward for good, obedient conduct. You committed an offense—we will deprive you of our favor: He who gave can take away. . . .

A: You are right. In the United States only naturalized citizens—those who were not born in the United States but who came there and were granted citizenship by the state—can be deprived of their citizenship. But if you were born in the United States the authorities can never, under any circumstances, deprive you of your citizenship, for citizenship there is an innate right; it is a person's inalienable right; it is "god-given."

And another matter—we need a democratic procedure for depriving a person of his citizenship. Not a decision made privately, albeit "from above," lacking clear arguments, but an open, honest court examination. . . .

Q: On the question of criticism. It is clear that societal control over the actions of the state on all levels is a condition for the existence of a rule-of-law state and that, in turn, one of the key factors in such control is the free press. There has been a great deal of talk here about the corrupt press in the West, but what can we call our press during the years of stagnation? And even now who is unaware that in the editorial office the telephone is more important than the teletype? The only thing that matters is how "loud" it rings: at a district newspaper—from the district committee of the party; at a regional newspaper—from the regional committee. If the newspaper is an organ, let us say, of the Executive Committee, then it is the Executive Committee at the other end of the line. In my opinion, subordination and democratization are in conflict with each other here.

A: At the 19th Party Conference the editor in chief of *Pravda* expressed what was, in my view, a productive idea: The press could play the role of a socialist opposition. A mechanism for the realization of this idea was also suggested at the conference: the transformation of the newspapers from organs of the party committees into organs of the party organizations, with editorial boards elected by all the Communists in the party organization. Under this scenario, the editorial board receives true independence and the opportunity to objectively evaluate the activity, in particular, of its guiding organ. The proposal was not accepted, but I hope that the matter is not closed forever. . . .

Indeed, democracy is the worst method of government. If you do not count all the others. If you do not count Rashidovism and Brezhnevism, Stalinism and fascism. Humanity has yet to come up with anything better than democracy.

We have already had the iron order. There has already been a wise man who said that he knew better than all the rest what must be done and would undertake to lead the people to a bright future, having shut everyone else's eyes. . . . And he led them—across seas of blood, as if on dry land. He shut not just the others' eyes but their mouths as well. We already know where this road can lead when we submit and obey.

A genuine rule-of-law state, functioning according to the principles of constitutionalism, is inconceivable without constitutional review. Today, many people are coming to recognize the necessity of introducing this kind of institution to the Soviet Union. In an interview in *Pravda* (5 December 1987), the chairman of the Supreme Court of the USSR, Vladimir Terebilov, supported the idea of constitutional review:

Endowing the Supreme Court of the USSR with certain rights in the area of constitutional review seems both timely and useful. . . . In my opinion, it should be done so that the procurator's protests about the illegality of enforceable enactments are brought before the court. The VTsSPS [All-Union Central Trade Union Council] and certain organs of the republics, for example, should be granted the right to appeal to the court with a request that it rule on whether a given enforceable act, statute, resolution, instruction, etc., contradicts the Fundamentals of Legislation.

If the Supreme Court, or, for that matter, other courts as well, in the course of considering a case, comes to the conclusion that certain resolutions or legally binding acts were promulgated by ministries or agencies in contradiction to the law, and a citizen has been called to account for their violation, the court should have the right to deem that they contradict the law, which means they are invalid.

Here is an excerpt from a conversation between the journalist Iurii Feofanov and the well-known legal scholar Boris Topornin in *Izvestiia* (12 January 1987) in which Topornin proposes several variants for putting into practice the idea of constitutional supervision:

> Today, during this period of perestroika, the need to strengthen legality, and thus to increase the function of constitutional control, has become particularly pressing. But how are we to inscribe it into our state structure? There are several variants.
>
> The first is the creation of a special organ under the auspices of the Presidium of the Supreme Soviet of the USSR or of the Supreme Soviet directly. This organ—let us tentatively call it "the Constitutional Soviet"—prepares resolutions and presentations about the constitutionality of a given act, but the Presidium or the Supreme Soviet of the USSR makes the final decision.
>
> The second variant is the formation of an independent Constitutional Court of the USSR.
>
> The third variant is the assumption by the Supreme Court of the USSR of the function of constitutional control. This would entail, of course, certain changes to its structure and composition. The advantages would be that the decisions about the constitutionality of acts would be made by a legal organ observing established procedure. The Supreme Court would review the legality of administrative acts according to a representation made by the procurator's office, the VTsSPS, and a few other strictly limited organs.

But a host of questions remains. Why are only legally binding acts discussed, and not laws? Does a mechanism exist in our legal system for independently verifying the constitutionality of laws? Why should the implementation of the procedure of constitutional review be the prerogative of institutions and organizations—the procurator's office, the

VTsSPS, etc.? In fact, the model presented automatically deprives citizens of the opportunity to appeal to the court for constitutional protection.

The realization of constitutional review by the courts is inconceivable without guaranteeing the complete independence of the judiciary from influences of any sort, which is, in its turn, inconceivable without a clear-cut demarcation of the functions of state-political institutions—in other words, without the separation of powers. Certain authors are turning to the idea of separation of powers refracted through the prism of the Soviet state system. Here is what Nikolai Popov wrote on this score in *Sovetskaia Kul'tura* (28 January 1988):

> The clear-cut separation of the functions of party (political), state, and judicial powers is essential for the development of democracy today. Under conditions of the democratization of economic reform, of changes that are on the whole revolutionary in the life of our society, the independence of juridical organs, of judicial power, from the other organs of power and institutions is essential. This is in order to guarantee that innovators, experiments, searching, and risk taking are protected from the opposition and arbitrariness of people who aspire at any price to stop the reform process. Today, ways to perfect the practice of the courts are being discussed: the possible introduction of trial by jury, the improvement of the work of the procurator's office, changes to the Criminal Code. It is important that these changes be made in advance of the other reforms, since it is precisely legal fairness that can ensure the execution of new laws guaranteeing the security of the organizers of perestroika.
>
> The separation of powers is likewise in keeping with the general direction of the development of democracy and the greater independence of enterprises and of the public. The separation of powers must be accomplished vertically as well—in the direction of greater autonomy and independence for local government organs from the "center," from Moscow. In our country's statutes and legal codes, this or that government organ is identified, more often than not, as "independent" and, in the next breath, as subordinate to a superior level. Either one, or the other: If it is in fact subordinate, then in what ways specifically? Under these new conditions we need to examine anew what exactly democratic centralism is and how it accords with self-government. . . . The development of self-government and of the separation of powers is closely bound up with and dependent on the principle of the legitimacy, or legality, of power. Theoretically, all relations between citizens and the authorities, and especially all actions taken by officials, should be based on precisely regulated statutes, based in their turn on laws.

Corresponding member of the Academy of Sciences of the USSR Boris Topornin expressed the following views on the subject of the separation of powers (*Izvestiia*, 12 January 1988):

Today it is especially crucial that we address the points of departure for our theory—in particular, the strictly scientific understanding of the idea of separation of powers. It must be said that this idea, which was first expressed by Montesquieu and assumed the existence in the state of three "powers"—the legislative, executive, and judicial—has not infrequently been interpreted as an appeal for the coexistence of the "powers" of various political forces and classes, including those that are antagonistic. On these grounds, the door was, so to speak, slammed in its face. As a counterweight it was emphasized that the power in a socialist state must belong to the working people and cannot be shared with anyone. Such a reading of the idea of separation of powers is, however, a simplification.

It is true that the power in our country is united and indivisible, and the people realize their power through the system of soviets. Our parliament does not restrict its activities to legislation but also fulfills the functions of supreme administration and control. But does this really eliminate the need for a government? Although it appoints the Supreme Court of the USSR, the Supreme Soviet nevertheless is not itself engaged in the examination of legal matters. In short, the separation of "powers," or, to put it more precisely, of state functions, has been and remains one of the foundations of the constitutional system.

How can the independence of the courts be guaranteed in practice? Here is the opinion of journalist Aleksandr Bovin on that question (*Literaturnaia Gazeta*, 3 February 1988):

Guarantees are needed to protect the judge from having to stand at attention in private offices with double doors and massive desks; from instructions, advice, and recommendations that exceed the limits of the procedural code; from telephone calls conveying "opinions" and "commissions"; from all sorts of "comradely" requests and wishes; from all the conceivable pressures and influences, which in most cases are ostensibly justified by urgent state necessity but in actual fact are only due to the direct and undisguised arbitrariness of a local authority.

What might such guarantees be like? They say that we need a law to punish those who interfere in the activity of the courts. It may in fact be necessary. Although how such a law could begin to be implemented, I honestly do not know. After all, both the trouble and the problem consist in the fact that interference in the activity of the courts is usually informal in nature, which means that to prove it, much less to stop it by legal means, will prove extremely difficult.

Yet if we do not find and establish reliable guarantees, if we do not ensure that judges have independence that is genuine and not just a word in slogans and on paper, there will be no real justice either, no matter how much we improve and perfect the organization and workings of the legal organs themselves. Because a judge who can be pressured, a judge who can be called out on the carpet, is no longer a judge but just another local bureaucrat, obedient and tractable. The kind of bureaucrat who fixed things up for a lot of people for a long time and who today is still sorely missed by many. They hope that maybe all is still not lost, that somehow they will manage to preserve the kind of pliable judge they can keep in their pockets to serve their own interests.

In fact they will preserve him, they definitely will, if we do not ultimately find firm and reliable guarantees to ensure that judges possess real, authentic inviolability and independence.

Today, many proposals are being made to increase the number of people's assessors as a means of guaranteeing the independence of the court "from within." At the same time some people believe that the increase in the number of assessors should also result in the division of functions between them and the judges: The assessors would decide the "questions of fact" (for instance, is the defendant guilty or innocent?), while the judges would decide "questions of law" (the appropriate classification of the crime and the determination of the punishment). Trial by jury? Why not? Igor Petrukhin wrote in *Moskovskaia Pravda* (17 May 1987):

> The advantage of an increased number of assessors lies in the collegial decision-making process, in the many-sided discussion of the fundamental question, which is the raison d'être of the entire process: Is the accused guilty? What is needed to answer this question is not so much legal expertise as broad life experience and a sense of truth. The judge, without himself realizing it, incorporates "yardsticks" and "standards," formed by the legal practice. The people's assessors are not bound by "formalism," and can therefore take a fresh look at things. It is unlikely that the telephone calls and other requests, which are sometimes addressed to a judge by representatives of the local authorities, will be able to influence the assessors. The court of the people is more independent and just. Research has shown that assessors are more humane in fixing the degree of punishment. Consequently, increasing the number of people's assessors will promote the further democratization of our legal procedure.

In the expanded panel of assessors the principle of unanimity or of a qualified majority (let us say a 2/3 vote) should be used in deciding the question of the defendant's guilt. This would create a solid barrier against the conviction of those who are innocent. The defendant should have the right to object to the people's assessors if he has begun to doubt their ability to decide his case correctly.

"A Speech in Defense of the People's Assessors" was the title given to an article in *Ogonyok* (1987, no. 39) by A. Move, a lawyer and chairman of the Criminal Law and Procedure Section of the Moscow College of Advocates. He too defended the idea, still unusual today, of the independence and autonomy of the people's assessors:

In discussing the causes of miscarriages of justice, many legal experts point, not without reason, to the fact that a judge's independence can be violated by "local influences." But if the fate of the verdict were actually determined not by a professional judge alone but also by people's assessors, that would be an additional guarantee of the elimination of such occurrences. . . . The development of Soviet legal procedure, as of every other science, should not be based solely on our own experience but should also absorb everything that is valuable, useful, and progressive in the storehouse of world experience, bearing in mind that to reject does not simply mean to say no, that all rejection incorporates continuity. . . .

The people's assessors, people who have been made wise by their life experience, are called upon—without going into the legal technicalities, but as students of life and human beings—to understand the events of the case and the character of the person who has been brought before the court. Is the defendant guilty or innocent (yes, no); should he be recommended for mercy or not (yes, no); is it necessary that he be isolated from society or is there no need to deprive him of his freedom (yes, no)? That is a rough list of the questions that the people's assessors should decide at the trial. The judge, the professional legal expert, should cloak their decision in the appropriate judicial form—the legal verdict. Strictly speaking, this was always in fact the essence of trial by jury, which divides the court, in accordance with the various tasks facing its different members, into two completely separate and independent parts: the panel of jurors and the state judges.

A sweeping change in the status and role of members of the legal profession could also influence the state of legality and the protection of citizens' rights and legal interests in significant ways. But what is being proposed? In an article about the legal profession (*Pravda*, 22 March 1987), Professor Valerii Savitskii expressed the belief that:

Our attitude toward the very function of defense must be fundamentally altered. The court must consider the defense attorney and the procurator as parties enjoying equal rights, each trying to prove his case in an open, public process.

The slightest deviation from this most important principle distorts the nature of justice itself. There is nothing more demeaning to judicial honor than when one participant in the proceedings is treated roughly while the other is treated with deference. There is no obstacle on the road to truth more dangerous than when the court adopts an unequal attitude toward the applications and petitions of the parties, when opportunities for uncovering the truth are curtailed in the interests of personal sympathies and antipathies, and as a result the verdict becomes at best a reflection only of a half-truth. . . .

It seems that in all criminal cases the defense lawyer should have the right to participate in the process from the moment when the citizen is charged with an offense or from the moment of his arrest. This would make it impossible to exert any sort of psychological or physical influence on the accused to force him to give "necessary" testimony. Other illegal methods would likewise have the carpet pulled out from under them.

The matter, of course, does not consist solely in permitting the lawyer to participate at the very earliest stage of the criminal investigation. The task at hand—currently being discussed on the pages of the press— is to radically raise the status of the bar as a whole: to unite the uncoordinated colleges of lawyers under the aegis of one organization encompassing all the republics—a Union of Lawyers; to impose no limits on the colleges in their determination of their own numbers; to protect them from overzealous bureaucratic administration on the part of the Ministry of Justice; to change the system by which lawyers are remunerated for their work; to give the lawyer the right to collect evidence independently while putting together his defense in criminal cases.

The weekly *Nedelia* recently published a selection of letters from readers who spoke out on the subject of the problems of the legal profession (1987, no. 22). Here is an excerpt that reveals an increasingly widespread point of view:

> I vote for the unconditional expansion of the "corpus" of lawyers and of the legal advice network until for every 200–300 (or at least 1,000) inhabitants, we have one lawyer. I vote for a permanent agreement with a "family" lawyer on whose fee no limitations would be placed. I vote for the expansion of the lawyer's rights, for his participation in all investigatory activities. That is just as essential as the lawyer's participation in the trial itself. Giving the lawyer access to the investigation will raise the prestige both of the employees of the

investigative agencies and of the court. It will eliminate complaints by the accused—both well-founded and groundless—of "psychological coercion," "unlawful methods of conducting the investigation," and so forth.

A. Petrushin,
Deputy Procurator of the Lenin District,
Moscow

Preparation of new criminal legislation has begun in our country. The directions and principles of the impending reform of criminal law can be discerned from the pieces dealing with the subject that appear periodically on the pages of our press. The newspaper *Moskovskie Novosti* (23 August 1987) carried an interesting interview on the subject of the reform with Doctor of Juridical Science Sofia Kelina:

Q: What stage is the work at now?

A: I will not take it upon myself to say how much time remains before the work will be complete. There are statutes that are adopted relatively easily, while others provoke long and stormy debates.

Q: You dot the final "i" and cross the final "t." Then what?

A: Our proposals will have to undergo approval in all the various departments. The practical workers in the provinces will become familiar with them. Then we propose to publish them. After that, there will be discussion, and at that point they will also be examined by the Commission on Legislative Proposals of the Supreme Soviet. A session of the Supreme Soviet is empowered by law to approve the Fundamentals of Criminal Legislation of the USSR and the Republics.

Q: It used to be thought that we had neither drug addiction, nor prostitution. We lived "without problems," and the question of criminal liability did not come up. How can you punish something that does not exist? . . . But now persistent demands are being heard for the introduction of criminal liability for prostitution and the use of narcotics.

A: Some legal experts are voicing these suggestions as well. That, in my opinion, does not speak well of them.

What does it mean to introduce criminal liability, for example for prostitution? Questions of a technical nature arise immediately: How can you prove it? Who will testify? One can make jokes about this subject, but it is a more serious matter than it seems at first glance. The extraordinary difficulty in proving the charge means that it is only punished selectively: some are brought to trial, others are not. The selective enforcement of the law amounts to arbitrariness.

However, even that is not the main point. Is immorality subject to jurisdiction? Should the laws of morality be lumped together with criminal laws? . . . So what is this, we should not fight prostitution!? We should. But without the participation of a judge. We are in fact proposing not to introduce criminal liability for prostitution. But of course we should punish those who keep the houses and who coerce others into prostitution.

I also think that we should not introduce criminal liability for the use of narcotics. That would have the most harmful consequences! People will be afraid to get medical treatment. A blind wall will grow up between drug abusers and those who can help them.

Furthermore, we are proposing to repeal the article dealing with homosexuality, leaving only coercive sodomy criminally prosecutable. . . .

Q: Are any sort of changes being proposed in the articles of the criminal code dealing with "dissidents"?

A: If you have in mind article 70 of the Criminal Code of the RSFSR concerning agitation and propaganda aimed at undermining and weakening the Soviet regime, then, in my view, it should definitely remain. The state has the right to self-defense. But in 1966, article 190.1 was introduced, making punishable the dissemination of fabrications known to be false, that are defamatory to the Soviet system. This includes both anecdotes and conversations that have no anti-Soviet intent nor the aim of undermining or weakening the system. This article seems excessive.

The question of the level of severity of criminal repression in light of the plans for reform of the Criminal Code was touched on in Aleksandr Iakovlev's discussion with a correspondent from *Ogonyok* (1987, no. 33):

Many people sincerely believe that the harsher the punishment, the lower the crime rate. An illusion! . . .

Excessively severe punishment provokes [criminals] to continue breaking the law; it spurs them on to more brutal crimes. When in the 1960s, under pressure from the public, the death penalty was introduced for rape, the concern was not, of course, for the criminal, but for the victim. But in reality in many cases this leads to a second crime—murder.

It seems to me that the demand for tougher laws is explained in part by ignorance of the true state of affairs: ignorance of the fact that we already have an extremely severe criminal code.

The death penalty has been completely repealed in the majority of developed countries, and the death penalty for economic crimes is already entirely our own "achievement." I am convinced that despite all the repulsiveness and gravity of, for example, embezzlement, one cannot equate a human life with any sum of money, no matter how enormous. Such an operation literally puts a price on life. Does this heighten respect for human life in the public consciousness?

On the whole, the death penalty somehow legitimizes murder, somehow lets murder in, allows it to enter into our morality. "Aha, that means it is okay in an exceptional case," the thought creeps into someone's consciousness, and there begins the independent determination of what constitutes an exceptional case. Human life is sacred, and nobody—not even the state—should have the right to take it away. . . .

Scholars are now proposing to change criminal legislation in the following manner. First, by applying punishments other than imprisonment more broadly; second, by reducing the maximum term of imprisonment—in the case of minors to seven years; third, by sending convicts to colony-settlements—where there is a certain latitude for making at least some sorts of domestic and economic decisions for at least some, if only a small, choice in their relations—not just for unpremeditated crimes but also for premeditated but minor offenses. . . .

To exaggerate the role of violence, injunction, and restriction is to show a simultaneous disdain for constructive changes. In my opinion, we have already paid dearly for such disdain. In staking everything on punishment, we unwittingly—or wittingly—deflect the attention and efforts of society from the perestroika of its very life.

In our press today the question of the implementation of the death penalty is being widely debated. On 19 April 1987, for instance, *Moskovskie Novosti* published an article by the writer V. Kardin in which he expressed his unconditional support for the repeal of the supreme penalty:

Human life is sacred only when no one dares to make an attempt upon it in neither word nor deed, when premeditated violent death is eliminated from practice and from intention, legitimized murder—the death penalty—is eliminated as well. . . . The perestroika which has begun of our consciousness and our economy is called upon to satisfy the moral and spiritual needs of the people, by whose enthusiasm and labor it is being realized. Its goal is the true elevation of the "simple person." The eyes of the planet are upon us. It is not for effect that we have today declared that the highest human right is the right to life. The repeal of the death penalty would serve as yet another weighty confirmation of the program of the most perfect system of life on earth.

Here are some lines from a letter written by Boris Lesniak to the *Moskovskie Novosti* (26 July 1987) in which he too speaks out against the death penalty:

The question of the implementation or non-implementation of execution as the highest method of social protection is, to my way of thinking, a partial question. One must talk about the entire judicial-legal system functioning in our country. This question is indissolubly connected with glasnost and the democratization of society, with its awakening from apathy and indifference. . . .

I think that a still so imperfect system of justice cannot be entrusted with such a sharp instrument as the death penalty. We cannot be certain that it will always be used in an entirely responsible manner.

Others, however, come out in favor of preserving the death penalty and of increasing the severity of legal measures in general—in the name of "law and order." Nostalgia for a strong authoritarian power and a rejection of the free expression of opinion splash over onto the pages of the press. Space is given to them; points of view should be compared. But how much Neanderthal conservatism there is in some points of view.

A. Konogov, assistant superintendent of a factory workshop of a large enterprise and secretary of the party bureau of the workshop, ended his article "We Need the Whip," published in *Moskovskaia Pravda* (2 September 1987) thus:

I am no fan of Stalin's. I believe that he caused people a lot of grief. But we had order under him, and how! Why? People were afraid. They knew: if you mess up your work—you will be taken to court. Today too we need to punish, to punish mercilessly, in order to teach others. As the saying goes, it is better to shoot one man, so that the whole regiment can fight normally.

Konogov's opinions were echoed by a like-minded thinker (*Moskovskaia Pravda*, 30 September 1987):

The author of the article "We Need the Whip" is perfectly correct in his warning that we can go too far. But I want to add that the game of democracy and glasnost that is now in high gear is advantageous not just to let slackers and ne'er-do-wells, as A. Konogov writes. That is not so very serious. Just take a look at what is happening now. In our country they have begun to organize open, virtually anti-Soviet public meetings and various assemblages; groups have appeared. The West, like an infection, has burst onto the television and the stage, where with its hoarse voices, its affectations and untidy clothing, it has overshadowed everything good and talented. We do not need this kind of "democracy" because it leads to pernicious consequences and the corruption of our young people. A. Konogov said it right: It is essential to institute the strictest discipline before it is too late.

E. Ivanov,
Member of the CPSU since 1954

Fortunately, however, the tone of the current discussions and plans for reform of the legal system is set by those who believe that the progress of our society must follow the path of the successive democratization of our country. Progress cannot be attained by punitive impulses.

On the tenth anniversary of the 1977 Constitution of the USSR the newspaper *Sovetskaia Rossiia* (7 October 1987) published an interview with the Academician Vladimir Kudriavtsev. The scholar declared:

> I believe that the constitution of 1977 as a whole created the essential preconditions for the further socioeconomic and political development of the country. But not everything was realized at that time. A number of progressive factors that were put in the constitution remained "on ice" for many years. The braking mechanism was at work. It is not enough to proclaim this or that political freedom, to create a legal institution. It is necessary to guarantee their fulfillment.
> . . .
> The sphere of juridical activity is the [sphere] most in need of democratization, of effective control on the part of society. Without this the strengthening of legality is inconceivable. How can democratization be realized here? It demands thorough study. . . .
> The edifice of justice is still under construction! Thus, during the preparation for the recent elections of judges and assessors by the workers, approximately 20,000 critical remarks and suggestions were made. We see that it is necessary to increase the number of people's assessors at complex trials. Or yet another question—with what can we oppose the arbitrariness of some administrative employees? With a generally high standard of legal understanding among the population! A zealous old boy breaks into an apartment without any legal grounds, or demands a passport on the street, and the person does not even know that he does not have to let him into the apartment and that he is not always required to present his documents. . . . There can be no excess of democracy. If the people are the source of power, then their free will in fact determines the level of democratization that they need at any given time. So this is a lively process, and to a certain degree changeable as well, reflecting the mood of the masses.
> . . .
> The people will not give up perestroika. There is no road back.

We do not want the reader to form the false impression that in our movement toward a rule-of-law state, toward a democratic system of justice and the guaranteed protection of inalienable individual rights, everything is proceeding smoothly and swimmingly. To begin with, the arguments and discussions themselves have still only just begun, and it is difficult, in advance, to be 100 percent sure which point of view will gain the upper hand. The belief in a "strong authority," which by virtue of its status is endowed with the right to punish and pardon, is implanted in the depths of our consciousness, of our psychology, of our political culture. Moreover, even a great many of those who are most inclined to the spirit of reform very often fail to thoroughly think through the logic of their reformism in the area of the justice system.

This was particularly evident during the debates on the drafting of the new Constitution of the USSR that took place in the fall of 1988. Many people preferred to remain passive observers. Others, including well-known legal experts, made critical observations (which were later partially taken into account) and expressed regret that their opinions were not taken into consideration beforehand. Doubts were expressed in particular about the degree of centralization and concentration of power that was proposed in the new constitution. But few people raised the question of what institutionalized guarantees can ensure this very constitutionalism and legality. In other words, from the proclamation of the idea of the primacy of the law to the real creation of a rule-of-law state, we still have a considerable road to travel. Open, public discussions, arguments, and clashes of various points of view are the essential condition for that.

FIVE

An Economy at the Crossroads

During one of his numerous interviews, Academy of Sciences member Abel Aganbegyan, "the father of economic perestroika," related the following incident:

> Once I was invited to a very serious meeting, at which a highly placed colleague (I won't name him, as he has since been relieved of his post) was addressing a group of economists. He began to lecture at them, sharply criticizing Hungary and that country's experience: "Do you have any idea of what they've come to? Any person can buy anything he wants in a store. Do you have any idea of what this will lead to?" At this point Academician A. Arbatov could no longer contain himself and interjected: "Well, what will it lead to? After all, that is socialism—when any person who has the money can buy what he wants. As long as that money has been earned by honest work . . ." You can imagine what followed!

This incident illustrates a particular economic ideology that developed over many years in our country: an ideology in which socialism was understood to mean chronic shortages and the administrative distribution of goods. That view has left its mark on all other societal relations and forms the basis for a certain model of consumption—a model that some have called the "socialism of shortage." It is precisely for this reason that economic problems are at the core of perestroika and will ultimately decide its fate.

Serious difficulties, however, stand in the way of real economic reform. To permit the screening of a film that was "languishing on the shelf" just yesterday, or to publish a novel that five years ago provoked outrage among adherents of ideological purity, requires courage and resolve.

But to tinker with the economy—to introduce genuine economic accountability not only for individual enterprises but for whole industries as well—is a complex and protracted affair: much more so than the publication of *Children of the Arbat* or the poetry of Joseph Brodsky. Economic reform involves changing the lives of millions of people. Furthermore, the rejection of dogma is significantly more difficult in the economic than in the cultural sphere, if only because the professional perpetrators of economic dogma are far more numerous.

It is therefore not surprising that changes in intellectual and cultural life are far more perceptible today than changes in the economic structure. Radical changes in the character, organization, and remuneration of labor still remain only a prospect. The consumer market, with minor exceptions, remains unchanged; the production of consumer goods grows slowly. Thus, the editorial departments of newspapers and magazines receive many letters whose authors complain bitterly that perestroika is skirting the heart of the matter, particularly in the economic sphere, that it dies out as it moves down the hierarchy from the "centers." In intellectual and cultural life, breadth and diversity of discussion are in themselves important goals. In the economic sphere, however, people expect debates to produce a direct, concrete, practical result: a clear-cut and economically workable strategy for restructuring the national economy. People expect not isolated, specific experimentation but an attack along the entire front.

We Speak About Our Difficulties and Problems

When the negative aspects of our national economy are discussed, those most often cited are the notorious performance indicators, which focus almost exclusively on "gross output" (*val*); the low quality of the goods we produce; the deficient price system; the slow adaptation of new and progressive technology; and the excessive expenditure of energy, raw materials, and labor (per unit of production) in comparison with that of Western countries. What is most surprising is that by the late 1920s and the 1930s, competent economists were already concerned about our unwarranted squandering of resources and the tendency to evaluate an enterprise's performance in terms of the value of the production it yielded. But many decades have passed and we see that *val* is alive and well. Our production methods remain wasteful and we still have a low level of efficiency. In computerization of the national economy and in scientific and technical progress we are far from the requirements of the age. And there is no need even to mention the quality of the goods we produce. What are the sources of our poor economic performance? Aganbegyan offered one answer to this question in his interview in the weekly *Ogonyok* (1987, no. 29):

> Our primary misfortune has been that we have tried for such a long time to preserve the old economic mechanisms. Those mechanisms served a specific function in other historical circumstances, when our industrial economy was being created. But those mechanisms have proved entirely unsuitable to new conditions. These economic mechanisms not only fail to help solve the new problems associated with a new environment, they impede such a solution. . . . It is not easy to change, because everything in the economy is interconnected. . . . This situation has been criticized, and justifiably, for years, decades. . . . But nothing has changed because the existing economic system is, in its own way, logical. It is based on administrative methods, and this principle is very consistently maintained. How is the work of the various economic organizations in our country planned? First, each of them has many directive tasks from above. They disaggregate assignments from above concerning the output of a whole range of products. Second, they also "release" resources from above: so many machine tools, so many chairs, so many typewriters, and so forth. Everything is noted down in great detail. And an application for these resources must be made a year and a half in advance of when they will begin to "fill your order." Third, under such a system every step is regulated. Tens of thousands of norms determine what can and can't be done by whim.

According to Aganbegyan, such a rigid bureacratic system of management has had many negative consequences. To make life more comfortable, officials padded capital and resource demands. In some places resources were amassed in unreasonable quantities. In other places serious shortages were experienced, resulting in still further efforts to create reserves as "insurance." The psychology of hoarding "in case of dire need" has led to a situation where total reserves of various types of raw goods and materials have reached huge proportions—estimated at 460 million rubles. In fact, however, these economic reserves of resources and materials represent dead capital, a tremendous economic loss.

> A similar picture—the loss of capital—has occurred here with capital goods. Our stock of machine tools exceeds that of the United States by more than two to one. But what is the point of all these machine tools if the coefficient of the average machine shift is hardly more than one? On our construction sites cranes and machinery stand idle. Road freight transport is greatly underutilized. . . . Tens, hundreds of millions of rubles are spent on the production of these machine tools,

machines, and equipment, but they have not had the anticipated effect. Somewhere, at some time, someone calculated what kinds of supplies were needed, in what quantity, distributed to whom. And when everything that had been so painstakingly divided up reached its destination, it turned out that there, at the site, they could not fully utilize them. Idleness and underutilization characterize every sector of capital goods use.

Many Soviet economists agree that our greatest misfortune is the dictate of the producer over the consumer. Take whatever is given you; otherwise you won't get anything at all: There you have the philosophy of the economic interrelations between enterprises and economic organizations. And enterprises are forced to take that which they don't need. After all, they're not going to be given anything else. This corrupts the producer, deprives consumers of their rights, stifles the desire to display initiative, and ultimately leads to great material losses in the national economy.

All past attempts to form a realistic assessment of our condition have ended in failure. It is sufficient to recall the fate of the economic decisions of the 20th Party Congress. Subsequent attempts at economic reform during the 1960s and 1970s met with the same fate. Over the course of more than thirty years, the process of reform of socialist society either did not develop at all or developed with unbelievable sluggishness. In Aganbegyan's view, it was because these efforts and decrees were:

palliatives, half-measures, miniscule improvements that did not guarantee a complete and fundamental solution to the problems facing our national economy. And the economy is the kind of force that can strangle and nullify any attempts that are based on incomprehensive, inconsequential measures.

These earlier efforts at reform also failed because they focused on separate, narrow sections of economic activity, leaving related issues unresolved. This is the explanation offered by Professor V. Dashichev, head of a division of the Institute of the Economy of the World Socialist System. He wrote in *Moskovskaia Pravda* (16 July 1987) that:

A return to the Leninist idea of cost accounting is unthinkable without destroying the old system of price formation. Expansion of the independence of enterprises would be futile without a fundamental reform of the system of supply and the introduction of optimal trade in spare parts, machines, equipment, and materials.

At present, continued Dashichev, perestroika encompasses literally all spheres of Soviet society. Economic reform will entail a sharp increase in independence for enterprises and a fundamental restructuring of centralized management. It will entail the reform of planning, price formation, and financial-credit mechanisms. Reform will also involve a switch to optimal trade in the means of production and a restructuring of the administration of scientific-technological progress. These changes involve a profound democratization of economic processes and procedures for making economic decisions. Enterprises are becoming independent and responsible actors in the economy, while previously they were primarily objects of the activity of higher organs.

> In this new way, the center of gravity of social activism is being decisively shifted directly into the productive sphere. The role of production collectives and [the role of] the individual are being fundamentally changed. Broad prerequisites for the elimination of one of the major defects of the old economic system—the alienation of the direct producer from the means of production—are being created. . . . The economy, founded on principles of strict centralization from above, most resembled some gigantic war machine with its battalions, regiments, divisions, and armies—the enterprises, unions, ministries, committees, and chief committees, with the figure of the commander in chief towering over all. Everything was subordinated to the fulfillment of the plan-command. But a society can't live and work by the laws of an army. . . . The individual in socialist society must feel himself not as a nonparticipating and indifferent fulfiller of an alien will but as an interested, responsible, and active master of production.

The majority of Soviet economists argue, with some slight disagreements, that the centralized system departed from Lenin's idea of self-management by workers. It lacked healthy material incentives to motivate workers, and it discouraged them from showing initiative, enterprise, and innovation. Economic responsibility certainly did not fit into it. Administrative centralization radically distorted the Leninist plan for cooperatives. Forced labor, total subjugation to the government, and submission to orders from above replaced the principle of voluntary participation and independence. It is difficult to believe that just a few decades ago, Soviet peasants were, as in olden times, bound to a particular area of land and received little or nothing for their labor on collective farms.

This kind of economic system was extensive and expenditure-heavy by nature. It permitted successes and breakthroughs only in narrow sectors where centralization made it possible to concentrate huge resources at the expense of other sectors of the national economy. According to Dashichev, Stalin's personal ambitions exerted the strongest influence on the formation of the administrative-command economic system.

> He placed personal power above all else. The psychology of centralism from above, despite the fact that it was by nature alien, even hostile to socialism, could not have fit in better with Stalin's interests and ideas about state management. This psychology permeated deeply into the very pores of society. . . .
> Although in the late 1950s signs of the failures of the economic system appeared, accompanied by a growing realization of the need for deep-seated transformations, the system continued to perpetuate itself and to grow in strength. The unproductive bureaucracy had grown to unprecedented dimensions. The bureaucratic fetters and petty regulations from above literally bound society. A situation had been created in which the development of our productive forces was being artificially contained. It is only thanks to our country's enormous resources that our economy was able to stay afloat.

Defenders of the old system do not want to ask themselves a simple question: Why has a country that is without equal in the world in its natural resources turned into a country of chronic shortages? Why do we have one of the lowest standards of living in Europe? This grave problem would seem to demand serious attention. But no, apologists continued to believe blindly in the old managerial mechanism. They refused to comprehend that it no longer served the interests of socialism and even threatened the governing position of the Communist party.

Writing on these problems in *Moskovskaia Pravda* (7 May 1987), Anatolii Butenko, a professor at Moscow State University, expressed the opinion that perestroika is progressing more slowly than is desirable because it is encountering obstacles that were not foreseen or were not fully exposed. Therefore, he considers a critical analysis of the entire development of socialism indispensable. Butenko believes that we cannot solve the problems of today and the future until we have an exact and complete picture of past mistakes and shortcomings.

> I would point to three factors that were not previously included in the party's documents. First, there was no recognition that indicators of a crisis within Soviet society were developing. This is important to establish, because it allows us to analyze the mistakes and shortcomings of the past more thoroughly and to draw the necessary conclusions.
> Second, serious shortcomings developed in the functioning of the institutions of socialist democracy, in political and theoretical prin-

ciples that are obsolete and at times don't even correspond to reality, and in the conservative management mechanism. All of this has acted as a brake on economic development and has been conducive to the growth of a crisis phenomenon.

Third, many of the mistakes of the past, as well as the braking mechanism that has taken hold, are directly tied to phenomena of the 30s and 40s and to Stalin's cult of personality.

In rethinking the various aspects of Soviet socialist management, we find that much was not done according to the socialist method; that is, according to socialist principles, norms, and mechanisms.

The braking mechanism took shape out of economic, political, social, and ideological forms, phenomena, means of control, and devices that prevented the full expansion of the possibilities of socialism, and checked the successful utilization of its advantages. Mistaken theoretical concepts, such as the psychology of idleness contributed to this braking mechanism.

Professor Butenko concluded his analysis thus:

I believe that this is what Marx, Engels, and Lenin warned about, a warning subsequently ignored in an oversimplified understanding of the building of socialism: Bureaucracy poses an enormous threat to the working class that has come to power. The founders of scientific socialism explained this by saying that at a certain stage in the transition from the old society to the new working class, the state will become essential. And the state, along with its organs, has a tendency gradually to become more and more estranged from society, to become an ever more independent force, threatening to place its own interests above those of society. For this reason Marx and Engels stressed: In order to protect the working class against such a danger, it is necessary from the very first to attract the workers to management, to develop their ability to govern themselves. This is the only way to create a counterweight to the formation of a bureaucratic state system.

In Search of a Strategy for Economic Change

Considerable consensus exists in discussions about the poor condition of the economy, but there is nevertheless great controversy over how to go about restructuring it. Virtually all believe that the economy must be changed, but in what way? Some propose radical recipes for all-encompassing economic restructuring; others limit themselves to proposals for specific changes. Yet a third group advises that the structure be left as it is but that the screws on workers be tightened so that people will work "as they did under Stalin." There is only one common theme inherent in all these proposals—that the economy, no matter how it is to be restructured, remain socialist.

It is appropriate to open discussion with a quote from Professor Nikolai Shmelev, who, in a widely discussed article, "Payments and Debts" (*Novyi Mir,* 1987, no. 6), proposed a logical system for the restructuring of the economy. This article provoked a tremendous response and became the subject of numerous and at times bitter discussions. Even Mikhail Gorbachev, in one of his meetings with the residents of Moscow, referred to it. Shmelev's views are captured in the following excerpt:

> No one is satisfied with the condition of our economy. Its two central built-in defects—the monopoly of the producer in a situation of general deficit and the uninterestedness of enterprises in scientific-technical progress—are undoubtedly clear to everyone. But how to rid the economy of these defects, what to do not in theory but in practice—I am certain that today there are no sages from above or from below who would assert that they completely know the appropriate formula. We now have many more questions than answers. We still have a lot to talk about, to argue, to propose, and to reject before we can discover the answers we need.
>
> The basic reasons for the clogs and slowed blood circulation in the country's economy are already apparent. The principle of "from *prod-razverstka* to *prodnalog*" has been put forward, signifying that administrative methods of management should be replaced by economic and financial incentives and policies. One could say that the path to common sense, at least on the ideal-theoretical level, has come to light. It is evident, however, that a restructuring on the scale we desire cannot be realized in one stroke.

We must acknowledge that the rejection of Lenin's New Economic Policy (NEP) drastically complicated socialist construction in the USSR. If we do not acknowledge this, we will condemn ourselves to halfway measures as we did in 1953 and in 1965; and a partial approach, as is well known, is often worse than inactivity. NEP, with its economic incentives and policy tools, was replaced by an administrative system of management. Such a system by its very nature was not capable of improving the quality of production or of raising productive efficiency, or of achieving the best results at the lowest cost. It assured the necessary quantity of *val* (gross output), not in agreement with objective economic laws but in spite of them. Achieving gross output in spite of sound economic laws resulted in unbelievably high losses in material resources, and more important, in human resources.

In order to inspire faith in economic recovery there must be success in the very near future, palpable and evident signs of an improvement in life. Above all, the market must be saturated with goods as soon as possible. This is not a simple matter, but with the necessary decisiveness it is possible. It is possible, however, only by way of "cost-accounting socialism," through the development of the market itself.

Consistent cost accounting does not require significant capital expenditures. All that is needed is boldness, firmness, and consistency in freeing internal economic forces. What hinders this? Above all, ideological overcautiousness, fears that we will let the evil genie of capitalism out of the bottle.

When speaking about the probable strengthening of spontaneous phenomena, one must take into account what our own economic experience has shown us. It is no secret now that efforts to exercise 100 percent control over everything have led to such spontaneity, to such lack of control, that by comparison anarchy would look like the essence of order. Elements of spontaneity will be unavoidable and in practice will be a minimal price for progress, for the revitalization of the economy. According to Shmelev:

> Things must be called by their proper names: stupidity—stupidity; incompetence—incompetence, vestiges of Stalinism—vestiges of Stalinism. Life requires that everything be done in order that our food market will be assured in the near future. Otherwise, all calculations based on the activization of the human factor will hang in midair; people will not respond. We should abandon our ideological childishness, which exists, to be honest, only in newspaper fairy-tale lead articles. People are stealing and enriching themselves more through this childishness than ever before. How much better it would be if those who desire to and can give society real products and services, real values, were to flourish. Only when we solve the task of securing daily bread, and not before, can we then decide how the large profits of the most hardworking and enterprising entrepreneurs can be prevented from leading to the formation of threatening capital. There are simple, effective means for doing this—taxes and the corresponding powers of the financial inspector (in measure and reason, of course, so as not to kill the goose that is just beginning to lay the golden eggs, which benefit everyone).

To those who worry that such economic reforms could lead to the emergence of unemployment in our country, Shmelev responded:

First, natural unemployment among people looking for or changing
their place of work already exists, although at any given time it is
less than 2 percent of the work force; the inclusion of unregistered
transients probably raises the figure to 3 percent. It is one thing to
discuss the problem, acting as if we have no unemployment, and it
is a completely different thing to surrender oneself placidly to the
idea that some level of unemployment exists and is inevitable. Second,
there are millions of unfilled and continually emerging new job
positions. With proper turnover, the level of temporary unemployment
may be estimated at 1 million. Naturally, this requires considerable
additional efforts by the state to retrain the freed work force, to transfer
it to other branches and regions, to stimulate organized migration,
and so forth. Third, we should not close our eyes to the economic
harm caused by our parasitic certainty of guaranteed work. It seems
clear to all today that we should be very concerned about loafing,
drunkenness, and bad workmanship. We must fearlessly and assidu-
ously discuss what a relatively small reserve army of labor may give
us, of course without the state surrendering itself completely to the
will of fate.

This discussion about the replacement of administrative compulsion
is a profoundly economic one. The real dangers of losing one's job,
going on temporary assistance, or being obliged to work where one is
sent are fairly good prescriptions for curing laziness, drunkenness, and
irresponsibility. Many experts believe that it would be cheaper to pay
such temporarily unemployed workers adequate assistance for a period
of several months than to retain a mass of brazen good-for-nothings
who could obstruct any economic accountability, any effort to raise the
quality and effectiveness of social labor.

Criticizing the conventional Soviet emphasis on quantitative output,
Shmelev argued instead for a more efficient use of existing resources:

Still greater possibilities for economic progress lay in the modern-
ization and rational use of the technology that we already possess.
We produce almost twice the amount of metal that the United States
does, and we do not need any more; we need another type of metal,
of another quality. We do not need more energy: Our national energy
capacity is almost one and a half times higher than that of the majority
of Western countries. But the introduction of advanced energy-saving
technology gives the same effect, but at a cost three to four times
cheaper than drilling for new gas wells. We do not need new areas
under forestation. Today we use, on average, only 30 percent of available
wood, but in the United States, Canada, and Sweden, the level of
utilization of raw materials in the forest industry is more than 95
percent. We do not need more water; we do not need any more river

diversions: We need to stop the waste and terrible losses of water allowed by current irrigational systems. In certain estimations, these losses make up 75 percent in total. We do not need to import grain and, consequently, to export gas in such quantities: The import of grain is actually equal to yearly losses in our own harvest. We do not need more tractors; we produce them in numbers six to seven times that of the United States: We need to ensure that our already existing stock of tractors works and not to let almost every other new tractor stand idle due to lack of spare parts. We do not need more machine tools; we have almost two and a half times more than the United States: We need machine tools of another quality to be used not just for one shift but for two or even three. And we do not need more shoes; we produce more of them than anyone else in the world—but there is nothing to buy in the stores.

In sum, we need not quantitative but qualitative growth, not an increase in any gross output in line with the bewitching magician of percentages but quality of growth. This new, technically advanced quality of growth may yield a negative result in terms of gross output—and what is so horrible in that? Qualitative growth is a guarantee that metal will not be produced simply to increase the weight of plate but to make new progressive types of machines. Qualitative growth will ensure that boots will be produced, not to rot on the shelves but for people to wear.

In an interview in *Sovetskaia Rossiia* (17 July 1987), Academician L.I. Abalkin explained his understanding of the new system of management and administration. It includes self-management, planning, the combination of democratism and planning, and individual labor activity. At the same time Abalkin took issue with Nikolai Shmelev on several points put forth in the latter's article:

> In N. Shmelev's widely discussed article, "Payments and Debts," it is maintained that the market must become the main economic regulator. But the evolution of bureaucratic deficiencies in the earlier system of planning is not reason enough to rush toward spontaneity. There are things that, in principle, the market cannot regulate. Spontaneity is good in terms of current demand, a quick change of juncture, the restructuring of production in accord with changing demands. But spontaneity is harmful in matters of a strategic character, developing fundamentally new directions in science and technology, and basic reforms in the economy. . . . To place one's hopes on the market is to experience nostalgia for past times, to which there is no return.

Socialism guarantees people numerous advantages and insures against possible economic disorders and unemployment. The individual is certain that tomorrow everything will be the same for him. But cost accounting and the independence of enterprises present the possibility of bankruptcy as well. How, then, are social guarantees to be understood? In answer to this question, Abalkin explained that:

> Every blessing, when extended beyond its natural limits, becomes a negative phenomenon. Social guarantees, which are inherent to socialism, are an enormous advantage of our system. But when we begin to represent all blessings as essentially gratis, then the individual, no matter how content he is with the state, begins to be filled with dependency, the wish to receive things without accounting for the expenditure of his own labor. Equality in distribution is widespread: Since everyone gets things from the state, from its riches, then each person claims a more or less equal share. Naturally, such a form of parasitical socialism does not correspond to the true nature of our order.

At the same time Abalkin stressed that one should not go to the other extreme: rejecting social guarantees in general. Every citizen of our society has the right to count on the state to ensure that he has a minimum living standard, that in his old age he will have a guaranteed income to keep him from being dependent on other people, even on his children. This is a minimal social security. Every individual should know that his real position, the entire range of material and even spiritual goods at his disposal, depends above all on the results of his labor. Of course, with the introduction of cost accounting, differentiation in wages should be strengthened. Some will receive more and some less than they have received previously.

Is bankruptcy for enterprises still possible under the system of financial responsibility? Won't it lead to a certain level of unemployment? N. Shmelev considers that, yes, it will lead to this, and he finds that it is a "fairly good way to prevent laziness" and provides a lever stronger than "any financial responsibility." Abalkin, however, does not think it necessary to use the word "bankruptcy." It would be better to emphasize the closing, the liquidation of superfluous enterprises:

> Superfluousness is a phenomenon alien to the nature of socialist economy. If there are hopelessly ailing enterprises, which essentially ride on the back of society, which live off the labor of others, then that enterprise must be liquidated, closed, and its property, naturally, sold. This also benefits socialism.
>
> With regard to workers, a person should have the possibility of getting work in line with his specialization if his old job becomes unnecessary. There should be a state system for reassignment, for the

retraining of cadres, and compensation for temporary unemployment. Even if an enterprise is liquidated, the individual should have a guaranteed income for a certain period of time until he gets a new specialization and finds a job.

In reacting to these conclusions, N. Shmelev introduced certain correctives to his own position, which appeared in *Sovetskaia Kul'tura* (17 October 1987):

Obviously, I am not being completely clear. I fear above all that I was not able precisely to describe the issue of rational employment. It is obvious that, having become somewhat distracted in the course of the discussion, I used words that have a definite connotation, such as "unemployment." I am convinced as a professional that unemployment as such is not a problem for our society.

For us, the question is something different. Huge forces lay idle in our industry, and at the same time significant unused reserves of the work force remain hidden in the existing ineffective system of management. If one could release these reserves and join them with the standing productive forces, the efficiency of the economy would sharply increase. In reality, of course, everything cannot be solved by a simple arithmetic equation: Scientific-technological progress creates the need to raise worker qualifications. A more mobile work force is needed, but in Central Asia, we argue, the number of workers is excessive, while in another place they are literally suffocating from a shortage of people. . . .

Unfortunately, we are impatient. If the reforms don't yield immediate results, if the shelves of the stores are not filled with goods, if the living standard does not jump up, if something does not happen, then we believe that perestroika isn't going as it should. As a matter of fact, there is nothing in the world as inert as an economic system. To move something that developed over decades, to switch the economy onto a new track, is a task of enormous difficulty, and to expect an immediate effect is simply unrealistic.

In the article "New Anxieties," which appeared in the journal *Novyi Mir* (1988, no. 4), and which continued the discussion began in "Payments and Debts," Shmelev frankly caused anxiety:

The more obvious it becomes that the deep restructuring of our social life is not a situational, tactical maneuver but is serious, the more fear for its fate grows. Anxiety is not spreading today among the most active part of our population alone. A certain lack of faith has been observed as well among the broad masses. On the one hand, they fear that efforts for curing the political and socioeconomic life of the country will turn out to be nothing in the end, but on the other hand, they fear the possible social consequences of restructuring.

Special anxiety is caused by a series of negative phenomena, which have worsened in the recent past. First, in several central ministries that claim to support perestroika, an obvious effort continues to emasculate reforms, to use bureaucratic measures to paralyze the Central Committee's stress on full cost accounting, independence, and self-payment and self-financing of enterprises. At the same time, hidden, and often open, opposition to perestroika is growing in regions and provinces among many local party, soviet, and economic organs. Second, acceleration thus far has been achieved largely through the growth in production of unneeded goods. Third, there is a widespread belief (perhaps connected with the growing expectations) that the supply of food and other goods in high demand has not improved recently but has become even worse. The lines in stores and the empty shelves are the same as before: Government food production has grown insignificantly; the quality of domestic high-demand items has not changed; and imports (including even such basic goods as tea and coffee) have declined markedly. Fourth, fears of a different sort have grown among the population connected with discussion in the press of particular economic measures that directly affect the social sphere.

> For instance, fears are completely understandable that the central issue of perestroika—the reform of prices and the subsequent possibility of increased prices for a whole range of food items and communal services—will be decided at a significant cost to the mass consumer. Fears exist that the state organs will not restrain themselves from their traditional temptation to resolve this issue at the expense of the people's interests, that the organs—simply due to hastiness—will fail to prepare and implement price reform so as to ensure corresponding compensation to the lower and middle levels of workers: pensioners, students, people living on supplemented income, and so forth. Rumors urgently circulate about the possible currency reform and, correspondingly, about the confiscation of a certain share of savings deposits. People are also frightened by the prospect of enterprise closings, the new demands for quality and more stringent discipline at the workplace, the necessity of requalifying or transferring to other regions, and the possible losses in earnings.

The present aggressive, revolutionary approach to perestroika has its minuses as well as its pluses. Such a focused effort has given many people unrealistic hopes for virtually instantaneous changes and has led to an underestimation of the difficulties of remaking our economic system. That system evolved over six decades and possesses an unbelievable force of inertia. Perhaps it would be more useful at present to concentrate the attention of our press and society on the difficulties of perestroika. Illusions and hopes for rapid results are dangerous. Also, one has to recognize that, fundamentally, economic reforms are only a part, and possibly not even the most important part, of the entire problem of perestroika. As has been repeatedly emphasized by higher authorities, economic reforms in the 1950s and 1960s were constricted because the political structure of society remained immobile. Today we fully recognize the vital necessity for democratization, openness, and the development of social initiative. Shmelev concluded his article as follows:

> First, we should infuse all spheres of social life with the understanding that all that is economically inefficient is immoral and, on the other hand, that which is efficient is moral. The economically inefficient situation of a general deficit of goods is, in my deepest belief, the main reason for theft, bribery, extreme bureaucratism, for every sort of hidden amoral privilege, for human animus. The economically inefficient spending mechanism of planning leads to thoughtless waste of our national resources, an immoral relationship to our natural resources; the fact that land and water were free led to such wild consequences as the degradation of entire regions of the country (for example, the Aral region). The economically inefficient restraint of popular entrepreneurial activity, equalization in production, the long struggle against all forms of individual and cooperative labor—these, I am sure, are the main reasons for the exacerbation of such social problems as idleness and drunkenness, which threaten our national future.
>
> Second, I am convinced that the most important moral defect of the "administrative economy" is the blind, burning envy of a neighbor's success. That envy has become (at almost all levels) the strongest brake on the ideas and practice of perestroika. As long as we do not smother this envy, the success of perestroika will always remain in doubt.

A revolutionary situation has truly evolved in the country. The "higher ups" cannot manage anymore, and the "lower levels" no longer want to live as they did. In their potential consequences, the decisions of the June 1987 Plenum of the Central Committee could have a truly revolutionary significance for the fate of the country. Revolution from above, however, is in no way easier than revolution from below. Its success, as in any revolution, depends primarily on the steadfastness and decisiveness of the revolutionary forces and on their ability to smash the resistance of anachronistic social attitudes and structures.

In *Izvestiia* (13 September 1988) Academician G. Arbatov, director of the Institute of the USA and Canada, posed a series of questions relating to the elaboration of a new economic strategy for the transition period:

> The conclusion suggests itself that reform is in any case more important than the current plan. The more so because this "child," as is already evident, is burdened with many genetic defects inherited from the administrative-command system: gross output indicators, distortions and disproportions of the structure, an orientation not so much toward the actual needs of society as toward the interests of the economic bodies, and just a nice figure for accounting purposes. . . .
>
> Another important question of economic strategy is how to switch over from the omnipotence of the economic organs to the independence of enterprises. This question is connected, in turn, to the readjustment of state ordering, the issue of liquidating unnecessary links of administration, and the reduction of the apparatus. Resolving these problems involves the fate of tens and hundreds of thousands of the unemployed. Here also it is necessary to make a difficult choice, and it is believed that it would be not only more humane but also economically more useful to make withholdings for the payment of more generous aid and pensions than to restrain the liquidation of unnecessary, bureaucratic organizations. It is necessary, as a rule, to get rid of that which is actively harmful as well as that which is not beneficial!

Arbatov's argument continued by addressing four other issues:

> First. On competition.
> We all are used to applying V.I. Lenin's remark that monopoly leads to decay only in capitalism. But for a long time we have not considered that the type of monopolization that we have is probably unmatched by any other country. And we should already have become convinced in practice that socialist monopoly is no less a source of decay than is capitalist monopoly.
> The second problem deals with the existence of extensive, deformed spheres of economic activity that have degenerated into parasitical, socially harmful forms. This is above all the case in trade and social nutrition, a significant part of the service sector. . . .
> The third problem relates to the living standard of the Soviet people. It's on everyone's mind, if only in connection with the ongoing discussion in the press about prices. It seems to me that a group of our economists look with horror upon the monster that they have helped to create: The reform they proposed for the system of price

formation has fallen into the bureaucracy and has been transformed into proposals for the raising of prices. . . .

In discussions about the reform of price formation, Arbatov stressed the improbability of the claim that perestroika should demand new sacrifices. Changes in prices should not occur at the expense of people's living standards but within the framework of its general improvement. This is a very important issue, not only in social but also in economic terms. Without raising the standard of living, it is impossible to go beyond the present contours of the economy.

The crucial questions of where to secure the means for forward economic movement were answered by Arbatov as follows:

> The most important of these means, and about this our economists are speaking more frequently and loudly, lies in the abandonment (fully and forever, rather than temporarily or partially) of many expensive but not very effective national economic programs and projects. . . . The means may also be obtained by rejecting excesses in the defense sphere through the active use of political possibilities for the attainment of security. . . .
>
> And the fourth problem. The administrative-command economy relied upon noneconomic compulsion—administrative and judicial repressions—as an essential instrument. These were used in various ways—from trials against dissenters (beginning with the trial of [Aleksandr Vasil'evich] Chaianov and [Nikolai Dmitrievich] Kondrat'ev) to the monstrous excesses of dekulakization and various forms of requisitionings and limitations of individual income. Persecution, reprisals against enterprising economic leaders, and the destruction of their work also became widespread.

Two new laws have been drafted to secure the basis of economic restructuring. These laws will help make the economy more flexible, mobile, and consumer-oriented and provide the conditions for each person to take advantage of all his possibilities so that he may work and earn more. These are the laws on state enterprises (amalgamations) and on individual labor activity.

The law on state enterprises, which went into effect on 1 January 1988, is very important politically as well as economically. It is important politically because it gives an unambiguous response to the question of whether the move toward radical economic reform promised by the 27th Congress of the CPSU is going forward. Otto Latsis, doctor of economics, wrote about this law in *Moskovskie Novosti* (15 February 1987):

A person unfamiliar with economic life may ask the following: Why is so much importance given to this law in particular? Is it really the first document regarding economic restructuring? No, it is not the first; in the past two years or so much new has been introduced into the economic system. Changes of one type or another have been introduced into the methods of planning and economic stimulation of the activity of enterprises in agriculture, construction, light industry, retail trade, and everyday services. The administration of foreign trade has been restructured and the rights of enterprises in this sphere have been broadened. Economic experiments are being broadened and deepened. The system of wages is being restructured. . . .

All this is so. However, what has been done thus far falls within the parameters of smoothing over the defects of the old economic mechanism, described at the recent January Plenum of the party Central Committee as a "braking mechanism." The realization of the proposed law on enterprises will signal a qualitative leap, a transition to a new mechanism. By its very designation, such a document will be the core, the heart, of an entire system of legislation that defines economic relations in the process of social production. In substance, the proposed project convincingly demonstrates a striving for radical reform.

The law defines the main task of an enterprise as satisfying consumer demands. It makes consumer satisfaction the norm for the activity of the labor collective, introduces an element of economic competition between enterprises for the most complete satisfaction of consumer demand, and obliges the state to reduce the monopoly position of enterprises as producers.

The combination of centralized leadership with socialist self-management of the labor collective is a novelty. Latsis further wrote that "Socialist self-management is realized through the participation of the entire collective and its social organizations in the elaboration of the most important decisions, in the control over fulfillment of those decisions, and in the election of leaders and one-man management in the enterprise." And there is yet another new conception: the labor collective council. The system for planning is being completely changed: Now the enterprise itself composes its production plan, operating on the basis of economic norms provided by the government, state orders (their fulfillment is obligatory), consumer orders, and free sales. A flexible price system will be established: Besides the centrally established prices, there will be contractual and independently established ones. The switch from distribution of material resources by stocks to optimal trade as the basic form of material provisioning is planned. The law rejects bureaucratic control over the enterprises. Professor Latsis wrote:

Social control by society will not become weaker but stronger when realized through economic norms, especially through the norm of distribution of profit between the state budget and the enterprise. Consequently, the price for lack of management will no longer be a formal matter. Fines will be paid and forfeits will come out of profits— that is, out of managements's own pocket. In response to long-term losses and insolvency, the lack of demand for its production, or the absence of measures to assure profitability an enterprise may be liquidated (although the labor position of those laid-off workers is guaranteed in accordance with the constitutional right to work).

One of the most important and novel positions in the law is the right of the labor collective to elect its leader. This is without doubt an extremely democratic practice. The collective, under the new system of management, is likely to be much more interested than before in the material results of their labor and to elect a leader who assures the maximum productive work of the enterprise. But, as with everything new, this practice runs into real difficulties. Valerii Nosov, the general director of Moscow's amalgamated State Ball-Bearing Factory No. 1, wrote openly about these difficulties in *Moskovskie Novosti* (8 February 1987):

> It is interesting to think about who our factory would have voted for two years ago when I was sent here as general director. In the past year we have been able to give the workers of the factory roughly the same number of apartments as they received for the entire last five-year plan. A chronically backward factory has begun to fulfill the plan, breakdowns have disappeared. . . . But workers probably would have voted for the old system because the paradox still exists that the worse the factory works, the more the worker earns. The plan at any price means constant overtime, higher rates at the expense of fewer days off.
>
> I think the experience of real elections is a difficult one—not mechanical voting for a single candidate or "a list issued from above," but an election that depends upon you and affects your job. People are not accustomed to being asked, to being listened to. Social passivity is also a fruit of the period of stagnation. Have a look, you will see that at the factory there are three vacant positions for heads of shops, and a chief engineer. . . . At the same time, more than 100 specialists with higher education work as manual operators. They don't want to be promoted: The higher the position, the greater the responsibility.

Nosov asked how it is possible to arrange elections when we could not even fill vacant positions from a single candidature? In his view competition for positions is the first condition for the election of a manager. Elections are necessary, especially on the lower levels of management. But not everyone, sometimes not even the most advanced and capable brigade leader, can become a boss. Management is not an assignment, but a science. Nosov continued:

> I myself began as a craftsman, an adjuster at the ball-bearing factory. My parents worked here and we lived nearby, but I was invited to the factory from another large enterprise in Moscow. In order to strengthen the collective I had to bring in a series of specialists from outside. I see that I was not mistaken in appointing them. But is such a personnel move possible under general elections?
>
> I am picturing what would happen if tomorrow at our factory a general director were to be elected. Can the majority of people objectively evaluate him, when almost 100,000 people work here? Perhaps in such large collectives we should talk not about the election of a single person but about a vote of confidence—an open one!—of this one person by everyone, after a certain amount of time in his position. . . .
>
> The right to elections is a wonderful right. It is the very essence of democracy. However, it is necessary to describe very clearly how it is to be used. My worry is that no false notes should be sounded in this matter.

The second law, which became effective on 1 May 1987, deals with individual labor activity. It introduced new economic, social, and moral norms into Soviet society. Why was this law necessary? First, as everyday life improves, a multitude of new needs are appearing that require an individualized approach instead of the standard bureaucratic one. Second, the need to meet demand for individualized, consumer-oriented production and services is becoming clearer. Finally, this is also a way to make full use of labor resources, to direct tremendous resources to the people, and to harness the enterprise, love of labor, and skill that have always blessed the Russian people.

Professors Vladimir Kostakov and Valerii Rutgaizer exchanged views on the private and service economy in the pages of *Sovetskaia Kul'tura* (8 January 1987):

> The mutual interest of certain people to receive services and of others to render them has turned out to be so strong and energetic that there has developed in this country a special, unofficial system of services for the population. According to current estimates, this sphere of activity involved nearly 2 million people in the mid-1980s. But this is a relative indicator reflecting the number of so-called half-time workers. In fact, the majority of the present participants work

occasionally, far from every day. The average number working in the service sector approaches 17–18 million people.

The volume of services in the "shadow" sphere of services was 14–16 million rubles in the mid-1980s—one-third the level of services paid for in the socially organized sector. The volume of everyday services was especially great: 5–6 billion rubles annually, or approximately half the entire volume of services received through the system of everyday services.

There is much to say about the harm caused to society by the "shadow economy." The state budget suffers, material stocks are lost, legality and the norms of social justice are grossly trampled upon. However, it is also evident that in years past the "shadow" sphere of services has also brought concrete benefits: the construction of dachas; the repair of apartments, automobiles, and televisions; and the production of many useful items. And if up to this point it has been difficult to separate the good from the bad, to distinguish clearly and consistently between honestly earned money and blatant nonlabor profits, then now the law on individual labor creates such a possibility for removing all "shadows."

But can individual labor activity generally be regarded as one of the fairly possible channels in securing the rational occupation of the population? To this question, we believe one should answer in the affirmative. We have not been accustomed to speaking about the problem of full employment; we were used to dealing with the shortage of workers, although already in the country today there are territories, as we have said, that have a surplus work force. But we are trying to look forward to the future situation. . . . There is good reason to predict that the presence of a developed, reliably organized sector of individual labor will provide flexibility and will remove a number of severe situations and contradictions in the sphere of labor. If the law carefully defines the zone of this activity, it is probable that within the next five-year plan period the circle of those engaged in individual labor activity will be expanded. It will appear necessary to do so to satisfy both personal and social interests.

Not everyone, however, agrees on the necessity of this law. Thus far, many letters have appeared in the editorial sections of newspapers and journals expressing the opinion that individual labor activity, cooperatives, and family contracts will lead us away from socialism and instill money-grubbing, the forgetting of social interests, and the pursuit of personal interest at any price. These feelings and anxieties were expressed with great force in P. Osipov's letter from Volgograd in *Literaturnaia Gazeta* (10 June 1987):

I am not against a private garden, kitchen-garden, cow, or any other type of household economy. There have been many turning points in our life, especially in the village, but to give "the whole spool" to all these individual small proprietors in the city as well as in the village is impossible. Look how many rubles they "knock down" from the Soviet people for flowers, for meat, for mandarin oranges. And we buy them—there is no other way out.

It will be the same thing with the law "on individual labor activity." The auto repairman will flay three skins from the auto owner for repairs and for acquiring deficit spare parts from the auto service or the auto stores where he or his friends work. The private doctor will give poor care in the hospital and good care at home, for pay. A cooperative cafe (will they really operate just to feed us? . . .) will steal from the state: They will get meat and vegetables in the store and sell them for three times the prices in their business.

Underground groups will appear—syndicates of shopkeepers: Try to control them all, especially now that they are defended in every way possible. . . .

And of course, most important is the impact on the psychology of people, on their consciousness. All these individualists, self-seekers, being "thrown into the river" of profits of easy earnings, will put away huge piles of money for a rainy day.

The NEPmen are on the march! None of them ever had any need of socialism, for which millions of people have perished in the past. . . .

And what now awaits us? Again, the stratification of society.

It is a good thing, of course, to stimulate the labor of the family field, the family contract, the family cafe, shop, restaurant, inn, and then later they'll own factories. . . . Further and further away from socialism.

Materialism and the demand for overseas joys have already affected many groups of youth. And we know about this, only we bashfully hold our tongues, and then they grow into such a life. What does the son of the owner of a family restaurant or a *shabashnik* [someone who works in the underground economy] have to do with the Komsomol, what solidarity does he have with those proletariat types? Even the family contract, in spite of all its economic progressiveness, will lead people away from the understanding of "ours" to an understanding of "mine." And what then of the whole theory of socialism, what of the subordinate component of this society—the individual, his consciousness? There are already many people today who, in their convictions, are further from socialism than people were in the 1920s, 1930s, 1940s, 1950s, and 1960s. . . .

Explain how everything will look in the future. But without shouts and mocking. What will this new economic policy mean with regard to the inculcation of socialist consciousness of our Soviet man?

The mention of the NEPmen in this letter is very symptomatic. Very many people today draw a parallel between the New Economic Policy (NEP) carried out in our country in the 1920s and the current reforms. For some this is a positive point, for others a negative one. Economists are also divided in their opinions. This is reflected in a discussion on the pages of the weekly *Sobesednik* between Academician S.S. Shatalin and Professor A.Z. Seleznev (nos. 25, 26, 1987). Beginning with the issue of NEP, these scholars speak to many of the vitally important questions of the present restructuring. Shatalin had this to say in his interview:

> Is it proper today to draw a parallel between those reforms planned for the next few years and the period of transition from "war communism" to the New Economic Policy? Is there a similarity between the early New Economic Policy and the present economic situation? Of course there is a similarity. What is most important at the present is the effort to adopt normative methods of management for the national economy. Now, as in the NEP, the enterprise's sociocultural and wage funds are planned on the basis of profits. The quantity is not specified in rubles but in terms of a share of deductions. Something like a tax is paid to the state, after which the plant, factory, or kolkhoz can distribute the remainder at its own discretion. Remember that during NEP in the 1920s grain surpluses were not confiscated from the peasant. Until the beginning of collectivization he paid a high tax, gave part of his grain to the state, but kept the remainder. And although the tax was significant, the peasant prior to 1927 could look to the future with optimism and strive to increase production. As a result, between 1922 and 1925 the production of grain and animal products in the USSR grew by one-third.

The second parallel with NEP is in the policy regarding trade-money relations. During NEP the country entered into a period of sharp trade expansion. Now, based on decentralization and the independence of enterprises, we are again widely expanding the sphere of trade. It is the market, and not orders, directives, and instructions "from above," that should define economic development. The role of the market should be much greater than it is today. The transition from "war communism" to NEP was precisely a policy of this type: not so much a "temporary retreat," as it is usually described in school textbooks, but a transition from "administrative-compulsory" socialism to "cost accounting," to the construction of new relations in society on a scientific basis that makes reasoned use of the possibilities of each person.

But is individual labor activity part of these analogies? Absolutely, stressed Shatalin:

When Lenin spoke about the transition to the New Economic Policy, he emphasized that there was no reason to fear private initiative as long as the commanding heights were in the hands of the dictatorship of the proletariat. And this was in 1922! What is there for us to fear in 1987?! Individual labor activity and cooperatives in the sphere of services and production of consumer goods do not threaten Soviet power in its seventieth year of existence. They will help to satisfy demand, to heat up competition, which we are clearly lacking, and to make a precise calculation of all consumer needs possible. . . . The "new" forms today are being integrated into the general system of socialist production, and the scale of this activity can be regulated without administration through a tax policy. Naturally, such a tax must be reasonable enough not to smother initiative, but to develop this sector.

A. Seleznev, in a letter to the editor, took issue with several of Shatalin's positions. Seleznev drew attention to what he sees as the latter's unjustified emphases in discussing the restructuring of the economic management system:

> It is incomprehensible why some prominent Soviet economists, considering themselves Marxists, do not hide their nostalgia for economic circumstances that give rise to a struggle of all-against-all competition. It seems to me that under the present conditions, one must speak not about heating up competition but about developing economic cooperation, which is organically inherent in socialism. . . . Unfortunately, for some reason economic cooperation is overlooked by proponents of competition, which inevitably gives rise to anarchy. It is certainly true that in contemporary conditions the character of competition is already far from that which characterized premonopoly capitalism, although today as well the losses from competition in the West, in Japan, and in the Scandinavian countries are great. Contemporary socialism cannot borrow this method of whipping up economic growth from the capitalist economies—it has its own inherent stimulators of growth, including economic cooperation.
>
> It also seems strange that, in arguing for competition, the author for some reason avoids the question of its "costs." But they are not insignificant. As a result of competition the owners of enterprises are ruined, excessive production is created, and thousands upon thousands of workers are thrown out of work. And without this element, competition is not competition.

Professor Seleznev went on to argue that just because individual labor is allowed, it does not at all follow that it is necessary to propagandize it in every possible way. It seems that one should also worry about a certain loss in the development of social consciousness. If one argues excessively for individual activity, it will work not as a supplement and continuation of organized labor but as a sphere of "extortion" of money from the consumer. According to Seleznev:

> Reasonable centralism is especially necessary in the future as well as now. The question is whether one may in general get along without the administrative system if the prerequisites for the withering away of the state have not yet been created. The state will wither away gradually, but this process will occupy an extended period of time. Authority is needed. This includes economic authority. We are told to completely forget about the word "subordinates." But, as is well known, Lenin demanded subordination to a single will, the compulsion to labor. Without subjection there is not and cannot be responsibility and discipline. . . .
>
> [Shatalin's] position on the issue of the market seems strange. No market policy, no market mechanism is capable of moving socialized production forward without strong centralized regulation, which allows for strategic decision making and concentrates the means necessary to realize them.

What is going on in practical economic life? Are there signs of something new here? Yes and no. Elements of a new system are appearing—the number of cooperatives is growing, more people are beginning to work in businesses (for some reason we continue to call it "individual labor activity"), enterprises are trying to carry out policies more independently of the ministries. But all of this is accompanied by enormous difficulty and conflict. Before discussing these problems, however, it seems appropriate to give the Western reader some basic ideas about the meaning of "cooperative" in the Soviet Union. This is explained in an article by the economist Pavel Bunich in *Moscow News* (1988, no. 10):

> Our limited experience in the '20s and the great experience of many countries, above all socialist, testify to the fact that the cooperative movement after the first, sometimes erroneous steps enters a healthy stage, and becomes a significant feature of the economy. We are basically familiar with cooperatives, and we approve of them. So, it makes much more economic sense to study and apply something that became established and justified itself a long time ago than to try to invent something new by ourselves. . . .
>
> Admittedly, some of the advantages of cooperatives over state enterprises should be curtailed. The cooperatives do not pay ground rent. The state enterprises also don't pay ground rent, but the state takes away all "extra" profits, while the cooperatives keep theirs. That's

why a cooperative renting out property on the Black Sea shore gets superincomes not through its own work, but rather like "manna from heaven." Those who have fertile subsidiary plots of land also get superincomes. The introduction of ground rent would do away with this unfairness in incomes and narrow the field of "easy" earnings.

Besides ground rent, cooperative enterprises should also pay taxes. Otherwise, they will again be in an artificially privileged condition in comparison to the state sector, where taxes are being introduced. License, ground rent, and taxes: Isn't that too much? All these are different factors that do not exclude one another. And in order to avoid taking "too much," the payments should be justified—not too low or too high.

Another unfair income advantage inherent in the cooperative movement is the lack of economic responsibility for the quality of output. As the cooperatives rarely use trademarks or labels, the customer does not know who to complain to about poor quality. On the other hand, wrote Bunich:

> Cooperatives do face limitations which are absent in the state sector. Members of cooperatives can be invalids, pensioners, housewives, students, or schoolchildren, and the people employed in the state sector can work in them only in their spare time. Such a limitation cuts off from the cooperatives many production areas calling for real manpower. This does not stop all cooperatives. For example, a shop preparing chips at the Verkhniaia Siniachinkha plant for making wood-shaving boards in the Sverdlovsk Region has become a cooperative. The former state brick factory in Neviansk, also in the Sverdlovsk Region, now operates on the basis of a cooperative contract.
>
> People use all sorts of well-known contrivances to avoid cooperative labor regulations. They try to get jobs which give them two to three days off for every workday or they conserve energy during the day, then go to their cooperatives to do all-out work; they bribe people to register them as employed in the state sector, where they don't work.

Generally speaking, measures are needed to put cooperatives and state sectors on a par with each other, at least at the beginning, to guarantee competition between them. The winner will be the one who works more imaginatively and efficiently, who honors his obligations to his suppliers and customers, and who sells his goods at the lowest prices. The idea that cooperatives always demand higher prices is groundless. When shortages of goods are overcome, the enterprises that hike prices lose their market and go bankrupt. At best, their turnover slows down and incomes decrease. That is why, even now, there are cooperatives that are lowering their prices. For example, the Alina shoe cooperative in Armenia is selling women's slippers at a lower price than the state does. In such conditions the state will also be obliged to lower prices because the market tends to level them. Where items demand a high level of production technology and large sums of "capital," the state enterprises will be able to take the initiative and make the goods at a lower cost as they have greater technical and financial resources and are capable of lowering overheads on account of mass output.

In spite of all the difficulties, our cooperatives are growing; slowly, but they are growing. All of them are basically in the services sphere. Recently, new forms of cooperative enterprises have been appearing. *Moscow News* (1988, no. 45) described this phenomenon:

> In something resembling an auction, the Main Department for Trade offered to lease shops including a bakery, groceries, domestic appliances, haberdashery, a center for empty bottles and jugs, and even a wine store.
>
> Why? Before the procedure started, the Department chief for labor and wages, Svetlana Korolyova, explained that the decision to lease out the shops was made because they operated at a loss and there had been complaints from the customers about rudeness and cheating among the staff. More and more shops are being leased in Moscow and this is proving to be an advantage. Indeed, lessees, as a rule, sell thrice as much, with half or one-third the number of employees.

This was the first such auction in Moscow, which is perhaps why the list of shops to be offered was so long. A shorter list would limit the choice and make for greater competition at the auction. How did the auction go? When officials of district departments of trade started to read out the names of the shops one by one, the bidders did not react but waited for more exciting offers. Then they started making bids on everything that came up. The reporter wrote:

> A young man sitting in front of me made bids for six shops at once—not the biggest number at the auction—but that committed him to nothing. "I'll go out and see them and perhaps make my choice," he said.
>
> This wasn't an auction in the proper sense. If, for example, the young man found that he didn't like any of the six shops, he could stake his claim on any other, including those that already had their bidders. The final say goes to the district trade amalgamations after the applicant's record, and that of his team, are studied, along with his program for the shop.

And another thing: The auction was not attended by a single member of the staff of those eighty-five shops, despite the fact that their future was at stake. Weren't any of them interested in leasing their shop? I phoned the food shop at 11 Obruchev Street and got such an earful of unprintable words that I gave up all attempts to phone any other shop. There was clearly a problem. The most important thing that the first auction has ensured is that eighty-five shops will now be staffed by people who welcome customers instead of hating them like sworn enemies.

It is in the agricultural sphere where the new entrepreneurship will be decisively tested. Today many Soviet specialists are convinced that we should place our hopes not so much on the transformation and reform of the system of collective and state farms as on the development of a parallel and competing system of farming. The first efforts have already been made, but they are also meeting with opposition—not only of local bosses but also of simple neighbors. The opponents accuse the new farmers of resurrecting *kulachestvo*, the so-called greedy exploitation of poor peasants by rich farmers. Moreover, the success of this farmer movement differs region by region. The following was reported from Estonia in *Moscow News* (1988, no. 45):

Dark green Lake Uhtjärve is surrounded by hills. It is deserted except for the occasional angler. Local foresters built a little hamlet on its shore only to see its residents disappear.

It was in this hamlet, five years ago, that Mart Saldre, the collective farm's supplies chief, bought a big house, a cow shed, hay sheds, and a barn. He bought two cows with a calf, two sheep, and enough hay to last the whole winter. The total cost was ten thousand rubles. The former owner, a woman, couldn't manage her farm single-handed. Saldre has no idea of the farm's real cost, but says it will cost a fortune soon. The most precious thing about it is that at long last his family has a home on Estonian soil after years of drifting from one communal flat to another.

As soon as the idea of lease and family contracts became a reality, Saldre approached the board of the Kuldre collective farm. He said it straight to the chairman Agu Truuts: "A lessee is essentially a predator because he leases a plot of land for a period. Let's sign a cooperation contract. I'll raise my own cattle and use my own feed and my own sheds. You help any way you can. As for the land. . . ."

The chairman said: "The land is being wasted anyway. Get it and use it. Would you like to lease the lake, too? The district authorities keep insisting on putting it to some use and I can't see how I can do this."

Said Saldre: "Later perhaps, let me first do something about the land."

So Saldre went to the district agro-industrial association; he consulted economists at Tartu University, officials at the district Party Committee, and the Republic's Agro-Industrial Committee. Thus, he secured the document cited above. I doubt though that every peasant could wade through this bureaucratic procedure and succeed.

"At first I planned to raise sheep," says Saldre. "Then I thought the land is ideal for raising cows. Excellent pastures with a watering place nearby and a small plot of arable land. I selected more or less plain plots to grow cabbage and potatoes because rich fodder is essential for cows, and I sowed the meadow with white clover and a mixture of grasses. The collective farm provided me with a tractor, a seeder, a mower, a set of implements and a five thousand–ruble credit as promised."

Saldre's wife, Riina, is a trained vet with three years of practical experience. Their daughters Maire, 14, and Merle, 9, help with grazing the cows, feeding the poultry and taking sandwiches to their father mowing hay in the meadow.

Last year, from his own farm, Saldre sold the collective farm nearly 14 tons of milk and 1.5 tons of meat. By October of this year the figures were 20 tons and 3 tons respectively.

"You can't make much money on dairy farming, but then that's not what we're after," says Saldre, picking up the ledger his wife keeps. "The most important thing is stability, confidence in tomorrow and an independent way of life."

The reporter went to the board of the Kuldre collective farm and was told that for each 100 hectares of cultivated land there were production means worth 255,000 rubles. For Saldre's farm, however, that figure was only 80,000. Kuldre produces 12,000 rubles of output a year, while Saldre produces 11,000 rubles. Kuldre gets 3,806 kg of milk from a cow while Saldre gets 5,000 kg.

"At the moment I have six milk cows," says Saldre. "Last year I sold the collective farm four tons of hay. This is waste. Given the amount of hay I have, I should have 15 cows and sell 100 tons of milk. I'm going to build another cow shed and get as many cows as I can feed, unlike the collective farm where they sometimes try to divide an armful of hay between 100 cows. But we shouldn't compete with the collective farm: we should cooperate. Each should bite off exactly as much as he can chew."

In other regions of the country farmers must overcome great opposition to establish cooperatives. They may even envy their Estonian colleagues, as Nikolai Sivkov, a farmer from Arkhangel'sk who was one of the forerunners of leasing in agriculture, expressed in a letter in *Moscow News* (1988, no. 45):

"You're a kulak, Sivkov—a farmer," I was told in early 1984, after I had made up my mind to take land to raise feed grain.

And who—from Moscow down to the district—invented objections? Bureaucrats, who owed their livelihood to us. Right before my eyes, many hard-working fellows boarded up their huts and went away to who-knows-where. How many smart men started hitting the bottle only because they no longer had their professions. . . .

I envy the Estonian farmer M. Saldre, because in his case the Soviet power is intelligent; they gave him land to use as long as he should live, sold him machinery. They told him to make the land produce. My son and I, too, have bought a tractor and a truck, and we've borrowed a mowing machine. The land has been transferred for unlimited use, but given to a cooperative. We are not yet recognized as essentially being farmers, so we had to set up a cooperative for appearance's sake. As if this will improve the appetites of our bulls. . . .

Now the district authorities are trying to make me hire a bookkeeper and accept a mountain of bookkeeping forms. But why? To check whether or not we are cheating?

There's land and there are farm tools, there is the worker and the state, and nothing else is needed to organize equitable, mutually beneficial relations between them.

Farmers ought to have legal rights!

We find new economic initiatives today not only in the area of services and agriculture. "Lease" is becoming a popular word in the vocabulary of restructuring. Here is yet one more article from *Moscow News* (1988, no. 36):

Seven-plus decades divide the appeal "Factories for Workers!" from the banner headline "Factories for Lease" over a full-page article in *Pravda.*

As recently as two years ago it seemed to us that we had found a perfect way to combine "common" property with individual interests: self-financing. But when the slogans started appearing in workshops: "Workers, Remember That We Are on Self-Financing," it became clear that self-financing didn't exist there. If it had, every worker would have felt it. Money was still not earned but distributed. On paper, enterprises were operating under complete cost accounting, and that could be reported to the top, but in fact their work was based on norms and plans drafted by the plant managers.

When the press started gushing about the introduction of the "lease system"—in services, agriculture, and industry—many were convinced that it would not go beyond the publicized "oases" in small-scale industry and individual villages. But then Vladimir Moskalenko, deputy general director of the industrial association in Sumy that pioneered self-financing, admitted in an interview with the newspaper *Sotsialisticheskaia Industriia* that he was keeping an eye on the integrated works in Butovo, which had pioneered the lease system in industry. It is an attempt to implement an idea that has clearly been distorted in practice. The desire to feel like a master is always frustrated by the fact that there always is a master—higher bodies of management. Any "feeling of being a manager" is just an illusion, and even that disappears after the first shout, order, or withdrawal of funds.

The author continued:

The real danger is not that the lease system will contradict our goals but that the bureaucracy will be discredited in one of two ways—both of which have been tried repeatedly.

The first way is by submitting reports about blanket lease-lending. According to weekly reports reaching the Regional Party Committee and Regional Agro-Industrial Committee, almost 1,500 work collectives in the Voronezh Region have converted to the lease-contract system with good results. But a *Pravda* correspondent could find only two collectives working under this system. Why do officials file such reports? Why are they needed? For what I call the "fundamental change" on paper. The only true indicator of change is the amount of goods on store shelves.

The second way builds so many conditions and restrictions into the lease system that it cannot function as such. Only the name would remain. This way seems particularly real today when departments are compiling instructions, recommendations, and provisions which might well turn into a Law on Lease which would contradict the very idea of a lease. . . .

The crucial question is: with whom should one enter into a lease contract? Today it is the corresponding branches' head departments and ministries. Which means that the departments—the economic management bodies—are the real property owners. "A contract is to be made with Soviet power," says Director of the Butovo Integrated Works Mikhail Bocharov, and economist Gavriil Popov arrived at this conclusion independently. Only Soviet power should be defined more precisely: if local enterprises can be leased from local authorities, what about huge enterprises of national importance? The answer is to combine the ideas "Power to the Soviets!" and "Factories for Workers!"

Even in its present tentative form, the lease is the best catalyst. If an enterprise were allowed to distribute its profits as it saw fit rather than according to orders from the top, the self-management would make sense. Profits and labour productivity would soar as if the next five-year plan were already in operation. Money to modernize the enterprise would be found somewhere. Then other things would come: lessees don't need a centrally-determined wage plan. Neither do they need a predetermined correlation between the growth of labour productivity and wages: this correlation would develop of its own accord. What is really needed is an insurance fund and reserves since wages cannot be guaranteed under the lease system, especially in large factories. . . . The lease will challenge the old system mainly because lessees—an entire plan's work force—will either be interested (unlike they are today) or return the leased factories and plots of land as a bad job. The nature of the ownership will determine the results of the reform.

Our foreign economic policy is also causing sharp disagreements and discussions. This is yet another problem that requires new approaches. Aleksei Kunitsin wrote in *Moscow News* (1988, no. 35):

I think that the time has come to assess soberly the situation and admit that our own technology is incapable of making Soviet industry top-quality and top-efficiency in any area of production. The problem isn't only the time limit: we don't have a proper economic mechanism.

For modern production, allied industries must be modernized and able to fulfill orders promptly for the necessary raw materials, supplies, intermediate goods and instruments. As we know, our domestic economy lacks this vital prerequisite. Any attempts to organize modern competitive areas of production inevitably run up against the problem of raw materials—the more ambitious the attempt the greater the problem. Given that other CMEA [Council for Mutual Economic Assistance] countries have some of the same problems we do, Western imports become the only practical solution. But since funds are limited, so are the competitive areas of production. Witness the commodity structure of Soviet exports to the West: four-fifths of it is fuel and raw materials; only three per cent is machines and equipment.

Thus any realistic program for "breaking through" to the world level must recognize the primary accumulation of currency as a key condition of the USSR economic openness abroad. Only to the extent that the Soviet Union can earn additional foreign currency can it (with a measure of economic safety) increase the imports of better foreign goods.

The author suggested the following ways of generating currency: through comprehensive scientific and technological programs set up independently within the CMEA framework and ultimately intended to produce exports; through stepping up the export activities of enterprises that already have permission to have an independent international outlet;

and through gradual inclusion in export activities of producers' and marketing cooperatives. To increase export in these ways would mean producing more modern types of industrial goods: machines, equipment, transport facilities, cooperative units, and parts and consumer goods.

Given the scarcity of currency and the important role of currency incentives, Kunitsin believes the following measures would be most advisable for the primary accumulation of currency reserves:

> Lift restrictions on the use by economic organizations of the currency reserves at their disposal, make their currency revenues fully tax-exempt, and cancel all currency deductions in favor of superior bodies. The proposed measures would increase the interest of state-owned enterprises run on lease contracts and of cooperatives working for export and encourage them to obtain currency revenues.
>
> But for these measures to be effective, we must give up the present restrictive policy in the field of foreign economic activity and go over to a policy under which the economic units themselves determine the expediency, scope and forms of cooperation with foreign firms. Firms should simply notify the superior bodies of international contracts, and the latter should not interfere in the firms' decisions.

N. Shmelev, writing in *Novyi Mir* (1987, no. 6) also touched on the issue of foreign ties:

> Isn't it time to consider what to do about the considerable debt of the Council for Mutual Economic Assistance, which has so far given nothing to us and little to them? Of course, debt is largely a political problem. However, it is probably possible to go about it in such a way that our debtors would find it profitable to gradually pay off their debt to us. To do so it is necessary to open the Soviet domestic market to any type of their production. If you want to earn a good profit in the USSR, then leave us a part of this profit as part of your debt repayment. . . .
>
> Naturally, opening the Soviet market and creating a "common market" of the CMEA countries is impossible without a change in the current exchange rate of the ruble and the introduction of its free convertibility within the CMEA. The existing, innumerably branched currency coefficients must be gradually abandoned, a single rate of exchange for the ruble must be introduced, and the free circulation of national currencies within the CMEA must be allowed. This matter is unavoidable, and there is no reason to put it off.
>
> It is also time for a definite reconsideration of our entire policy of economic cooperation with the socialist and developing nations. In the final account, this costs us billions. Too many objects that have

been created with our participation have not yet been of any real use to us or to our partners.

We have decided to go ahead with the creation of enterprises with foreign participation on our territory. But it is difficult to attract considerable amounts of foreign capital. It is yet more difficult to assure that mixed enterprises can easily exist alongside our system, that foreigners will readily reinvest the profits they receive into our industry. According to Soviet specialists, it might be worthwhile, therefore, to consider the creation of "free economic zones." If we were to achieve visible success in this area, we would not only be able to accelerate the saturation of the domestic market but also to strengthen markedly the country's export position.

Who Is Hindering Perestroika?

The reader may have the impression that everyone in the Soviet Union is in favor of perestroika. And, in actuality, the overwhelming majority are "in favor." But there is also open opposition to these reforms. In our society there exist powerful forces that are vitally interested in retaining the status quo and will do everything possible to surreptitiously interfere with the process of change. These forces will do so because the old system guaranteed its representatives essential well-being with a minimum of work and responsibility. These forces are concentrated primarily in the bureaucracy. Much is now written about this problem. L. Egorov's article in *Literaturnaia Gazeta,* for example, dealt with these questions:

> For the past few years we generally related the bureaucrat to red tape, a bursting briefcase or, at best, with bureaucratic self-satisfaction. The severe and merciless profile of the bureaucracy has somehow slipped away and become hidden in the shadows. The essence of its character is reflected by the principle of hierarchy, in the faultlessly laid out scheme of "from above to below."
> A decisive shake-up is now necessary in order to dismantle an outdated anachronism affecting all aspects of our society. It is also precisely this anachronism that more than anything else opposes the new times, the new winds, or better put, storms. Only now do we feel the weight of the Leninist warning that the struggle with the bureaucrat requires a long siege demanding many efforts.

Many believe that the struggle with the bureaucracy requires not only a limitation of its activity but also the training of a new type of manager— one who possesses a new mentality that is flexible, prepared to make changes, and does not fear responsibility. S.S. Shatalin, in the article in *Sobesednik* cited above, dealt with these issues well and concisely:

> Radical changes in all spheres of life in our society require no less a struggle for change in the individual himself: for his emancipation, the use of his entire creative potential. It is worth remembering this at all times. Otherwise perestroika will be realized at too high a price. . . . Yes, it may not even be realized at all if we do not change the individual's view of his role in society. One must begin with this and for this. And the first priority is to dispel the feeling of being a cog in the big state machine, to give him a feeling of himself as an individual. But many, many stereotypes that have been taught us and that we hold strongly prevent this from happening. We were accustomed to a model of our socialism that was basically, even entirely, created under Stalin, an undemocratic socialism, economically ineffective, extremely centralized, dogmatic. . . . It seems to us, or at least it had seemed, that it was precisely this model that was solely correct and true. Up until this time we have voluntarily or involuntarily compared everything against this instead of looking forward or even looking to the side. And we are still continuing the search for a philosophical foundation.

N. Shmelev called attention to other difficulties in his article in *Sovetskaia Kul'tura* (17 October 1987):

> The two most serious dangers that today threaten restructuring consist of the following: babbling about perestroika and smothering it quietly, little by little.
> It is also necessary to overcome the opponents of economic reform who agree to reform and nod their heads while little by little they try to drown it in red tape, let everything go through the usual route. Some in our administrative structures don't understand that the economy has been switched to a new policy in a serious and long-standing manner and that no other way exists out of the precrisis situation, a situation discussed at the June Plenum of the Central Committee.
> It is also understood that of the 18 million higher- and lower-level supervisors in our country, a significant number of them simply aren't necessary. Of course, these people fear for their fate; they don't want to rearrange their lives or leave their jobs and, naturally, they therefore try to hinder anything new that could threaten their social prestige, financial situation, and usual way of life.

Many are also interested in the tempo at which perestroika should be implemented. Some call for rapid and sharp changes. Others, anticipating the dangers of such a path, propose a course of slower and more gradual reforms. The essence of the discussion is best expressed by the president of the Soviet Sociological Association, Academic Tat'iana Zaslavskaya, in *Izvestiia* (20 April 1987):

> In principle, perestroika can be carried out either quickly and radically, or gradually. It seems to me, the first variant (with the simultaneous implementation of radical reform in social relations) is fraught with certain dangers. Principal among these is that science has not had time to provide the needed bases for it, and reform is again going forward by the method of "trial and error."
>
> Moreover, in conditions of haste, real changes can be undermined by bureaucratic reports. Real reform activity is replaced by pseudo-activity, the fulfillment of "lowered" indicators. This seems paradoxical, but bureaucratization of the very process of democratization of society presents a very real threat. As a result, the principal ideas of perestroika may be compromised.
>
> But gradual restructuring presents as many dangers. This can be judged from the Hungarian experience. There, particular changes were introduced in the economic mechanism in an uncoordinated way over a long period of time. This did not allow, in the opinion of scholars, the achievement of qualitative improvement in the system of economic management. Incremental implementation lowered the general effectiveness of reform. The prolongation of reforms may create popular dissatisfaction, and under certain circumstances, a gradual abandonment of the goals set forth: a "dying out" of perestroika.

T. Zaslavskaya's main point is that the optimal strategy must propose above all a profound scientific elaboration of the principal issues, the formation of a reliably based conception that encompasses all the basic elements of reform. This is the first thing. The second matter is the comparatively rapid (in the course of one to three years) coordinated reform of the system of socioeconomic relations.

> One of the important prerequisites for choosing the most effective strategies for perestroika will be the carrying out of methodologically reliable and representative sociological studies of social groups. Wide discussion of the results of such studies will promote the deepening of social self-understanding and the development of democracy.

In the debate on perestroika, there exists a consensus that it must not dismantle the basic structure of socialism. Socialist relations in all of these proposals are retained. But socialism is not a rigid monolith; rather, it is a developing and changing system. Therefore, it would be a mistake to believe that socialism has achieved the highest level of its development and that there is nothing further to change in it. At the time of the "roundtable" reported in *Literaturnaia Gazeta* (3 June 1987) on the problems of the new economic mechanism, the editor of the economic section of the newspaper, A. Levikov, had the following to say:

> In speaking about socialism, some maintain that "everything was built in strict accordance with a project." But I don't believe this. Such representations are not constructive; they deny socialism the possibility of development, the possibility to change, to become better. This, it seems to me, is a form of dogmatism, like an exercise in formal logic: either-or, the plan or the market; no third alternative is given, as when it is said that "it is impossible to be a little pregnant. . ." In the economy there is no "either-or." Nowhere in the world is there a "pure market" or a "pure plan." The capitalists have learned how to plan fairly well—both within the framework of state orders and within the confines of the most powerful corporations, comparable to our branches, and in socialism both the plan and the market are possible and necessary.

Levikov is supported by the writer-publicist G. Lisichkin, but Lisichkin puts the question more radically: "What do we want to achieve by our restructuring? What do we need to achieve it?"

> After we have basically eaten our fill of potatoes and bread, the question of "what do we want?" becomes more and more complicated. In point of fact, do we really know what we want? How many things can be named that, after a short period of time, turn out to be unnecessary! Money is frittered away. Why? Because we don't have a mechanism for the establishment of goals; we don't think about their priority; we don't know how to define priorities. At times, we define our goals by looking at what kind of hats the bourgeoisie wear. We see it and we run after it: ah, robots, ah what other wonders! We hurry to catch up, although we do not always have the technical, social, and personnel conditions needed to catch up to the next novelty, and we end up looking ridiculous.

Lisichkin asked a fundamental question: What, above all, is needed in our society today? He believes that the division of labor where one part of the population is narrowly specialized in the production of national income and the other part spends it must be changed. What is this "other part"? It is the incredibly cumbersome administrative apparatus pervasive in all spheres of activity—not only the economic sphere but also ideology, culture, science, education, leisure, health, and so forth. The obvious surplus of "stages," the multitude of unproductive organizations of all stripes and classes, inflated personnel in pursuit of their appetites and ambitions—all of these hang on the neck of the producers of national income. We have put ourselves in a position where the state should feed, dress, and house all of us. And it feeds us from the general pot to which everyone contributes: One puts in a lot, working by the sweat of his brow, another throws in a few cents at best, and another nothing at all. Everything is eaten without a sense of personal responsibility. Let a person who works industriously receive 1,000 rubles for his labor, but also let him build his own house and buy milk and meat at full price. It is a typically parasitical society where each person, as in front of a church displaying his sores, yells out: Give, give, give! It seems to me that the understanding of socialism as a shared pot from which the people draw and thank the state for its concern is a fairly primitive one and is nothing other than a vestige of feudal consciousness.

As we can see, discussion about the issues of restructuring the Soviet economy, the transition to a new economic mechanism, has begun and is continuing. But this is only the beginning, the first steps. We have tried to present a variety of views to show different approaches to economic restructuring among leading Soviet scholars and specialists. Yet we haven't spoken yet of what is perhaps most important: What is essential for success? Many have analyzed the various essential links in the chain of reforms. In our view, T. Zaslavskaya best addressed this question (*Izvestiia,* 20 April 1987):

> Without an understanding by the laborers of the real social-political state of affairs, without the development of their social self-consciousness, it will be difficult to expect that the majority will give active support to perestroika. In this situation one cannot depend upon an authentic democratization of society either. It is precisely this developed social consciousness of the rank and file that is the main guarantee of the irrevocability of progressive social change.

The overwhelming majority of the population is made up of people who are willing to follow rather than lead. But if the majority of people clearly recognize their interests, society will not "recoil" toward a limitation of democracy. Conversely, people who do not understand their own role in the processes of social development most often tend to make peace with events in whatever direction changes occur.

> "What kind of people must we be in order to strive for this? What can we do?"—this is their typical position. Many of these people passively and at the same time impatiently wait for changes to be

made by others. ("If they are going ahead with this restructuring, then why is there still no meat in my refrigerator?" such people often ask). . . .

I am convinced that the collective will of all citizens will become the decisive factor in the success of perestroika. Included in this, however, are those who so far have not clarified their attitude toward the process of social recuperation, who have not taken a definite place "in the ranks." The social passivity of a huge number of people is not at all neutral but is an active braking factor in perestroika. . . .

In conclusion, it seems appropriate to look ahead, to make some forecasts about the possible development of economic restructuring. By the early 1980s, we found ourselves in a blind alley; our immediate task was to get out of it while keeping the inevitable costs to a minimum. We already knew what needed to be reorganized, what was obsolete and slowed our progress, what was a mistake and what was correct in the theory and practice of socialist construction, especially in the economic sphere—the foundation of our existence.

Perestroika is not simply the result of good will. It is a process predicated on needs for the positive development of society, though it is going slower than we would like. In our complex world no one is allowed to lag behind, to become too easily satisfied. No one will be able to sit it out, walling themselves off from the urgent problems of the present. We have undertaken a complex revolutionary matter, and without popular support our goal will not be realized. The image suggested by T. Zaslavskaya nicely sums up the situation:

> Picture a ship that sails along the shore in calm seas, and then goes out into the open seas and falls into an area of turbulent currents. Previously, it was enough that the captain and several officers of the watch be on deck; the rest could relax. Now the undivided, unremitting attention of the entire crew is needed, and every sailor must have a grasp of the situation.

SIX

Nationality Relations in the Age of Glasnost

A central myth of the Brezhnev era was that the nationality problem in the USSR had been resolved once and for all and that the construction of a "society of developed socialism" had resulted in the emergence of a "new historical community—the Soviet people." According to this myth, all the nations of the Soviet Union—and there are more than 100 of them, large and small—are in harmony and enjoy relations based on "eternal, inviolable friendship." With glasnost this myth has been shattered. Glasnost has brought into our vision the real state of affairs in the sphere of national relations and has dispensed with the fiction that was invented by the ideologues of stagnation.

The flagrant errors of Stalin's, and later of Brezhnev's, nationality policies, which either underestimated or completely disregarded the national consciousness of the peoples inhabiting the Soviet Union, led to a heightened sense of resentment among ethnic groups. In the absence of democracy, and with no freedom of speech, this feeling could not find an outlet. Under glasnost, many regions immediately experienced an abrupt, explosively charged exacerbation of national conflicts that for decades had remained imperceptible (or, more precisely, had gone unperceived). These conflicts were most acute in places where national frictions had historical roots, and they were exacerbated by economic dissatisfaction.

The Uzbek writer Timur Pulatov sought to explain the upsurge of national tensions and called for a new and more thoughtful approach to national relations in an article in *Moskovskie Novosti* (3 April 1988):

In the beginning the problem of perestroika was fully "contained" in the dual formula of fundamental economic reform with deep, all-around democratization of social life. Now, at last, we have "opened" the nationality question—more specifically, the problem of national relations.

It has become an ingredient of perestroika. We have to deal with it very fundamentally from every angle—in theory and in practice. For most always around the nationality problem there is an open or hidden struggle of the old with the new, of the proponents of perestroika with its opponents. Here one has to keep in mind that the enemies of perestroika might be the first to discover still another side to that problem. The priority of such a discovery they always try to use for their own conservative interests, for the discrediting of the very idea of perestroika.

It seems to many that the nationality problem has suddenly gotten worse in connection with the democracy that has begun in our society. Dark, conservative forces already accuse the forces of renewal of a "weakening of screws," diligently noting in their "register of wisdom" everything that glasnost has brought to the surface that, in their opinion, is "loosening the foundations." This is a lie calculated on a lack of information. Those who are informed know that the Crimean Tatars all the more insistently stated their case twenty to twenty-five years ago, when in Central Asia the first postwar generation of forced migrants was born and spiritually formed. They also gathered in a demonstration, organized by their leaders, among whom were also extremists. Emotions, driven inside, turned into a sickness, although even then it was obvious that you cannot walk away from "burning" questions anyway; you cannot put off their decision any longer, once again neglecting the legal demands of the Crimean Tatar people.

The very fact of the creation of a commission of the Supreme Soviet of the USSR, which is studying the question, inspires hope that its resolution can be a standard for all analogous cases. . . .

Those who have brought our multinational country to the brink of crisis, garbling the facts, now try to deny it correct bearings, deny us the pure and honest, albeit romantic, belief in change. The real tragedy for our multilingual Fatherland would be a return to the Stalinist methods of resolving nationality arguments. . . .

Sociologists have computed that according to contemporary time-tables for the maturing of national consciousness, every nationality question rises up most sharply on average five years after it has first been raised publicly. As a rule, it is raised by writers, who are most sensitive to language and cultural movements among their own people. Then the broader intelligentsia are drawn into the arguments, and their ideas and thoughts flow out among the broad masses. It was precisely writers two years ago who were the first to speak out about the coming ecological catastrophe for the peoples of the Urals region. Five years ago Grant Matevosian told me with bitterness that owing to the efforts of local bureaucrats, books of contemporary Armenian writers practically do not reach the residents of Nagornyi Karabakh, whom they artificially separate from their native language. That is when the problem ripened. . . . But no, the propagandists act as if there are no problems, continuing as before to toast the honor of the inviolable friendship of the peoples. Maybe they are waiting for "orders from Moscow" before they understand the reasons for the tensions in relations among nationalities. They are still living in the times of the cult of the personality, when instead of thoughtful and painstaking work in the sphere of national relations, one campaign "for the struggle with bourgeois nationalism" replaced another, no less brutal, for the "struggle against cosmopolitanism."

Nagornyi Karabakh

The eruption of national tensions was especially dramatic in Nagornyi Karabakh, the territory in Transcaucasia where the latent conflict between the Armenians and the Azerbaidzhanis is many decades old, dating back to tsarist Russia. The source of the conflict in those distant times was largely religious discord: The Armenians are Christians and the Azerbaidzhanis are Moslems. Religious conflict served as one of the causes of the massive slaughter of the Armenian population in 1915 carried out by the Turks. Armenian historians maintain that Azerbaidzhanis participated in these pogroms. In the Soviet era, a situation rife with conflict was created in the 1920s when Nagornyi Karabakh—which the Armenians assert is historically Armenian territory—was, by Stalin's decree, placed under the jurisdiction of the Azerbaidzhani Soviet Republic. Since then, the Azerbaidzhani minority has become virtually the ruling nationality in the region, gradually forcing Armenians out of leading posts in state institutions and industry and limiting the development of Armenian culture: The Armenian language was almost entirely supplanted by the Azerbaidzhani language.

The age of glasnost has permitted the Armenian population of Nagornyi Karabakh to publicly raise the issue that has continually disturbed the consciousness of the nation—the reunification of Nagornyi Karabakh with Armenia.

The entire country was stirred by the tragedy in Sumgait, the Azerbaidzhani city in which a wave of violence led to the deaths of nationalistically motivated Azerbaidzhani bandits and dozens of Armenians and citizens of other nationalities. At first, the media were silent about the dramatic events. As *Moskovskie Novosti* (3 April 1988) wrote:

Looking at the February and March files of newspapers you might come to the incorrect conclusion that the quietest period was in the last days of February. The central newspapers and the press in Armenia and Azerbaidzhan printed letters devoted to the friendship of peoples, talking about the laboring achievements of workers and collective farmers of both those republics. There were no reports about meetings and marches in Erevan, where out onto the street came hundreds of thousands of people. The Sumgait newspapers uttered not one line about the pogroms and outrages going on in the city. Thousands of people looked to the soldiers entering the city for salvation and protection—we found out about that only later in the Moscow newspapers.

Only now is it becoming clear that from the very beginning we somehow underestimated the possible consequences of the nationality problem. Moreover, only gradually and with difficulty did it become an object of glasnost. But we need not merely information (even though we cannot get by without a truthful and full account of the events that brought on the crisis) but analysis taking into account the real complexity of the problem and the impossibility of a simple resolution. For now we are trying, having surmounted emotion, to understand what is happening in many of our republics, to listen to the voices of various sides.

A report by the journalist Aleksandr Guber published in *Novoe Vremia* (1988, no. 38), expressed the dilemmas:

> An appraisal of the situation in Nagornyi Karabakh depends very much on who looks at it and from what point of view. From Moscow it is considered one way, from Baku another, from Erevan a third. In Nagornyi Karabakh itself the same thing. Three-fourths of the population of the autonomous region are Armenians. All Armenians with whom I spoke in NKAO [Nagornyi Karabakh Autonomous Region] are decidedly for the secession of Nagornyi Karabakh out of the Azerbaidzhan SSR and for its annexation to Armenia. Practically the entire adult Armenian population of the region at one time or another has signed an appeal to the central organs with an analogous demand. This is a factor that must be taken into account.
>
> On the other hand, the Azerbaidzhanis living in NKAO are just as unanimously in favor of the region remaining in the structure of Azerbaidzhan. They number about one-fourth of the population there. The position of the Azerbaidzhan part of the population also must be taken into account.
>
> I happened to read the recently published works of Armenian and Azerbaidzhan historians in which one and the same facts of history, one and the same findings of the archaeologists are treated differently. In this, basing themselves on one or another measure of reliable sources of far-off centuries, they make conclusions about a burning

issue of the day: To whom should Nagornyi Karabakh belong? It does not appear that a solution lies down that road. For even if competent, disinterested specialists came to the same conclusion based upon history, what would that change today? Would both peoples accept their conclusion, when one of these without fail is bound to feel wounded? . . .

There are various points of view about how justified are the demands of the Armenian population of Nagornyi Karabakh and to what extent they should or should not be fulfilled. From afar, in many ways it all looks like the work of a group of extremists, both local and arriving from Armenia. This is not so. The main problem lies not with them but in the fact that this is a real mass movement.

The nationality conflict in certain conditions will blaze up quickly, and to extinguish it will be long and difficult. Let me relate a general impression: The representatives of both sides, even the best of them, are beginning to lose a sense of measure. Any, even the most minor, conflict, any publication in the newspaper or television broadcast is seen by them through the prism of national relations. One and the same stories, one and the same anecdotes, one and the same pretensions to one another. In sum, the figure of the enemy, which we renounce on the international scene, is building up in one people to another. The seeds of mutual mistrust, hostility, and even hate for our general misfortune are already penetrating the souls of children and adults.

In its October issue, the journal *Vek XX i Mir* (1988, no. 10) published two pieces on the subject. The first is a letter to the editor sent by Suren Zolian, chief of the department of Russian language of Erevan University. It is truly a cry of pain.

What is happening to us?

For already half a year now the single "we" increasingly is fractioned into "we" and "you," "we" and "they." . . . What is happening to us today cannot but disturb us. But why do we worry so diversely, and why do such diverse things worry us? Why, instead of trying to understand our feelings, did you, as much as can be judged from the means of mass information, prefer to distance yourselves from us? We read and hear only the appeals: Settle down and do not get agitated! . . .

The problem that alarms us and excites the entire country is the problem of Nagornyi Karabakh, the entire population of which is 180,000 people and which without difficulty could fit into one city square during a meeting (in Erevan there have been meetings even more populated). The solution to that problem demands justice and not the opportunistic considerations and deep-rooted habits to decide without changing anything. Such a habit is extremely dangerous. . . . Those who wished to hush up the problem of Karabakh also had to be silent about Sumgait. As a result the problem has become today much sharper and more painful, and for many reached yet a totally inadmissible turn: Who will conquer whom? Armenia-Azerbaidzhan, or Azerbaidzhan-Armenia?

The Russian intelligentsia, with rarest exception, distanced itself from the problem of Karabakh: We did not create it, they say, and we do not have to solve it! Meanwhile, this same intelligentsia with its ability to escape ready-made labels and to seek nonstandard solutions should have helped the leadership work out something more constructive than the notorious "who is getting whom." Instead the problem has now become much greater in scope, not only before the leadership but also before the whole country: the problem of Armenia, that same "Armenian question" that was one of the key questions of European politics and diplomacy in the nineteenth century.

What prevented in the twentieth century, under the piles of unburied bodies, the permanent burial of the Armenian question? Not only the Armenian instinct to survive, acquired over many years of distress, but also the voice of the community, including Russian public opinion. As early as 1895, the Russian intelligentsia, shaken by the horrors of the first, and what then seemed unprecedented, slaughter of Armenians, came out decidedly in support of them. There were not many in its ranks, but the intelligentsia did everything it could. "Brotherly Assistance to Armenians" was the name given to the collection, published for charitable ends, in the creation of which took part all leading Russian writers, poets, and publicists. In the historical memory of Armenians it was that book which made an impression and not the dispatches of the Ministry of Foreign Affairs, not the embittered fables of the untalented but celebrated poet [Samuil Vasilevich] Velichko or the instructions of the governor of the Caucasus, Prince [Dmitrii Mikhailovich] Golitsyn, about the exile of refugees to Siberia.

So is it possible that now the only things that will become achievements of history are the letters that we receive from acquaintances and strangers and that are returned from all editorial offices with the note: "We share your feelings, but we cannot publish this"? Or they are simply not returned. One way or another these letters reach us. We are thankful to their authors, and we find in them that which we have not enough of today: hope and the belief in justice. . . .

What will the future historian say about our society when rummaging through piles of newspapers for the year 1988 when he is surprised to discover that letters of condolence and indignation at the goings on in Sumgait can be found only in personal archives? What will that historian say when he finds out that Sumgait refugees, the very poorest, contributed money to those who lived through the railroad catastrophe in Arzamas while he looks in vain for mention in any newspaper of the relief fund for the Sumgaits?

I am a person who has devoted himself to the teaching of the Russian language in Armenia and the translation of the classics of ancient Armenian literature into Russian. For that reason I am especially bitter and hurt not only for my compatriots, from whom you are trying to fence yourselves off, but also for you. Because your position is reason to doubt your sincerity and honesty. Understand— we share problems with you, and the main one is the problem of a just perestroika of our society.

In the same issue of the journal is an analytical article by Viktor Sheinis, doctor of economic sciences, that attempts to penetrate into the cultural and psychological mechanisms of the crisis.

The events in Karabakh signified the deepest political crisis in the course of perestroika, from which it is necessary to draw lessons.
. . .
The most obvious of these lessons is that any situation is easier to take under control before it deteriorates. In the meantime, there was revealed in nationality policy, and not for the first time, an inability to notice in time the growth of a crisis situation. The conviction that as long as we have not recognized it, the thing does not exist fully corresponds to the stereotypes of the previous political thinking and behavior, but it is inexplicable in conditions of the dismissal of dogmas. It is still more difficult to explain the inactivity at the center and locally once the conflict already was out in the open. The expectation that everything would take care of itself, that the pressure would ease when fatigue took its course, resulted in a loss, not a gain, of time. The situation in the Caucasus in the course of the whole first half of 1988 quickly became heated, and with every month, to find and bring to life a peaceful and just solution became all the more difficult.
. . .
It was not sufficiently appreciated what a deep impression the tragedy of Sumgait had on the development of events, what kind of wave of despair and protest it called forth in the consciousness of the Armenian people, who applied to it the historical memory of the genocide of 1915. In my opinion, the reaction to Sumgait outside Armenia was and remains inadequate to the outrage. The events, which heated up emotions, in fact cannot leave reason or conscience in peace. Of course, one cannot place all the responsibility on the people of Azerbaidzhan. But Azerbaidzhan families protecting their Armenian neighbors from pogromists acted more bravely and worthily than state power, which showed incomprehensible timidity in the political evaluation of events, as if fearing to excite anyone's emotions.

The appropriate general humanitarian approach, it would seem, should have made clear that it was necessary as a first act to publish the list of names of victims of the Armenian pogrom in Sumgait. This could have immediately removed the argument about the number of deaths, not to mention that the meaning of the events and the elementary feeling of solidarity demanded the declaration of a national period of mourning (which, by the way, we have called in recent years on less important occasions). But if the first reaction still can be explained by the elementary confusion, then one cannot understand why judgment on the participants and organizers of the mass distur- bances and banditism (and not simply hooliganism) was not given appropriate social sounding, and glasnost was as if smothered. Up to now no clear answer has been given to the question of who is responsible and how it could happen that decisive measures were taken only on the third day of a pogrom going on near the Azerbaidzhan capital. Political and moral deafness prevented timely bridge building between Erevan and Baku.

Any solid and just decision of nationality conflicts should rely upon compromise and not the "victory" of one side or another. It is important to be aware that the Karabakh crisis placed the central state power in a difficult situation: Both sides appealed to it and on it lay the responsibility for the preservation of order, for the restoration of the normal rhythm of economic life. In addition, the field of possible political solutions of the center were extremely limited. The violent suppression of the peoples' movement for the reunification of Karabakh with Armenia (a method to which they did not fail to turn in past years) would have had catastrophic consequences for perestroika. But you also cannot, with a simple decision of the center as occurred in the past, change the borders of a republic if both sides do not approve. Finally, it is vitally important to prevent the development of a chain reaction of nationality arguments and pretensions capable of destroying glasnost.

Sheinis went on to argue that we should view independent movements that express the expectations and demands of many people and adhere to peaceful, nonviolent action not as destructive but as a constructive force working for perestroika. It is the nucleus of a reviving civil society, one of the forms of the realization of political pluralism.

The political potential of national self-awareness must not be forced into opposition but used in the interests of perestroika, democracy, and socialism:

In my view, the right of a nation to self-determination is higher, and in principle more significant, than state sovereignty, and this should be reflected in the amended constitution. This corresponds to those ideas which Lenin stood for at the beginning of the century and also to the general democratic legal consciousness that is estab- lishing itself in the world as this century comes to an end. Not emotions, not the impulsive redrawing of boundaries, but the turn to reason, they tell us, is needed today. But reason cannot but take account of emotions, and in the Karabakh conflict an insulted and alarmed national feeling of a people with a difficult historical fate clashed with territorial ambitions and falsely understood notions of prestige. I deeply believe that the Azerbaidzhan people can recognize how unequal these values are and see that it is better to have a friend near one's home than to forcibly hold another people in it.

At the same time it is necessary to consider that the ethnic map of the USSR today fundamentally differs from the administrative-territorial division. This disparity, apparently, will grow stronger over time. The number of areas with mixed national composition will grow. In order to solve the rising problems related to this in satisfactory fashion, a consistent course must be followed toward economic and political decentralization, toward broadening the competence of local organs and intensifying the direct links in the economy. . . . But territorial autonomy must be supplemented by national-cultural autonomy, which can find adequate reflection in the structure of organs of state power and, in part, in the reform outlined by the Soviet of Nationalities of the Supreme Soviet of the USSR. Radical elimination of crises and acute situations in relations between nationalities can be achieved only within the framework of deep democratization of political life.

The Baltic Republics

The Baltic Republics are another "tinderbox" on the map of the multinational Soviet Union. To this day the wounds inflicted on the Lithuanians, Latvians, and Estonians during the years of Stalinist dictatorship are still gaping and the grievances connected with the irresponsible economic and social decisions that were made during the years of stagnation are still fresh. The People's Fronts, new unofficial mass organizations pressing for greater republic autonomy and a restoration of national symbols, culture, and language, may well be the prototype for future political parties, which will not necessarily be in opposition to the Communist party because they already include a number of Communists among their members. Leonid Mlechin depicted the development of these movements in *Novoe Vremia* (1988, no. 43):

Sitting in Moscow one cannot understand the scope of what is happening. You need, apparently, the almost everyday effort of television and the press in order to get across an adequate picture of the events, the changes. It is not enough simply to describe the daily, morning-to-evening heated arguments at the Freedom Monument in Riga or the continuous collection of signatures under various appeals in Old Tallin. Just familiarize yourself with the programmatic documents of the republican Peoples' Fronts. . . . It is not enough to read in the party newspaper the official statement about how the government of the republic, at bottom, reports on the economic questions to the Latvian Movement for Perestroika (analogous to the People's Front). One must imagine an unprecedented rise in the activity of the people, when all conversations are not about prices, not about coupons for sugar (already introduced) and meat (which, judging by the rumors, they want to introduce in places) but about that political struggle which has seized the entire Baltic region and is the main content of her life. . . .

The socioeconomic situation in the republics in no way can be called disastrous—in comparison with other regions of the country. Not at the level of everyday consciousness (how many people have always come to the Baltics, if not to find work, then at least for a vacation, to eat tasty things and to buy something good), not according to statistical reports. However, average Soviet [socioeconomic] levels have not been taken into account here. First, because, as they always say, before it was better. Second, because the state independence in force here for two decades after World War I and also the circumstances of the incorporation in 1940 into the structure of the USSR were perceived by the national consciousness not exactly the way they have been written about in the school textbooks. Third, because the integration of the republic into the single economic mechanism of the Union was effected, as is becoming clear, not in the most reasonable ways and was perceived here by many as a denial of the republic's independence and even as Russification.

For those who visited the Baltics before, the dissatisfaction with the methods of central leadership was obvious. It existed at the level of everyday life and manifested itself in an inhospitality to visitors that was noticeable in even the phlegmatic Latvians, Lithuanians, and Estonians. In those years it could be understood as dissatisfaction with the mass inflow of vacationers and tourists in the summer season. In fact that was only the external side of a process that has deep roots. . . .

The situation in the republics can be characterized thus: a crisis of trust toward the existing powers. This formula resounded, let us say, at the Plenum of the Central Committee of the Communist Party of Estonia. It is expressed not only in ultimatums to the chairman of the Soviet of Ministers of the republic to step down and in the unexpected, I would say, tone with which the republican press addresses local leaders but above all in the fact that the attention of people is turned not to official structures, from which people expect nothing, but to the political movement called the People's Front (or the Movement for Perestroika).

The People's Fronts in all three republics were born as a result of mass dissatisfaction with the way the republics were run, with the level of socioeconomic development; a dissatisfaction strengthened by the desire to experience their own sovereignty and independence.

Perestroika and democratization have now opened up such a possibility.
. . .

It must be stated clearly: The People's Front, as a movement in support of perestroika, has won to its side hundreds of thousands of people thirsting for a renewal of life. They see in the People's Front not only a powerful catalyst of the perestroika processes but also a form of participation in those processes comfortable for the broad masses. That is why the republican party organizations supported that broad people's movement. At the same time they warned against any form of extremism and nationalism. The activities of the People's Front, awakening the social activity of the masses, and everything it does in the interests of the people deserve every possible approval. But this approval does not only not exclude—but does just the opposite: it presupposes—the thoughtful conception of programs and goals of the People's Front, which, at home (in the republic), to put it mildly, is not deprived of its fair share of the attention of the press, but of whom in the central newspapers a critical analysis is for some reason lacking. . . .

The proclaimed task is to strive for the sovereignty of the republic. The People's Front of Latvia proposes in the union and republican constitutions to limit the competence of the federation and the republics, providing the latter the right of veto in the resolution of questions important to it, and also the right independently to enter into relations with other state and international organizations. The People's Front of Estonia proposes to strive for the unambiguous priority of the interests of the union republic before the Union as a whole. The Union will be left with the problems of defense and diplomacy, which does not exclude the recognition, in some forms, of the republic on the part of any state or international organization.
. . .

A reflection of the general discussions in our society regarding military service was the proposal to introduce a compulsory labor duty for youth who for religious and other convictions reject military service; to demilitarize school, to liberate schoolchildren from military preparation and students from real military service; to offer conscripts the possibility to serve in their native republic with the use, along with Russian, of their native language. The PF of Latvia considers it necessary to restore the right, recognized by the previous constitution, of a republic to a territorial military formation in which the citizens of the republic can fulfill their obligatory military service. . . .

The core of the proposals of the People's Front is the economic program of regional cost accounting, about which there is talk not only in the Baltics. . . .

All economic questions [would be] decided by the republic itself, without any kind of interference from the center. Trade-economic ties with other parts of the Union are to be only those of market relations. The full freedom of action on the world market. . . .

All enterprises, including those subordinate to the Union, are to be transferred to the control of the republic. It would receive the right independently to use its natural resources. . . .

Favorable conditions are to be created for the investment of foreign capital, especially the capital of émigrés. A market of free buying and selling of currency is to be opened, and republican money is to be introduced. The question of the transformation of all Estonia into a free economic zone with its own customs and tax legislation is to be studied.

Also a more sweeping reform of the economic system is proposed, including free development of cooperative, individual, and private ownership. . . .

The draft program of the People's Front of Estonia underscores the intention to fight for peace; it proclaims all the Baltics and the entire Baltic Sea as part of the nuclear-free north and calls for the removal from the territory of Estonia of all nuclear weapons placed there.
. . .

Finally, the most important question for the People's Front, the nationality question.

The demands of the Baltic People's Fronts summarized by L. Mlechin hardly sound extremist or provocative. The published programs of the People's Fronts, however, immediately stirred up harsh criticism and tension. The growing tension in nationality relations that spread throughout the Baltic republics can be traced by looking more closely at the example of Latvia.

In early October 1988 in Riga, the capital of the Latvian Republic, the Constituent Congress of the People's Front of Latvia held its meeting. The program of the People's Front was published in many Latvian periodicals, including the monthly magazine *Daugava*. One of the activists of the Front, A. Iakuban, provided a brief introduction to the publication of the program, writing, in part:

It would appear that the kind of political void that was created by the overly bureaucratized side of the party was conducive to the birth of the People's Front. It only stimulated perestroika. The People's Front appeared in a vacuum created by the extraordinary apathy of the trade unions and the theatrical animation of the Komsomol. . . . The openness [glasnost] at the congress was all-embracing. Many were troubled by this, but many were filled with amazement: Pluralism had gone so far that it was even encroaching on some of the fundamentals.
. . .

For some, the People's Front has become the star on which they, full of euphoria, train their hope-filled gazes. For others, the People's Front represents a marvelous opportunity to flap their tongues and sit through long meetings until total stupefaction sets in. Still others are dying to do something. But others are frightened by both the congress and the program. A few not entirely successful, rhetorical planks of the program have become a dangerous stumbling block, although we should not forget that not long ago the program of our Communist party promised, in all seriousness, that today's generation of Soviet people would live under communism. . . .

In its "General Principles," the program states that the People's Front is a popular social-political organization of the republic that has sprung up as a result of the people's political activity. This activity consistently supports fundamental perestroika in Latvia based on the principles of democratic socialism and humanism. The section "Democratization of the State and Society" declares, in part, that:

The People's Front is fighting for the dismantling of Stalinism and the administrative-bureaucratic system of neo-Stalinism and for the transformation of the USSR from a centralized, federative state into a union of sovereign states; for the guaranteeing of the republic's sovereignty, proclaimed in the Constitution of the Latvian SSR; and for the restoration of Leninist principles of federalism. The citizens of Latvia should be masters in their own land and decide all questions independently. . . . The republic must be granted the right of veto when questions are being decided that affect its interests. It must also have the right to enter into direct relations with other states and international organizations (the United Nations, Comecon, UNESCO, the International Olympic Committee, and others). It has become necessary to define the status of citizen of the Latvian SSR in the Constitution of the Latvian SSR and to pass a law concerning citizenship in the Latvian SSR.

A special section defines the People's Front's attitude toward problems of human rights, saying, in part, that "in defending the most important human right—the right to life—the Popular Front is fighting for peace. It consistently comes out in support of disarmament and the demilitarization of society and supports the declaration of the Baltic and Scandinavian regions as nuclear-free zones. Moreover, the People's Front supports the withdrawal of weapons of mass destruction from the territory of Soviet Latvia and the reduction of conventional types of armaments there."

On the nationality question, the People's Front comes out in favor of preserving and enhancing distinct national cultures:

The People's Front considers it essential to fundamentally reevaluate nationality policy, which has been primarily supported by Stalinist dogmas and doctrines. . . . The People's Front does not support a nationality policy that is based on the conception that social progress inevitably entails the disappearance of national traits. The People's Front favors the preservation of national diversity as a storehouse of civilization's values.

All nationality problems in Latvia should be approached in a manner that takes into account the democratic rights of all the nationalities living in that territory. The People's Front, however, proceeds from the notion that the Latvian people have a special status in the republic because Latvia is the historical territory of the Latvian people, the only place in the world where the Latvian nation, the Latvian language, and the Latvian culture can be preserved and developed. On this basis, the People's Front calls for representatives of the Latvian nationality to be guaranteed a majority of mandates in all the elective organs of the soviets and demands that the Latvian language be designated the official language of the territory of Latvia. At the same time, however, it guarantees that:

> Citizens, in their dealings with the state organs, institutions, or-ganizations, or enterprises of the Latvian SSR, can use either the Latvian or the Russian language and get official documents in either language, according to their preference.

The problem of immigration from outside the republic's borders occupies a special place in the program of the People's Front because the influx of a Russian (or Russian-speaking) work force led to a situation where, by the early 1980s, Latvians constituted less than 50 percent of the republic's population.

> Uncontrolled immigration has made the Latvian people, for the first time in their entire history, a national minority in their own territory. Their further existence and statehood are jeopardized. The People's Front supports the immediate cessation of this immigration.

The program of the People's Front makes special note of the circum-stances of Latvia's entry into the USSR in 1940. The People's Front believes that an objective treatment of these events is essential and that their political, economic, and social consequences be "honestly and openly" analyzed and understood. It must be acknowledged that "force was used to bring the Latvian Republic into the USSR and that the opinion of the people of Latvia was never elucidated" (*Daugava*, 1988, no. 12).

In the same issue of *Daugava*, Viktor Avotinsh, member of the Duma—the guiding center of the People's Front—commented on the results of the Congress of the People's Front of Latvia. He dwelt on the most acute question—relations between Latvians and Russians.

> Essentially, after the war we did not have a normal experience of national relations even on the cultural level. The administrative policy of the republic created, seemingly intentionally, various situations that were conducive to the hostility of the Latvians toward the Russians, on the one hand, and that, on the other hand, did nothing to promote the stabilization of the cultural consciousness of Latvia's Russian population. Moreover, the centers of Russian collective culture were extinguished. That is in fact one of the reasons why there is unequal participation of Latvians and Russians in the People's Front.

In fact, the overwhelming majority of members of the People's Front in Latvia are Latvians; there are literally only a handful of Russians. The People's Front has therefore acquired a reputation not just as a social-political movement but as a national-political movement as well. Indeed, V. Avotinsh predicted that immediately after the Congress of the People's Front, alternative groups based on nationality would appear.

> Even if the situation does give rise to such groups, I do not see any sense in placing them in opposition to the People's Front. If they really feel the need, let them form a group with its own charter that would stipulate those views that differ from the general direction of the People's Front. But let it work jointly with the PF, not counter to it. Who needs that? If we are going to create movements for perestroika, each in our own niche, we will smash this perestroika into pieces. (*Daugava*, 1988, no. 12)

These expectations were quickly realized. During the fall and winter of 1988, the International Front of the Workers of Soviet Latvia—a movement similar to the People's Front but uniting under its auspices the Russian-speaking population of the republic—rapidly gained strength.

The editor of *Daugava*, Vladlen Dozortsev, observing the first actions of the International Front, shared his impressions about the events in Latvia with readers of the *Literaturnaia Gazeta:*

> The present "Russian point of view" is that we, they say, were not invited. We were not in the organizing bodies, and we are not in the Duma. The front is not ours, and the Duma is not ours, and the program is not ours.

This is all more or less true. The question is simply why we were not there, and where we should have been. . . .

I will venture to express the conviction here that it was not the document, or the program, of the PF that has excited the passions of the Russian community, but the Congress of the PF.

V. Dozortsev wrote that he was a delegate at the Congress of the People's Front and spent two days sitting at sessions feeling like "a poor, naked person at the marketplace beneath the fierce wind blowing from the rostrum." Certain gusts of that "wind" struck and disturbed him:

No, I am no cynic, and I understand how much discontent and bitterness has accumulated in the people's hearts and how many decades we have been unable to say what we were thinking. But I know something else as well: A word, once hurled from the official rostrum, has consequences for the program. What has been said cannot be unsaid. One of the delegates is now sending verbose letters to the editorial department explaining what he meant when he said that, "on the whole the Germans were not bad guys in those places where there were no partisans." But it is too late. You cannot erase tactlessness and idiocy with repentance after the fact. Whoever yelled out at the congress, "We have had enough of the workers' power; we had it for seventy years and look at the result," probably regrets that the sentence reached the people's ears, since he himself knows full well that the workers are not the issue here, it is the Zhdanovs and Suslovs who were using them as a cover. But what is the use of his regretting it? The People's Front is accused of having a policy that is anti-worker. Did the person who declaimed from the rostrum, "Go home," understand the kind of reaction he provoked? Now we can try to explain our point of view on the problems of migration till we are blue in the face—they will not hear us, because a politically crude remark was hurled from the highest rostrum of those days.

At its first post-congress session, the elected Duma of the People's Front (101 people) passed a resolution that repudiated all the extremist statements made at the congress that were not in conformity with the program and the charter of the People's Front. But, V. Dozortsev emphasized, an opposing movement had already sprung up:

The first anti-meetings and the first anti-appeals, which were extremely aggressive in their emotions and demagogic in the character of their arguments, were held to the tune of slogans like "There are more of us so don't touch us!" and "Down with the creeping counterrevolution!"; of demands to expel from the party virtually the entire

Central Committee and bring in troops; of the conviction that "we should all join the People's Front in order to blow it up from within" (an actual quotation). That wave later subsided somewhat and gave way to attempts to get a grasp on the documents of the People's Front and to draw up their own. (*Rigas Balss*, 6 January 1989)

The International Front began as a response to the extreme, nationalistic views held by some members of the People's Front, but it gradually began to take shape as an actual opposition to the People's Front as such.

V. Dozortsev recalled his attendance at an Interfront meeting at a large factory in Riga. When he appeared in the hall a provocative note was sent up to the presidium: A member of the People's Front Duma has paid us a visit, it said, are we going to kick him out of the hall? Although the leaders of the meeting had sworn their adherence to pluralism, V. Dozortsev was still not allowed to speak. In recognition of the fact that in Riga the Latvian population amounts to less than one-third of the total, and in some other Latvian cities even less than this—15 percent, a retired Air Force major general demanded that radio and television broadcasts in the Latvian and Russian languages correspond to this ratio of the nationalities. A certain student "of working class origin" at the Latvian State University demanded . . . "[that we] remember the Baltic conquests of the Russian Empire."

One of the leaders of Interfront, Aleksandr Belaichuk, denied that the organization was established as a counterweight to the People's Front. In his speech to the Constituent Congress of the International Front, convened in Riga in January 1989, he asserted:

> We call our front international not because we want to oppose it to other social and political organizations. The "Internationale," both as a concept and as an anthem, is the flag of the workers, united in defense of their working interests. The name of our organization is based on the assumption that all workers are equally interested in seeing Soviet Latvia flourish.
>
> Interfront should not be viewed as an organization created as a counterweight to the People's Front. (*Sovetskaia Molodiozh* [Soviet Youth], 10 January 1989)

While criticizing the People's Front for erecting "barricades of mistrust," the leader of Interfront pointed to the existence of common goals in the struggle for perestroika:

> In organizing Interfront, we take as a starting point the idea that, on the whole, the interests of workers of various nationalities coincide,

and that the differences between those interests are not antagonistic in nature and are considerably smaller than the common ground that unites them. That is what our internationalism is built on. At the same time, the differences between the interests of the workers of a given nationality and the interests of the nonworking, corrupt elements of that same nationality are antagonistic in nature and are considerably stronger than that which unites them on the basis of nationality. As recent history has demonstrated, the interests of nonworking and corrupt elements of various nationalities, wherever they might live, coincide, and we are opponents of their "Internationale."

Belaichuk openly admitted that Latvians feel limited and frustrated in their own homeland. He also acknowledged that this feeling had developed under the yoke of Stalinist oppression and had remained to this day. The equilibrium of languages in Latvia had been disturbed, with Russian becoming more widespread than Latvian in some areas.

We now have a situation in which it is very difficult to live in Latvia without a knowledge of the Russian language, while one can manage without knowing Latvian. This is an important distinction between Latvia and such republics as Armenia and Georgia. The situation is such that there are people who were born and raised in Latvia, some of whom even have "Latvian" stamped in their passports, who do not know the Latvian language and who are almost entirely unfamiliar with Latvian culture. The question is, what provided the basis for this situation? The answer is obvious: It is all a consequence of the total disregard shown for Leninist principles during the periods of Stalinism and stagnation. Our task is to correct these mistakes in a relatively short period of time.

Although A. Belaichuk resolutely declared that "because of the great number of Russians living in Latvia, we are conducting a campaign for the recognition of Russian as the second official language of Latvia," he stipulated that, at the same time, Interfront supports the adoption of laws that would give priority to the Latvian language. He concluded his speech with an appeal for reconciliation and cooperation:

We believe that the presence of various fronts, associations, and informal bodies is a guarantee against the monotony of thought that we had, until recently, in our public life. There should be many ideas. On the other hand, let us not forget that practical actions are needed as well. Let us be tolerant in our relations with each other. After all, it is often we ourselves who are perestroika's opponents—when we lack sufficient tact, when we lack self-control, when we do not take responsibility for the consequences of our speeches and actions, when we are uncivilized in our relations.

But the rest of the congress, which lasted two days, virtually repeated the confrontational tone that had marked the Congress of the People's Front. The Congress evoked a critical reaction from the republic's Latvian population and from a portion of the Russian population as well, although sentiments were far from unanimous. The newspaper *Sovetskaia Molodiozh* published a number of readers' reactions to the Interfront Congress:

We think that the Interfront Congress was directed at preserving the old ways (with some minor cosmetic repairs). We think that after the congress it will be difficult to speak of any sort of normalization in relations between the nationalities. We are quite certain of this.

With the exception of a few speeches, nothing constructive or new concerning Latvia's problems was heard at the congress.

The Ponomarev family,
Riga

I am a Latvian and I work as a brigade leader at a kolkhoz. I have not joined any of the fronts. The Interfront Congress represented many, many steps back into our past with its slogans about the glittering heights of communism.

I.Ia. Ozola,
Orskii region

The Interfront Congress is over, and I am sure that it left many Latvians offended, to say the least.

. . . There was much talk about language, about bilingualism, but only for their own narrow advantage, without taking into account the indigenous nation and forgetting that this republic is Latvia. Hypocrisy—there is no other name for the speeches on language made by the Interfront members. After all, everyone knows that nearly all Latvians speak fluent Russian, and as far as the use of language in their territory is concerned, only Latvians can be the injured party, not Russians.

Let us look at the composition of the congress. The majority of the people are over fifty; most are bureaucrats. There are almost no peasants or Latvians and relatively few workers. Can this movement really call itself international and perestroika-oriented?

Every movement in the republic will die if Latvians do not participate in it, but it can provoke and strengthen discord between nationalities. Yes, the Interfront Congress caused offense, but fortunately not all Russians, including my friends, are like that.

A.P. Kravalis,
Ogre

———————

Interfront does no harm to anyone. Its ideas and activities are reasonable; it does not ignore our government or use the expression "demands" in its program like the PFL does in its documents. I think it is time that everyone came to their senses, stopped stirring up enmity between people, and started fighting evil, parasitism, alcoholism, drug abuse, corruption. . . . We must restore Riga's former reputation as a clean and cultured city. But ignorant and lazy people exist in every nationality. They are the ones who need to be brought to order.

A. Bekkere,
Riga

———————

I am opposed to fronts. A front is a confrontation, and that, in our Soviet conditions, always leads to nationality-based confrontations. I am firmly convinced of this. Who needs it?

Ia.A. Kreitsberg,
Riga

———————

In my opinion, the Interfront Congress was conducted, with a few exceptions, intelligently, correctly, and in a friendly and well-organized fashion.

I have been living in Latvia for twenty-six years. I came here with my parents to the Pliavinsk hydroelectric power station construction site. My husband is also a hydro-construction worker. Unfortunately, we do not know the Latvian language well: There are few Latvians working in our sphere, and in many respects that determines our "language of contact." How will we translate our recordkeeping into

Latvian? It is a good thing that someone finally brought up this problem.

I. Pestova,
Riga

We formed the strong impression from the Interfront Congress that we, Latvians, by our mere existence, what we symbolize, our language (which we think has rights, too), are very much preventing the comrades of Interfront from living peacefully and feeling at home in Latvia. At least, this was apparent in many of the speeches that were made and it was expressed in accusations and slander. Like it or not, Latvia is first of all for Latvians—an ancient home where we want to live in peace and friendship with those representatives of other peoples who respect our land, its ancient culture, and the Latvian language. Those who try so stubbornly to present Latvians in the image of the enemy, pinning on them the "labels" of nationalists, fascists, or at least suspicious people, we answer by rallying ever more closely around our culture, our traditions, our languages, and our symbolism. We rally around the People's Front of Latvia, which is the true defender of Latvians and all the peoples living in Latvia. We rally around the Forum of the Peoples of Latvia, whose documents express the genuine interests and aspirations of the peoples living in Latvia.

Representatives of the Collective of
the Institute of Inorganic Chemistry of the
Academy of Sciences of the Latvian SSR
(27 signatures)

Apparently, the leaders of Interfront themselves also felt that the delegates had obviously "gone too far" at the congress, and shortly thereafter they came out with an official document appealing for reconciliation.

As the programmatic platforms of the People's Front and the International Front in Latvia and of similar movements in Estonia were revealed more and more, it became clear that the chief dissimilarity in their programs was not so much national as political in nature. This was a conflict between two approaches, two points of view on perestroika: the radical (supported by the People's Fronts) and the moderate (espoused by the Russian-speaking opponents of the People's Fronts). The advocates of radical perestroika in the Baltic republics insisted they were fighting for the development of the national-cultural uniqueness of all nations, including Russia.

The Russian Nation

In opening discussion of many aspects of nationality policy long hushed up, perestroika and glasnost also focused on a central issue in the USSR today: the relation of the Russian nation to the Soviet state. For decades it was believed, both here and in the West, that the Russian nation, the Russian language, and Russian culture were, so to speak, the dominant ones in the Soviet Union and that the forcible "Russification" of other cultures was the goal of Soviet policy.

In recent years, as scholars, cultural figures, and writers in Russia began to discuss the pernicious consequences of the national nihilism and national assimilation that were carried out during the Stalin years and the era of stagnation, some began to argue that the Russian nation was itself the greatest victim of Soviet policy. What looked like Russification in fact meant the assimilation of various national-cultural traditions and the creation of something like a universal "Esperanto" in which the unique traditions of Russian culture themselves disappeared. Moreover, the assault on the peasant village intensified as a result of collectivization. The destruction of the environment caused by unbridled industrial development and the erosion of traditional moral values and social solidarities had undermined the foundations of Russian national culture. Deep concern over the degeneration of Russian national culture and the fate of the Russian nation has been vividly expressed by a number of distinguished Russian writers, including Valentin Rasputin, Sergei Pavlovich Zalygin, and Vasilii Ivanovich Belov. This concern is expressed in a variety of forms and covers a broad political spectrum, from liberal and reformist advocates of Russian national revival to chauvinistic and xenophobic proponents of hatred of other groups. A common theme, however, is the view that Russian national interests have been trampled by Soviet policy.

In Moscow, in a number of major cities in Siberia (particularly in Irkutsk), and in the cities of central Russia, the creative intelligentsia has for many years tried to persuade the public that "In the family of peoples of the USSR, Russia has ended up in the position of Cinderella." This sentence appears in a lengthy open letter written by Russian writers to the Soviet government that was published in the newspaper *Literaturnyi Irkutsk*. Focusing on economic policies that place the Russian republic in a disadvantageous position, they argued:

> We, Russians, denying ourselves in everything, buy citrus fruits at exorbitant prices for our children and our sick ones from southerners [namely, the inhabitants of Central Asia and Transcaucasia who bring their fruits and vegetables to markets in Russia] who do not hide their

disdain for our poverty. Even in the store the prices for such fruit exceed by twenty to thirty-five times the cost of bread or potatoes—products that are cultivated by the workers of Russia. After all, it takes the same amount of work to produce either one!

The Russian Federation occupies a leading position both in the development of the country's economic potential and in the USSR's state budget, but the standard of living in the republic is the lowest. . . . The southerners have a higher living wage, better housing, and better roads. Practically every family has cars and the like.

The letter went on to argue that a major factor in the economic disparity among the republics is the Law Concerning the State Budget, as the most privileges are enjoyed by the republics that make the smallest contributions to the all-Union budget.

Criticism is leveled not only at the inequitable distribution of economic resources but also at the industrial policies pursued during the first decades of the Soviet Union's existence:

> Starting in the 1920s and continuing right up to the present day, Russia became an arena for dubious economic and scientific-technical experiments that undermined its economy and destroyed its ecology: hydroelectric power, which rendered unusable the most fertile lands, water resources, the fish industry, etc.; the introduction of harmful projects like the rerouting of the northern rivers; the erection of atomic power stations using an unresearched system for the burial of radioactive fuel wastes and in defiance of scientific recommendations not to build near major cities and at the sources of large rivers.

Turning to an analysis of the socio-demographic situation in Russia, the authors pointed out that today Russia has the lowest birth rate in the USSR; that with the low wages in effect, men cannot provide adequately for their families; and that the percentage of defective births is growing, as is the infant mortality rate. Is this really where our future lies? asked the authors.

> The future of a people who thrice saved themselves and Europe from the Golden Horde, Napoleon, and Hitler? A people who were able to bring to life Humanity's dream of justice and who created the most advanced socialist system in the world?
>
> Russians have been squeezed out in all the spheres that comprise the pinnacle of the so-called social pyramid: in government, science, creative organizations; in short, where national consciousness is formed. The certification of scientific personnel became a powerful mechanism of discrimination against Russians. . . . In accordance with the principle of "freeing science from the Russians," a recertification was conducted

in the institutes of the system of the USSR Academy of Sciences. In many cases, Russians were removed from their posts or transferred to lower positions, while representatives of other nationalities were promoted.

In the opinion of the letter's authors, discrimination against Russians is observed in the political structure of the Russian Federation as well:

> In Russia there is no Republican Central Committee of the Communist party, no KGB or Academy of Sciences, no Academy of the Arts, no Conservatory, and so forth. Essentially, at the present time the situation conforms to the Trotskyite-Zionist program—"a Federation for the 'nationalities' with separate centers, without a separate center for the Russians"—which was, in its day, debunked by Lenin. Now Russians have wound up without rights in their own country.

The defense of Russian culture and values is here linked to a conservative attack on the influence of Western decadence, with anti-Semitic overtones:

> In the realm of ideological life the situation has become extremely acute. The organs of the mass media—television, radio, the press—have embarked on an open course of Russophobia, boycotting defenders of Russian culture while giving the "green light" to its detractors and even to traitors to the homeland. . . . Western tastes are being inculcated through a consistent attack of imperialism: rock music and abstract, unprincipled, and formalistic art that includes pornography in paintings and sadism in cinema. . . . This Russophobia, which is being skillfully manipulated by the forces of international reaction—headed by the conductors of imperialist aggression, the Zionists—is directed primarily against Russia as the standard-bearer of communism. . . . These forces realize full well that once they have destroyed or at least weakened the Russian people, they can guarantee themselves the positions of worldwide mastery of capital that were badly shaken after the October Revolution.

The authors concluded with a number of demands, the fulfillment of which, they are convinced, can further the preservation of the Russian nation as an ethno-cultural unity. Among these demands is, specifically, the suggestion that "the Central Committee's control over radio, television, and the press be strengthened," that "musical drug addiction (rock music, hard-core rock, heavy metal, and so forth) be outlawed," and that "a barrier be erected against the propaganda of Western artistic tastes, in affirmation of the national traditions that have been developed during the Soviet era and whose efficacy has been vindicated over centuries."

What immediately strikes one in reading this declaration is the fantastic blend of the rhetoric of Stalin and Brezhnev (even on the level of phraseology) and of the mentality characteristic of Stalinism and the era of stagnation. The paradox consists in the fact that the authors of the letter, while they correctly pointed out many economic and social problems experienced by Russians, refused to see these problems as resulting from the deformations of socialism that have caused suffering to all of Soviet society and to representatives of many, many peoples. The idea running through this letter like an undercurrent is that there is an all-but-unconscious activity among certain enemies of the Russian nation, non-Russian representatives of Russia, whose aim is to "force out" the Russians. No less evident is the tendency toward cultural isolationism, the identification with the Russian nation, and the struggle to preserve Russian culture combined with the struggle against other cultures perceived as hostile.

In this document, however, one senses the extremism only in the subtext. These extremist inclinations are openly revealed in the public speeches and publications of the so-called historical-patriotic front Pamiat (Memory), a group that advocates doing absolute battle against the "enemies" of the Russian people and the Russian nation. Indeed, one of the central arguments asserted by the leadership of Pamiat is that the nation is threatened by a conspiracy of "Masons-Zionists-imperialists."

A multitude of critical articles about Pamiat has appeared in our press saying that the organization is trying to substitute chauvinism, anti-Semitism, and dogmatism for the popular desire to preserve the Russian cultural heritage. For example, *Izvestiia* (2 June 1987) reported:

> In Moscow and several other cities, the informal association Pamiat talks about itself all the louder. It is a historical-patriotic association, its activists stress. In a number of places it has conducted a series of thematic evenings, and in the beginning of May in the center of Moscow, on the square in front of the Manezh, there took place a demonstration of its activists, about which the press has reported. Slogans were raised demanding official recognition of Pamiat. . . . There were slogans such as: "The memory of the people is holy!" and "Down with the saboteurs of perestroika!"
>
> In the ranks of the demonstrators there stood out a person giving orders:
>
> "Turn around! Hold up the slogans! The banners of Russia forward!"
>
> Toward him—it was D. Vasil'ev, one of the leaders of Pamiat— turned the curious Moscovites and guests in the capital, including

foreign ones, with questions: What kind of demonstration is this? He answered that onto the square had come the "people"—the "courageous part of the people," who no longer have any strength to tolerate bureaucrats and other enemies who "destroy our history, our culture."

"They tell us that there are no enemies, but there are, and not only external, but also internal. . . ."

If someone chooses to express doubt about the conclusions of D. Vasil'ev and those with him, then the cries begin:

"Comrades! He is a CIA agent, do not listen to him! . . ."

Conversing with people who have heard the "revelations" of Vasil'ev and the other leaders of Pamiat, you feel that they are really troubled by many genuine problems. But at the same time, with surprisingly unthinking trust, they relate to the strange world of loud words that the Pamiat society creates around itself, to a world where just about everything around is full of a certain subtext, connected with the activity of all those "dark forces." For instance, a newspaper, if you look at it in the light, can reveal a certain new meaning—a signal, by means of which secret forces are communicating. Or take a memorial to a leader: If you search for and find a certain foreshortening, it turns out this is not simply an error but a conscious distortion in order to demean all of us. The hand of secret forces edits even the speeches of the general secretary, shortening all the good things said about the Russian people.

In general, as is said in the appeal of Pamiat to the people, the Motherland is in danger. We must "expose the conspiratorial apartments" of the enemy, "unite in battle formation." And this is my and your "national spirit"! Reading, listening to such a thing, you become convinced that it is something that has gone beyond the borders of the rational, turning into its opposite. The high turns into the low. Patriotism into shrill fanaticism. Vigilance against the penetration of alien ideas into our culture into fussy hysterical suspiciousness. Which tells us that the development of glasnost, the widening of democracy, bring diverse fruits, among them shrill, "vulgar" self-expression and pretense. . . .

Many newspaper articles written in a similar spirit were published. The time has come, though, for sociologists and philosophers to conduct a more serious investigation of this sociocultural phenomenon in order to understand the motivating forces behind this and other manifestations of national extremism.

The Jewish Problem

Although the leaders and members of Pamiat assure us that the "cosmopolites" of international Zionism—i.e., simply put, Jews—represent the greatest danger to Russian culture, Jewish culture in the Soviet Union has in fact been one of the cultures most discriminated against. A wave of state anti-Semitism in the late 1940s and early 1950s played a vital role in this discrimination. On Stalin's order, a campaign was initiated against "rootless cosmopolitans"—representatives of Jewish culture in the USSR. This campaign reached its apogee in 1952 with the provocative "doctors' plot," in which Jewish doctors were accused of attempting to poison Stalin and other highly placed leaders of the Soviet state. At the same time, many prominent Jewish cultural figures were executed; writers and theatrical figures were charged with "treachery" and "betraying the Motherland." Yet another impetus for anti-Semitism was provided by the war in the Near East in the late 1960s, when another propaganda campaign against Zionism was launched in the Soviet press.

The result was that for Jews in the USSR it was virtually impossible—although there were no legislative prohibitions—to study or develop their national culture, language, and history. This in turn led to the painful problem of emigration and "refuseniks." It is only in recent years that we have begun to have the opportunity to openly discuss the course of the Soviet Jewish community's struggle for its cultural-national rights.

In their most radical form, these questions are posed by the journalist Iu. Pelekhova in her article "Jews and the 'Question,'" which was published in *Vek XX i Mir.* The author noted that the democratization of Soviet society during the perestroika years has brought a number of problems to light. "But," she wrote, "these very problems either confound us or elicit a purely instinctive hostility. One of these palpably disagreeable subjects is the Jewish question. . . . The question of the Jews, raised by the Jews themselves."

The author further said:

> The spurts of activity, the "initiatives from below"—for instance, the idea of creating a Jewish cultural association, or the call for the formation of a society of friendship and cultural ties with Israel, etc.—provoked suspicion and an attempt to make them fit into the comfortably familiar framework of the formal structure of our society. . . . I remember a fairly well-organized meeting, devoted to the fortieth anniversary of the formation of the state of Israel, held in a forest on the outskirts of Moscow. . . . The wonderfully melodic Jewish national songs resounded in the forest glade. The lectures on the history of the Jewish state were also very interesting. In the speeches and interviews a number of demands were expressed, which were also repeated at the next meeting of this sort: a guarantee of opportunities for the development of the national culture; the creation of Jewish

organizations such as a Jewish historical society and a society for lovers of Jewish music; the "legalization" of the Jewish Museum and Library; the opening of Jewish schools; the publication of literature in Hebrew. What was striking, however, was that these proposals, which were on the whole reasonable and constructive, were put forth by people who had already virtually broken with our country.

In referring to the "refuseniks"—Jews who have decided to emigrate from the USSR, but who, for various reasons, are not given permission to leave, Pelekhova recalled that the persistent demand for the creation of a friendship society with Israel came from Iulii Kosharovskii, a "refusenik" of many years who had made a firm decision to leave the Soviet Union. One might ask why he cared whether the Soviet Union had such a society? Pelekhova ascribed this aspiration to man's capacity for conviction. She called upon us to assume a calm and understanding attitude toward this "strange," to use her words, combination of "refusal" and concern with the development of Jewish culture in the USSR. She corrected herself immediately, however:

> It is not really so strange when you consider that for a long time in this country only someone who had nothing more to lose could allow himself to talk about the revival of the Jewish nationality. The status of a "refusenik" was equated with an antisocial element. The only thing left for members of this "element," forced out onto the edge of society, was to seek comfort and support for themselves in the organization of circles to study the Torah or a legal seminar on the problems of "refusal." Veterans of "refusal" were also inspired by the development of Hebrew instruction and the study of the history of Judaism.

Pelekhova asked a question she could not answer: What ultimately caused the prohibition against the study of the language, culture, and literature of the Jewish people that existed until very recently? She believes that the national-cultural movement of Jews in the Soviet Union, dubbed the "Jewish question," has long been in need of serious public discussion—"not just at meetings in the woods." The author also asked another, more concrete, question: Who or what is preventing the immediate creation of a Jewish cultural association? She quoted Mikhail Chlenov, a researcher at the Institute of Ethnography of the Academy of Sciences of the USSR and organizer of a movement to create a Jewish association, who characterized opponents of the idea as representatives of the "middle bureaucratic level." In other words, the Soviet regime does not object to it, but the bureaucrats are erecting obstacles on their own initiative.

But the problem does not lie only in the bureaucratic sabotage of the Jewish association. The history of the "purgatory" endured by the association's organizers is typical of many initiatives relating to the sphere of independent public activity. The first meeting of the organizing group was fixed for mid-May of 1988, but it fell through due to the lack of a hall. When the association's organizers found three halls in Moscow and rented them in advance, the rental agreements were all canceled for obscure reasons on the eve of the meeting. Finally, in the summer, the organizers decided to meet in a small cafe. But just as the meeting was about to begin, some defects in the plumbing there were discovered. Consequently, the meeting of the founders took place in a private apartment, and so the association's proclamation was not issued at that time. "I wonder," Pelekhova asked ironically, "whose hand was behind this orgy of 'refusal'?"

The organizing group of the Jewish association puts out a samizdat publication, *Yevreiskii informatsionnyi biulleten'* (The Jewish Information Bulletin), once every two or three weeks in an edition of approximately 100 copies. "Again I cannot understand," said Pelekhova, perplexed, "why it could not be published 'legally,' even just once a month? . . . The worst thing that can happen now is to pretend that the problem will resolve itself in time. Experience has shown that national problems do not resolve themselves with time, but just become exacerbated" (*Vek XX i Mir*, 1988, no. 9).

The persistent struggle for the national-cultural revival of ethnic minorities in the USSR is finally bearing fruit. Although progress in the creation of national-cultural associations is proceeding unevenly in the various regions of the Soviet Union, by the beginning of 1989 Jewish associations had been formed in Moscow and Leningrad as well as in the Baltics. The history of the Latvian Society for Jewish Culture is described by one of the movement's activists, Zalman Kats, in the Latvian newspaper *Sovetskaia Molodiozh* (10 January 1989):

From the mid-1970s to the present day a seminar called "Rizhskie [of the city of Riga] Readings in Judaica" has been operating. When the state and the community could offer the Jews only two places for contact—less frequently, the synagogue; more often, the cemetery—a few of them found a third place. They offered their apartments—which, by an irony of fate, were usually communal—for the seminar. There were few of them for two basic reasons. First, assimilation, the isolation from their spiritual soil, from their language and culture, had taken its toll. We cannot be silent about the other reason. Many were afraid. Afraid because to take part in the languages, history, culture, religion, or traditions was always considered a regrettable affair by the authorities, and sometimes criminally punishable as well. For that reason the first to come to the seminar were those for whom the choice had already been made: They had decided to emigrate.

During the years of its activity, wrote Kats, the seminar collected an extensive library, which contains such rarities (impossible to find in ordinary Soviet libraries) as the *Jewish Encyclopedia*; the ten-volume *History of the Jewish People* by Simon Dubnov, who perished during World War II in the Riga ghetto; and works published abroad on the history of the culture, philosophy, and religion of the Jews. In addition, there are five folders of typewritten Jewish samizdat publications from the 1970s, including the "seditious" informational bulletin *Jews in the USSR—A Collection of Materials on the Culture, History, and Problems of the Jews of the Soviet Union*, published in Moscow by Aleksandr Voronel and Viktor Brailovskii; chapters from the book *To Jerusalem and Back* by Saul Bellow; an article by one of the most important philosophers of our time, Martin Buber; and commentary on anti-Semitic literature written by authors of our own country who, not infrequently, alas, have Jewish names.

Amid rising concern about the national and cultural rights of groups living outside "their" republics, in late 1988 and early 1989, in the major cities of the USSR, other national-cultural associations were established as well. As a multitude of problems in relations between nationalities began to be exposed, social scientists, psychologists, and journalists began to devote considerable attention to the sources of the conflicts and contradictions in order to find acceptable democratic ways to resolve them peacefully. Often such discussions touch on the very fundamentals of national-administrative organization in the USSR and on the principles underlying the creation of the Soviet federal system in the early 1920s.

In the last 1988 issue of *Vek XX i Mir*, summing up the very stormy period of the rebirth of consciousness among the "small" peoples of the USSR, Moscow sociologists and activists in the national-cultural movements discussed many aspects of the nationality problem at a roundtable:

G. Starovoitova: If perestroika had not had its beginnings in the economic or social sphere, it could have had them in the sphere of national relations—so acute and urgent have the problems lurking there proven, and so vital the interests of the millions of people affected in this sphere. It is now becoming clear that these interests cannot be reduced to purely economic or social interests.

It so happened that the illegalities committed in the Stalinist era with respect to the fates of individual people were repeated in the fates of entire peoples. One can recall such tragic pages from our history as the announcement that entire peoples were "enemies." The so-called "punished" peoples were transplanted from their primordial ethnic territories in accordance with the principle of collective guilt. Historical justice is, in many respects, far from being restored here.

Starovoitova had in mind the mass resettlements to Siberia, to the Gulag, of peoples like the Crimean Tatars, Germans, and Chechens, whom Stalin accused of collaborating with the Nazis during the years of the occupation. During the period of Khrushchev's thaw, some of these peoples were "pardoned," allowed to resettle once more in their historic territories, and regained their statehood. But others remain "punished" to this day. However, this is not so much the result of malicious intent on the part of the authorities as the fear of violating the status quo. Hence the insistence on the "inviolability of borders" that complicated the situation in Nagornyi Karabakh in 1988.

Other participants in the roundtable focused on other aspects of current problems in national relations. A. Prigozhin singled out three aspects of the nationality problem for particular attention:

First, democracy is conflict. We have to get used to that. Admit it and accept it. Conflict that is open, in many cases—incessant, but, as distinct from conflicts that arise in a despotic system, peaceful conflict. Conflicts among nationalities are the norm under democratic conditions. It is another matter to be able to solve them by democratic methods.

The second principle is that in nationality conflicts one must separate the horizontal from the vertical. The horizontal means relations that are strictly between nationalities, while the vertical means power relations, political relations. What do I have in mind?

In the situation surrounding Karabakh, I see the refraction of the vertical relation into the horizontal. For quarrels among nationalities, . . . demands represent a channel for the expression of discontent that has been worked out over centuries and that is close to the common man, while vertical relations in our society are blockaded, not serious, and inactive.

Prigozhin cited as an example the anti-Russian disturbances in Kazakhstan in December 1986, when the Kazakh party leader of the republic, D. Kunaev—a true comrade-in-arms of Brezhnev—was removed from his post and replaced by a Russian. Prigozhin believes that the Kazakh-Russian disturbances were a reaction to the unacceptable, essentially undemocratic method of political struggle with the "veterans" of the period of stagnation but that the protest took a particularly nationalistic form.

Third, the basic outlines of the problems of relations among nationalities. I think that Russian ethnos occupies the primary place in terms of the problems in relations among nationalities. The leadership is composed of Russians; they predominate among the heads of the primary organs of power, in the Academy of Sciences, in the Central Committee, in the All-Union Central Trade Union Council, and so forth. But even in the national republics Russian leaders occupy a special position as well.

To put it another way, they are a people who are patrons with respect to other nationalities. . . .

But besides that, the people-patron turns out to be the people-mediator as well. Because the language that connects the Baltics, for instance, the only common language, is Russian. The same is true among the Transcaucasian peoples and the Central Asian peoples. The Russian territory somehow connects all the others, which are situated on the outskirts, on the perimeter of Russia.

The growing grievances of the "indigenous nationalities" are directed against the Russians because it is precisely with the Russians that they associate all the economic, social, and political problems from which the national republics suffer. Anti-Russian inclinations have intensified noticeably in the Baltics, Transcaucasia, and Central Asia, and strangely enough, Russophobia even occurs in Byelorussia, which is closest to Russia both ethnically and historically.

I. Krupnik: First of all, where did this explosion, this wave of nationality problems come from?

Aren't we simply encountering the normal phenomenon of the reappearance of ethnicity in our lives, the backswing of the pendulum after the very long time during which ethnicity as such was, if not expelled completely, then forced out onto the periphery of spiritual life?

Is our situation so unique? The entire world has been experiencing a return to ethnicity since the end of World War II. At first it was in the splash of the anticolonial, national liberation movement in the Third World. After that, the developed, industrial nations also found themselves, to their own surprise, at the center of a storm of nationality processes in the 1960s. We studied and described this without relating it to any process within the USSR. We are now paying for that, paying in the sense that processes that, in other countries, took decades, are happening twice as rapidly here.

M. Chlenov: I think that it must be acknowledged that the definite explosion of ethnicity that is occurring today in our country is a quite natural reaction to the crisis of internationalist ideology. It was provoked not by its essence but by its practical realization over the course of many years.

In discussing the crisis of internationalist ideology, Chlenov argued that for many years nationality policy took the form of ethnocide: a policy and practice aimed at the extermination of the specific ethnic and cultural character of a given people. (Ethnocide is, therefore, different from genocide—the physical extermination of peoples.)

Chlenov also discussed the fate of dispersed groups, i.e., peoples who do not have their own national-state autonomy. The Jewish problem, in his view, remains one of the exceptionally important problems that has thus far been ignored in the Soviet press. One of the manifestations of that problem is anti-Semitism and Zionism and the attitude of official circles and popular opinion toward these seemingly opposite, but actually interdependent, phenomena. For Chlenov believes that the official battle with Zionism is the hidden cause of the dissemination and tenacity of anti-Semitism in the Soviet Union.

Recently, I asked various people who have nothing to do with Zionism what they thought the word meant. No one told me that it was the "ideology and practice of the worldwide Jewish bourgeoisie." But they all said that Zionism is extreme Jewish chauvinism. When I asked them, however, to give examples of this extreme chauvinism, they told me: well, for instance, the appeal to the Jews of the USSR to leave and go to Israel. Recently on the television program "View," there was a speech by a censor who spoke about the fact that censorship has been lifted from everything here, except from Zionist and anti-Zionist literature. Why? After all, there are many different nationalities, but only this one is for some reason singled out.

Until recently, by this watchword, everything [in libraries] relating to Judaism was sent into "special storage," and this includes a Jewish cookbook I saw there myself. The confusion around the concept of "Zionism" creates the threat of an entirely inadequate perception of the problem and the creation of an anti-Jewish stereotype and "image of the enemies." Strictly speaking, Zionism in the USSR is in fact the classical image of the enemy.

O. Pchlintsev: I would like to dwell on a question raised by G.V. Starovoitova at the very start: ethnos and territory. It is important not only in the theoretical but also in the practical respect, and it also touches on the sphere of certain kinds of political decisions.

Generally, the problem of relations among nationalities ultimately boils down to the choice of the optimal form of national existence, self-determination that is not to the detriment of other nationalities.

Some participants in the discussion advocated the idea that citizenship, rather than national identity, be treated as the basis of the Soviet system, as in the "American" model. A. Fadin proposed:

> The separation of a nationality from the state is the key question in the existence of the USSR as a state. Because we are limited to just two alternatives for development. If we follow the path of national-state pluralism, then truly, as in the inevitable renewal of the agreement about the creation of the USSR, there is no other way. We must again raise the question of our existence as a state and confirm the voluntary nature of the Union.
>
> That is one logical path for development. It is more traditional for the Soviet path of development. The other—let us call it, provisionally, the "American path"—is the autonomy of territories with any and all national associations being voluntary in nature. But in that case, insurmountable, fatal problems arise. Will the small nations, which today exist only thanks to artificial state guarantees, want to lose those guarantees?
>
> But it is impossible to develop along both paths. An attempt to sit on the fence results in what we have in Karabakh.
>
> **N. Rudenskii:** If you want to talk about the Western experience, let us recall that in Great Britain and Canada referendums have been held on the separation of major national territories (Scotland, Wales, Northern Ireland, and Quebec.) Separatist inclinations did not find the necessary support, but the authorities were not afraid to hold such referendums. I think that we could be bolder too. Our fear of this precedent found vivid expression in the state commission's announcement on the Crimean Tatar question, which stated that the national-administrative borders had been created long ago and were fixed in the constitution and that all problems could be resolved within that framework. Only in archaic societies is it believed that this or that social institution is good because it has existed for a long time. It is likely time to change that way of thinking.

The participants in the roundtable concurred in the opinion that "democracy is conflict." As life has shown us, it is impossible to "resolve once and for all" the nationality problems. But in conditions of genuine democracy it is essential to create the kind of flexible social, political, and legal structures that would promote the mitigation and "demilitarization" of clashes between nationalities and to channel them toward a more peaceful course.

SEVEN

What Is New About New Political Thinking?

Soviet Society and Foreign Policy Decisions

With the arrival of glasnost and the unusual animation of debates on domestic issues, international affairs began to be seen as the refuge of the old rhetoric. Some defended the situation, arguing that "you cannot change everything at once," that you cannot carry out reforms "on two fronts"—simultaneously in domestic and in foreign policy—and that continuity with previous approaches and evaluations in foreign policy must be preserved so as to balance the abrupt changes in domestic approaches and evaluations.

But as time passed, the words "new political thinking" appeared more often. More and more people began to get used to the thought that if the time of "double standards" within the country was past, then we could not leave the sphere of foreign policy untouched. The time had come to begin a serious rethinking of our place in the world, of our interests and goals in the world arena, and of the means to attain them.

In his article "Glasnost, Negotiations, and Disarmament" (*Izvestiia*, 17 October 1988), Academician Georgii Arbatov, the director of the Institute of the USA and Canada, wrote frankly about the need for extending glasnost into the foreign policy sphere.

If, in our domestic affairs, glasnost has developed simultaneously with perestroika and at times has gone ahead of it, in our foreign policy things developed in a more complex way. There were various reasons for this. Most important was the limitation on information. Of course, in previous periods, information on domestic policy had also been mercilessly covered up. But the changes in that sphere proceeded more quickly than in foreign policy and especially military affairs.

This is naturally justifiable in some ways—these affairs have their own character, which does not allow for revealing everything to the public eye or for guaranteeing complete "transparency." Because in the world arena we come up against not only friends but also opponents, against whom we are really struggling, and it is not in the rules to lay out all our cards. And also because foreign policy issues have touched, and still touch, the interests of third countries, demanding a delicate approach to public discussion (and also a temporary abstinence from such discussion). And also, in some cases (sometimes in many) it was habit, the force of inertia, or even some officials' vested interest that prevented candor. . . . Nonglasnost in the foreign policy and military spheres—this is the heritage we are rejecting.

In calling for the extension of glasnost to foreign and military affairs, Arbatov deplored the fact that policy-making in these areas remained a closed process excluding broader participation by experts and legislators. Glasnost in foreign policy, he suggested, was inseparable from its democratization:

It is obviously important to take into account that we have entered into an era of glasnost and that glasnost must extend not only into domestic but also into foreign affairs, including military and disarmament affairs. Why is it that what we tell the American negotiators has usually remained secret even from the experts who are supposed to explain and defend the Soviet position? Why is it that delegations from the U.S. Congress regularly come to the negotiations, but never delegations of the USSR Supreme Soviet? Why, finally, does the Supreme Soviet's foreign affairs commission "get involved in" a problem when it comes to the ratification of an agreement but does not even have the possibility of expressing its opinion on the progress of the talks, as it has on many other important political questions? And, perhaps, would there be any sense in establishing in the Supreme Soviet a commission on defense questions?

The time has come, it seems, for us to answer these and other similar questions within the framework of the planned political reform, democratization, and the broadening of glasnost. . . .

As Arbatov's remarks suggest, the new political thinking in international affairs is inseparable from glasnost and the democratization of the foreign policy process. Yet it did not emerge all at once as a fully developed and complete program. Expanding the discussion of the Soviet Union's priorities in the foreign policy, military, and ideological spheres is a long process that is only now really beginning. What distinguishes the new approach from the previous ones is the recognition that the USSR has no monopoly on the new thinking. On the contrary, it is understood that new thinking arises as an international, global phenomenon. Attempts are still made to interpret the boundary between the old and the new thinking in international affairs "geographically"— to say that the Soviet Union has completely gone over to the new thinking while the United States and other Western countries remain the refuge of the old thinking. However, the view that increasingly predominates understands the new thinking as a result not only of Soviet efforts but also of the efforts of many politicians, movements, and social organizations of the West as well as of the East. That means that the struggle of ideas is developing not so much among various states but within each society, including Soviet society.

"Politics is the privilege of all." This title of an article by the famous poet Yevgeny Yevtushenko, one of the informal spiritual leaders of recent decades, disputes the familiar formula according to which politics—especially foreign and military policy—is the exclusive prerogative of the government. At the end of the 1970s, after the shock of Vietnam and Watergate, the Gallup Institute concluded that American society ceased to believe that the "President knows best" what the nation needs. Something similar is happening in the Soviet Union today. People are coming to understand that questions of foreign and military policy in today's world cannot remain only the object of "chess games" by diplomats and generals. They touch the interests of life itself, of the security, well-being, and individual conscience of each person, and therefore we need democratization and glasnost in international policy, a sharp increase in the role of society, and a feeling that each person is involved in the affairs and problems not only of his own society but of the world community as a whole. Yevgeny Yevtushenko wrote in *Literaturnaia Gazeta* (22 July 1987):

> In order that the semi-science of today's politics becomes a science, we must introduce into its teaching a new discipline—toleration, that is, patience. We must heal ourselves of ambitious attempts to appear, in our own and others' eyes, to be the truth in the final instance. Politics is not an elite privilege of professional politicians. Politics is the privilege of everyone. This privilege is dictated not only by spiritual but also by physical necessity. This privilege is the instinct for self-preservation of humankind from nuclear catastrophe. This privilege is also that new thinking, of the necessity of which the Soviet leader persistently speaks. The times when narrow nationalism could be progressive are historically past, for any nationalism, armed with the atom bomb, is internationally dangerous. More than that, aggressive nationalism with the atom bomb ceases to be nationalism, because it

is suicidal also for one's own nation. The division of the world into so-called "three worlds" is historically conditioned. But nevertheless, in perspective it is unnatural. These three worlds are actually only three various ways of seeking the future. It is possible that one of these models will triumph, convincing the other societies of its superiority. But it must convince only without forcibly imposing, for to buy anybody's love with government bribes or to achieve that love with rockets pressed to the throat is in the end a hopeless cause.

Glasnost and democratization in foreign policy—these are the important recipes in the cause of turning the people away from mutual distrust and suspicion of the enemy and from ideas of the omnipotence of secret new weapons and secret diplomatic springs. But openness in foreign policy matters is unfamiliar, and wide social discussion of foreign policy alternatives has few precedents in our history. Would not glasnost itself tell too much to the "enemy"? Yevgeny Yevtushenko answered:

> The main strength of man is not to fear to speak of his weaknesses. . . . At the same time as secret services achieve great perfection in listening in on each other, nations lose the opportunity to listen in on the beating of each other's hearts. Many political negotiations founder precisely because they are built on mutual accusations and not on confessions. The fear of the so-called loss of face in itself leads to that loss. The world will be saved only if politics will mutually build itself on the reciprocal courage of admitting one's own mistakes and not on the comfortable cowardice of considering one's partner the symbol of all the world's evil. We need to unlearn mutual ill-will. Mankind is one body, and it would be a criminal absurdity if broken legs tried to dance a victory dance celebrating the ulcer of the small intestine, and if gallstones jumped for joy learning of the inflammation of the lungs. No country can find healing for its own illness in the illness of another country. In this sense, all people on earth, including politicians, must be wise doctors rather than gloat about others' diseases.
>
> Now the main task is to stop nuclear war, taking the risk of trusting each other. The risk of trusting is the only risk that is not dangerous, if, of course, it is taken mutually.

But trust among peoples and governments of various countries requires first of all the trust of each country in the foreign policy of its own government. In past years, in commentaries on international themes, one of the frequently encountered stereotypes was the phrase about the "unanimous support by the Soviet people" of one or another foreign policy decision made by the government. On some issues this support did exist. On other issues opinions differed. More often we encountered simple apathy and indifference. But is it not natural that the opinions of the Soviet people should vary according to age, nationality, social position, and level of education?

"There is no decision that is unanimously supported by the whole Soviet people!" wrote sociologist Nikolai Popov in the newspaper *Sovetskaia Kul'tura*. Any statistician will tell you that in all cases some percentage of the audience either does not have a clear opinion, is uninformed of the essence and even of the existence of a given issue, or is for various reasons against the decision. If we really want to base our policy on the interests of the people, then we must study this public opinion.

If a wide range of opinion exists even on the simplest questions, then it is doubly complex in a multidimensional sphere where many interests clash, as in foreign and military policy. One cannot expect people instantaneously to support such innovative, unusual, iconoclastic principles as those of the new political thinking. Glasnost requires an understanding of the various points of view held by Soviet citizens on the goals, interests, actions, and initiatives of the Soviet Union in the world arena.

Entitling his polemical article "The 'Voice of the People' in Conditions of Glasnost," (*Sovetskaia Kul'tura*, 12 June 1987), Popov justly emphasized that a government that makes decisions without real study of popular opinion cannot expect true popular support for its policy. He wrote:

What, exactly, did we fear? That the people would not support the policy of the party and government? Seventy years of life under a socialist order and the armed defense of Soviet power at the cost of tens of millions of lives should have, it seems, been proof of the people's loyalty to the chosen political course and to a certain complex of ideas of social justice, humanism, inviolable rights, values, and principles of the organization of society. As for the concrete plans of development of one or another branch of the country's life, as for large and small projects, here there does not have to be complete unanimity, "universal" support. Here there can and must be dissent, various opinions. More than that, the presence of open and, most important, audible criticism of this or that project can in itself play the role of a safety mechanism built into the system, to speak in technical terms, that warns if not all of the mechanisms are working correctly. . . . Unfortunately, the development of democracy is a far from speedy process. As we often say, "See, he alone is marching, and nobody else is in step with him." In the army when walking in ranks it is necessary for everyone to march all with the right or all with the left, but in society it is also possible for only one person to be right. But, most important, he must have the right to express his opinion openly and without fear. One of the familiar cliches is that the people are always right. (In the historical plan, yes, but in concrete instances, large groups, classes, and peoples can make mistakes). If a person or a group of people has an opinion different from the commonly held one, their views and activity have often been labelled "anti-popular." This prefix "anti" (often fateful for people in the past), attached to other terms as well, has more than once been used to characterize people with "uncomfortable" views.

Popov acknowledged that in view of the sharp struggle that is going on in society, we also need to hear the views of those who are not rushing to restructure themselves:

> Of course, the opponents of perestroika or of the new thinking in foreign policy do not live in any one place, do not wear a common sports uniform, and do not go, probably, to demonstrate in front of the Moscow Soviet, as do members of the Pamiat society. However, their voices must be heard in the current, more and more polyphonic choir of society, even if it seems that they are ruining the melody. Inasmuch as there are people who, all the same, "protest in action" (or inaction), then it is better fully to know such opinions and moods. In order not to repeat old mistakes, we need to work out a tolerant attitude toward those who disagree (even toward those in disagreement with a good cause), if only in the name of developing traditions of democratism and glasnost and so as not sometimes to chill the opponents of the next bureaucratic or technocratic adventure.
>
> We must realize that the voice of the people is not always pleasant, that we may hear something "unripe," something unforeseen, something that does not fit into the schemes of civics textbooks. And that public opinion will contain contradictory opinions, because in society there are many contradictions.

There is not and never has been a monolithic, noncontradictory public opinion. The refusal to notice the variety and contradictions, the struggle of opinions, is not at all the same thing as "unity" of opinions. Therefore, today we are paying much more attention to surveying public opinion, even on questions of foreign policy; we try to take into account various, often diametrically opposed points of view. We all know that the heterogeneity of opinions in the USSR on all kinds of foreign policy, ideological, and military questions has always existed and exists now. But it is one thing to reveal this with the help of anonymous surveys; it is another to meet open expressions and clashes of opinion in public debates, to draw various political and social groups with their views and programs into a real process of working out foreign policy decisions.

The journal *Vek XX i Mir*, which has become one of the most independent, original Soviet publications of the period of glasnost and perestroika, published a letter to the editor by Aleksei Pankin (1987, no. 5) that provoked pointed debates. Reminding the reader that for many long years Soviet society was put in the position of giving "prescribed approval" to any and every foreign policy step by the government and that journalism and propaganda strongly supported the image of an "absolutely consistent, uncontradictory, and infallible" foreign policy, Pankin spoke frankly of the difficulties created by the new situation:

Let me focus on my own experience. When, during lectures on the international situation, questions are asked about the military balance, I invariably end up in a tight corner. There is not a lot of official information about Soviet armed forces (although the amount of published military statistics has increased in the past five to seven years). There exist, of course, Western estimates, but can they be trusted? (In general, in this field, it becomes absurd: We know Soviet rockets best by the names given them in the West.) Just in case, I, as a rule, take care to limit myself to general reasoning.

There is, in my view, yet another reason for our passion for general, and thus not always convincing, reasoning. It is that, when we begin to ground the completely true principles of the new thinking, we discover that even the leadership of our country has perhaps not always followed them. And to admit mistakes in foreign policy here is still somehow not customary. Indeed. In 1983 the USSR walked out of the talks on reducing medium-range missiles in Europe and began to place additional SS-20 missiles in response to the appearance in Western Europe of American cruise missiles and Pershing-2s. Sometime afterward, we renewed talks and dismantled the extra missiles. The question arises: Does this not mean that our response measures were superfluous? Now the USSR has agreed not to count, for a rather long time, the nuclear weapons of England and France and is negotiating in order to remove from Europe the American and Soviet medium-range missiles; that is, in effect, to return to the situation of the mid-1970s, before the beginning of deployment of the SS-20s. Were those missiles really so necessary at the time? No matter what the responses to these questions, it is simply illogical not to ask them.

I think that greater openness and glasnost in the discussion of Soviet defense and foreign policy make the new thinking more convincing and more comprehensible to society as a whole and that our internal discussions will become more mature.

Some time ago on "Mayak" I heard a commentary dedicated to the Korean War of 1950–1953 under the rubric of "Chronicle of Crimes of Imperialism." The commentator kept talking about the "American aggression" against the Korean People's Democratic Republic, not once mentioning that the invasion was carried out under the UN flag and that there participated in it, albeit basically symbolically, military contingents from England, France, Australia, Belgium, Colombia, Canada, Ethiopia, Greece, the Netherlands, New Zealand, the Philippines, Thailand, Turkey, Luxembourg, and South Africa. Why did it ignore these facts, which were essential for understanding the situation? Was he too lazy to glance at a history textbook? Or did he think that a reminder of them would justify the crime of imperialism? Then it would have been more honest to share his doubts. How many times has it been said that one must not correct history by throwing out real facts? And imagine the perplexity of a Soviet person who, after that commentary, heard, let us say on Voice of America, that the Korean aggression was an "international mission of the UN."

TASS's accounts of many important foreign policy announcements of Western leaders sometimes give the impression of wide polemical commentaries on barely accessible texts from which only a few lines have survived. From year to year we read about the "unrestrained growth of American military spending," about the immeasurable swelling of their military budget, although in real measurements it has not actually grown for several years. And is it not worthy of explanation to the wide audience that a significant part of the U.S. military budget goes to pay for the upkeep of its military personnel, to pensions for retirees and veterans? The awareness of that fact allows one to take a calmer attitude toward the gigantic figures for military spending by the United States. It would be all right if somebody had prohibited divulging this. But no. Soviet scholarly journals write about these things; they are analyzed in Soviet books. And the fact that they are only with difficulty making their way onto the pages of the mass press is a result, I think, of some kind of unconscious internal orientation of many internationalist journalists that forces them to edit the picture of reality; it is a manifestation of an inertia built up in past years from which they free themselves with more difficulty than do journalists writing about domestic themes. . . .

The Soviet people, it seems to me, are predisposed to the new thinking, but still its dissemination and propagandization are a very difficult business demanding a reevaluation of many values, a review of customary ideas; in other words, demanding perestroika. This process has already begun and is gaining momentum, and the moral and political duty of Soviet peace advocates consists in making their contribution to it, and making it irreversible.

The publication of this letter provoked a variety of responses from readers. The majority favored the inclusion of society, as far as possible, in real discussion about foreign policy decisions. But there were those who accused the letter's author of seeking to prevent the government from conducting foreign policy appropriately and independently. One of the respondents insisted that as far as he could tell, "in all the time of its existence the Soviet Union has not committed a single mistake in its foreign policy."

To take another example, at the beginning of the 1980s, many Soviets viewed "citizen diplomacy" with caution, considering it inappropriate to create an alternative to official diplomacy. Others called citizen diplomacy a cunning trick of the West. Many simply did not wish to enter into discussion about foreign and military policy, inasmuch as they did not have any experience of direct contact with foreigners and did not have at hand the information necessary to arrive at their own opinions about foreign policy and military questions.

Now the situation is changing before our eyes. Citizen diplomacy is being transformed from a "foreign wonder" into a familiar, customary means of intercourse with other peoples. Many dozens of trade unions, cultural associations, youth organizations, and initiative groups are involved in diverse contacts, dialogues, and joint initiatives with foreigners, including Americans. The democratic idea of transforming traditional interstate relations into genuine international relations, relations betweens peoples, is beginning to be realized.

New Approaches to the Problems of War and Security

What principles of the new thinking in foreign policy are at the center of current discussions in the Soviet Union? Are the discussions of new thinking merely a propagandistic trick, and if not, what is the principal novelty of these ideas?

It may be that the most important principle here is the recognition of the primacy of universal, global interests over the interests of any government, nation, or class. Nikolai Sokov wrote along these lines in the journal *Vek XX i Mir* (1987, no. 3):

> The rapid development of the interdependency, the interconnectedness, of the various sides of international relations requires the introduction of substantive changes in the foreign policy process on the scale of worldwide cooperation and of each of the governments that are a part of it. There is a great need today for the internal elites and society, in shaping the essential directions of foreign policy of our government, to instill within themselves the need to consider the other's point of view, to understand this point of view, to have a certain level of flexibility and globality of thinking, a universal approach to their foreign policy. . . . Just as in its own time the Ptolemaic theory of the solar system was overturned and replaced by the theory

of Copernicus, it has come time to recognize that any government, large or small, is above all a part of the association of governments and no single one must claim that the others revolve around it and should subordinate their interests to those of its own.

Messianic ideologies have often led different peoples and political forces to efforts to dictate to the rest of the world how to live and what kind of political or social system to choose. The echoes of such approaches have often been heard as well in the ideological opposition between the capitalist and socialist countries. Today the question is not about the renunciation of one's own interests but about a deeper, broader understanding of what these interests are.

> A kind of rule of foreign policy of any government must be a clear understanding that no single people, no single political actor, possesses an exclusive right to the truth unless it is guided by the interests of all mankind. Efforts to appropriate the right to absolute truth in the creation of a world order (and such a right is never granted by anyone but is only appropriated) lead to a clash with the objective truth that no single government of the world can have special rights, or even a special responsibility for the fate of others, insofar as it almost inevitably brings with it a "right" to interfere in the affairs of others. Even the most powerful governments are able to bear only one responsibility—for the protection of peace on Earth, for the building of a more just world order, for the solving of global problems without the infringement of any rights—and all this on an equal basis with all the governments of the world.
>
> Naturally, it would be a mistake to deny that, above all, the quickest reduction and liquidation of nuclear weapons must be carried out by the nuclear powers, especially the USSR and the United States. However, because of its super-global character, this problem affects everyone.

Has not the question of universal interests been posed in a similar fashion in the Soviet Union before? Practically not. "In the Political Report of the Central Committee [of 1987] a distortion was corrected, through which the antagonism of the two world systems—socialism and capitalism—was considered without their interdependence," remarked Academician Evgenii Primakov, director of the Institute of the World Economy and International Relations of the Academy of Sciences of the USSR. In his article "The New Philosophy of Foreign Policy" in *Pravda* (10 July 1987), Primakov maintained:

> It is important to note that the growing interdependence of the contemporary world is reflected not only in the problem of survival

shared by all but also in the existence and development of a worldwide economy, the presence and intensification of universal interests connected with the preservation of the natural environment, the overcoming of the backwardness of the so-called Third World, the victory over disease, the discovery of new sources of energy, the use of space and the Pacific Ocean for the progress of mankind, etc. An understanding of all this lies at the base of the new foreign policy philosophy.

The statements by Gorbachev in his speech at the UN on 7 December 1988—which were widely discussed in the Soviet press—represented a new step in recognizing international interdependence and the common interests consequent upon it. "The scientific-technological revolution," declared Gorbachev, "turned many problems—economic, food supply, energy, ecological, information, demographic—that we treated as national or regional problems until recently into global problems."

He continued: "It is as if the world has become more visible and tangible to everyone, thanks to the latest means of communication, mass information, transportation. International relations have been simplified to an unprecedented extent." Therefore, Gorbachev drew a conclusion that is extremely important for the Soviet Union, "the preservation of any sort of 'closed' society today is nearly impossible." The gradual transformation of the Soviet Union into a more open society is the most important guarantee of the irreversibility of the reforms taking place in the country and of glasnost itself.

The new political thinking proposes the working out of a new view of the world and our position in it. And that in turn is unthinkable without a reevaluation of several traditional stereotypes, as Academician Georgii Arbatov pointed out in an article in the weekly *Moscow News* (1988, no. 39):

I will start with . . . our concept of the world. For a long time we saw it split into two hostile and opposing camps—capitalist and socialist. It was thought in the USSR that an irreconcilable struggle between them would determine the main direction of the world's development.

The reality turned out to be much more complex than this scheme, although an irreconcilable strife, alas, did, for many years, poison East-West relations. The scheme was incorrect because it transferred, mechanically and with oversimplification, the laws of internal development to international relations. At the same time, the more important features of the modern epoch were ignored. Today we see the world differently and think that it is one. Despite the existing contradictions, differences and disagreements, it is a single whole, and moreover, very fragile and ever more interdependent world.

Another important problem giving rise to arguments and disagreements is the interrelationship between war and politics in the nuclear era. Above all, it is a question of the applicability of the famous formula of Karl Clausewitz to the nuclear era. Is it possible to attain political goals through the massive use of nuclear weapons? Among Soviet authors today there is no unanimity in response to this question.

Moskovskie Novosti, under the rubric of the "Discussion Club," presented (on 26 April 1987) the opinion of foreign policy expert Daniil Proektor, who straightforwardly called the classical formula an "absurdity" in contemporary conditions:

> We are living in an epoch of the most profound reevaluation of ideas in all spheres relating to peace and war. There is reason for a terrible uneasiness about the protracted period for the realization of new objective realities in this mortally dangerous sphere. . . .
>
> It is natural and logical that the profound restructuring going on in our country also includes a new intellectual theory about the main categories of world politics, security and military policy. A general reevaluation of the old is going on, thinking in the sphere of politics and defensive philosophy is being carried out in complete accordance with the dynamics of the modern world, with the discoveries of the natural sciences, above all nuclear physics, medicine, space science. Can such a new understanding be made universal?
>
> The ideas of Clausewitz were interpreted and embodied in practice in Europe in the most varied situations. But now, in our view, there can be no disagreement. After the newest discoveries of natural scientists about the probable consequences of such a war, after Chernobyl and Challenger, it has become clear that nuclear war is the continuation of the absurd. . . . It cannot have anything in common with politics as such.
>
> But perhaps those who consider that for Europe not a general, but some sort of local, limited nuclear war could become an accepted means of politics are right? Or a traditional, non-nuclear war?
>
> . . . 17,000 nuclear charges are directed at this continent from land, sea and air. By means of what sort of politics could a war begin in which the sides would begin to shoot "only a part" of their arsenals at each other, for example 5,000 or even 200 warheads? Ancient Europe, with all the brilliance of its civilization, has come to the point when war has become synonymous with "the end."
>
> Conventional war in Europe is also an absurdity. One cannot even remotely imagine, for instance, what would occur if only non-nuclear rockets of high accuracy were to smash 200 European atomic electric stations to dust.
>
> Not only technology changes over the course of history. Man improves. People of yore lived in vague anticipation of general destruc-

tion, Armageddon. "The Last Judgment" of Michelangelo or the second part of Verdi's "Requiem" perhaps most expressively of all bring to painting and music the idea of the general final hour. But we do not believe in it. No matter how difficult and dangerous the path, a "revolution of the mind" is unavoidable. And it cannot help but bring to mankind, presently reinterpreting peace and war, emancipation from the complex of worldwide catastrophe. The wise "teacher of war" Karl Clausewitz has become anachronistic for Europe. A peaceful nuclear-free Europe is possible.

The invention of all-new "nuclear doctrines" is not capable of resolving the absolute contradiction between the grandiose volume of built-up military strength and the complete impossibility of using it in the capacity of a "continuation of politics." There remain only the highest and singular means—"the use of the force" of reason in the name of a great political goal—the destruction of force itself. But this is already "Clausewitz reversed." And only in that form is it acceptable for Europe at present and in the future.

But Proektor noted that Clausewitz's ideas retained some validity in relation to nonnuclear conflicts and wars outside the boundaries of Europe:

> Our world is unbelievably complex; it is not only Europe. In accordance with our calculations, in the regions of the world outside of the zone of East-West opposition from 1945 to 1982 there have been 253 wars and conflicts. That is where Clausewitz is still alive and, unfortunately, will continue to live.

The historian Anatolii Utkin, in the same discussion on the pages of *Moskovskie Novosti*, emphasized that all members of the "nuclear club" do not yet refuse to recognize nuclear war as a rational means of politics:

> There is no doubt that Clausewitz's formula has lost its sense in the modern nuclear world. Its realization is equivalent to suicide.
>
> But if we rest on this statement, we elucidate only a part of the problem of international security. The simple statement of the unacceptability of war is like atheistic propaganda among nonbelievers. We believe and hope that a nuclear catastrophe will pass us by, but in order confidently to assert that nuclear war is an absurdity, it is necessary that this point of view be shared by all five nuclear powers. In order that this assessment becomes a law of European life, it is necessary that it be shared by those who have nuclear arms either in Europe or merely directed at it. But some nuclear powers allow the possibility of using nuclear arms. Moreover, they make the most

important part of their strategic planning the use of nuclear arms in the very earliest stage of conflict.

Of the four nuclear powers possessing nuclear weapons in Europe only the Soviet Union has officially declared that it will not use them first. Three powers—the United States, England and France—on the other hand, do not contemplate the carrying out of military action, in any case on a large scale, without the use of nuclear weapons. It is the governmental policy of these countries, and no matter how much we talk about the destructiveness, suicidal nature, and unacceptability of nuclear conflict, this does not negate the fact of the preparedness of these three countries' troops in Europe to use these weapons.

The most "rigid" of positions is held by France, which is prepared to use nuclear weaponry immediately after the beginning of conflict. This is its official doctrine and in this regard it diverges even from the general NATO doctrine of "flexible response" shared by the USA and England.

We are speaking of the need for new thinking, the type which [Albert] Einstein dreamed of. We are struggling for the affirmation of new thinking which excludes the possibility of the carrying out of politics through rocket-atomic means. But we must not give ourselves over to illusions. The idea that nuclear arms can exert a revolutionary impact on the thinking of everyone is excessively optimistic. The old is not given up without a struggle.

Soviet foreign policy in the framework of the new thinking is directed toward the liquidation of nuclear arms, and we believe that the forty-year peace in Europe is due not to nuclear weapons, as official Washington, London, and Paris assert, but to realistic and cautious politics, at the basis of which lies the conscious or compelled rejection of Clausewitz's formula.

But are we not simplifying the real picture when we say that the USSR simply does not recognize the rationality of nuclear war while the Western powers consider it a means of politics? In the West, as in the East, there are those who reject the use of nuclear weaponry for political goals, but there are also those who retain the old approaches.

The new departure in Soviet thinking can be seen in the fact that the political leadership of the country, in the person of Mikhail Gorbachev, made an official announcement that nuclear war is not considered a rational extension of politics. But several participants in our discussions consider that such an approach does not by a long shot require a change in all traditional assessments.

General Nikita Chaldymov wrote the following in the armed forces newspaper *Krasnaia Zvezda* in an article entitled "The First Responsibility Before the Peoples" (22 August 1987):

What is the essence of war today? The desire to issue a new word in the development of the bases of political thinking often leads other theoreticians to the unproven destruction of everything created earlier in the theory of military policy. This above all relates to the assertion that, as a result of the catastrophic nature of the consequences of nuclear war, the latter has ceased to be an extension of politics. The authors of this point of view have lost sight of the fact that the reality of war includes two elements. First, the properly political [element], defining the reason for the existence of war as a social phenomenon and its political content, and the second element, defining the means (that is, armed force) through which political goals are achieved by war. Obviously, nuclear war has ceased to be a rational means of attaining political goals. In this sense nuclear war, if one were to break out, would not be an extension of rational politics insofar as it would be a catastrophe for mankind, and in such a war neither side could win. But rocket-nuclear war, if it is to be suffered by mankind, has its causes, precisely the adventuristic, militaristic politics of re-actionary imperialistic circles. And if today we are to remove completely the idea that the essence of war is politics, we would also conceal the reason for the possibility of the appearance of new wars; we would remove the responsibility from imperialism as a source of wars in the modern epoch.

General Dmitrii Volkogonov, in *Argumenty i Fakty* (1987, no. 25) also defended the view that the "good old" formula of Clausewitz is still of service:

In our opinion, it is not worth calling this formula "absurd" as does the well-known historian D. Proektor. It is not even that present insignificant merit overturns authorities of long ago, but that the position about the relationship between war and politics in the nuclear age is considerably more profound than it appears at first glance.

I will explain this idea. Nuclear weaponry has "outgrown" the goals in whose name it was created. A qualitatively new level of development in military technology has placed the issue of the fate of war itself on a new plane. In essence, a border, limit, boundary of war (here we mean nuclear war) has appeared. From this point of view Clausewitz has become hopelessly anachronistic. If one speaks about the functional side of the phenomenon of war, it has ceased to be a reasonable, rational means of politics. . . . It is thought that this is the main thing in the present definition of the relationship between war and politics.

On the other hand, if one defines the essence of an unthinkable, but possible, nuclear war, then henceforth, with its help it is only possible to continue stupid, criminal, adventuristic politics leading to oblivion. As to the argument, "what kind of extension of politics is it, if in such a war everyone perishes," it is the result of a criminal politics. In this way, war may be a monstrous extension of criminal politics. The exercise of our struggle for peace requires the tireless unmasking of those who generate such a type of politics.

In a word, the discussion of this problem is not yet concluded; various, as yet mutually exclusive, points of view continue to clash.

Heated arguments are provoked by other questions as well—for example, are there values more important today than peace? Not everyone is ready to recognize the consequences that flow from treating the preservation of peace as the highest priority. Not everyone believes that there are not some values for which it would be acceptable to risk confrontation, including a military one. In the Soviet press a polarization of opinions on this question is apparent. A position close to pacifism is held and defended, for example, by the Byelorussian writer Ales' Adamovich. In a public discussion in a Moscow forum for a nuclear-free peace and on the pages of *Moskovskie Novosti* (8 March 1987, no. 10), he described his understanding of the problem as follows:

What I wanted to speak about at this forum and to continue here in this article is the conversation regarding the fact that the new thinking is nothing less than a new logic. And a new morality, a new feeling, and a new literature.

It can also frighten, this new political thinking. It is not a simple thing to understand fully the notion of a thermonuclear age.

I had a conversation with a commander of a modern submarine.

"Is it not difficult for you to understand what cosmic power you control?"

Answer:

"Someone has to control it, once it exists. One must restrain oneself from superfluous thoughts."

"Well, and if you could imagine," I hurried to elucidate everything at once, "that those whose doctrine allows a first nuclear strike were to carry it out. Or if an accident, mistake, would cover half the world with a fiery sandstorm. And it depended on you: would you respond or not?"

Suddenly a woman present at the table spoke up:

"Of course! They would kill us, they would kill everyone!"

These hurried voices are from the previous, pre–nuclear war.

The commander of the nuclear submarine was silent. Then he asked me:

"And would you push the button?"

"Me—no. Otherwise the destruction of mankind would be carried out by my hands. By my second strike."

Besides that, I remembered and reminded him that their retribution would come even without a responding strike—in the form of the deadly radiation from their own warheads and bombed atomic reactors.

"I will keep silent all the same," said the military man. "No one, especially they, should know how I will respond."

Yes, we do not want to take part in the murder of mankind, neither by a first nor a second, nor any strike, because we are for the complete liquidation of nuclear weapons, we are ready with relief to part with nuclear "power," we are not at all gladdened by rocket pseudo-biceps, we do not cling to the status of a nuclear power—all our propositions, moratoria, and practical steps toward the other side speak for themselves.

Yes, the new thinking is not a mental exercise. It requires courage.

For the military man, it is the courage to recognize the foolishness, absurdity, inhumanity of this very "matter"—of war. That is, it is as if a devaluation of their very profession. To me, personally, there is no one more brave or worthy than those military men, like the retired generals, who devote their military knowledge to the antiwar movement.

This last assertion brought forth an especially stormy reaction. However, Adamovich continued:

Now we return to the question: is the new thinking advantageous? It would seem that it could be more advantageous for all to survive, instead of everyone burning in the nuclear fire. But this is what we see time and again: the flight, the running away from a higher interest for any petty "advantage," political, class-economic, and so forth. Remember that in the fifties the following model for the behavior of the competing systems was drawn: two cars on one road are heading toward each other, who will turn away, who will lose his nerve?

The path of non-military solutions to any problems is not only preferable in these circumstances, but it is the most rational according to the highest calculation—from the point of view of the interests of mankind and of each of its peoples, and of any of its classes or groups. But precisely because of that, agreement is necessary on the problems of peace and disarmament of the great powers, in order that the most acute problems of the development of all nations without exception may be settled quickly.

That is what courage is. Let us too try to demonstrate it ourselves as well. There is the question of the co-existence of different systems: And if here too we more bravely look precisely from the positions of the thinking of the nuclear era? Have we not kept silent too long, losing the sense and what is yet more dangerous, losing the chance to agree about what is important—the survival of the human species itself?

The new thinking is thinking through to the end that which previously no one brought themselves to think through. For example, the question of local wars and, in connection with this, of just and unjust wars. That there are, occur, just wars—to reject this idea today would be unjust (in relation to the victims of aggression, force, and exploitation in Africa, Latin America, the Near East).

But in this question as well, in the age of the nuclear bomb, it is not the same as it was before the bomb.

In our own ongoing war with the partisans there have even been cases in which even experienced demolition experts have perished from their own mines, and the fault for that was the safety fuses: among them were fast-lighting ones. A person calculates on the basis of three minutes, but the ignition occurs in a moment.

General Dmitrii Volkogonov attacked Adamovich's approach, criticizing his views as abstract pacifism and capitulation:

The new political thinking is not a new worldview; it is a new level that enriches our understanding of the objective requirements of the nuclear age. The conception of the new thinking does not contradict Leninist teaching about the defense of the socialist Fatherland. It is important to emphasize—as lately in our press there have appeared publications that, in our opinion, present the phenomenon of war in a distorted way—the military-political situation and the social role of the Soviet armed forces.

Unfortunately, certain authors concentrate their efforts only on the condemnation of war "in general," at the depiction of its apocalyptic consequences, without a clear indication of who is to blame for this global threat. It is similarly an aimless condemnation of nuclear arms outside of the political context. For example, one can thus assess the printed statement of the well-known Soviet writer A. Adamovich, who sees the duty of literature to "create a moral atmosphere in society, in the world, on the planet such that it would not be prestigious to have the bomb, but that it would be no less shameful than to have a concentration camp, a factory of death, an Auschwitz?!" In this way the author says that in order for the opposing systems to "cease to be mutually threatening," we must start with ourselves. But did we not begin to struggle for peace already in 1917? As if there has not been and is not a well-known Soviet plan for the gradual liquidation of nuclear weapons on the planet by the beginning of the next century! If one were to follow the logic of this writer, then only unilateral disarmament (since the West thus far has not taken any countermeasures) is capable of freeing us from the "shame" of possessing nuclear weapons. (*Krasnaia Zvezda*, 22 May 1987)

Volkogonov also said that Adamovich's position is ideologically incorrect:

> It is difficult to understand an author who writes that a "general worldview foundation" is necessary for the construction of a demilitarized world. The worldviews of the two worlds will remain different. But this, however, does not exclude the possibility of developing a single view of nuclear war as an unacceptable means of politics. And not only such a view, but real actions, directed to the exclusion of nuclear war from the life of human society. So far only socialism is prepared for this. This is the whole issue. . . .
>
> Just as it is impossible to clap with one hand, so it is impossible to create a nuclear-free world through unilateral efforts alone. Whether we want to or not, we cannot but take this reality into account. Unfortunately, assertions are allowed like the one written by a Soviet author, that there will be no peace while "each social system insists on its 'beloved ideals.' " That is, that the possibility for the preservation of peace is conditioned upon the rejection of one's ideals and spiritual values. The unacceptability of such an approach is obvious.

Volkogonov defended a different understanding of the role of the armed forces in today's society, one that does not assume that the Soviet and American militaries are "on the same level":

> The armed forces, which have been an instrument of force and war over the course of the entire history of human civilization (so they remain as well under capitalism), in socialism were transformed into an instrument of peace. But if the authors of the conceptions of "massive response," "deterrence," "flexible response," and "star wars," having once crossed the Rubicon dividing peace and war, went over to monstrous actions, Soviet soldiers and officers controlling strategic power would be compelled to fulfill their duty to the end. So the positions of our military doctrine are prescribed.
>
> Unfortunately, several authors have placed the correctness of this conception in doubt. For example, the writer whom we mentioned in the beginning of this article considers such an approach absurd and preposterous. In his words, for him "today there is nothing more brave and worthy than those military men, like the retired generals, who devote their military knowledge to the antiwar movement." At the same time the writer believes that there should not be any kind of response strike. In essence, by his reasoning he leads the reader to the following thought: Once a response strike is senseless, is preparedness for it even necessary?
>
> This point of view is not original. These so-called "nuclear pacifists," largely people from a religious circle, assert that the use of nuclear weapons even for self-defense or retribution is amoral.

New articles by the participants in the debate followed, and then the correspondent of the weekly *Argumenty i Fakty* (1987, no. 25), in the course of an interview, turned to Volkogonov with the question:

> **Correspondent:** Many readers did not fail to note your polemic with the writer A. Adamovich at the plenum of the Writers' Union of the USSR on the question of the paths of survival for mankind. What is the principal difference in your approaches?
>
> **Volkogonov:** I can tell you immediately: I respect the writer for the open presentation of his views, although I am not in agreement with him in principle. If one were to synthesize the ideas, the statements of Adamovich on the problem of survival, they can be reduced to the following: "survival at any price." He considers that it is not even necessary to retain preparedness for a response strike. To have an atomic bomb is "shameful." Military men are good only in the garb of pacifists. Upbringing should be "anti-militaristic-patri-otic" and so on. By the writer's logic, we should not even stop before unilateral disarmament.
>
> I think that the writer does not have the basis to consider that his opponents are less qualified than he to evaluate the real danger. One must not fall prey to intellectual confusion. I remember that the first time I was at a military rocket complex containing charges of fantastic power, I experienced very complex, contradictory feelings. Human genius had created these unimaginable means of destruction. . . . Could there be anything more paradoxical in human experience? But Adamovich himself says that in this matter emotions are a poor adviser. We should not be condemned for possessing nuclear weapons. If the United States in 1946 had agreed to the USSR's proposal to forbid forever the "nuclear club" (an expression of then-President H. Tru-man), then today the situation would be completely different. It should be "shameful" only for those who do not want to liquidate nuclear arsenals on an equal basis. We acquired nuclear weapons as a forced response to the exceptionally dangerous call from the side of the United States. How can this not be taken into consideration?
>
> As far as a realistic approach to the survival of civilization is concerned, it was completely grounded in our Party Congress. It is important to survive without surrendering one's ideals, principles, and spiritual values. And our government and party consider that this is possible. Our class approach to peace does not contradict a universal approach but coincides with it. A socially worthy path of survival lies on the plane of compromises, negotiations, mutual concessions. But only on the basis of the principle of equal security.

Social scientists were also involved in the debate. Two Byelorussian philosophers, V. Begun and V. Bovsh, also attacked Adamovich on the pages of *Sovetskaia Kul'tura* (10 December 1987):

The essence of our polemic with A. Adamovich touches, in particular, upon the response to nuclear aggression, the advisability of which the writer argues against in political and moral terms. . . .

The truth about response consists in [the fact] that its inevitability is a factor capable on a decisive level of obstructing a potential aggressor from carrying out his plans. In this way, the issue here is not about "finishing off" but, on the contrary, about the saving of mankind.

It stands to reason that the inevitability of response to aggression alone still does not secure a strong peace. For this it is necessary to eliminate war from the life of society, forever having destroyed its material attributes, among them weapons of mass destruction. The practical initiatives of the Soviet Union on this score are well known. Our new political thinking ties the peaceful perspective of mankind with the disarmament and peaceful coexistence of governments, with the decision of other global problems in universal interests.

Along with this our new political philosophy, based on Leninist ideas, is permeated with the concern for the defense of the socialist Fatherland, of the socialist achievements of the fraternal peoples. "It is no secret," it was noted in the political report of the Central Committee of the CPSU at the 27th Party Congress, "that we do not have plans for a nuclear attack." From this stems our preparedness for a response strike. It is also one of the realities, which cannot but be taken into account by the new political thinking, but there are no objective bases for carrying it, as does A. Adamovich, to the prenuclear era.

One must also speak about the humanistic side of the problem. A. Adamovich is inclined to see the rejection of a response to nuclear attack as an act of humanism. Can one agree with this position? Of course not. The fact is that the realities of the nuclear era, if one speaks about it in all seriousness, leave their impression on our understanding of humanism as well. It, as never before, becomes active and simultaneously extremely "squeezed," "concentrated," directing all one's energy toward one goal—the prevention of nuclear conflict—for the chances for the preservation of the human species are directly dependent on the prevention of the threat of nuclear war. If mankind has to cross over the dangerous threshold, then the arguments about humanism lose any sense. We will not comfort ourselves with the illusion that it could be different. Genuine humanism is indivisible.

A. Adamovich, . . . having heard about the "nuclear winter," cannot, naturally, know also about those in the West who in all seriousness hope to "survive" this "winter" and therefore are concerned not with the problem of the prevention of a cataclysm but with the building of fashionable shelters. The "I would not push the button" of A. Adamovich, whether the writer intends this or not, objectively corresponds to the interests of these masters. If one is to be completely open, in the given case one must talk not so much about abstract humanism so much as about the current cosmopolitanism.

This reference to "cosmopolitanism" conjures up old associations. Some forty years ago, using the slogan of the struggle against "rootless cosmopolitanism," the Stalinists carried out their recurrent purges and defamed and repressed numerous people. But here is Adamovich's response:

> For some reason I do not want to dissuade Bovsh and Begun, to prove that I am not "unpatriotic," not a "cosmopolitan," and that I do not work for those who plan nuclear destruction for us, hoping to sit it out in "comfortable shelters."
>
> Nevertheless, I will answer their letter. No, I will not answer them, but those who, puzzled, look, listen, and read: What are they actually talking about? What does all this—"to push the button," "not to push the button"—mean?
>
> Everything seemed simpler ten to twenty years ago: "They" struck— and received the same. And it was calculated as to what percent of the population would be left in each of the countries. In our time, given the present arsenals and knowledge of the consequences (especially secondary), it is obvious: No one will be left, not only in these two countries but on the planet in general. . . .
>
> Not immediately and not by everyone has the main truth of the nuclear age been grasped: neither victories, nor awards and knowledge, nor pensions. Not for anybody. But how many colonels' dissertations and generals' books about the future triumphant seizure of the "nuclear heights" are there in the world?
>
> These people will not immediately part with the retaliation doctrine, even when the political mechanism of disarmament is created.
>
> But in order to create such a mechanism, and not to be too late in creating it, we need preliminary work in the souls and brains of people. Not seeing, not understanding the whole amorality and dangerous absurdity of the currently existing doctrine, how many people will continue to hold onto it? Although already today it is fatally dangerous for the human race. (*Sovetskaia Kul'tura*, 10 December 1987)

Another famous writer, Vasil' Bykov, also commented on the debate in *Sovetskaia Kul'tura* (10 December 1987):

> Alas, here there is no hint of the new consciousness. Everything here is from the mossy "stagnation" and "prestagnation" periods, when aphorisms like this one were so familiar and natural: "Yes, life is

worth defending in view of its uniqueness in the universe." "But whose life?" query the distinguished authors with striking naivete. The life of the human race, I answer. Can it be that this self-evident truth still needs to be explained to the learned philosophers from the Byelorussian Academy of Sciences?

This argument has not come to an end. The question of whether one can count on winning a nuclear war is one of the most important criteria of the difference between the old and new thinking. As an abstract principle everyone admits that a nuclear war can have no victor. But the distance between a political declaration and the inculcation of the principles of the new thinking in people's consciousness is not short. Perhaps this process is most complex for military professionals, which is understandable. Here, for example, is what Rear Admiral G. Kostev wrote in the journal *Kommunist Vooruzbionnykh Sil* [Communist of the Armed Forces] (1987, no. 6):

> In the nuclear age, when imperialists prepare for an uncompromising and shattering war (they themselves do not deny this), the moral-political and psychological preparation of the defenders of the Fatherland for carrying out decisive, military actions has an inestimably important place. In this context, pacifist moods among military men are unacceptable, because in the moral-psychological plan this lowers the military readiness of the armed forces. Why? Because for success in battle, in a confrontation, it is obligatory to have inculcated in every soldier the ability to fight to the last drop of blood and the readiness for self-sacrifice. One must prepare for victory in both the tactical and the operative plans without any reservations, taking into account the application of any type of weapon. Without such an approach, the attack, combat, and battle operations will be lost even before they begin. This is the axiom of the military art. Let us remember our basic principles: "The troops need to learn what is necessary in war." Without observing this, one cannot attain victory in battle, and in peacetime its violation lowers the level of specific elements of the fighting potential of the Soviet armed forces, such as military craftsmanship and loyalty to one's patriotic duty. And, as a result, the effectiveness of the manifestation of the human factor of the Armed Forces is lowered.

The change in attitudes toward war, victory, and security also entails a change in attitude toward the role of the army in society, toward military service, and related issues. Widening discussion of these issues was triggered by an article in *Literaturnaia Gazeta* (13 May 1987) entitled, "Why Do We Have Few Truly Educated People?" Academician B. Raushenbakh, corresponding member of the USSR Academy of Sciences M. Volkenshtein, and Doctor of Philosophy V. Mezhuev proposed that the needs of the military, specifically for manpower resources, must be critically evaluated in relation to broad social needs:

V. Mezhuev: The recently inaugurated practice of drafting first- and second-year students as soldiers is completely incomprehensible. Military service is the constitutional obligation of every young person. But not at the expense of normal study! Can it be that our society has a greater need of soldiers than of young physicists, biologists, engineers, and social scientists who have been educated at an appropriate time? . . . Forcible removal from education is not conducive to . . . success. Besides, many people do not return to the institutes after army service—time has gone by, new cares and problems have arisen, and sometimes the interest in study has fallen behind.

B. Raushenbakh: Education must certainly not be interrupted. At our institution there are kids who come here after high school and kids entering from the army. Those who come after army service are excellent performers, excellently organized, but they never turn into Newtons. Apparently there is an atrophying, a numbing of the creative abilities.

As a result, after ten years there will be nobody to do fundamental science, and that is dangerous. Also for defense.

M. Volkenshtein: After the First World War, in which Germany, as everyone knows, was defeated, science in that country grew to a much greater extent than in England and France. Why? Because the Germans did not give up their intellectuals, their scholars, to be soldiers. But the French and English did. As a result, a whole generation of talented scholarly youth was knocked out. It is an elementary thing people do not think about here. Therefore I am absolutely in agreement that this is stupid and shortsighted—to draft students into the army.

Sharp disagreement with this position was expressed on the pages of the newspaper *Krasnaia Zvezda* (22 May 1987) by Volkogonov:

Inasmuch as we cannot get by without our defensive might, then we cannot underestimate the inculcation in the Soviet people of preparedness for the defense of socialism. This is not only a sacred duty but also a deep vital necessity. In this light, the conclusions of a group of scholars that were published in a popular newspaper are mistaken. Abstracting from social, demographic, and other factors, they characterize the drafting of students for military service, carried out in complete accordance with our laws, as a "stupid and short-sighted" decision. They say that, during service, "there is an atrophying, a numbing of creative abilities." One of the participants of the roundtable in the newspaper, in fact, poses an unacceptable question: What does our society need more, soldiers or scholarly specialists? If for that scholar this is a problem—that's not so bad. But how will such an opposition allow one to understand the role of military service? Especially in light of contemporary realities?

In *Literaturnaia Gazeta* (3 June 1987) an article by the vice chief of the General Staff of the Armed Forces of the USSR, General M. Gareev, was printed under the rubric "There is Another Opinion." In this lengthy article, more than ten times longer than the scholars' discussion that started the debate, he offered this criticism of the opinions expressed by the scholars:

In the remarks of Doctor of Philosophical Sciences V. Mezhuev, Academician B.V. Raushenbakh, and Corresponding Member of the USSR Academy of Sciences M.V. Volkenshtein, there is in essence a negative attitude toward service in the armed forces in general, and not only toward the drafting of students into the army. The participants in the discussion, in completely unacceptable terms, criticized Soviet laws regulating the procedure for drafting youth into the army. M.V. Volkenshtein spoke most categorically, flatly declaring that " . . . It is stupid and shortsighted to draft students into the army."

Our democracy provides for wide discussion of projected laws, but when they are accepted, they must be carried out. Of course, the question can be raised about the perfection of existing laws, but then we need concrete and well-founded proposals, taking into account the interests of the state as a whole, so that appropriate competent organs can review them. While I was preparing this article people tried to explain that the participants in the discussion were only saying that it is not expedient to cut short students' study in institutes of higher education, and they were not against army service altogether. Perhaps this is true. But then why do they speak about military service as something unworthy of an educated person, about its negative influence on the nurturing and education of the personality? On the one hand, they seemed to be admitting that "service in the army is the constitutional obligation of every young man." On the other hand, they raised the contrived, rhetorical question: Who is more necessary to our society, soldiers or young scholars? At that, they spoke about service in the Soviet armed forces in language common to prerevolutionary Russia, when the tsarist army was a weapon for oppressing and suppressing the toilers ("forcible separation from education," "drafting to be soldiers," etc.). When it says in the discussion that in some states "they did not give up their intellectuals, their scholars, to be soldiers," while other states did give them up, the conversation is supposedly about bourgeois countries, but the conclusions are applied to our army.

In a careful reading of the text of the discussion, one cannot but notice that the whole tone of the remarks of some of the discussion's participants is such, as if military service in our time is something alien and not very necessary for our society. One cannot just pass this by, also because recently in our press there have appeared many other articles with similar arguments.

Despite my respect for the honored academicians and scholars, I cannot agree with their assertion that kids coming to an institute right after graduating from school will turn into Newtons while those who went through military service experience an "atrophying, a numbing of the creative abilities." One is forced to wonder: If there are such negative results with young people who have served only two years, then what must become of those people who spend practically their whole lives in military service?

Historical experience shows that the solution of military tasks, which often determine the fate of a state, demands no fewer gifted people than in any other branch of science or practical activity.

The discussion of the role of the army in Soviet society and the call for reassessing and altering it was taken up by Academician Andrei Sakharov, the world-famous fighter for human rights. In an interview with the journal *Novoe Vremia* (1988, no. 38), he proposed that the length of military service in the USSR be cut in half for the following reasons:

> Actually, at the present time the Soviet Union is not threatened by any aggression. There are no Hitlers now. I am convinced that the great tragedy that happened to us, to all of humanity, as a result of Hitler's coming to power and the onset of the Second World War is to a large degree tied to a whole network of mistakes and crimes of Stalinism. I will not here analyze in detail the events of that time; I will only say that they elicited terror of the USSR in the West, made difficult any real cooperation of Western countries with the Soviet Union, and still earlier, in Germany, set Communists against the then Social Democrats. The results of all this sad combination of events was war.
>
> Now, I repeat, the situation is completely different. I consider that now there is really no country that could threaten the USSR with an attack. No! Even with a halving of the Soviet armed forces, [such an attack would be] absolutely excluded. And such a cut would have a colossal international significance. It would improve conditions for the solution of the problem of reducing conventional arms in Europe and in the whole world. And it would beneficially affect the possibility of developing a fruitful dialogue on deep nuclear reductions. Besides that, it would also have very great social and economic effects within the country, a great significance for domestic politics. This would be important for a more rational use of the labor resources in the country, for students, and for the healing of the atmosphere within the army.

One must not think that these are simply the nonprofessional musings of a civilian person. No, even among professional military men we are now seeing attempts at a new approach toward defining the role of the army in society, toward the construction of the armed forces itself. At present these are not the views of the majority of military people. But this makes the appearance of these points of view in the open press all the more remarkable.

Lieutenant Colonel Aleksandr Savinkin in *Moscow News* (1988, no. 45) wrote:

> The strength of the armed forces lies in popular support. However, it's impossible to ignore the armed forces present drop in prestige among civilians and young men's dwindling interest in army service. "Illnesses" in society and within the armed forces have manifested themselves, but these are being removed in the process of perestroika. However, a certain dislocation of relations between Soviet society and its armed forces nevertheless remains. There are several reasons for this: armed forces' state-political estrangement from the people has been taking place at various periods of this country's development; the contradiction between the comparatively quicker and essential restructuring of society, in general, and its comparatively slower spread to the military sphere where changes are largely carried out through administrative actions; the controversial influence of the events in Afghanistan on people's conscience; and the insufficiency of information about the processes going on in our defence policy and in the life of the armed forces, and so on.
>
> Of course, there is a way out of this predicament. Complex changes dealing with the social and state system are needed, and they are underway. The need for a military reform has become urgent (it is my personal, and therefore arguable opinion). The restoring of the Leninist image of the socialist army, the developing of its truly nationwide popular, democratic and humanist character is hardly possible without taking such a resolute and serious step. I think that the absence of any immediate threat of aggression, plus the favourable situation in the country, are propitious for carrying out the reform in a relatively short time. This will ensure a gradual transition to a new model of the armed forces.
>
> The military reform core, as I see it, is the transition to a *professional-militia army,* in other words, to a relatively small, perfectly technically equipped, professionally trained and mainly voluntarily staffed military organization supported by a broad network of local militia formations. Such a system, I believe, would allow us to reduce standing military components without any detriment to the country's security, and provide a better cohesion between the army and the people. As a result, a democratic military structure integrated into society would

be created, providing an opportunity for solving a number of problems, including the security and inner stability for the country, as well as enforcement of law and order carried out by citizen-militiamen themselves. The professional-militia army will combine the ideal of a democratic military defence system with the real possibilities for reshaping the armed forces in keeping with the principles of sufficiency and the strategy of military defence. In the course of disarmament, the system can be transformed into a militia army highly geared to productive work. That army with short terms of reserve military service and a high patriotic spirit will have no regular military organization.

The transition to the new system in the course of the Soviet armed forces buildup would upgrade the *quality and orderliness of the armed service,* as well as *boost its appeal.* It would become possible to do away with the overcentralized and cumbersome administrative-command control system. It could be replaced with a flexible control structure based on scientific analysis, automation and elements of public control and self-management. The direct linkage between the armed forces and all strata of Soviet society would be strengthened.

That is my vision of an armed forces model suitable at this new stage of development of socialist society. This model would respond to military-political detente, ensure effective safety for the country and boost the prestige of the armed forces. An increase in the aforementioned tendency to reduce and restructure the armed forces internationally would represent a triumph for the new political thinking.

Aleksandr Prokhanov, however, holds a very different view of the role of the military in society. He openly delights in the strength of the contemporary weapons of mass destruction, sees in the army a salutary force that can save society and offer a model for social emulation. In his article "Defensive Consciousness and the New Thinking" (*Literaturnaia Rossiia,* 6 May 1988), he posed this question:

> In what direction is criticism of today's army, today's defensive ideas, heading? In my view, there are a few of these.
>
> First, it is confirmed that the army seems an awesome, terrible, negative force, which led to the militarization of the world, to the militarization of history, to the militarization of life. And precisely it, the army, wielding death-bearing weapons, put the world on the verge of the final catastrophe, on the verge of destruction.
>
> Second, it is considered that the army, due to its lack of flexibility, its super-conservatism, and its closedness, is the source of everything stagnant, conservative, everything that is not accepted by the new thinking, perestroika, and the new, experimental models for the behavior of a country and state. That is, they are nearly beginning to equate the army with an enemy of renewal.

Third, they accuse the army of the fact that supposedly in recent years it has grown lazy, frittered away fighting experience and therefore cannot deal with its military obligations: It leaves the border with "holes" for the airplanes of other countries (for example, in the Rust incident, which dealt a very serious blow to our prestige), often does not know what it is doing (we remember the situation with the South Korean Boeing).

And, finally, the direction of criticism especially strong in recent weeks concerns the army and the problem of Afghanistan. The liberal flank of our society, most active today, criticizes the army because it went into Afghanistan and considers this step impermissible, mistaken, and harmful, and in connection with this, lays all sorts of faults on the army.

Some part of society, on the contrary, considers the withdrawal of troops from Afghanistan a mistake that will be surrounded by political and military-strategic complications.

Further, Prokhanov gave his version of the responses to all four questions:

What can one say in response to the first claim—that the army has militarized the world and placed it on the brink of global catastrophe? It seems to me that it is not the fault of the army but the whole course of world history of the past thirty years, conditioned by the idea of total confrontation—the confrontation of societies, the confrontation of two superstructures. Besides, the addition into this confrontation of fast-acting means of technology gave it an extreme, I repeat, not only military but total human potential: means of propaganda, ideological doctrines, and whole economies worked for it [i.e., the confrontation]. And culture also, in many ways, worked for it.

I summarize: The army helped us to preserve ourselves as a sovereign society that the powerful civilizations of the West could not crush. In other words, the army has fulfilled its mission.

Second, the opposition of the army and the military complex to the new thinking. I undertake to confirm that the new thinking as a practical way of acting on the world scene has become possible and [that it] turned from an abstraction into a reality only after the attainment of military-strategic parity. . . . As long as there was no parity, as long as the West had the upper hand (more warheads, more means of delivery, superior technological equipment, when they dominated in the most important regions of the world, when we had no atomic fleet, etc.), in a word, when all these factors worked against us, there could be no discussion about the new thinking, because one of the sides (in this case, their side) was always ready to use the trump card of its superiority. . . .

Next, the reproaches that the army has become lazy and cannot deal with its obligations, that social chaos and unauthorized relations reign there—perhaps these are to a large extent justified. The manifestations of stagnation in society naturally spread, could not help but spread, also to the army.

Lastly, Afghanistan. For almost nine or ten years of the war we practically did not talk about this. And in order to come to an understanding of the problem, we need unceasing discussions, analysis, and the exchange of conceptions. And though everything that now, at first, will be said about Afghanistan may have a preliminary, dilettantish, emotional character, often sorrowful, colored in blood, tears, and indignation—nevertheless, this must be done, must be begun. This is, after all, ten years of our country's history, very terrible and awful years.

In this connection, A. Prokhanov touched upon another major problem: *afghantsy,* i.e., the soldiers who arrive from Afghanistan. According to him, Soviet "liberals" are trying to inculcate in them an inferiority complex, to make them a sort of social sacrifice laid at the altar of an unnecessary and terrible war, almost calling them "cannon fodder," a lost generation. And, thus winning their sympathy, to influence, with their help, social-political processes in the country.

On the other hand, said Prokhanov, Soviet "rightist extremists" are also ready to use this contingent for their own purposes. It is very advantageous to have in one's ranks an organized detachment steeped in the cult of power if one can introduce into it one's own ideology. Finally, the bureaucrats, for whom the appearance of these people means extra work, try to disassociate from them, not to notice them, to lose them, to assimilate them as quickly as possible and as widely as possible.

But the *afghantsy* themselves do not want to assimilate. They are undergoing a most interesting process of crystallization. They prefer to consider themselves a sort of community, which has shifted from purely economic demands—give me an apartment, give me a job, give me an artificial limb, give me a wheelchair, give me a pension—to ideological concerns. The *afghantsy* are becoming an ideological force. They are beginning to interest themselves more and more not in the problems of their invalids' wheelchairs and pensions but in problems of social justice, problems of the state system, of ecology, problems of monuments of culture, of historical treasures. And, being filled with ideology, they are becoming a real force. They are not set aside in some kind of reservation—some of them work in factories, others on collective farms, others are returning to the universities; there are already *afghantsy*-journalists, and there will soon appear *afghantsy*-writers. And all of them, entering into various pores of society, retain solidarity. And in ten years, when many of them will have leading positions in the economic, party, and ideological apparatus, this will be a consolidated force, steeped in the idea of suffering, struggle, in the idea of stoicism. And the state must take advantage of this force, must use it in a positive sense. For if, God forbid, some crisis happens, the state will be badly needing tested people who are ready to sacrifice themselves. I do not think that the pacifist-inclined youth—rockers, break-dancers, punkers—will be those who will sacrifice themselves in the name of saving the Fatherland. If there comes a time when they will have to shed bloody sweat, they may turn out to be unprepared for this. Therefore, the *afghantsy,* potentially prepared for sacrifices, must be watched over, cared for, cherished, and surrounded by ideological and social care, creating for them a regime of the highest favor.

Widening public discussion of the Soviet involvement in Afghanistan offers a particularly vivid demonstration of the gradual extension of glasnost to international and military affairs. Although it is now the sharpest and most burning question for the Soviet public, open discussion and disagreement on this subject were absolutely unthinkable until recently. But already we are encountering various evaluations and a range of opinions in print.

The discussion was opened by Aleksandr Prokhanov in *Literaturnaia Gazeta* (17 February 1988) when he called into question the political assessments underlying the Soviet involvement:

As the Geneva dialogue moves along, questions are accumulating. You cannot get away from them. They are asked in family circles, in private conversations, and they are already beginning to be sounded in public meetings—tomorrow they will spill out into the press, breaking the spell of many years of silence.

Why did we send in the troops? What goals did we pursue? Did we attain these goals or not? What will happen after the withdrawal of the troops? What was the cost of the presence in Afghanistan of our limited military contingent? All these questions will be asked severely, and I foresee that the answers to them will create a painful battlefield of polemics that will not soon die down. . . .

We, having introduced troops, thought that their presence would balance out the powerful pressure from abroad and that the internal civil strife would in the end quiet down; that the victorious party, the NDPA, defining the path of state development, would know how to create a capable structure extending over the whole country, the entire territory, all social layers of society, and that stability would triumph.

This did not happen. That initial project of development was not realized. The NDPA did not become a power recognized by the entire people.

Why?

. . . Mistakes in the political line, false recipes for the direct implantation of socialism in that "non-Afghan," "non-Islamic" form that insulted tradition, ended up in force and repression. In the persecution of mullahs, in the trampling of rites and ceremonies. . . .

The factional struggle in the bosom of the party, eating away at it, corrupting it, paralyzing it, bringing chaos, factional egotism, and intolerance, and as a result—internal repression, the destruction and removal of leaders, a numbing fear, a shortage of creativity, against a background of which there was bureaucratization, the unwillingness to sacrifice oneself in the name of the revolution, the fear of going into a crowd of Muslim Christians, the inability of finding a dialogue with the people—all these qualities of a certain part of the party prolonged and strengthened its political drama.

Is a durable political structure of socialism possible in a country where an innumerable number of tribes, nomads, agglomerations, leaders, and satraps constitute a continuous soup, a thick social broth, swelling in an instant with bursting bubbles? In this jumble worthy of the Middle Ages there have only just been extracted forms consonant with the contemporary world, and yet on this marshy swamp it was conceived to build a socialist building.

After those December days when troops of the USSR went into Afghanistan, the political course of the Kabul government changed in many ways. State forums were advised by the prayers of a mullah. The flag ceased to be red and included in it the green Islamic fragment. The star disappeared from the coat of arms of the country. The party stopped talking about the creation of a socialist society. It denounced the monopoly on power. It called for pluralism. It invited a hostile foreign opposition to participate in the government; the possible return to the country of the aged king was studied, who in his day overthrew not Taraki, but Daoud—the return to the foundations of fifteen years before. And the main thing—a policy of national reconciliation was declared, unprecedented compromise with the enemies, the readiness to see in them not enemies but patriots, coworkers in the future traditionally Islamic, nonaligned Afghanistan, slowly healing the wounds inflicted by war.

All that taken together allows one to say: The initial goals of the NDPA were not achieved. The party itself, the revolutionary government itself, renounced them. And if this is so, then the presence of Soviet troops in the country loses its sense. A withdrawal is unavoidable, logical.

Does that mean they were brought in vain? I do not think the question can be put that way. There was an incorrect prognosis. The experts were mistaken in their evaluation of the situation in the country. There were mistakes made by our specialists on Islam, by diplomats, politicians, and military leaders. Because, I repeat, the basic goals were not achieved.

. . . When the last soldier crosses the border at Kushki or Termeza, the "Afghan" question will be closed, a page of our history will be turned; this will not mean the conclusion of the "Afghan theme." It will all the more strongly and obstinately resound in culture, in internal politics, and in social relations, because Afghanistan tragically passed through itself a large part of our generation, gave birth to tragedy and pain in families and a special "Afghan pathos" in those who returned from the sniper-filled villages.

Prokhanov's article prompted an unusual commentary on the policy-making process leading up to the decision to send troops into Afghanistan. Academician Oleg Bogomolov, director of the Institute of Economics of the World Socialist System of the Academy of Sciences of the USSR, published an article entitled, "Who Erred?" in *Literaturnaia Gazeta* (16 March 1988):

In Aleksandr Prokhanov's article . . . questions are asked concerning events in Afghanistan. Questions overdue. But that is not the fault of the author. The topic was for a long time simply closed. Only now do we begin to consider the circumstances, reasons for, and results of our participation in those dramatic events; we try to understand why and how the decision was made eight years ago.

Aleksandr Prokhanov writes: "There was an incorrect prognosis. The experts were mistaken in their evaluation of the situation in the country. There were mistakes made by our specialists on Islam, by diplomats, politicians, and military leaders." In connection with that I want to point out that although the Institute of Economics of the World Socialist System of the Academy of Sciences of the USSR does not directly deal with the region, [it] did not stay on the sidelines but expressed its very negative attitude toward the introduction of Soviet troops into Afghanistan. Taking the initiative, in a memorandum given to the appropriate authorities on 20 January 1980 it spoke of the hopelessness and harmfulness of that action. The note contained ten points in which it gave an evaluation of the situation. In one of these it said: "In addition to two fronts of resistance—in Europe against NATO and in Eastern Asia against China—for us there has arisen a third dangerous center of military-political tension on the southern flank of the USSR, in disadvantageous geographical and sociopolitical conditions, where we still have to face the combined resources of the United States and of other countries of NATO, of China, of Australia, of the Muslim governments, and of the rebellious army of the Afghan feudal-clerical circles commanding the strongest influence among the Afghan people. For the first time after the Second World War we face the possible prospect of a local military conflict in which, unlike

Korea, Vietnam, and others, we will have to fight with our own troops."
The memo said that as a result of that action, détente was blocked
and the political preconditions for disarmament had been liquidated;
that there had occurred a significant consolidation of the anti-Soviet
coalition of governments encircling the USSR from west to east; that
the influence of the USSR on the movement of the nonaligned had
suffered, especially in the Muslim world; and that the conditions for
a possible normalization of Soviet-Chinese relations had disappeared
for a long time.

In other notes and reports addressed to the highest authorities much
earlier, in the second half of the 1970s, it was pointed out that it was
necessary to show restraint and caution in the turbulent zone of the
developing countries in order not to threaten the easing of tensions
and the cause of disarmament.

Formerly, the leadership of the USSR ignored such warnings because
it viewed foreign policy to a considerable extent through the prism of
the ideology of confrontation—the class approach carried over into the
international sphere. In his speech at the UN in December 1988,
Gorbachev summed up the rethinking of a significant portion of the
country's previous foreign policy principles, formulating the goal of
foreign policy in a fashion fundamentally different from that of his
political predecessors. Namely, he spoke of "the search for a consensus
common to all mankind in the movement toward a new world order."
Two months after his address at the UN, the last Soviet soldier was
withdrawn from Afghanistan. That was one of the steps toward a
"consensus common to all mankind," steps that went beyond the former
stereotypes and the old understanding of foreign policy and ideological
goals. How many more such steps lie ahead?

The Code of the Nuclear Era

At a time when Soviet and American leaders are groping toward
political paths that will lead to a safer world, many Soviet writers,
publicists, and social activists are discussing in the press the ideological
and cultural implications of the new political principles. How to destroy
old stereotypes and develop a new code of behavior suitable for the
nuclear era are central themes. The writer Iurii Slepukhin set off such
a discussion with the publication of his article, "Do We Believe in the
Reality of the Threat?" in the journal *Vek XX i Mir* (no. 4, 1987):

> The new thinking—which is truly new and rests on a sober as-
> sessment of all the realities of the current world situation—must above
> all look in a completely new way at the problem of the opposition

between two social-political systems. Thinking in the old way, we often perceive them to be polar opposites and mutually exclusive, although we speak of disarmament and coexistence (not forgetting, by the way, to emphasize that in the sphere of ideology there can be no disarmament: Is it not because of this that [such a disarmament] remains an unattainable dream?)

Now we simply cannot—we do not have the right to—comfort ourselves with naive thoughts about the differences between the systems, among which one is subject to all kinds of ailments while the other has an unshakable, absolutely reliable immunity. We all are subject to ailments to some degree.

Today's world is one whole, one single system of elements communicating among each other. Some are linked directly, and changes in one part of the system immediately affect the neighboring parts. In some places the linking canals are so narrow as to be more like capillaries, and then the average [*usrednenie*] of the parameters in various parts is accomplished very slowly, sometimes unnoticeable for the viewer. But it is nevertheless accomplished—inexorably and irrevocably, like entropy.

Squabbles about who is more to blame for the nuclear arms race of the four preceding decades now seem fruitless. Some think that the arms race was started by the imperialist ambitions of Truman; others blame Stalin, with his tenacity on certain questions of postwar foreign policy; and this dispute, in its insolubility, evokes the scholastic discussions on the famous theme of the chicken and the egg.

The author proposed that the real threat comes not so much from the arms race itself but from the attitudes underlying it:

They say that a weapon starts to shoot by itself when too much of it accumulates. The other variant is more likely: The weapon begins to kill when too much fear and mutual distrust accumulate in the souls of those who own them. The tragedy of our epoch is that a monstrous surfeit of arms, able to turn the whole planet into ashes, has been controlled by a sick society that is unsteady and unpredictable in its actions.

By "society" I mean not the citizens of any one country or group of countries but the totality of the population of that enormous cultural-historical arena [*areal*] that was once called the Christian world. All the misfortunes of our time have sprung from one common root— they were born of the spirit of impatience and antagonism, enmity between peoples, races, political systems, and ideologies. In the nineteenth century, politics was subordinate to economics; wars were fought primarily in the name of profit. Territorial acquisitions, the seizure of colonies, squabbles over markets—this was understood; it had its own brigand logic, barbarian but easily explained. And how do we explain what is happening today?

The problem of détente is first of all a problem of trust. It is useless to talk about disarmament, even partial, while both systems distrust each other, while a blind atavistic feeling of mutual fear remains the main characteristic of relations between the two nuclear superpowers. It is irrational—it has no logic nor any sober understanding of the situation; logic should tell us, first of all, that today nobody can desire a nuclear war or consciously bring on such a war. The danger of the sparking of conflict (and this, by the way, makes it especially threatening) lies in the fact that it can happen by accident—either by a technical mistake, or because somebody's nerves give out.

And anybody's nerves could give out. We all live in conditions of constantly growing psychological stress when each of the sides, through every means of influencing the mind and feelings, inculcates in its citizens the certainty of the existence of some kind of diabolical conspiracy against their country, their children, their future. If in the West much anti-Soviet literature is published and films such as *Red Dawn* and *Amerika* are widely shown, likewise in the Soviet Union a sharp anti-Western tendency in all information policy has also become a tradition. These phenomena are very different, and I am not drawing parallels between them, but we will be honest with ourselves and admit that the cause of peace does not benefit from this propagandistic wrangling.

Therefore, any détente must begin with a healing of the international atmosphere on this psychological plane. Such a healing can be accomplished, but only if its necessity is understood by both sides and if Moscow and Washington take some concrete steps in that direction. Today one cannot solve anything simply through appeals.

Speaking out against the over-ideologization of international relations and against the mistrust and suspicion between peoples living with various social systems, the writer spoke out against an oversimplified "black-and-white" picture of the world in which one side assumes for itself the name of absolute good and labels the other as absolute evil. A renunciation of this black-and-white picture of the world is another important principle of the new political thinking.

We have no time left for empty arguments. If the disputants really want to come to an agreement—and to agree is essential, that is the most important, most categorical imperative of the present moment— one must first cease to comfort oneself with mutual accusations. There is no better way to deliberately make any agreement unattainable than to declare oneself, again and again, the monopolistic holder of truth.

A conflict situation in which one side is absolutely right and the other absolutely wrong is theoretically possible. But in practice this does not happen on any level of the structure of human society: not within the family, not between two families, not between two states. In every real case of conflict, as a rule, one can only talk about who is more right; that means that, even if one considers oneself conditionally "right," one must admit a certain amount of correctness in one's opponent. Only this can be the path to compromise, to an agreement, to harmony.

The famous Soviet political commentator Aleksandr Bovin developed this theme further in the article "From the Art of War to the Art of Negotiation" (*Izvestiia*, 3 June 1987) where he reminded the reader that even the most noble and righteous goals, such as peace and progress, must not be insisted on by one side in the form of an ultimatum without consideration of the interests of the other side:

> One of the manifestations of V.I. Lenin's political realism was his sharply negative attitude toward ultimatums. Already on the day after the victorious uprising, delivering some final words of his lecture on peace, Lenin decisively expressed himself against making the demand for peace into an ultimatum.

Although Bovin recognized that Lenin's flexibility may have reflected the weakness of the newborn Soviet state in 1917, he went on to argue:

> Lenin's thought is not only tied to the needs of the moment. It has a more general character: Every ultimatum—where the sides are equal—limits the one who declares it. An ultimatum locks one in, freezes one's position, hinders one from considering changes in circumstances, disrupts the feedback loop that allows one to correct one's policy. It narrows the space for political maneuvering, which gives the partner clear tactical advantages, allows him to back away from a concrete discussion pointing to the inaccessibility and implacability of the side that declares ultimatums. The inevitable withdrawal of one's ultimatums, called forth by the pressure of circumstances and by one's own interests, may be essentially beneficial and effective but will appear to be a retreat, a loss of face, etc. The long-term minuses inherent in ultimatums clearly outweigh their short-term, mostly propagandistic, pluses. . . .
>
> Of course, each partner has a limit to his concessions defined by the higher interests of state security and alliance obligations. But to a significant degree that limit is subjective. For it is defined not by one's interest "in itself" but by how that interest is understood and formulated.

The principles of the new thinking compose a sort of code of political behavior of states in the nuclear age. This is not a collection of laws and documents; it is, rather, a complex of new principles by which states with varying social systems and ideologies can achieve a peaceful, civilized coexistence and, most important, adapt themselves to the conditions of the nuclear era.

"What could be considered correct before the appearance and accumulation of nuclear arms must not necessarily be considered correct after that watershed event," wrote President of the Soviet Association of Political Sciences Georgii Shakhnazarov in his article "The Logic of Political Thinking in the Nuclear Era." Here he developed his concept of the code of political and ideological behavior of states in the contemporary world (*Voprosy Filosofii*, no. 5, 1984):

> It is enough to review in one's mind the traditional concepts and rules of behavior on the international arena, so as to be convinced of the necessity of more or less essentially correcting them, taking into account the fact of nuclear danger. In the world over which has been hung the threat of destruction, some concepts, which used to serve as a more or less reliable instrument of orientation, begin at times to play a directly contradictory role, as a demagnetized compass: That which was effective can become pointless, strength can turn into weakness, profit into ruin, gain into loss, murder into suicide. And there is only one way to save oneself from such irrationality: to place one's customary concepts into a new system of accounting, to review them from the point of view of the logic of political thinking in the nuclear era. "We must learn to think in a new way"—thus was this demand formulated in the remarkable Manifesto of Bertrand Russell and Albert Einstein. . . . In conditions when the most effective (and practically the only) factor holding back the outbreak of nuclear war is the threat of a counterstrike (or, more simply, of revenge), the concept of "individual" national security loses its meaning. Potential participants in the conflict are forced to reckon with the security of the other side as well as with their own. This formal mutual dependence demands the acknowledgment and admission of the fact that in the nuclear era only collective security is possible. . . .

From the logic of political thinking in the nuclear era flow demands that could be formulated thus:

- The level of security in conditions of nuclear confrontation is inversely proportional to the quantity and quality of means of mass destruction accumulated in the world;
- National security becomes a fiction if it is not drawn within the bounds of collective security. . . .

. . . It is generally accepted that a result of the stormy development of the international division of labor has been the high level of mutual dependence of states. The economic, political, and spiritual existence of certain countries has become so close that a basis has appeared for talking about the formation of a world community. . . . The logic of political thinking in the nuclear era imperiously demands:

- A renunciation of national egoism, . . .
- The unconditional precedence of the international interest over the national one, which in effect means the precedence of true, long-term national interest over transitory, short-term interest.

It is clear that the imperatives of the nuclear era set substantial limitations on the political acts of states in the nuclear arena. But it often happens that internal social transformations in certain societies, particularly revolutions, lead, or can lead, to serious international conflicts with the use of arms. Angola, Grenada, Nicaragua, Afghanistan— these are only a few examples. What political needs and norms should guide the activities of the nuclear powers if they are drawn into complex conflicts of this type? Shakhnazarov continues:

Nobody can ever halt the struggle of peoples for freedom, equality, material well-being, and other ideals of a just social order. That is an objective process in which, along with the conscious factor, there always exists an elemental factor, and thus, any attempts to place it under anyone's absolute control are doomed to failure. . . .

Does that mean that revolutionary and progressive movements can neglect to take account of the realities of the nuclear age because their causes are right? Of course not. The issue is not that they, like any other social force, have an inherent instinct for self-preservation. Striving to transform the world on principles of justice, nurturing a confidence that the future is on their side, these forces, more than anyone else, have a vested interest in averting a nuclear apocalypse.
. . .

In its general form, one of the imperatives of the nuclear era can be formulated thus: There exist no political goals justifying the use of means capable of leading to nuclear war. . . .

Humankind does not have time to spare. The logic of political thinking in the nuclear age must be understood and assimilated in a short space of time because on this depends the overcoming of the nuclear era and the dangers connected with it.

The Image of the Enemy

Perestroika and the development of glasnost raise anew the question of how the United States and the Soviet Union must relate to each other, how to free ourselves from the "image of the enemy." In February 1987, more than 200 Soviet and foreign journalists, publicists, and scholars gathered in Moscow for a conference called "USSR—USA: How We View Each Other." The participants admitted that in order to create a climate of trust in Soviet-American relations, much needs to change in the images each has of the other side.

In his article "'The Image of the Enemy' and the New Political Thinking" (*SShA: Ekonomika, Politika, Ideologiia*, 1988, no. 1), Andrei Melville wrote:

Today, when the political stakes are so high, when a wrong decision based on outdated prejudices is capable of leading to a mistake fatal for all humanity, especially dangerous is the dehumanization of the opponent, turning the other side into a symbol of "absolute evil," seeing in him only the "absolute enemy," deprived of any human characteristics. Here there is also needed a radical break from traditions of the past and the working out of new attitudes toward partners in the international arena; there is needed a break from traditional political thinking, according to which your opponent in the world arena is perceived as an "enemy."

The "image of the enemy" throughout history has traditionally been one of the most important components of international tension, conflicts, and wars.

Over the course of centuries, in various societies and cultures, there were various definitions for those states and peoples who were considered hostile. Various reasons pushed people into conflicts, rivalry, enmity. And, of course, the conflicts and wars themselves never were a direct product of the "image of the enemy"; they had various class characters and various social-political content. But nevertheless, that situation of international tension in itself, especially leading to armed conflicts, has engendered and, in its turn, reinforced itself with the "image of the enemy," which formed in the mass consciousness and lay at the base of the special psychological hostility and hatred toward other countries and peoples.

At bottom, the whole logic of the traditional political thinking leads to the formation of a certain psychology of "Homo hostilis," "hostile man." "Homo hostilis" perceives his environment, a priori, as hostile and full of enemies. This admittedly paranoic picture of the world is reinforced by a double standard in the evaluation of one's own and others' actions. Furthermore, the consciousness of "Homo hostilis" ends up under the power of what psychologists call cognitive dissonance when the "image of the enemy" calls forth admittedly unwise and unjustified actions, which in their turn are justified by ascribing to the "enemy" even more evil intentions, as a result of which arises a vicious cycle of hostility. . . .

Evidently it would be naive to count on the "image of the enemy" being replaced by the "image of the partner" in the near future. Rather, one should speak of a gradual crowding-out of the "image of the enemy," and especially of its extremely ideologized forms. It is important to take into account that the "image of the enemy," especially in that artificially ideologized, moralistic form in which it is known to us today, is not so much an inherent aspect of consciousness as it is primarily a product of deliberate manipulation of it.

"The image of the enemy" has always been an important part of the moral-psychological preparation of troops for war. But with the development of the system of mass propaganda, especially in its totalitarian, Goebbelsian variation, addressed to the whole nation, there arises the task of the moral-psychological cultivation not only of troops but also of the whole population—both one's own and the opponent's. Such manipulation, primarily through media of mass information, is carried out today by those social-political forces that are directly, one can say materially, interested in pumping up international tension and continuing the arms race, justified by the existence of an external enemy and an external threat.

As regards the United States of America, here these forces comprise primarily the professional military establishment, politicians who represent regions where military industry is concentrated, and finally, the military industry itself, guaranteeing itself gigantic profits through military procurements. In essence, this is the military-industrial complex, and for those rightist politicians the "image of the enemy" is necessary as an important component of the ideology of militarism and of the ideological and psychological preparation for war—a component which, both in its importance and in the spending of resources on it, is today commensurate with real military might. In these ranks are both professional anti-Communists and anti-Soviets, including those in academic circles.

And is everything fine on this plane in our country? Do we not remember our own posters and caricatures, excesses of rhetoric and oversimplification, selectivity in our approach to the portrayal of the other side—this and much else, which poured oil on the flames of mutual accusations, suspicion, and hostility? Even now, in the period of perestroika, our international information and journalism too often do not keep up with the stormy tempo of the changes in our social life and social consciousness.

But this problem also has another, practical side. This [has to do with] our internal factors, which in a certain sense facilitate the formation in the American mass consciousness of the "image of enemies" in the Soviet Union. Here we have an absolutization of the differences and contradictions between the two social systems and accordingly the two countries; the ideological rudiments of a theory of "world revolution"; an obsession with secrecy and suspicion that is hard to overcome; and the somnolent monolithism of the period of stagnation. Certain real events of our history also could not but give the Americans a negative perception of the Soviet Union (ranging from the excesses of collectivization and of Stalin's purges, to the excesses connected with the known position of [Andrei A.] Zhdanov in the area of literature and art, to the early tendency to interpret human rights only in quotation marks).

It would be interesting now to ask oneself: How would we ourselves have reacted to all that if we looked at ourselves from the outside? Mutual understanding was hardly helped by the rhetoric of our military leaders, who spoke of a victory in a possible conflict with the West and, later, euphemistically, of a "crushing second strike." And did not our orthodox social scientists, covering themselves with the armor of quotations, not paint the world in exalted moral hues as the arena of a struggle between "good" and "evil"? . . .

But not everyone agrees with this perspective. Posing the question in terms of the "image of the enemy" calls forth criticism from other Soviet authors. Thus, for example, Volkogonov wrote in *Krasnaia Zvezda* (22 May 1987):

> It is vexing that, in discussing the theme of the "image of the enemy" (by the way, in our propaganda, even our military propaganda, in peacetime that term is not used), conclusions are reached that do not take reality into account. For example, in the . . . discussion on this theme that was held in one journal, in the statements of many participants were heard ideas with which it is difficult to agree. In particular, one of the publicists asserted that, "in times of political frigidity, the editors are swamped not with analytical articles but with letters from readers and with caricatures. These materials are literally on the borderline of fighting, front-line propaganda. This is what I would like to warn of." The speaker, knowingly or unknowingly, "warns" Soviet people away from showing alertness, a direct class reaction, and caution. He "warns" Soviet people, who have more than enough grounds for soberly judging the intentions and deeds of the imperialist circles.

Aleksandr Bovin, in his interview in the journal *Ogonyok* (1987, no. 34), spoke about the difficulty of restructuring, of changing the traditional approaches of our international journalism in regard to the portrayal of the other side:

> **Q:** Sometimes it is said that, in contemporary conditions, international journalism lags substantially behind journalism that deals with domestic themes. What do you think?

A: I think this is true. This lag exists, and the "crack" between them is not yet narrowing.

First, there are themes, and not just a few of these, which are in fact closed to thoughtful, objective journalistic analysis. One may "touch on" these themes, but only superficially, on the level of banal truths.

Second, the activity of the administrations connected with carrying out foreign policy is also beyond the limits of journalistic possibilities. This makes an analysis one-sided, flat, and inflexible.

Third, we often primitivize our opponents and consider them stupid. Let's say, a commentary on a recent speech of the opponent is printed. But from the commentary it is impossible to understand what they are saying, what motivates their position. By omitting the opponent's argumentation and motivation, we are really doing battle with a shadow. And because such a battle doesn't require arguments from our side either, they are replaced with a choice of sharp epithets: "malicious," "slanderous," "provocational," etc. The reader, of course, feels the falsity of the situation and does not thank us.

Fourth, we do not have enough discussions and arguments, even though we have all the objective conditions for a comradely polemic. I do not know of any major international problem on which—in an analysis under a general principled approach—the opinions of specialists completely coincide. Thus, there is something to argue about. Evidently we are hindered by the force of inertia left over from times past.

Thus it happens that we give a totally incomplete picture of world events; we deprive that picture of many of its colors; we free it from the contrasts and contradictions of shades and halftones.

The broadening of glasnost in information has also created new opportunities for foreign correspondents and scholars of international affairs. Many briefings are now held for foreign correspondents in Moscow; they have much more open access to various institutions; and they do not need "permission" for interviews with Soviet citizens. Contacts between foreign journalists and Soviet citizens have broadened. Developing new forms of international informational contacts, a series of Soviet newspapers have begun to provide a place on their pages for journalists and commentators from Western countries to directly address the Soviet readers with their evaluations of various events.

One final point should be emphasized in our discussion of the new political thinking. We have already said that the new thinking is not a conception formulated once and for all. Rather, it is a dynamic search for new ideas and new approaches that assumes internal development and the clashing of positions. One of the most important decisions along this path is whether to give priority to universal human values and interests over any class, national, political, or ideological values and interests. For this, one must pose the question of the role of class struggle and ideological struggle in the international arena.

Aleksandr Bovin, in his article "The New Thinking—New Politics" (*Kommunist*, 1988, no. 9), wrote the following:

> The choice posed by the new political thinking is based on the fact that no class or group interests, no ideology, is worth collective suicide. Survival and the preservation of civilization is a universal human interest, a more "weighty" interest than the interest of any class or social group. V.I. Lenin wrote: "From the point of view of the basic ideas of Marxism, the interests of social development are higher than the interests of the proletariat. . . ." (*Polnoe Sobranie Sochinenii*, vol. 4, p. 220). Time has infused a much richer content into that formula than [Lenin] had in mind at the turn of the century. Only by taking a stand for the priority of universal human interests can one correctly approach the whole problematic of war and peace in its current content and correctly evaluate the danger created by the contradiction between the development of the technosphere and the preservation of the biosphere or come to a decrease and eventual liquidation of the ecological, social, and cultural gap between the North and the South. However, [although] paradoxical at first glance, it is precisely the universal human approach that serves as the main guarantee of social development in our world, which is steeped in class and social contradictions.
>
> The placing of universal human interests in first place, the approach to problems of world politics from the point of view of such interests, does not mean a renunciation of class orientation in social analysis and in social practice. The interests and demands of social groups continue to play a decisive role in social life. They determine the content of political decisions. But at the same time there has arisen and broadened a sphere of universal human interests, a sphere of problems whose solution accords with the interests of all classes, all social groups. Furthermore, in order to solve universal human problems successfully, it is necessary to take under control and to subordinate class contradictions to the higher goal. In this is the sense of the priority of universal human interests.
>
> If the thesis about the priority of universal human values is not to be "balanced" with the class analysis of current events, there arises the temptation to cast doubt in the antagonistic character of relations between capitalism and socialism on the world arena, and on the class nature of the policy of peaceful coexistence. From the world-historical point of view, capitalism and socialism are not two parallel variants of civilization but two steps, two stages, of civilization, one of which will replace the other. This is the deepest content of their antagonism. The policy of peaceful coexistence does not remove this

antagonism but proposes to give a civilized form to the struggle and competition of civilizations.

The more we have recourse to peaceful coexistence, the more significant becomes the necessity of all-around cooperation—in economics and politics, in culture, and even in ideology. However, precisely that incontestable fact that we are dealing with the cooperation of various classes occupying conflicting historical positions, necessarily burdens this cooperation with competition, opposition, the desire to outflank one's partner, to draw society to one's own side. Exclusively peaceful forms of struggle and a policy dictated by the presence of an objective limit to confrontation will stimulate economic competition and ideological struggle.

Furthermore, the struggle of ideology is not simply an opposition of words, slogans, and ideas. It is above all the opposition of lifestyles in the widest sense of that word (material provision for people, civil rights, the possibility for spiritual and physical improvement of the individual). The real lifestyle is the main reservoir and generator of arguments that influence people's mind-sets.

Here, it seems, one must touch on the following issue. As is known, the new version of the CPSU platform omits the definition of peaceful coexistence of states with various social structures as a "specific form of class struggle." This innovation has been called to emphasize that there has appeared an objective limit to class confrontation in the international arena—the threat of pan-destruction. In this way is accented again and again the peace-loving character of the political strategy of the CPSU, the firm intention of the USSR not to carry class confrontation to that limit, to put in first place that universal interest, that which unites the worldwide working class and the worldwide bourgeoisie—the aspiration to survive and to continue history.

At the same time, Bovin's interpretation of this issue is not the only one, even among the advocates of the new thinking. Let us emphasize that today our disputes and debates develop not only between advocates and opponents of the new thinking but also among "new thinkers." For example, Andrei Kozyrev, vice chairman of the Administration for International Organizations of the USSR Ministry of International Affairs, in his article "Trust and the Balance of Interests" (*Mezhdunarodnaia Zhizn'*, 1988, no. 10), expressed a more radical point of view and, in fact, polemicized with Bovin:

I can already predict the question: Is a balance of class interests on the international arena possible at all? For a long time, the answer given to that was unconditionally negative. This was based on a simplified idea that class struggle between socialism and capitalism is, in essence, the question of "who is getting whom?" and if that was so, then this struggle must have a consciously unreconcilable character. Of course, it was explained that the form of this "class confrontation" must be peaceful coexistence of states with various social structures. Furthermore, the dialectical Leninist conception of international trust, which was full of living force, turned into a deadening black-and-white scheme of orthodox theory. In practice, this spilled over into confrontation along the whole politico-geographical system of coordinates.

It is not surprising that, following the logic of anti-imperialist struggle, we, against the interests of our Fatherland, allowed ourselves to be drawn into the arms race and helped to instill the "image of the enemy," to establish technological and cultural barriers between the USSR and the United States, between two systems. The result was the incarnation of the Kiplingesque formula: East is East, West is West, etc.

The whole thing is complicated by "questions of principle," which must be answered once and for all. For example: Can one speak seriously of trust toward the class opponent? Unfortunately, we used to answer that question more often "by the book" than according to life. It is alarming that even now, when the 27th Congress of the CPSU excluded from the party program the definition of peaceful coexistence as "a specific form of class struggle," attempts are made to interpret this only as an acknowledgment that there has appeared some limit to class-ideological implacability in relations between states of different systems—the threat of nuclear catastrophe. And only that. But on such a basis a world free from nuclear weapons—and, even more, a nonviolent world—cannot be achieved! For it follows that without this threat, class and global confrontation again would become a reality. And this means that Mrs. Thatcher is absolutely correct: Without "the bomb" humanity must return to an epoch when wars, not only in the "Third World" but in the whole world, would be seen as a means of policy.

The same logical chain also tangles the thesis about the priority of universal human values, explaining it approximately in this way: The USSR will not carry class confrontation to the brink of catastrophe. Putting into first place those universal human values that unite the worldwide working class and the worldwide bourgeoisie, [the USSR] wants to survive, to continue history. The conclusion is the same: If we liquidate nuclear weapons by the end of this century and preserve our ecology, then in the twenty-first century the universal class confrontation will return to its prominent position. . . .

But the party has something else in mind. The new political thinking, as the 27th CPSU Congress emphasized, demands not simply not bringing confrontation to the ultimate limit but "laying down a constructive, creative interaction of states and peoples on the scale of the whole planet"—that is, to turn peaceful coexistence into the highest universal norm of international relations. In this consists a true class interest, which is also the universal human interest of all countries—socialist, large and small capitalist, and developing countries.

A paradoxical situation has developed when the most innovative and radical ideas come not only from scholars and publicists but from the political leadership itself and, in particular, from the leadership of the Ministry of Foreign Affairs. An unprecedented talk by Foreign Affairs Minister Eduard Shevardnadze at a conference of the Foreign Affairs Ministry in July 1988 (*Mezhdunarodnaia Zhizn'*, 1988, no. 9) significantly widened the boundaries of the new political thinking. Shevardnadze directly spoke of the appropriateness of a pluralism of opinions; of the appearance, with glasnost, of various, sometimes diametrically opposed points of view; of the necessity of renouncing primitive ideologized approaches; of the democratization of the process of making and carrying out foreign policy decisions as a condition of overcoming the alienation of the people from foreign policy and of foreign policy from the people. However, perhaps the main political and ideological problem, in Shevardnadze's view, is the overestimation of the issue of class struggle in the international arena:

> This "image of the enemy," on the development of which we are spending so much energy, has developed in counterbalance to the real image of the Soviet people, despite and in contrast to its friendliness, bravery, wisdom, and self-sacrifice. A belief in its creative peacefulness was undermined by repressions, by declarations of the type, "We will bury you," by incorrect steps toward friends, and by the preaching, during the détente period, of a mistaken and, I would say, un-Leninist orientation toward peaceful coexistence as a specific form of class struggle.

In his opinion, the new thinking views the philosophy of peaceful coexistence as a universal principle of international relations:

> Completely justifiably, we refuse to see in it a specific form of class struggle. Coexistence, which is based on principles that are primary for everyone, such as nonaggression, respect for sovereignty, national independence, noninterference in internal affairs, etc., must not be equated with class struggle. This, of course, does not abolish the naturalness [*zakonomernosti*] of class struggle and of the thesis that a state's policy is determined by the interests of its ruling classes. But these class interests can and must have, as their common denominator, universal human interests.

In general, the equating of international relations with class struggle is hard to reconcile with an acknowledgment of the real possibility and inevitability of peaceful coexistence as the highest universal principle and mutually profitable cooperation of states with different sociopolitical systems. . . .

In order to correctly evaluate and provide for one's own national interests, it is essential to recognize the tendencies and understand the direction of movement of humanity as a whole.

If the thesis is correct about the increasing unity of the world, about its diversity and interdependence—and it certainly is true—then it follows that our national interests, too, demand that this process be helped along.

If the thesis is correct that nations can realize themselves, following the historical logic of social development—and this also is certainly true—then our interests consist in being one of the uniting forces of the world, in facilitating the development of integrational principles in the spiritual and material spheres of common human existence.

If humanity is moving toward a unity in diversity, toward a community of equals that are freely choosing their own paths—and it is certainly moving toward this—then our interests consist in strengthening, in every possible way, our own unique socialist individuality and essence, increasing their attractiveness for the rest of the world.

If humanity is capable of surviving today only in conditions of peaceful coexistence—and it is certainly incapable of guaranteeing itself a future in conditions of permanent confrontation—then does not this conclusion suggest itself, that the opposition between two systems can no longer be seen as the leading tendency of the current epoch?

It is clear that even this is not the last word in the development of the new political thinking. Ahead lie new ideas and new disputes.

EIGHT

We and the Outside World

The problem of the relationship of the Soviet people to the outside world occupies, on the whole, a smaller place in ideological and political discussions in our country than discussions, say, on questions of ecology, the legal system, democratization, or the preservation of our historical heritage. But this important question nonetheless merits separate treatment because, until now, the theme has been almost completely closed to discussion. There have been denunciations of émigrés, of course, as well as of Western capitalist countries, and self-glorification has long been a staple of the Soviet media. But the whole complex of issues involving the meaning of patriotism, the nature of human rights, and the place of the USSR in world civilization could not be freely discussed until the development of democratization and glasnost, and until the new thinking about foreign relations began to shatter the "iron curtain" that isolated our society from the outside world.

On Emigration and Patriotism

The subject of emigration has been a sensitive one in our society, and for a long period émigrés were treated as virtual traitors. Open discussion about the subject is relatively recent: It was touched off by the showing on Soviet television of an American documentary about the lives of former Soviet citizens in the United States and by the news that some émigrés want to return to their homeland. One article, which conveys the spirit of many of its kind, was published in *Literaturnaia Gazeta* on 14 January 1987 under the title "What He Realized Across the Ocean":

> The other day, several families of former Soviet citizens returned
> from the United States to the Motherland. Among them is the family

of singer-composer Anatolii Gross, who wrote under the pseudonym Dneprov. Immediately after passport control at Sheremetevo airport, an *LG* correspondent interviewed Gross.

"I left with my family for the United States in 1979, having succumbed to the persuasion of my father-in-law, Paul Leonidov, who at that point had already been living in the United States for some time. He painted a picture of a beautiful, paradise-like life, with full freedom of creative self-expression. Disillusionment set in almost from the first day of our stay abroad. There was indeed more creative freedom than one knew what to do with, but it turned out that, regardless of how talented you were, there you created only for yourself or for a narrow circle of people who knew you well. For a composer, and even more for one who works in the choral arts, having an audience and its support is of special importance. Besides that, it was necessary to earn a living. For four long years I had to earn a living behind the wheel of a New York taxi. Later, things went a little better, and I was able to appear with my songs in restaurants and cabarets. But this kind of work somehow could not bring satisfaction. How many times I recalled with bitterness what huge audiences there were for my songs in the Soviet Union.

With time I realized that, not only in the United States, but also in the West generally, talent is only a meager, insignificant part of what makes for the success of a composer or, let us say, a singer. The main thing there is money. Money means a name, money means universal recognition and love. Producers, who might have helped me in my creative work, calculated that in order to reach a wide public, I would have to raise around two million dollars!

And then there are the relations among people who work in the arts, especially if they have some kind of name! It is hard even to imagine the toughness and even cruelty of their relations with one another.

However, I did not decide to return to the Motherland because my material situation was really so difficult. Ultimately, we managed to adjust and came to earn enough for a living. That was not where the problem lay. A composer, poet, or writer, lacking the soil on which he grew up, loses, if not all of himself, then something irreplaceable and essential, without which it is impossible not only to work but also to live. Nostalgia forcefully enters into every day of your life. My wife and I expressed these ideas in a song we wrote in New York, "My address—Rus' ": It was written from the heart to the place of our "childhood," which we nowhere got away from. Left behind in Russia were happiness as well as sadness. It was written from the heart to the address "Rus'."

Many friends came to see me off to the Soviet Union. They were happy for me and envied me. Many of them would give up everything in order to be in my place and return to the Motherland. Now I envy myself: It is even hard to believe that I am home."

The meaning of patriotism was the theme of another article by Vera Tkachenko entitled "The Motherland is Given to Us Once and Until Death" (*Pravda*, 21 August 1987):

> *Rodina* (Motherland) is a given. You do not choose her according to your taste and desire, just as you do not choose a mother for yourself: Whatever kind of mother she is, your mother is the one and only among all the living; she cannot be compared with anyone, for all comparisons are blasphemous and insulting to the one who gave you life, fed, nursed, and raised you as best she could. . . .
> . . . We ask ourselves: Are there things about which we Soviets are proud? Oh, yes! Now, in the time of glasnost and perestroika, some of us, perhaps, have become somewhat drunk from the opportunity to say openly what is on our minds and in our hearts, disagree, argue and quarrel to the point of being hoarse, orally and in writing, and in the heat of emotion have begun in some ways to go too far in the line of exposure and repudiation of everyone and everything. . . .
> Yet not by a single criticism of shortcomings in the distant or recent past will we be able to progress farther! Not only that, but do not those who investigate and collect at the same time openly savor the errors of the past? Yes, in my time, serious and at times tragic mistakes were tolerated. We do not justify and will never forgive what happened in the years 1937 and 1938. But this cannot discount, and must not cross out, what we have achieved after seventy years of Soviet power; all that we have and are proud of was created by the party and the people while going through the most trying experiences. We are proud of each of the days we lived through, even if they were most difficult. . . .
> Unfortunately, some publicists appear to have forgotten about pride and about the victories and achievements of our great Soviet people. Involuntarily you fall to thinking: Does not this discredit the history of the Motherland—which was difficult, at times incredibly trying and tragic, but uniquely heroic? Sometimes you read with bitterness kinds of apologies to the respectable West for the fact that, in the years after October, we, with the possible exception of NEP, were, it turns out, very bad and weak and that we, as they say, must make amends. . . .
> Let them say what they want in the West; that is their business. But, really, it is distressing when you encounter in several of our publications articles where, using glasnost, they practically wash away our indisputable political and moral values. Why do some of these people compete with one another in striving to be the most biting, caustic, and malicious in poking with the scorching iron pin of exposure? It makes me want to say: Ease up, ease up, comrade compatriots! The Motherland, like a mother, needs compassion, filial love, and active assistance above all. I repeat: We must not see in our

history only minuses; there was and is also much good about which we are rightly proud. We will not discard this from the records. It behooves us in the first place to concern ourselves with the augmentation of the good, and without love for our native country, nothing will come from this.

The publication of Tkachenko's article evoked numerous readers' responses, some of which were published by *Pravda* on 7 September 1987. For example:

I read with great attention and emotion the work of Vera Tkachenko. I fully agree with the author and am convinced that the editors were absolutely right to have published this material.

Criticism of shortcomings is, of course, necessary, but it should not be an end in itself, and if criticism meets the approval of bourgeois statesmen in the West, I think that should put us on our guard.

> With respect,
> V. Kriuchkov,
> Moscow

No less important is another question—that of the "rolling stone" people. To me personally, they are deeply offensive, and I believe that the country does not need them. Let these people without roots be borne abroad—let them go their way: It is really impossible to rely on them in any situation. Humaneness is an honorable quality, but it should not go so far as slobbering. To abandon the Motherland—which is not a worn-out shoe to be kicked off one's foot—a person must answer for such a decision first of all to his own self. Returning must absolutely be earned and gained through suffering, not merely material deprivations.

> Z. Levit,
> Party veteran,
> Leningrad

In recent times, many critics have subjected everything to being run down, as if they were and are detached observers and everything that has been done and is being done does not concern them; their task is to run down, to slander. The question arises, how do they understand glasnost? Glasnost is, surely, a rational illumination of our affairs in the interest of strengthening the Motherland and increasing her authority. So, the interests of the Motherland must be the basis for all public statements. But we see outright competition over who can spread the most vile slander about the country. It seems that we all do the wrong thing and in the wrong way. One of these articles went so far as to write that our soldiers in the years of the Great Patriotic War advanced under the muzzles of machine guns, which followed and frightened them; another went so far as to say that industrialization should not have been carried out at such a rapid pace, that collectivization was little other than a mistake, and that the kulak did not himself present a real danger and should not have been touched.

Your article reproduces extracts from a letter in which the author says: . . . We must not turn the Soviet Union into a thruway for people who live by the principle: "A homeland is wherever one can live well . . ." I subscribe to this opinion. Nothing about them is shown on television; they pose before the lens as heroes.

A. Kravchenko,
Lvov

I read the important article "The Motherland is Given to Us Once and Until Death." It provokes an argument, it seems to me. Most of all, by the way the meaning of the words "Soviet patriotism" are explained to us. Yes, our past is behind us. Though not in a romantic, legendary sense, moving from achievement to achievement, but a living history, which is often rough and not simply heroic, . . . with mistakes, with justice—and with injustice as well. To give the appearance that it is not so is, to some extent, impractical: Thus we wittingly doom ourselves to repetition of mistakes in the future. Are these the errors of "some organs of our press," which supposedly have forgotten about pride and victories?

It seems to me that love for the Motherland is not a matter of shedding quiet tears of tender emotion in connection with the "mushroom spirit" and taking to the land. It is not a matter of, having forgotten about the building, feverishly touching up the facade. It also does not lie in delicate efforts to obscure—not cut out, just obscure a little bit!—the unpleasant and uncomfortable facts of history.

If we are a vital and healthy people—and I do not doubt that—we must relentlessly lance the boils that have accumulated in great numbers on the holy body of the Motherland. Yes, lance them and do not say "Fie, how unpleasant this is"—do not hold your nose at this.

A. Konev,
Engineer,
Yaroslavl'

On 18 March 1987, *Literaturnaia Gazeta* opened a new column under the headline "Readers Disagree" that carried three letters about attitudes toward the return of émigrés. One of the readers opposed granting permission for émigrés to return; the other was more favorably inclined but had serious reservations. The third letter expressed a point of view not reflected in *Pravda*:

> I think that if you do not like our way of life and do not want (or are unable) to work for its improvement or alteration—well, then, leave and try out something different.
>
> But the implementation of this principle alone does not fully resolve the problem. A complete solution of the problem entails recognizing that every former Soviet citizen must have the right to come back. Denial of homecoming is regarded as a punishment for treason. I personally think that leaving is not treason but stupidity. It is a mistake to which people are pushed by greed, envy, and dissatisfaction with their situation, in combination with overvaluation of their own individuality and being insufficiently informed.
>
> Emigration from the Soviet Union has seemed to confirm the slander of bourgeois propaganda. But returning refutes this slander! A person who returns from emigration thereby himself acknowledges his fault and mistake. If everyone who wants to starts to return from over there, that will be the strongest argument against leaving.
>
> I believe in the advantages of socialism and think it is necessary to make use of these advantages.
>
> A. Negodenko,
> Altai region

Discussion of this theme was continued in the 1 July 1987 issue of *Literaturnaia Gazeta*, and a survey of readers' reactions was published. This excerpt conveys something of their tone:

> "The people do not forgive, but you print: The Motherland forgives—forgives whom? Did you ask honest toilers, on whose necks sit the 'former citizens'? The people schooled, clothed, fed, and provided for them, gave them palaces, not apartments. . . . What did they lack? . . . We now have enough of our own spongers, writers, artists, musicians, and other spiritually enriching people. . . . How dare our correspondents go to meet with these people? . . . Glasnost, such glasnost! Excuse me, *LG*, but I am a longtime reader of yours, so publish my note without any alterations." . . .
>
> In the mail received there are letters that are frankly vulgar, and there are also the vilely anti-Semitic, right up to the Black Hundreds' call: ". . . save Russia!" They are few, but they exist. Just where do they come from, from whence did this filth crawl out? Well, it did.

In the stagnant mire of the previous period, it did not strike one's eye, but in the churning rapids it has started to come to light. . . .

Glasnost and democracy do not mean either cannibalism or that everything is permitted. There is no place in the newspaper for statements in the spirit of the "Union of Mikhail Arkhangel" or for sermons of misanthropy. Not today, and not in the future.

Another thing—the letters are full of sincere bewilderment or incomprehension of what is happening. Such letters, perhaps, are the most common of all. Blame for this, one should think, lies not with the authors themselves but with the former attitudes of the press (not excluding even our own newspaper): the persistent striving to over-simplify the question and to pass off emigration as something uniformly contemptible, greedy, and hostile. That is to say, among the "former citizens" you often find not the better representatives of the race of humanity: both scroungers and unrecognized "geniuses," and also outright traitors. All the same, historical reality was and remains much more complex. "The Motherland is not a shirt to put on if you want and take off if you want" (V. Savenkov, Yakutsk). "The Motherland is not an apartment that can be exchanged several times" (E. Melikhov, Moscow). "You can take offense at your boss, your friend, or the weather, but you cannot take offense at your Mother and Motherland" (K. Medyanskaia, Estonia). These would seem to be copybook truths. But what if someone else's shirt turns out to be unbearably tight? What if the "change of apartments" resulted from a mandatory order? Finally, what if Mother in unkind years conducted herself at times like a stepmother—and it was enough for her to smile, just to smooth out the severe wrinkles between her brows, in order for the spark of filial love to blaze up anew and heal old wounds. Do you think: It is not possible? But why, as a matter of fact, do you think that? Because one is not supposed to talk about it out loud?

. . . But opponents here again respond. Some of them are not at all averse to placing their objections on a theoretical basis and raising them to gigantic height. In what way? Take the following example: "The return of the 'lost sheep' from the West calls to mind the last war and how soldiers absent without leave were shot while former POWs were sent to Siberia. Discussions about humaneness supposedly obliging us to accept the émigrés are sinful, rotten hypocrisy. This understanding of Soviet patriotism in no way accords with the Helsinki agreements, which stipulate freedom of choice of a homeland. Spe-cifically, these agreements constitute one of the reasons why appearing before audiences of well-informed people who read the press with lectures on the inculcation of Soviet patriotism is becoming very difficult. There is no demand for this topic now anyway.

"I think that if foreign political circumstances force us to make certain concessions to the West, it is still better to limit permission to leave. The return of the 'differently minded' inflicts irreparable harm to traditional Soviet moral values.

> A. Rusakova,
> Moscow"

Many of these statements reflect a widespread view that almost all of the problems of the Soviet Union are brought to us from beyond our borders. In the face of hostile ideological invasion, the Soviet people in the best case become passive victims, and in the worst, willingly lose their spiritual innocence. This point of view is expressed particularly clearly by a number of famous and popular writers, including Sergei Vikulov, whose speech to the plenum of the board of the Writers' Union of the USSR included the following passage (*Literaturnaia Gazeta,* 6 May 1987):

> Our ideological opponent does everything in order that our future will not be as we have planned it. The impression is created that he works significantly more actively than we do, especially in the sphere of mass culture. How else to explain that he and only he appears in a legislative mode, particularly in the past decade? In music, in style of behavior, in clothing, in dance we appear only in the role of a miserable imitator, able to adopt others' grimaces but not able to think and create, to fashion our own culture in the national traditions and socialist in content. Vocal-instrumental ensembles on the Western model, with voiceless performers who shamelessly pose as asexuals, occupy so much television time that it hardly suffices as a way to congratulate the return of the "expatriates," who once betrayed the Motherland and now without a shadow of embarrassment resort anew to her altar.

The problem of dissidents and the "differently minded" merits a separate discussion. At present there are not very many articles on this theme, but they do appear. For many, emigration is simply associated with dissidence. But another point of view was expressed by V. Borev in the journal *Sotsialisticheskii Trud* (1987, no. 10):

> Often criticism is taken as a personal insult. This is typical for our society. It is still not old enough and has not accustomed itself to a normal perception of criticism as a rational activity directed at the improvement of the general situation. Here it is appropriate to recall how intolerantly we reacted to the expression of criticism of bureaucratic procedures, local governments, and the leadership of separate artistic unions by some of our writers, scholars, and poets in the 1970s. Often we forced people to become embittered. I am far from the idea that in our society there are principled opponents, enemies of Soviet

power, but those people who in the 1960s and 1970s talked with pain and grief about one or another process in the life of our country, these people were turned into enemies of the country, renegades, and dissidents by the bureaucrats. The problem of dissidents, in part, in my view, was in its time far-fetched. In any case, if we think about those who spoke with bitterness about what has happened in the Fatherland, then we will see that all of these people were in general well taken care of. Among them were academics, generals, literary figures, actors, and producers. All of them, being well-off, could have gone on quietly living comfortable lives. But they were concerned not so much for themselves as for others, for the social surroundings of their lives, for the state. We should remember also that they addressed their appeals in the first place not to the foreign press and "the Voices" [e.g., the Voice of America] but to their own leaders. But, as I said, even today we react to criticism with indignation, animosity, and intolerance. This can also be said about the past years. . . . Many worthy people were accused of not being patriots, although all of their statements were dictated by the most patriotic feelings.

An article in the weekly youth magazine *Sobesednik* (September 1987) expressed a similar idea, in a deliberately provocative form, as if to throw down a challenge to the organs of the press:

> I am a member of the Komsomol but do not believe in communism: In my opinion, it is a utopia, and to live in a society where all is ideal is simply uninteresting, boring. It is impossible for everyone to be equal. I am not infatuated with material possessions, but freedom to go abroad is good; hence you must write about it. Indeed, even V.I. Lenin often left the country and hid in Paris from the tsarist government. The tsar was bad, but the borders were open—and that is how it should be. But you do not write about this. You are afraid! Perestroika is perestroika, but do not say that which is forbidden.
>
> A. Gurko, 26,
> student, Kiev

The spectrum of positions on the question of emigration is much narrower than on many other problems. Many of these statements have a common initial premise: Emigration is treason, betrayal, in the best case—guilt before the Motherland. Americans may find it particularly difficult to believe in the sincerity of such views, but they may have a historical and cultural explanation. The United States is a nation of immigrants; the USSR is a country that over the course of centuries was the object of threats and attacks from many directions. In the Soviet Union people gradually developed a special, negative conception of those who want to leave the country. This problem is not so much rational (there is no rational argument against emigration as such) as emotional, psychological. Such is the reality, and we must reckon with it.

Soviets Abroad

The trips of Soviet citizens abroad is another question that has become a subject of discussion today. If before glasnost at least something was written about emigrants (basically criticizing without the right of reply), as a rule the normal departure of Soviet citizens for foreign countries (whether on official trips or as tourists) was always covered with a halo of secrecy. Today people have lost respect for secrets of this type; they not only openly discuss them in writings but also do not hide their own opinions, which are most often critical. Moreover, the travelers gain a new perspective from which to view our own society.

In his article "Our People Abroad," published in *Literaturnaia Gazeta* (26 August 1987), Leonid Pochivalov asked directly: "Are we really like that there?"

> From the first years of Soviet rule we have become accustomed to "overcoming difficulties," to "storming," to a constant state of mobilized readiness. This preparedness for "overcoming" is carried abroad.
> . . .
> Still another trait peculiar to our people abroad, which, I think, was created over the course of decades and perhaps even centuries, is the conditioning to patience, to being content with little. I was struck in several African countries by the fact that the buildings of our embassies and trade delegations, especially their residences, are more modest than you would think, huddling people together in regular black settlements. Aren't there too many difficulties "to overcome?"
> Such orphan-like unpretentiousness reflects not only on the prestige of our individual citizens but also on the prestige of the whole country. "Oh! Russian!" For them the hotels are cheaper and the food simpler, and desk clerks fling their belongings as if they were worthless—take them all! The semi-literate, unscrupulous small shopkeeper who is like a missionary, somewhere in the port of Tangiers or Singapore, looks condescendingly at Russians as if at indigents. Alas, our people do not go looking at the sparkling windows of expensive shops in Piccadilly but search for simpler stores on the outskirts—the expense accounts for official trips are tight. It is wounding to one's self-esteem that our low standard of living demonstrates itself particularly there, abroad. This often comes into conflict with our national pride, with our patriotism, which is founded on a just consciousness of the might and unlimited possibilities of our great country. . . .

At the dawn of Russian statehood, *zagranitsa* (the outside world)—that is, that which was beyond the limits of control by outlying Russian patrols—more often threatened us with troubles than it offered friendly intercourse. Since ancient times, the feeling of caution and distrust toward the outside world has been instilled in the Russian people. Probably the most painful lesson inflicted on our psychology came from the invasions of the Golden Hordes . . . and that more ancient, latent consciousness of weakness, despite the brilliant flights of the creative national spirit, lived on in hearts, was passed on as an inheritance from generation to generation, and has been preserved even to our day as a bitter seed in the most spiritual depths. . . .

. . . Much in our relationship to the outside world needs to be reconsidered today. It seems necessary for us to move more quickly to deliver ourselves from some chronic habits, prejudices, and stereotypes which are really not at all in keeping with the spirit of the times. . . . We are talking now about the necessity to repudiate stereotypes of thinking formed over the years that made us more primitive and did not allow us to show better qualities. Striving to present a false front is an old illness that we are now striving to shake off most of all. Yet efforts to present a false front have appeared not only on our own soil but also abroad. Indeed, it is especially there that we have sought, not to present ourselves as we are, but to exhibit for foreign observers a fabricated slogan-placard model.

In our own time, as a result of straightforward propaganda, there arose—and with the years it was all the more strengthened—the conviction that we Soviets are loved throughout the world, that we are everywhere admired and imitated. Of course, the imperialists, the warmongers, hate us and are ready to trip us up, but the "ordinary people," especially blacks and colored people in general, are all for us. In a gush of starry-eyed idealism, we reach out with a brotherly embrace of friendship and try to palm off our cheap mass consumption goods. Then we are surprised when we do not meet with the reciprocal affection that we expect. In fact, it turns out that far from everyone— even "simple people," even Africans—loves us, and many simply . . . know little about "Soviets." We still have not earned the universal love of the "ordinary people" throughout the world and, unfortunately, have not yet become an example that someone would want to imitate unreservedly. It is easy to deceive ourselves. Time teaches one to evaluate reality soberly. We are now paying dearly for earlier illusions.

In recent years in the Soviet Union, and not least under the pressure of public opinion, much has been done to simplify our very archaic, multistaged procedures of official registration for foreign travel. The rules for registering as a tourist to a socialist country are being simplified, but all the same there remains the requirement that one's place of work must endorse the trip. Moreover, the system for approving applications for travel to capitalist countries is an assault on human dignity, as Elena Katasonova made clear in her letter to *Moskovskie Novosti* (12 July 1987):

You say that now there are no zones or themes closed to discussion? Well then, I will try to touch on some themes, about which it has not been acceptable to talk.

An orientalist by profession, translator of books, author of three stories and many articles, a member of the Union of Journalists of the USSR since 1965 and of the Union of Writers of the USSR since 1984, I travel a lot around our country and, as a tourist, abroad.

You are guessing, probably, what I want to talk about? Namely, about the official registration of tourists, about the exhausting procedures, one of which—the composition of an application—you will not be able to comprehend in your whole life: What is the sense of all this?

Explain to me why I, a non-party person, in order to go to England and see the country on my own money, have to get somebody's recommendation? They are not sending me, and it is not a reward for something. I do not represent anyone except myself, as a tourist. Why, then, does my trip depend on them?

I have been repeatedly convinced that there is no way you can type up the application only one time: something will be found to be not in the proper form; and again you re-type, in four copies, everything about yourself.

Then they take you to the district committee, tearing you away from all of your most pressing work—you and someone from the party bureau. You sit there half the day, because people, the masses, have been brought there for show. Behind closed doors sits the commission. Then we enter, and again the application is read, and they ask me questions, the gist of which is: Do I know the country to which I am going, and what do I know about events in the world? What kind of connection is there here to tourism? Why do they subject me to this examination?

Who are these people, sitting behind a long table, the rulers of my fate? If they wish it, I will see England; if not, I will not get a glimpse of that country. It is said that these people are prominent citizens. If that is so, how is it that in the procedure for departure of a tourist to foreign countries the focus is bureaucratic red tape and disrespect for individuality?

On the form which we fill out, there is everything about us: when we were born, which nationality, where we studied and worked, whether we have stood trial or been a prisoner (more than 40 years after the war!). Everything about parents, children, brothers and sisters. It is very difficult for me to write about my father, who died in 1972, where and in which cemetery he is buried. I found out about the cemetery this year from a set of instructions handed to me, not in a remote province but here in Moscow, at the Union of Writers! Someone is keenly interested even in the cemetery.

Furthermore—in addition to the application and questionnaire—you have to write an autobiography, in which you repeat the same things in the questionnaire and application: where, when and why you were born, and so on. Every time you write this, you think: The person who invented all this did it in order to justify his own idleness, to create the illusion of furious activity, to waste precious paper (none of the forests of Siberia suffice for this writing), and to humiliate people, who are guilty only in that they want, not to buy expensive furniture, but to travel.

There is no need for a tourist to get recommendations or write autobiographies, and if a questionnaire is required, it should be minimal: information necessary for a foreign passport.

Answer this, those who are concerned with tourism: What does abolition of this pandemonium depend on? Such people say, like a law of nature: That is how it is done—and that is all.

In the issue of *Moskovskie Novosti* for 16 August 1987, Viktor Sukhoteplyi, head of the administration of Soviet tourism abroad, VTsSPS, attempted to answer some of these questions:

> Until recent times, the procedure for official registration of tourists going abroad really did suffer from impersonal bureaucracy and red tape. The Ministry of Public Health alone, for example, required that a person visit sixteen doctors. . . .
>
> What, then, figures in the replacement of the numerous papers? A compact document—with everything on one page, the content of which is at the moment being developed. It will look roughly like this: on one side—questionnaire data necessary for registration for a foreign passport; on the other—a medical conclusion, for which a simple visit to a physician and the permission of the worker's collective will be sufficient. Last, in point of fact, the same recommendation, simplified and shortened, it is true, to several sentences. Why has the recommendation of the collective been retained? Unfortunately, for now a tourist voucher is still not sufficient. For this reason, it is also necessary to pass selection. Remember that in our country every second worker receives this voucher on advantageous terms, paying only half the cost of foreign services. The enterprise pays the rest, and understandably it is interested in seeing to it that voucher recipients receive what they deserve.

Yet the questions still remain. N. Popova, in the article "After Typing Ten Times," published in *Sovetskaia Kul'tura* (10 November 1987), wrote:

Not for nothing do they say that it is better to see once than to hear a hundred times. This is true both in relation to foreigners who are interested in the USSR and in relation to Soviet people, who must have a greater opportunity for acquaintance with different countries. Let our people judge for themselves, and not by hearsay or from newspaper articles, about life abroad. The development of all forms of tourism and international contact does not weaken but strengthens the position of our state.

When we become more deeply acquainted with the conditions of existence of ordinary people in the West, inquire into their problems, learn by what efforts and often exhausting labor they earn much higher wages than we do, how the budget of an average family is planned, how much they spend on an apartment, education, medical services, and so on, then we begin to value more the advantages and stability of the socialist system. The main thing is having a calm confidence in tomorrow. This trait of our society is noted—not without a feeling of envy—by many foreigners who visit the USSR.

However, there is also something for us to learn abroad. I have in mind not only the achievements of science and technology, the level of service, organization of publishing, and commerce. It is worth our while to study even the relations to the very labor by which no honestly earned kopeck is considered dishonorable. . . .

The very history of our culture testifies to the utility of international cultural and literary connections. But while developing international contacts and tourism, it behooves us to review the relations to official foreign trips that have arisen in recent years. After time-wasting paperwork and various commissions, we have started to forget the only important question that must determine the sending of people on official foreign trips: Does it have a concrete and real use for the institution, department, or ministry? In the period of stagnation, the people who were sent on official foreign trips were not always the most full-of-initiative, creative, and businesslike workers. For many people (with splendid questionnaires and applications), such official trips turned into pleasant tourist excursions at state expense, with a zero coefficient of useful activity. . . . Briefly stated, less bureaucracy and slackness but more faith and creative efficiency! These, in my opinion, are the principles that must govern our international contacts in the epoch of glasnost and democratization.

Popova also expressed serious criticisms of the Department of Visas and Registration (OVIR) in her article. There followed an answer to her from A. Logvinov, head of the main administration for the maintenance of public order of the Ministry of Internal Affairs of the USSR, in *Sovetskaia Kul'tura* on 4 February 1988:

The article "After Typing Ten Times" (10 November 1987) was discussed at an expanded meeting of officials of the service of the General Office of Internal Affairs (GUVD) of the Moscow City Council, at which, yet again, the attention of the people present was directed toward the need to decisively eradicate red tape, to improve manners in work, and to constantly manifest respectful and tactful relations to citizens and their declarations and requests. At the present time, the MVD [Ministry of Internal Affairs] of the USSR, with the participation of other ministries and departments, is completing work on a significant simplification of the formalities connected with the receipt of citizens' documents for foreign travel. The stated changes have been reported repeatedly in the press, at press conferences, and on television.

It was thought necessary, also, to pay attention to the one-sided and subjective approach to the complex question involved in the article, which creates for unsophisticated readers an incorrect impression of the situation in the area of the development of foreign contacts.

The last paragraph is disturbing: All too often in the past, such rhetoric was used to suppress criticism and dissatisfaction. But today people want to speak openly about the problems that have accumulated. In the very same issue of the newspaper, readers' letters on the subject were published:

When I read N. Popova's article, a lump stood in my throat. I myself went through the humiliating procedures, the cold looks and caustic retorts to me from the "girls" who sit in the OVIR office. Every time I went to them, my legs were literally paralyzed. I registered to visit my daughter—a Soviet citizen who is married and has lived abroad for five years now. They advised me: Let her go her own way! Or, rejecting me for the umpteenth time, they alluded to my "access to secrets" (I am an artist) and so on. Finally, they let me go, and out of happiness at seeing my daughter, I forgot all the insults, and abroad at the Soviet consulate I extended the period of my stay, at which I was asked several times whether this would not bring me trouble later. I answered with a smile: "Everything is done in accordance with the law; do not worry." At work I had been granted leave at my own expense and vacation time. But when I returned, at OVIR I was asked severely to explain in writing why I had extended the period of my stay. Of course, because I had not seen my daughter in four years! Really, they have instructions instead of hearts! But even with this the affair was not finished. In the name of the director of my enterprise came the inquiry: On what basis was I given leave on my own account? What saved me was that I have worked here for twenty-five years and have a good record.

Now, when times have changed, but those people who occupy their former positions are not prepared to change (since they simply are not able to), what are we to do—ordinary Soviet people? As before, endure all the humiliations? I hope that this article and our letters help to simplify the "thousands of instructions" and questionnaires. But really, they humiliate us everywhere: in hotels, at the post office, in stores. Still, one hopes to see the day when times change for the better! But meanwhile I write to you under a pseudonym because the bureaucrats are very vindictive, and I am afraid of them.

> A. Nadezhdina,
> Leningrad

Thank you very much for the article "After Typing Ten Times." I think that it accurately illuminates the obvious discrepancy between what is said at the very highest level and the senseless, expensive procedure of official registration documents for going abroad. It will be interesting to see whether sometime there will be radical changes in this sphere. We all urge one another to move from words to deeds, but this is obviously a case where action does not depend on us.

I am not writing you because I desperately want to travel abroad. It might happen, even after the tearing down of the fence of instructions, that I will not prepare an application. The issue is trust in people. You see, in practice, we ourselves by such prohibitions foster in people the illusion of a "utopian life," which they glimpse "there." And how! Even traveling at one's own expense is considered a privilege to our ideological "opponents"! For some reason we still hold on to absurd and absolutely illogical instructions. Are they really justified? Why, then, among our people abroad do there turn out to be the so-called "failures to return"—though they successfully filled out the questionnaires and gathered all the signatures and stamps? In any case, it is clear that the existing practice of departure is obsolete. (Restrictions on leaving must apply only to people privy to state secrets, but this is a fairly narrow circle of people.) Official registration documents must be reduced to a minimum. . . . The gathering of signatures and feeling of dependence on someone's subjective will (it must be agreed that relations at work take shape in different ways for everyone) only irritate, and even these signatures in essence do not guarantee anything. Surely, we are all adults and must be responsible for ourselves.

> Iu. Novgorodtsev,
> Reshety Village,
> Novosibirsk province

The impact of travel abroad on evaluations of Soviet society was frankly discussed by Liudmila Saraskina in the journal *Vek XX i Mir* (1987, no. 10):

I have heard many times from people who have often been abroad about the complexes of Soviet people who encounter much higher standards of living than we have at home. Our propaganda and mass media successfully teach us to think about the outside world, especially the capitalist world, in terms of "glaring contrasts," "social vices," "class conflict," and the "dark side of life." The ideological purpose of a negative evaluation of the other world has worked smoothly for too long; the older generation remembers too well the suffocating atmosphere of mutual suspicion in connection with the notorious "groveling before the West"—a malicious term of the Stalinist epoch, so costly for our intelligentsia and our whole people.

Now, finding himself in a highly developed industrial country and having usually very little money, our average man, if he is not a cynic or an unbridled intriguer, experiences sharp mental discomfort. If everything is so bad in the "rotting West," if the West, according to the diagnoses of television, radio, and newspapers, is experiencing a severe recurring economic crisis, then where does this exorbitant abundance come from? Accustomed to thinking about the outside world in an exclusively negative scheme, a visitor from our country is inclined to see in the very abundance almost a deformity. A society with surplus wealth produces in him a confused and complex feeling: a combination of envy, confusion, the unquenchable ambition of a consumer, and internal protest. This distinctive kind of culture shock provokes, as if in answer, a reaction of irritation and often even animosity. As a rule, these are fully controlled emotions, but still they demand some kind of psychic compensation. As if at a performance of "black magic," here, abroad, the observer craves unmasking. Striving to satisfy his patriotic feeling and sensing an insult to the nation, our traveler searches for—and of course!—finds "contrasts," the negative balances, which must explain everything and balance and soothe his agitated imagination. Our man begins to think in terms of notorious self-deceiving stereotypes, in the manner of the illogical thinking of competing women, each of whom is in the opinion of the other "ugly, but also stupid."

Fearing being exposed in "uncritical relations"—from one side, in "slandering"—from another, and this has started to happen—both in vulnerability to propagandizing and in ideological weakness, and remembering instructions, written who knows when or by whom, that contain innumerable "don'ts" and "not recommendeds," a person involuntarily changes his character. This is also how they perceive him in the West; this is what they strive to portray in innumerable propagandistic clichés: watchful, "vigilant," expecting provocations from all sides, and for that reason—reticent, unsociable. "The Russians are terrible to themselves"—this ironic expression, which characterizes the behavior of Russians abroad (coined, incidentally, in self-criticism by us ourselves), is, of course, not at all flattering, nor funny. It only describes that degree of constraint, which originated not in illusory but real fear, too deep, whose disfiguring traces are left in the consciousness of people.

Today we are beginning to deliver ourselves from this sticky, paralyzing feeling, from its obvious and hidden complexes. In combination with this liberation, the cliché that is humiliating for us is crumbling into the dust: We want to enter into contact with humanity not in the form of sullenly self-satisfied savages on tanks but as people normally different, and in our variety possessing great human potential.

Today it has become a little bit easier to look the world in the eyes. We are freeing ourselves from our own prejudices and stereotypes and striving to help our neighbors to do this. Of course, we are only at the beginning of the path, and before us is still the entire road.

The problem we are discussing has another side: Do we treat foreigners who come to the USSR the same way we treat our own people? A stimulus to the discussion of this question was provided by an article from film producer Stanislav Govorukhin published in *Sovetskaia Kul'tura* (13 July 1987). The article had a striking title: "Welcome, or Entry Prohibited," and it was devoted to the moral costs of the existing system of special services for foreigners in the USSR:

> At one time, I loved staying here [in Yalta]. But with the years such trips stopped providing happiness and later even began to produce only irritation and offense. Much has changed for the worse since that time, both in big things and small details. . . .
>
> Yes, it is uncomfortable to be a citizen with a Soviet passport in your pocket in this town. It is true there are sanatoria, tourist centers, and spas open to them here. In the final analysis, local residents accommodate even social outcasts for a price. But still, how many places do you think there are for Soviet citizens in hotels with elementary conveniences? Go ahead! Stretch your imagination! We are talking here about greater Yalta—a huge city, which has doubled or tripled in size in recent years and is the center of attraction for vacationers from all countries. So, how many?
>
> As the first secretary of the Yalta Party City Council, A. Kriachun, informed us, ninety-four places. Upon inquiry: Rooms with only one washbasin are considered rooms with conveniences. That is how it is!
>
> Meanwhile, in the past fifteen years in Yalta, hotel construction has been in full swing. But here is the paradox: The more hotels that are built, the fewer places remain for Soviet citizens. Quite recently, two famous hotels were at the service of visitors—Oreanda and Tavrida. Oreanda has been reequipped and made into a luxury hotel. Now only wealthy foreigners can stay there. The same fate awaits Tavrida. In the meantime, she houses an "Intourist" hostel.

Eleven years ago, when the sixteen–story mass of the hotel Yalta had just been erected and around it seethed work on building a pool, sauna, and tennis courts, Soviet citizens were allowed in the hotel. Somehow this was understandable to us ourselves, since our people—"are used to everything." To them, the crashing of jackhammers and grinding of steam shovels is not a hindrance; let them be grateful that they were just allowed to stay. But as soon as work around the hotel was completed, access to the hotel was closed to citizens with Soviet passports. No, no, we will be just until the end and admit them sometimes. Out of season, or if the big foreign reception area is torn down—then they will be allowed. Grudgingly, as if doing people a favor, with sour expressions and haughty little smiles—they register them. But then it is necessary to be prepared for all kinds of humiliations.

In the first place, they give you a visitor's card in a different color than for Intourist. This is to signify that you will be served last and that not all of the conveniences of the hotel are meant for you. For example, on this visit they would not allow you on the comfortable beach of the hotel Yalta—it is for foreign tourists. . . .

. . . It is striking what perceptible differences there are between foreign citizens and our own natives, and not in clothing, of course—in attire and such we are equally respectable—but in manner of behavior. Foreigners are carefree, relaxed, talk loudly, and feel themselves masters of the area. Our countrymen, though, hug the walls, look timid in the cafes and restaurants, and enter the pool apprehensively . . .

. . . How many times in conversations with Intourist workers have we run across the remarks:

We do not want rubles. We need foreign currency!

Yes, the state needs foreign currency—marks, pounds, francs, dinar, dollars. With them you can buy computers, machine tools, medical equipment, clothing, perfume. But is not this foreign currency too costly to us?

When a waiter, porter, or manager wags his tail in front of a foreigner but talks rudely, disrespectfully, boorishly with Soviet citizens, in my eyes he looks like a slave. He is a slave; he has the psychology of a slave. Just think: We do not prevent such a stratum of human slaves from arising, under our own eyes, in our own society. . . .

The state needs foreign currency, of course, but even more necessary to it in this complex moment of reconstructing our whole way of life are people who will carry out perestroika in practice. It is essential that they know that their labor will be rewarded, that their efforts will be compensated, that society cares about them, and that no one will dare to humiliate them or treat them with insufficient respect.

Is it not time, finally, to restore respect to the Soviet passport?

Let us think about our children. Let them not envy foreigners in any way!

In their responses, sent to *Sovetskaia Kul'tura* and published on 3 October 1987, readers supported S. Govorukhin:

> The author of the article raises a global question—about the degradation of the human dignity of Soviet citizens. He does it through the specific example of the "Intourist region."
>
> I want to share my own memories, too. I once stayed in the Hotel Yalta, which is mentioned in the article. Everyone was scrutinized there. A person could return from the beach with the idea of dining and relaxing in a comfortable room, but receive from the attendant on the floor instead of a key a *pokhoronka,* or "killed-in-battle" notice (that is how they referred there to official orders from the management about the urgent freeing of rooms). No one was concerned about what a person who suddenly received such a *pokhoronka* would have to do. Pursuing the matter with the directors was useless.
>
> O. Gaplichuk, engineer,
> Kiev

> What S. Govorukhin wrote about has, of course, long been well known. It is merely the first time it has been said aloud, though it is also accurate and graphic.
>
> Last year, my wife and son and I, having come to Moscow, wanted to visit the A.S. Pushkin Museum. How we anticipated seeing the beautiful exhibits!
>
> While we stood in line, busloads of foreign tourists arrived one after another, and the foreign guests entered the museum without difficulty. But our line did not move forward even an inch.
>
> Thus we did not get into the museum. We will probably not have another chance—since we are rarely in Moscow.
>
> Ivanov family,
> Saratov

The residue of cold war psychology and bureaucratic logic, especially where foreigners are concerned, has not yet been eliminated from Soviet life. Its consequences are described by V.V. Ustich in a letter to *Ogonyok* (no. 48, 1987):

> For around four years I have worked as a translator in the section of the chamber of commerce of Krasnodar concerned with the assembly of various types of equipment. A variety of people visit us, but I formed good, friendly relations with a few, with those who are interested in our country and sympathize with us. When our son was

born, we received congratulations from friends and acquaintances, including some from abroad.

One of the West German specialists, with whom our family had long been in correspondence, was to travel through Krasnodar to Novorossiisk. He informed us of this by telegram and asked to visit us. He wanted to come here to deliver a present on the birth of our child—a romper suit and matching booties, but he had to travel to the center of town to the chamber of commerce, which is located not far from our house. The specialist from West Germany asked an acquaintance, A.C. Zapunian, for permission to drop in on us for 10–15 minutes to congratulate my wife personally, deliver the present from his family, and take photographs with us. From the first to the last minutes of his visit with us—about 25 minutes—Zapunian was present, and he wrote down the data from my passport, although he had known me for three years already.

A week later, we said farewell to the specialist from West Germany, and at the airport, in the presence of Zapunian, gave him a set of knives and forks as a keepsake.

On May 8th of this year, I was summoned to the police station, where an official of the OVIR, Nina Nikolaevna Kirichenko, in the presence of the deputy chief of the OVIR in Krasnodar (whose name I did not catch) "talked" with me about violation of the law and about the depravity of friendly relations with citizens from abroad, especially from capitalist countries. The "conversation" went by the book: "They killed 20 million of our people, . . ." "To sell the Motherland for finery," "What kind of a suit is that you are wearing?" (I bought it, incidentally, at a shop here), "With him everything is clear."

Nina Nikolaevna read me the law that I allegedly had violated, but out of everything enumerated: assignment of a dwelling, services, deals—I had not violated a single condition. In the end, the deputy chief of the OVIR dwelled on the fact that I had created the preconditions for a violation—a deviation from the program.

"We have warned you the first time," they said to me in conclusion. "In your free time, you do not have the right to meet with foreigners. All the same, we will know who visits you. The second time, the fine will be 50 rubles." They poured out further threats in connection with my future.

This is how I turned into a criminal and internal enemy of our country. The head of the chamber of commerce, I.V. Milovanov, prohibited everyone from giving me even written work. Some acquaintances began to avoid my area. How can one correlate what happened to me with our initiatives and directions on trust in collaboration in the international arena, or with broadcasts in which it is said that people from different countries must get to know one another better, or, finally, with the simplification of the procedure of official registration for travel to socialist countries?

V.V. Ustich, age 33,
Krasnodar

Experience shows that the best means of breaking up archaic prejudices and stereotypes are direct contacts between ordinary people, Soviets and Americans. Extracts from an article by Vladimir Bogdanov, who walked with the rest of the participants in the Soviet-American March for Peace from Leningrad to Moscow, convey an impression of the enormous good will of ordinary Soviet people for Americans (*Vek XX i Mir*, no. 9, 1987):

At first no one believed in it. The view was expressed that to unite in one great action representatives of peoples as different as Americans and Russians appear to be is just as impossible as to unite "ice and fire." That is precisely how some mass media in the West characterized the first-ever Soviet-American March for Peace, which walked the route from Leningrad to Moscow between June 14 and July 8.

Two hundred and fifty Americans and 150 Soviet citizens walked together along the old roads of Russia through ancient Russian cities—Leningrad, Novgorod, Valdai, Torzhok, Kalinin, Klin, Moscow. . . . Mark Twain was right when he said that traveling is fatal for prejudices. Participant in the march Arthur Nelson, a professor of theology from Chicago, said in an interview with journalists that when he decided to set out on the march through Russia, his ninety-year-old mother worried that it was dangerous. But after thinking about it, she told her son: "No, you should still go. Go, since the time has come when Americans and Russians must work together." . . .

The three weeks spent on the march helped Russia to open herself to the Americans. It had to be seen, how the visitors were greeted in villages. Old men and old women came out with pies, set up samovars, brought out milk, some came out with icons, and, as was since ancient times the custom in Old Russia, blessed the travelers. The elderly embraced them and were not ashamed of tears of joy. The young enjoyed themselves, sang, and exchanged addresses. Many joined the march, and the column stretched for several kilometers. The march departed from the scheduled itinerary, but later even stern guardians of order smilingly observed the happy scenes of brotherly interaction.

I remember how cheerfully Soviet and American journalists laughed when they were present at a telephone conversation of Gary Shapiro, correspondent for several American radio stations. He persuaded his boss: He had not found here what he had earlier feared he would see; here there are normal people, who speak openly, and in the tents there are no eavesdropping devices (he personally verified this). Agents of the KGB, apparently, had turned into mosquitoes: The damned insects bite more viciously here than in America. . . .

We also opened ourselves anew to the Americans, and not in the fashion of the ritualized scenario "strikes—police—unemployed—arms race." We encountered ordinary people, who raise children and play basketball, fall in love, travel . . . and they want to learn more about us, to push beyond the limits of "études in red tones," according to which life in the USSR is a solid mass of vegetating underdeveloped people under the vigilant eye of the police and KGB.

As is evident, the relationship of Soviet citizens to the outside world is complex. There is an odd interweaving of sincere interest and sus-piciousness, openness and suppression, complexes of inferiority and superiority, strivings to learn and desires to teach. Such relations did not arise yesterday, and they have been discussed in the past. Relations to the outside world have developed largely under the influence of the notion that the USSR is situated in a hostile encirclement. The Soviet people traditionally have feared and been put on guard by the distrust and suspicion that the countries of the West show toward our country. We have responded in kind. Restrictions of democracy in our country have often been justified by a foreign threat.

It is most difficult of all here to overcome inertia. Today, when the general political and psychological atmosphere in the country has changed in a radical way, when the leadership itself actively encourages expansion of contacts between people on the most varied levels, we nonetheless often observe the recurrence of old thinking: The bureau-cracy is not really hurrying to facilitate contacts between people, and it is very common for contacts between Soviets and foreigners to be perceived by some as almost a crime. This is often not a result of somebody's evil will but behavior that to many people seems natural.

Is there hope for overcoming attitudes of this kind? Undoubtedly there is. First of all, the contemporary world demands ever greater internationalization of thinking and the widening of political, scientific, cultural, and human contacts. The free movement of ideas and people between borders must become the norm of the future. Only the gradual overcoming of prejudices on both sides, and the overcoming of hostility between our two systems, will allow us to come nearer to these goals.

The fact that problems of relations with foreign countries and foreigners is now openly discussed in the USSR is in itself a big step forward on the path to this norm. The state of social consciousness and its sore points are coming to be better understood, and consequently, attempts to make changes may be more purposeful. The present political will of the leadership, we hope, will overcome bureaucratic resistance and inertia. Improvement of relations between East and West will help to remove many real and imagined fears and anxieties from the consciousness of the people. Many notions adopted in the time of the cold war will clear up by themselves as they are seen to be groundless.

Finally, perestroika and glasnost have awakened a feeling of personal dignity and civic activism among people. There is still much nonsense in our lives, but people are no longer willing to be resigned to it. Relations with the outside world are becoming demystified. An ever-increasing number of people are striving to overcome blind admiration of the outside world without replacing it with either a feeling of superiority or jingoism. People are becoming more independent in their judgments and less inclined to accept on faith any kind of dogma. This process has begun and is continuing, however slowly and agonizingly, with retreats simultaneously from above and from below. An analogous phenomenon—establishing more normal and healthy relations with the East—is gradually taking place in the West. One wants to think that these processes are intersecting movements that in the course of development will strengthen one another.

ANDREI MELVILLE

Conclusion

My colleagues and I have been working on this book for some two years, and in all candor we could not have predicted that it would prove to be such a challenging enterprise. It has been difficult not only in the technical sense: choosing the articles, selecting the quotations, writing the comments, translating the entire work, editing and reediting it, adding new materials, using overseas mails and FAXes, holding working sessions in Moscow, Berkeley, and Stanford. The most difficult, almost impossible, part of the job was to keep up with the incessant flow of events, with the interminable changes, the ups and downs of current Soviet life, the ebb and flow in the public mood.

These days everything in Soviet society seems to be changing so quickly that for those of us who have worked on this book it is hard to avoid a feeling of frustration as we register that something is no longer newsworthy, something else is already outdated; new problems appear on the agenda and at times new ideas as well.

Even so, we are convinced that what we have tried to do is useful. We have tried to provide the American reader with an outline of the major ongoing debates and the logic of the arguments and counterarguments presented in them. These arguments continue to be voiced in the current discussions on perestroika and glasnost. They still mark the dividing lines between different political and ideological camps in our society. Meanwhile the public debate is evolving further. It is becoming sharper and less inhibited; new participants get involved; the spectrum of problems under discussion is expanding; and new ideas emerge. Here are a few examples.

Two years ago, to ask whether Afghanistan had not been a tragic mistake in Soviet foreign policy was to test the limits of glasnost. Today more and more people ask that the courts impose penalties on those responsible. Demands for the conversion of the military-industrial complex to peaceful uses have become much more pronounced, and practical proposals concerning such conversion are being widely discussed. Until recently, the history of Soviet foreign policy was another taboo. It is now becoming the subject of heated discussion: the Molotov-Ribbentrop Pact of 1939, for example, the fate of the Baltic states, and Soviet intervention in Hungary in 1956 and in Czechoslovakia in 1968.

The virtual explosion of national tensions within the Soviet Union has produced crisis after crisis and has stimulated a search for new approaches. In the process, participants in our public discussions have called into question the constitutional basis of our union, the principles underlying our federalism, and the legality of past actions in this field.

There are scarcely any "sacred cows" left in the debates over Soviet history. It is symptomatic that this reevaluation has spread from personalities to historical categories and events, such as the collectivization of agriculture and industrialization during the first Five-Year Plans. The notion of *alternativnost'*—the premise that history could have gone along different paths—has for the first time encouraged public discussion of the alternatives that existed in Russia in 1917, at the time of the October Revolution. The very idea of political opposition—both past and present—has gradually been legitimized. The whole process of historical rewriting has not been simply a repainting in opposite colors: Yesterday's villains are hardly emerging as today's heroes. It is, rather, a sense of tragedy that pervades the new understanding of our history. One thing is clear: The social amnesia typical of our past is no longer possible.

In the discussions of economic policy, a general tone of pessimism and dissatisfaction has become prevalent, the obvious reasons for this being the deteriorating economic conditions and the insufficiency of the proclaimed reforms, which are being blocked both by the bureaucratic apparatus and by the existing social and economic institutions. There is now a growing awareness that in the economy there are no quick fixes and that we face a long and painful period of stringency in the years ahead. As a result, people are more prepared to consider options that were hardly imaginable a few years ago—like the introduction of private ownership of land and reliance on the market as a neutral and value-free mechanism. Moreover, an entirely new reality has been created by the unprecedented series of well-organized and massive strikes, beginning with the miners, which prompted another round of public discussions and debates.

The list of issues under discussion keeps growing. Old and new arguments continue to clash, but many of the earlier illusions and expectations of easy and rapid solutions have vanished; optimism has diminished; resentment and fatigue have increased. Moreover, new challenges seem to appear before the old ones are disposed of. Hence a growing feeling of social overload, which contributes to an ambivalence about the future: People have high expectations for tomorrow and yet a growing fear of it. The old social guarantees for tomorrow are now being called into question, creating a sense of insecurity very alien to the traditional Soviet psyche.

When perestroika was first launched, many regarded it as a miraculous panacea for all the ills and problems of the stagnant system. Glasnost likewise was endowed with the qualities of political magic: All that was needed was to curse the crimes and errors of the past and to proclaim the new verities, and reality would miraculously be transformed into a new world of justice and abundance. In other words, glasnost was widely regarded not as a precondition of perestroika but as its guarantee. Alas, the miracle did not occur.

So people came to understand that the long-awaited glasnost would not work its magic, would not create a new and very different society by instant exorcism. We would not find any shortcuts around historically inevitable obstacles on the long and wearisome road to democracy.

That road has already produced its obvious rewards. It has also demonstrated their high price. There is no doubt that we now live in a much more open society. We are able to express our views freely, and we have begun to experience and value basic political freedoms. But glasnost is not the only measure of current Soviet life. We also live amidst strained and even violent interethnic relations, unprecedented strikes, spiraling inflation and rising prices, and a rapid social and political polarization that undermines the traditional Soviet ethos.

If glasnost deserves the credit for the broadening spectrum of public discussion, it also leads to a hardening of political positions and the intensification of political struggle in a polity that lacks both consensus and the tradition of democratic conflict resolution. The result is a growing destabilization of our society.

Conservative stalwarts and other opponents of glasnost use this as a pretext for critical attacks on glasnost itself, which they blame for the destabilization, for the loss of "law and order," for the critical conflicts of interest, for the fragmentation within our society, and for the deterioration of civic morale and public virtue. In fact, however, glasnost, as an integral element of and a precondition for democratization, did not create these cleavages but merely brought them to light, lifting the repressive lid that in the past had forced conflicting tendencies to remain out of view.

There are other, independent variables that fuel the present crisis. A major one, widely discussed to the point of becoming a cliché, is the resistance to perestroika and to the changes it seeks to bring about.

There is no doubt that the discontent of the bureaucracy is increasing. But this is not the only group opposed to radical change. A broad coalition of unskilled workers as well as the "workers' aristocracy," organized and semi-organized social and professional groups with diverse interests and aspirations, is united by their nostalgia for a past in which they thought they were better off. The rise of a conservative wing of Russian nationalism that seeks to unite all these forces is another ominous trend.

At the same time, we learn something else as we advance along the road of perestroika: Change itself proves, paradoxically, to be a source of crisis. To be sure, this is a very special sort of crisis caused not by the immobility of a stagnating and repressed society but by the very efforts to democratize it and bring about radical change. This should not have surprised us. Both political history and political theory teach us that the democratization of formerly totalitarian regimes is never a smooth and simple process. Not only does it include an authoritarian stage but it typically balances on the brink of social, economic, and political chaos. The aggravation of this systemic crisis has in fact led a good many people to wonder whether we have not moved from a period of stagnation to a period of social disintegration and collapse. One of the dangers is that such a crisis shrinks the space for political maneuver for the major driving forces of perestroika. As a result the authorities propose half-measures that cannot lead the society out of this crisis.

Very few people would have expected that after four or five years of perestroika they would see signs of a new erosion of power, a disintegration of old power structures before new ones had emerged. The current worries about social chaos are fueled by the perceived weakness and near paralysis of the political center, surrounded as it is by opposing and extremist forces, from conservative bureaucracy to radical intelligentsia and from nationalists of all sorts to populists. But whatever the reasons for it, and remembering that the chaos is as yet only the nightmare and not the reality, there is the general sense that the social overload is becoming unmanageable.

The delegitimation of traditional social and political structures—in the first place, power and ideology—has reached a point of no return. Rather than trying to galvanize them, the solution is to create alternatives to them. Today parallel and alternative sources of social and moral authority in the country are regarded as perfectly legitimate and no longer marginal. Thus in Soviet public opinion the ideas of an Andrei Sakharov or a Boris Yeltsin are seen as equally legitimate as those of a Yegor Ligachev.

Within the ruling party one can hear sharply contradictory voices. Perhaps even more important, one can clearly see different wings or political orientations within the party, and all of them are perfectly legitimate today. A good case can be made that a de facto multiparty system has emerged within the single party. Although perestroika was begun from the top down, today the party cannot claim a monopoly on "restructuring." Too many other forces outside the party, including those at the grass roots, have become actively involved in radically reshaping Soviet society.

It is also important to mention a significant increase of discontent with perestroika, above all, with the way it is carried out. This discontent comes from two opposing but mutually reinforcing sources. Conservative advocates of the status quo ante are expressing increasing alarm at the dangers of what they call the "excesses of democracy" (modest as it is in the USSR today); very often they are led to use practically the same language as American neoconservatives did in the 1970s. Their opponents on the left, previously passive social and political groups now dissatisfied with the modest pace and scope of perestroika, are for the first time being roused to democratic activism and are calling for its radicalization. To these two politically and ideologically motivated sources of discontent one must add those with grievances over the deteriorating economic situation and the quality of life, those alarmed about prospects for the future, and those troubled by the uncertainties of the current scene. This tension encapsulates the central dilemma of transformation: radicalization of reforms versus social stability. What balance to strike between them will be one of the most challenging tasks for Soviet statesmanship.

It may be safe to predict that the discontent will most likely manifest itself in a further radicalization of the population rather than in attempts to return to a conservative status quo ante. More than that, within a broader framework, this dilemma—stability versus radicalization—ought to be overcome because the conditions for the self-preservation of the system are changing. Today, ensuring stability is possible only by radicalizing the reform agenda. Otherwise, radicalism will feed opposition, in turn adding to political and social destabilization.

Another problem arises from the fact that effective reforms from above require a strong leader. Yet the logic of reform is precisely to activate societal forces that demand a voice in influencing its direction, pace, and scale. This creates a dilemma for the leader. To accept the logic of democratization is to recognize the many new players in the political arena who have their own interests, goals, and constituencies and who may very well seek to go their own way. To accept this fact is obviously not so easy for an ardent reformer at the top.

Such hard choices have become even more pressing since the first Congress of People's Deputies in 1989. Even if the elections and the course of the Congress itself failed to fully live up to a democratic ideal, they were an unprecedented development in the politics of Soviet reform. They marked a watershed after which society and politics would never be the same again. It is no exaggeration to speak of the Congress as our school for democracy and our battlefield of democratization.

In particular, it stimulated a further democratic activism from below. And it legitimized a broadening of the political and ideological spectrum of contemporary Soviet society. As a result it also legitimized the position of those who stand for more radical reforms than Gorbachev as the national leader is able to promote in the current situation.

The Congress can also be regarded as a means of institutionalizing glasnost. Many of the authors quoted in this book became deputies and began to play active political roles in Soviet life as participants rather than merely as observers. One result of the unprecedented openness and sharpness of the debates during the Congress is that glasnost acquired a life of its own, with its own rules and logic. While there are still limits to glasnost and a few "sacred cows," its scope keeps expanding and, perhaps even more important, the fear of taboos is vanishing.

We are often asked whether glasnost has become irreversible. I suppose everything in politics is reversible, and there are still influential forces of restoration in Soviet society. But one doubts whether such a reversal is either probable or feasible. An attempt at restoring the old order would exact an unbearable price economically, politically, socially, and morally, for society as well as for those in power. At the same time, I would argue that glasnost will be irreversible only after two conditions are met: first, when legal guarantees of glasnost are established (including stable and secure mechanisms for the unimpeded collection and dissemination of information); and second, when the need for glasnost becomes a staple of mass political culture. That, it must be admitted, has not yet occurred.

Nonetheless, it is safe to assert that glasnost has awakened Soviet society. It will never be the same as before: One might even be tempted to introduce a new abbreviation in Soviet historiography: B.G. and A.G. (Before Glasnost and After Glasnost). What the future of glasnost and of the Soviet Union will be remains impossible to fathom. That is why we would like to conclude our *Glasnost Papers* with the words, "To be continued."

Sources

Journals

Daugava, Latvian Writers Organization

Druzhba Narodov [Friendship of Peoples], Organization of Writers of the USSR

Kommunist, Central Committee of the CPSU

Kommunist Vooruzhionnykh Sil [Communist of the Military Forces], Ministry of Defense

Literaturnye Pamiatniki [Literary Heritage], USSR Academy of Sciences

Literaturnyi Irkutsk [Literary Irkutsk], Organization of Writers of the RSFSR

Mezhdunarodnaia Zhizn' [International Life], Novosti Press Agency

Molodaia Gvardia [Young Guard], Central Committee of the Young Communist League

Moskva [Moscow], RSFSR Writers' Union

Nash Sovremennik [Our Contemporary], RSFSR Writers' Union

Nauka i Religia [Science and Religion], Znaniye Society

Nauka i Zhizn' [Science and Life], Znaniye Society

Neva, Organization of Writers of the RSFSR in Leningrad

Novoe Vremia [New Times], Novosti Press Agency

Novyi Mir [New World], Organization of Writers of the USSR

Ogonyok [The Light]

Oktiabr' [October], Organization of Writers of the USSR

Raduga [Rainbow], Central Committee of the Estonian Young Communist League

Sobesednik [Interlocutor], Central Committee of the Young Communist League

Sotsialisticheskii Trud [Socialist Labor], USSR State Committee on Labor and Social Questions

Sotsiologicheskie Issledovaniia [Sociological Studies], SSA and the Academy of Sciences of the USSR

Sovetskaia Molodiozh [Soviet Youth]

Sovetskaia Yustitsiia [Soviet Justice]

Sovetskii Shokhtior [Soviet Miner]

SShA: Ekonomika, Politika, Ideologiia [The USA: Economy, Politics, Ideology], Academy of Sciences Institute of the USA and Canada

Vek XX i Mir [Twentieth Century and Peace], Soviet Peace Committee

Vestnik

Voprosy Filosofii [Problems of Philosophy], Union of Philosophers of the USSR, Academy of Sciences

Voprosy Istorii [Problems of History], Academy of Sciences of the USSR

Yunost' [Youth], Central Committee of the Young Communist League

ZhMP

Znamia [Banner], Organization of Writers of the USSR

Newspapers

Argumenty i Fakty [Arguments and Facts], Znaniye Society

Izvestiia [The News], Supreme Soviet of the USSR

Knizhnoye Obozrenie [Book Review], Organization of Writers of the USSR

Komsomolskaia Pravda, Central Committee of the Young Communist League

Krasnaia Zvezda [Red Star], Ministry of Defense

Literaturnaia Gazeta [Literary Gazette], Organization of Writers of the USSR

Literaturnaia Rossiia [Literary Russia], Organization of Writers of the RSFSR

Moskovskaia Pravda [Moscow Truth], Moscow Committee of the CPSU

Moskovskie Novosti [Moscow News], Novosti Press Agency

Moskovskii Komsomolets [Moscow Young Communist], Moscow Committee of Young Communist League

Nedelia [The Week], Supreme Soviet of the USSR

Pravda [Truth], Central Committee of the CPSU

Rigas Balss [Riga's News], Central Committee of the Latvian Communist Party

Sotsialisticheskaia Industriia [Socialist Industry], Central Committee of the CPSU

Sovetskaia Kul'tura [Soviet Culture], Supreme Soviet of the USSR and the Ministry of Culture

Sovetskaia Rossiia [Soviet Russia], Supreme Soviet of the RSFSR

Vecherniaia Moskva [Evening Moscow], City Committee of Moscow Central Communist Party of the Soviet Union

About the Book and Editors

This unique compendium of Soviet thought and dialogue introduces Western readers to the broad range of current debates in the Soviet Union concerning the past, present, and future of the country and its people. Andrei Melville, the Soviet academic who spearheaded this work, is convinced that Mikhail Gorbachev's initiatives have led his country to the brink of a domestic transformation, one that will lead to an entirely new stage of development. Melville chronicles the societal ills—repression, crime, and apathy—and the structural flaws—corruption, a stagnant economy, a monolithic bureaucracy, a stifled flow of information—that have undermined the foundations of the existing system. In response to this crisis, Gorbachev conceived of the idea of perestroika—a program for the revolutionary restructuring of the whole of society, a wrenching process that has led to intense conflicts and strong disagreements between the guardians of the old and the proponents of the new.

This book presents all facets of the debate, drawing on articles and letters extracted from dozens of major Soviet periodicals, including statements by political analysts, economists, historians, journalists, and writers, interspersed with excerpts from readers' letters published in the media. The extracts are placed in context by original essays that focus on the themes underlying all discussion of the implications of reform. The book paints a rich portrait of the diversity of opinions—from reformist to conservative—expressed in the public debates unleashed by glasnost.

Andrei Melville is vice-president of the Soviet Peace Committee. **Gail W. Lapidus** is a professor of political science at the University of California–Berkeley and chair of the Berkeley-Stanford Program in Soviet Studies.

Index

Humor, glasnost, 54

Iakovlev, Aleksandr
  interviews of, 165–166, 183–184
Iakuban, A., article by, 240–241
Idealism, 321
  worship of, 116–117
Ideology, 5, 272
  economic, 189
  flexibility in, 23
  perestroika and, 133
Immigration, problem of, 242
Individual labor, debate about, 211–213
Individual rights, 114, 140–141, 149, 170, 187
  importance of, 5
  protection of, 150, 180
  See also Human rights
Infant mortality, 251
Innokentii, Fr., article by, 130–131
Intelligentsia, democratization and, 8–9
Interdependence, growth of, 271–274, 310
International Front of the Workers of Soviet Latvia
  Constituent Congress of, 245
  goals of, 245–246
  growth of, 243
  review of, 247–249
Internationalism, 261, 333
  building, 246, 301
International prestige, concerns about, 57–58
International relations. *See* Foreign policy
Interrogation, illegal methods of, 161–163
Intourist, 328–330
Ioffe, Genrikh, quote of, 88
Iskander, Fazil', 35
Isolationism, tendency toward, 253
Ivanov, E., letter by, 185–186
Izvestiia, 24, 29
  articles from, 156, 176, 178, 224, 226–227, 253–254, 263–264, 299

interviews in, 156–157, 204–205
  poll in, 168–169

Jewish problem, 254–258, 261
  See also Zionism
Journalism
  changes in, 33, 304–305
  See also Media
Journal of the Moscow Patriarchate, 146
Judiciary
  criticism of, 158–159, 168–169
  independence of, 177–180
  See also Defense lawyers; Law enforcement; Legal system
Jury trial, debate over, 179–180
Justice
  extracting, 168
  miscarriages of, 158–159, 161–163, 180
  perception of, 149–150

Kaganovich, L., 109
Kalachev, V., letter by, 159
Kalashnikov, Evgenii, corruption of, 161–162
Kaltakhchian, Suzen, 127
  articles by, 125, 126
Kamenev, L.B., distortions about, 85
Karacharov, Iurii Gregor'evich, 138, 140
Kardin, V., article by, 184
Karpets, Igor, article by, 157
Karpinskii, L., quotes of, 45, 46
Karpov, V., 35
Katasonova, Elena, letter by, 322–323
Kats, Zalman, article by, 257–258
Katyn massacre, 25
Kazakov, Ignatii Nikolaevich, 103, 107
Kelina, Sofia, interview of, 182–183
KGB, 164, 333
  glasnost and, 13
Kharchev, K., article by, 141–142
Khodasevich, Vladislav, 34
Khrushchev, Nikita, 23, 44, 50, 93